50

12

Fallen Eagle

The Last Days
of the Third Reich

Robin Cross

CAXTON EDITIONS

First published in Great Britain in 1995 by
Michael O'Mara Books Limited
9 Lion Yard
Tremadoc Road
London SW4 7NQ

This Edition published 2000 by
Caxton Editions an imprint of
The Caxton Publishing Group
ISBN 184067 1548

A CIP catalogue record for this book is available from the British Library

1 3 5 7 9 10 8 6 4 2

Maps by Stephen Dew

Designed and typeset by Florencetype Ltd,
Stoodleigh, Devon

Printed and bound by Creative Print and Design,Ebbw Vale (Wales)

Contents

'A few friends came round yesterday evening. At 8 o'clock we had the usual raid, which left a lot of broken windows as a New Year's greeting. At midnight all was still. We stood with raised glasses, hardly daring to clink them together. A single bell tinkled in the distance for the passing of the year, and we heard shots, and heavy boots crunching on the splintered glass. It was eerie, as though a shadow were passing over us and touching us with its dark wings.'

Ursula von Kardorff, 1 January 1945

Acknowledgments

The author and publisher have made every effort to contact the copyright holders of material reproduced in this book, and wish to apologize to those they have been unable to trace. Grateful acknowledgment is made to the following for passages reproduced on the pages given below:

pp. 3, 18, 78, 173, 198: Hans-Georg von Studnitz, *While Berlin Burns*, Weidenfeld and Nicolson, 1963

pp. 10–11: Roger A. Freeman, *The Mighty Eighth*, Macdonald, 1970

pp. 17–18, 172, 241: Ursula von Kardorff, *Diary of a Nightmare*, Rupert Hart-Davis, 1965

p. 20: Martin Gilbert, *The Holocaust: The Jewish Tragedy*, HarperCollins Publishers Limited, 1986

pp. 38, 49–50, 50–51, 230, 243, 249: V. I. Chuikov, *The End of the Third Reich*, Progress Publishers, 1978

pp. 55–6: Janina Bauman, *Winter in the Morning*, Virago Press Limited, 1987

pp. 72–3: Guy Sajer, *The Forgotten Soldier*, Harper & Row, 1971

p. 73: Christian de la Mazière, *The Captive Dreamer*, Dutton, 1974

pp. 88–9: Alexander McKee, *Dresden 1945*, Souvenir Press Limited, 1982

pp. 117, 165–6, 166–7: Max Arthur, *Men of the Red Beret*, Hutchinson, 1990

p. 124 (top): Charles Whiting, *The Battle of the Hürtgen Forest*, Leo Cooper/Pen & Sword Books Limited, 1989

pp. 124–5: James M. Gavin, *On to Berlin*, Viking Press, New York, 1978

pp. 125–6: *The 43rd Wessex Division at War*, Clowes, 1952

p. 131: Charles Whiting, *Siegfried: The Nazis' Last Stand*, Leo Cooper/Pen & Sword Books Limited, 1983

p. 134: Charles MacDonald, *Company Commander*, Ballantine, 1958

p. 136: John Foreman and S. E. Harvey, *The Messerschmitt Me262 Combat Diary*, Air Research Publications

pp. 147, 148 (top): Peter Allen, *One More River*, J. M. Dent, 1980

pp. 148 (bottom), 251: H. Essame, *The Battle for Germany*, B. T. Batsford Limited, London, 1969

pp. 158–9: Pierre Clostermann, *The Big Show*, Chatto & Windus, 1951

p. 177: Heinz Guderian, *Panzer Leader*, Michael Joseph, 1952

pp. 186–7: John Erickson (ed), *Main Front*, Brassey's (UK) Limited, 1987

pp. 189–190: Margaret Bourke-White, *Dear Fatherland Rest Quietly*, Simon & Schuster, 1947

pp. 210–11, 229: Gerhard Boldt, *Hitler's Last Days*, Arthur Barker, 1973
pp. 226–7, 248, 260: Vera Bockmann, *Full Circle: An Australian in Berlin*, Wakefield Press, Netley, South Australia, 1986
pp. 239, 241, 244: Pierre Galante and Eugene Silianoff, *Last Witnesses in the Bunker*, Sidgwick & Jackson, 1989
p. 245: James P. O'Donnell, *The Berlin Bunker*, J. M. Dent, 1979
pp. 260–2: The Diaries of Lieutenant-Colonel R. L. H. Nunn housed in the Imperial War Museum

The author would also like to thank the following for giving permission to reprint extracts from the documents below, which are housed in the Imperial War Museum:

Pamela Wright for passages from Colonel Peter Earle's diary
Ian Whittaker for quotations from Major Whittaker's diary (PP/MCR/292)
D. Evans for passages from his unpublished manuscript (92/371)

Finally, the author would also like to thank James Lucas for permission to quote material from *The Last Days of the Reich* and *Das Reich: The Military Role of the 2nd SS Division*

PICTURE ACKNOWLEDGMENTS

The publishers are grateful to the following sources for permission to reproduce illustrations in the plate section:

Hulton Deutsch: pp. 1, 2 (below), 5 (above), 6 (below), 7, 8, 9 (below), 10 (above), 11 (below), 12 (above), 13 (above), 16
Süddeutscher Verlag: pp. 2 (above), 3
Novosti (London): pp. 4, 5 (below), 6 (above), 9 (above), 11 (above), 12 (below), 13 (below), 14 (above), 15 (below)
Mirror Syndication International: pp. 10 (below), 14 (below), 15

CHAPTER 1

Lost Victories

'Never in my life have I accepted the idea of surrender, and I am one of those men who have worked their way up from nothing. Our present situation, therefore, is nothing new to me. Once upon a time my own situation was entirely different, and far worse. I say this only so that you can grasp why I pursue my goal with such fanaticism and why nothing can wear me down. No matter how much I might be tormented by worries, even if my health were shaken by them – that would still have not the slightest effect on my decision to fight on. . . .'

Adolf Hitler, 28 December 1944

IN THE LAST week of August 1914, in East Prussia, General Paul von Hindenburg and Major-General Erich Ludendorff encircled and destroyed the Russian Second Army. At the Battle of Tannenberg they won one of the most complete victories in military history. Russian captives totalled 125,000 and the unknown number of dead included Second Army's commander, General Alexander Samsonov, who wandered into a forest and shot himself. The Battle of Tannenberg cleared German territory of Russian troops for the duration of the First World War. Later a great monument was raised at Tannenberg, and Hindenburg and his wife were buried there.

In January 1945 the Russians were back in East Prussia. This time it was defended by Colonel-General Hans Reinhardt's Army Group Centre, fielding approximately 600,000 men, 700 tanks, 800 artillery pieces and 1,300 aircraft. Facing Reinhardt's command was the combined might of General Ivan Bagramyan's First Baltic Front, General Ivan Chernyakhovsky's Third Belorussian Front and Marshal Konstantin Rokossovsky's

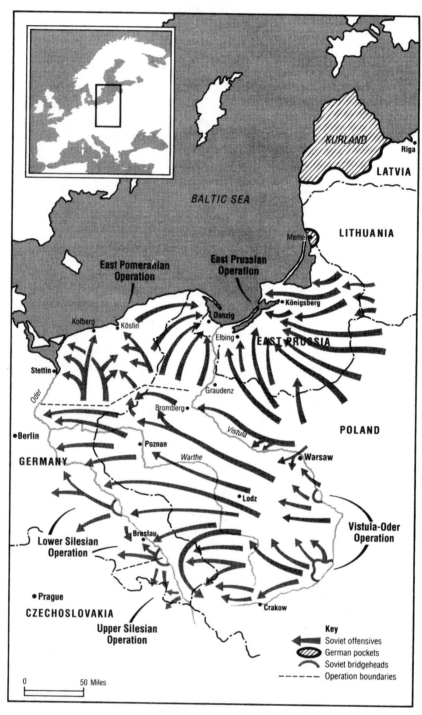

An overview of Soviet operations, January–April, 1945.

Second Belorussian Front. Between them the three fronts could put into the field 1.7 million men, 28,000 artillery pieces, 3,300 tanks and 10,000 aircraft, a measure of crushing Soviet material superiority. There would be no repeat of Tannenberg.

Time was running out for the monument to the victor of Tannenberg. On 21 January Rokossovsky's Second Belorussian Front took Tannenberg. The retreating Germans had dynamited the monument and removed the remains of Hindenburg and his wife and the colours of the regiments he commanded.*

News of the destruction of Hindenburg's tomb filtered back to Berlin, where it was noted in the diary kept by Hans-Georg von Studnitz, a thirty-eight-year-old official in the information and press section of the German Foreign Ministry. His entry for 25 January reads:

> The streams of refugees are interfering with military operations, dis-organizing the lines of communication from which some counter-stroke might be launched, and are denuding the East of its German population. In the midst of all these terrible tragedies childish actions still abound. For example, German troops were ordered to destroy the Tannenberg memorial, in order to prevent the Russians from demolishing it. Whether they have done so or not, God only knows. But in any case, the Russians can now with justice assert that, by themselves they have destroyed the memorial. The Germans have admitted that they have no hope of returning to East Prussia. The goods wagon in which Hindenburg's body is being brought back would have carried 60 refugees to safety. We would have rendered a greater service to the future of Germany by rescu-ing that number of refugees than by sending the Field Marshal's corpse round the country.

Germany's future looked increasingly grim on both the Western and Eastern Fronts. In the West the German offensive launched in the Ardennes on 16 December by Sixth SS Panzer and Fifth Panzer Armies and Seventh Army had been contained and then rolled back by the Americans and British. By 16 January 1945 the bulge which had been driven sixty miles into the fifty-mile front held by General Courtney Hodges's US First Army had been eliminated. The fog which had grounded Allied aircraft at the start of the offensive had lifted, enabling fighter-bombers to strafe German traffic routes and supply convoys. The roads on which the Germans withdrew were soon littered with the

---

* They now hang in the hall of the Officer Cadet School at Hamburg.

blackened hulks of Hitler's armoured reserve. The German losses of 800 tanks were irreplaceable. The Allies made good similar losses in two weeks.

On the Eastern Front, Germany's strategic position had been reduced to ruins by the destruction of Army Group Centre in July-August 1944. At the turn of the year the remnants of Army Group Centre, redesignated Army Group A, held a line along the River Vistula less than 400 miles from Berlin, the flat expanse of the Polish plain at their backs and no obstacle but the River Oder between them and the capital of the Reich. Two Red Army fronts,* Marshal I.S. Konev's First Ukrainian and Marshal Georgi K. Zhukov's First Belorussian, had been ordered to advance across western Poland and into Germany. Both commanders enjoyed an overwhelming material superiority over the enemy and were now displaying a new mastery of mechanized warfare. Konev opened his offensive on 12 January and Zhukov followed two days later. Within forty-eight hours they had broken through the crust of the German tactical defence zone and their armoured formations were moving at speed across open country. To the north the Soviet drive to the Baltic, spearheaded by Third Belorussian and Second Belorussian Fronts, sent millions of refugees fleeing westward to the Reich or northward to the Baltic ports.

On the southern sector of the Eastern Front the situation was equally grave. In August 1944 Romanian guerrillas had staged an armed rebellion in Bucharest, taken control of the city, arrested the puppet dictator Marshal Ion Antonescu and overthrown the government. King Michael had then formed a new government, negotiated an armistice with the Allies and declared war on Germany. By the end of August most of the German occupying forces had left Romania, and on the 30th Soviet troops entered Bucharest without meeting any armed resistance.

Hitler's Balkan strategy was falling apart in his hands. The German occupation of Greece had been fatally undermined by the capitulation of Italy in September 1943. Just over a year later, on 12 October 1944, German Army Group E began a fighting withdrawal from Greece to link up with Army Group F in Yugoslavia.

There were some crumbs of comfort for Adolf Hitler as he surveyed his war maps. North of the Carpathians, Army Group South, which had

---

* A Red Army front was the equivalent of a German army group. It usually consisted of some five to seven armies with one or two tactical air armies and special armoured and artillery formations in support. An entire front could total up to 1 million men and extend over a battle frontage of up to 150 miles with a depth – if one includes the rear zone of operations – of up to 250 miles.

narrowly escaped destruction in August 1944, was now close to holding its own in Hungary. Budapest, which had been encircled by Russian forces at the end of December 1944, might still be relieved. In Italy Army Group C had halted British Eighth and American Fifth Armies at the Gothic Line, a string of heavily fortified positions stretching from south of La Spezia, on Italy's western coast, to a point on the Adriatic between Pesaro and Cattolica.

It was against this discouraging strategic background that, on 25 January, the German Army's Chief of the General Staff, Colonel-General Heinz Guderian,* paid a visit to Foreign Minister Joachim von Ribbentrop in his official residence on Berlin's Wilhelmstrasse. It was an uneasy encounter. Guderian proposed that Ribbentrop accompany him to see Hitler and urge him to seek an armistice 'on at least one front'. By this Guderian meant an armistice in the West, before the Western Allies could take up their march into the heart of the Reich. Ribbentrop squirmed at the suggestion, protesting, 'I can't do it. I am a loyal follower of the Führer. I know for a fact that he does not wish to open any diplomatic negotiations with the enemy, and I therefore cannot address him in the manner you propose.' To which Guderian replied, 'How would you feel if in three or four weeks' time the Russians were at the gates of Berlin?'

---

* The German Army's leading expert in armoured warfare, Guderian had been appointed Inspector-General Armoured Troops in March 1943. In July 1944 he replaced Colonel-General Kurt Zeitzler as Chief of the General Staff.

CHAPTER 2

The House of Cards

'The worst is now over. We have succeeded in holding and pinning down the enemy both in the East and the West. We have had to take some heavy blows ourselves in the course of the fighting but I happen to know that the situation is still worse in the enemy camp. It is just a case of staying the distance.'

Heinrich Himmler, December 1944

ON 1 JANUARY 1945, the British writer and politician Harold Nicolson wrote in his diary:

Viti [his wife, Vita Sackville-West] and I hear the new year in crouching over the fire in the dining-room. I turn on Berlin, the *Deutschlandsender*, and then Hamburg – and we get Hitler's horrible but unmistakable voice. The reception is not good and he gabbles off his piece so fast that I may have missed something. But it seemed to consist entirely about reflections upon Germany's fate if she loses her moral staunchness. . . .

The broadcast to which Harold and Vita were listening in mild discomfort was the first the Führer had made since the unsuccessful attempt to assassinate him at his East Prussian headquarters on 20 July 1944. He told the German people:

. . . This nation, this state and its leading men are unshakeable in their will and unswerving in their fanatical determination to fight this war to a successful conclusion in all circumstances – if it means taking in our stride all the reverses which fickle fate may impose on us . . . we are resolved to go the extreme . . . whatever our enemies smashed was rebuilt with superhuman industry and unparalleled heroism and this will continue until one day our enemies' undertaking comes to an end.

Hitler stubbornly clung to the conviction that Germany would emerge victorious in spite of the terrible pounding the Reich and its armed forces had received at the hands of the Allies. But the conviction was wavering. Three days earlier he had confided in General Thomale, Chief of Staff of the Inspectorate of Panzer Troops, 'The war will not last as long again as it has lasted. That is absolutely certain. Nobody can endure it. We cannot, and the others cannot. The only question is who will endure it longer? It must be he who has everything at stake.'

Time, however, was running out faster than Hitler either imagined or was prepared to admit. On Christmas Eve 1944, Colonel-General Guderian arrived at the *Adlerhorst* (Eagle's Nest), Hitler's headquarters in the Taunus Mountains ten miles north-west of Bad Nauheim. It was from the Adlerhorst that the Führer had presided over the defeat of France in the summer of 1940. Now he had returned to direct the Ardennes offensive.

Guderian had travelled overnight in his command train from the OKH* headquarters at the Maybachlager in Zossen, south of Berlin. At Zossen Guderian had 'observed with a heavy heart the progress of our offensive in the West'. By 23 December it was clear that the Ardennes offensive was running out of steam. Once the first shock had passed, the Allied commanders moved swiftly to contain and then defeat the German spearheads. It was only a matter of time before they went on the offensive. Guderian's mission was to persuade Hitler to break off the battle and transfer all the forces which could be spared to the East to counter the massive Soviet build-up north of the Carpathians against Army Groups A and Centre. He had been provided with some heavy ammunition by General Reinhard Gehlen, commander of the Russian section of OKH's Foreign Armies (East) Department, who predicted that the Russians would attack on 12 January with a superiority of 11:1 in infantry, 7:1 in tanks and 20:1 in artillery. An evaluation of the enemy's total strength gave him a superiority of approximately 15:1 on the ground and 20:1 in the air. For Guderian the question was simply one of 'to be or not to be'.

But before Guderian could fight a battle in the East he had to fight a battle with the Führer. The meeting at the Adlerhorst on Christmas Eve

---

* Oberkommando des Heeres, the German Army high command, whose sphere of operations was confined to the Eastern Front.

was attended by Hitler, Field Marshal Wilhelm Keitel, Chief of the High Command of the German Armed Forces (OKW), Colonel-General Alfried Jodl, the OKW Chief of Staff, and General Burgdorf, Hitler's adjutant. Guderian ran straight into trouble. Hitler refused to call off the Ardennes offensive and poured scorn on Gehlen's figures, claiming that the Red Army's rifle divisions had a strength of only 7,000 men* each and its tank divisions no tanks. According to Hitler, the Russian build-up was the 'greatest bluff since Genghis Khan'.

At dinner Guderian was seated next to Heinrich Himmler, who had by now gathered to himself the offices of Commander-in-Chief of the Home Army, commander of Army Group Upper Rhine (a formation whose principal tasks were the defence of the river and the rounding up of deserters), Minister of the Interior, National Leader of the SS and Chief of German Police. Himmler leaned over to Guderian and reassured him in the familiar schoolmasterly tones, 'You know, my dear Colonel-General, I don't really believe the Russians will attack at all. It's all an enormous bluff. The figures given by your department Foreign Armies East are grossly exaggerated. They're far too worried. I'm convinced that nothing is going on in the East.'

Guderian was wearily resigned to higher idiocy of this kind, but he had a more formidable opponent in Colonel-General Jodl. OKW had no authority on the Eastern Front, where the war was run by OKH. In consequence Jodl regarded Guderian's travails with studied indifference. He was fully aware that the Ardennes offensive was bogged down, but he believed that a series of subsidiary attacks in this theatre – the first of which, codenamed *Nordwind* (North Wind), was to be launched in Alsace-Lorraine towards Strasbourg – would wear down the Western Allies. Guderian countered by pointing out that the heavy industry and transport systems of the Ruhr had already been paralysed by Allied bombing, rendering all the more important the industrial region of Upper Silesia, which lay directly in the Russians' path. The loss of the region, which was now the centre of the German arms industry, would lead to defeat in a matter of weeks.

The Eastern Front would have to take care of itself. It would have no reinforcements from the West[†] nor from the units disengaging from

---

* In fact Hitler was closer to the mark than anyone around the table realized. The establishment for a Red Army rifle division provided for 11,780 men, but the average ranged between 3,000 and 7,000 men.

† With the active help of Field Marshal Gerd von Rundstedt, Commander-in-Chief West and his Chief of Staff, General Siegfried Westphal, Guderian eventually secured the release of three divisions from the Western Front and one from Italy. But this 'wretched pittance', as Guderian called it, went to Hungary.

Finland, which were passing through Norway. Hitler also refused to countenance the withdrawal of the twenty-six divisions of Colonel-General Ferdinand Schörner's Army Group North which the Soviet Baltic fronts had cut off in Latvia's Kurland peninsula. The Führer was pathologically incapable of yielding ground, but he also wanted to retain access to Baltic waters for the training of crews for the new Type XXI and Type XXIII U-boats. Guderian went away empty-handed.

The next day, when Guderian was on his despondent way back to Zossen, Hitler ordered the transfer of IV SS Panzer Corps, deployed north of Warsaw, and two panzergrenadier divisions to Army Group South for the relief of Budapest. Later Guderian reflected, 'Two of the fourteen and a half panzer or panzer grenadier divisions assembled as a reserve against the impending Russian attack were sent to a secondary front. Only twelve and a half remained for a front of approximately 750 miles.'

Hitler's preoccupation with Budapest reflected the importance he placed on the Hungarian oilfields at Nagykanizsa, south-west of Lake Balaton, which were still in the hands of Army Group South. They were virtually the last of the Reich's natural oil assets, and oil was the key to survival. Without it Hitler's remaining panzers could not roll nor his Messerschmitt Me262 jets fly against the waves of Allied bombers crisscrossing the Reich by day and night. A dramatic decline in oil production had begun in August 1944 when Colonel-General F.I. Tolbukhin's Third Ukrainian Front captured the Ploesti oilfields in south-east Romania. Thereafter increasing reliance was placed on the programme to disperse, repair and build synthetic oil plants. However, the plants were extremely vulnerable to air attack, and by the autumn of 1944 the Royal Air Force's Bomber Command and the United States Army Air Force (USAAF) had brought German oil production to a standstill. With the onset of winter weather production crept back up again to 24,500 tons in December, just enough to launch the Ardennes offensive but not enough to sustain it. As Field Marshal Gerd von Rundstedt, Commander-in-Chief West, commented after the war:

> Taking account of the extra difficulties likely to be met in a winter battle in such difficult country as the Ardennes, I told Hitler personally that five times the standard scale of petrol supply ought to be provided. Actually, when the offensive was launched, only one and a half times the standard scale had been provided. Worse still, much of it was kept too far back, in large truck columns on the east bank of the Rhine. Once the foggy weather cleared and the Allied air forces came into action, its forwarding was badly interrupted.

The Germans fought hard to protect their fuel supplies. There were no fewer than 506 anti-aircaft guns around the much-raided oil plant at Merseburg, which explains why in August 1944 US Eighth Air Force lost 131 aircraft to flak compared with thirty-nine to day fighters. The anti-aircraft guns, grouped in thirty-nine batteries and firing a concentrated pattern of bursts with a shotgun effect, were defending the big IG Farbenindustrie plant at Leuna, three miles south of the town, which produced an estimated 10 per cent of the Reich's oil, half the ammonia and a score of chemical by-products. On 29 August Lieutenant Gordon Courtenay, a bombardier with 398th Bombardment Group, flew one of his first missions over this target. Ahead of him he saw what he assumed to be a pall of black smoke hanging over the target. In fact his B-17 Flying Fortress was approaching the smoke of several thousand shell bursts aimed at the preceding group. As Courtenay observed, 'The sight of those ugly black bursts leaves you with a numb helpless feeling. All you can do is concentrate on your job and pray that in all that steel there isn't a piece with your number on it.'

Running the gauntlet of the Merseburg flak is vividy caught in the diary kept by Second Lieutenant William Duane, a navigator with 388th Group who flew against this target on 28 September:

> Up early for an 03.30 briefing. Take off at at 07.10. Again I'm navigator and not minding it too much. With this being our 13th mission, I anticipated a hot one but didn't say much to the crew. I guess they were sweating it out enough themselves. . . . After plenty of flying we reached the IP [initial point, from which the bomb run began]. The bomb run was about 13 minutes long. About 2½ minutes before 'bombs away' we got intense and very accurate flak. About a minute later, at 12.00, King [engineer] was hit in both legs. He fell down in the passageway, crawled forward and I plugged in his oxygen mask. . . . I took off my flak suit, grabbed a knife, and cut open five layers of clothes. After noticing the extent of the bleeding I applied a tourniquet. All this took place in some very intense and tracking flak – and me without my helmet. I applied a gauze dressing and tried to get blankets and morphine. Interphone shot out so I started back to the flight deck to inform the pilot. The co-pilot was cranking closed the bomb doors so I got on his interphone. I got down in the hatchway on an oxygen bottle and stayed there relaying messages back and forth between the nose and the pilot. Finally came the blanket and the first-aid kits. King had a piece of flak go right through the meaty part of his upper left leg and puncture his right leg. Bleeding was not arterial so it stopped soon. I was pretty cramped in the

passageway where I was for more than an hour – until 13.30. In the meantime I had given King some morphine, but it was a hell of a job as it froze up and we had to experiment several times jabbing King's leg before I had finally discovered just how it worked. Hoff [bombardier] was giving most of the actual first aid while I wrapped King's legs in blankets and tried to keep them warm as he was complaining about them being numb with cold. . . . We fired a couple of red flares over the home field. Upon landing we got King into the ambulance OK and then taxied back to the hardstand. I was really tired after this mission so I took a good stiff drink to make me forget what was the worst flak I had ever seen. At first we had nine crews missing, but that narrowed down to six by midnight. Some of the boys had landed in Belgium. . . . Three ships went down over the target after a collision. I hope that we won't see anything like this again.*

By the end of December 1944 renewed heavy bombing had destroyed all but one of Germany's principal synthetic plants, and about 20 per cent of the smaller ones. Although Army Group South clung on to the oil fields at Nagykanizsa, the loss of the refineries in Budapest meant that the gasoline output was not sufficient to meet even Army Group South's requirements.

Throughout 1944 German industrial output had withstood the worst the combined bombing offensive could throw at it. Under the technocratic stewardship of Reichsminister Albert Speer, Hitler's Armaments Minister since 1942, war production steadily rose. In September the Reich's aircraft plants produced 3,000 fighters, a wartime peak. Production deliveries of the jet-powered Me262 fighter began in May but had subsequently been held up by Hitler's insistence on converting the aircraft to a bombing role. Nevertheless, in December 1944 fighter production was higher than in any month before May of that year. In the same month another wartime high was reached as 1,854 armoured vehicles rolled off the production lines. Impressive though it was, this achievement masked the remorseless erosion of Germany's industrial base. The armoured vehicles' heavy components had been fed into the pipeline months before to meet the long lead times required in the manufacture of such weaponry. But by the end of the year Allied bombing of the Ruhr had reduced pig-iron, crude steel and rolling-mill production to about one-third of the levels of January 1944. The effect was immediately felt in areas of production with short lead times. The output of trucks,

---

* On another mission five days later the co-pilot was fatally wounded by flak, and Duane watched the man die as he administered first aid.

previously boosted by the rebuilding of all the disabled army trucks in Germany, fell away rapidly. In December only 3,300 trucks were produced to meet a monthly requirement of 6,000, and of these over two-thirds were allocated to the Ardennes offensive. At the turn of the year the truck strengths of the depleted panzer divisions were reduced by 25 per cent, and panzergrenadiers* were issued with bicycles.

In 1944 Albert Speer had achieved a kind of industrial miracle, principally with a policy of dispersal, and it is perhaps ironic that by dictating the terms on which German war industry should be organized, the Allied bombing offensive succeeded in making it more efficient. But dispersal bred its own problems. Economy of scale was sacrificed and greater demands were placed on badly stretched skilled labour resources. Moreover, dispersal increased the chance of the interruption of the production flow by the bombing of communications. Between July and December 1944 Allied bombing reduced the number of rail wagons available to the state railway, the Reichsbahn, from 136,000 to 87,000. By February 1945 this figure had fallen to a mere 28,000, about 10,000 fewer than were needed to sustain 25 per cent of industrial production and 80 per cent of public facilities – the bare minimum for survival. As the railway system collapsed, the heavy weapons produced in the last surge of German war production lay stranded in their factory yards. For all the organizational genius of Albert Speer, his achievements had been no more than the feverish rally of a dying patient.

The disintegration of Germany's industrial infrastructure was paralleled by the haemorrhaging of her military manpower. In 1944 106 divisions were destroyed, three more than had been mobilized in 1939. In the summer and autumn of 1944 total irrecoverable losses on all fronts were 1.46 million men, of which 900,000 had been lost on the Eastern Front. At the beginning of October German strength in the East stood at 1.8 million, of whom about 150,000 were 'Hiwis' (*Hilfsfreiwillige* or voluntary aid) – Russian volunteers who were given line-of-communication duties. This represented a drop of 700,000 on the figure for January 1944, a time when troops in the Western theatre could still be used as a reserve. These grim figures served only to drive Hitler deeper into the military fantasy world he increasingly inhabited. In December 1944 he told General Thomale:

> There is no foreseeable end to reorganization. Everything is in a process of flux – our national production, the state of training, the competence of commanders. But this is nothing new in history.

---

* The motorized infantry component of an armoured division.

Only just now I was reading through a volume of letters of Frederick the Great. This is what he writes in one of them, in the fifth year of the Seven Years' War: 'There was a time when I went on campaign with the most magnificent army in Europe. Now I have a heap of rubbish – I possess no more commanders, my generals are incapable, my officers are no longer proper leaders, and my troops are of appalling quality.' You can't imagine a more damning indictment, and yet this man stuck it out through the war.

Hitler was constantly comparing himself to Frederick the Great, but his method of dealing with the manpower crisis flew in the face of military good sense. Since the spring of 1943 the high rate of casualties on the Eastern Front, and the lack of reserves, had made it impossible to bring depleted divisions up to strength. Logic dictated that divisions should be merged to maintain a sustainable ratio between combat troops and those in the auxiliary tail. This would have encouraged the economical use of experienced officers, NCOs and specialists, and the more effective employment of motor vehicles, equipment and horses.* Hitler's obsession with numbers frustrated any such rationalization. He insisted on replacing each of his lost divisions with new ones. For the Führer what mattered most was the number of divisions in the order of battle, not their strength or quality. Of this *rage de nombre*, Albert Speer gloomily observed, 'New divisions were formed in great numbers, equipped with new weapons and sent to the front without any experience or training, while at the same time the good, battle-hardened units bled to death because they were given no replacement weapons† or personnel.'

As the German Army burned away at its core desperate measures were introduced. Conscription was extended to bring in sixteen- and fifty-year-olds. Military hospitals were trawled for convalescing soldiers strong enough to hold rifles. They were drafted into the sardonically named 'stomach' and 'ear' battalions, made up entirely of men suffering from stomach complaints or defective hearing. All the while Hitler was juggling with numbers, reducing infantry divisions to six battalions, authorizing artillery corps with brigade strengths and transforming regiments into divisions. In November, he agreed to allow Hiwis to fight in the front

---

* Nine out of every ten divisions in the east were unmechanized, and at the beginning of January 1945 the Wehrmacht had just over 1 million horses on its strength, of which 923,000 were on active service with the field army, suffering losses of about 1,000 a day.
† In September 1944, of the 26,000 machine-guns and 2,090 80mm mortars produced, only 1,527 and 303 respectively were sent to front-line units while 24,473 and 1,947 went to newly formed divisions.

line, a decision which led to the creation of the Russian Army of Liberation, led by General Andrei Vlasov, who had been captured near Sebastopol in May 1942 when commanding the Russian Second Shock Army. Vlasov did not receive the first division of his army until 10 February 1945, at which time it still lacked half of its clothing and equipment and virtually all of its motor vehicles.

The summer of 1944 saw the introduction, under the direction of Heinrich Himmler, of the Volksgrenadier divisions, the name emphasizing their links with the German people rather than the Wehrmacht hierarchy which Hitler had come so heartily to loathe and distrust. The Volksgrenadier divisions were scraped together from replacement units, badly mauled divisions and depot staffs. Each approximately 6,000 strong, they were of scant military value in spite of Himmler's assertion that their close links with the Waffen-SS, with Nazi Party ideology, and with the people counted for more than military professionalism.

Addressing Volksgrenadier officers on 26 July 1944, Himmler left them under no illusion about the rigours of the Eastern Front, where life expectancy for a company commander was no more than three months. A battalion commander could expect to survive for four months at most before being killed or wounded. Nevertheless, Himmler concluded:

> ... So long as the Aryan lives, so long as our blood, Nordic-Germanic blood, lives, so long there will be order on this globe of the Lord God. And this task, from eternity out into the eternity of our *Volk*, is placed in the hands of each generation, especially ours. And when you see these periods of time, timeless, then I believe that each of you in the hour of difficulty and danger will realize what a short second that is in the life of the earth, in the life of our *Volk*. And during this short second the only thing that matters is that he who lives precisely there [at that time] now does his duty. . . .

Also answering a less rhetorically high-flown call to duty were the men and boys of the Volkssturm, the German equivalent of Britain's Home Guard. Established in September 1944, the Volkssturm was drawn from all males between the ages of sixteen and sixty who were not in the armed forces but were capable of bearing arms. Lists of those liable for service were compiled by local Nazi Party organizations and its predominantly politically reliable officers appointed by *Gauleiters* (provincial governors) and their subordinate *Kreisleiters*. Eventually the Volkssturm's battalions contained 1.5 million men. Like their British predecessors, they were in no way equipped to meet a determined and victorious enemy. Unlike 'Dad's Army', however, the baby-faced youths and veterans of the Volkssturm were to find themselves in the front line.

Veterans of the Grossdeutschland Panzer Corps encountered a Volkssturm battalion in the yard of an East Prussian factory:

> Some of these troops with Mausers on their shoulders must have been at least sixty or sixty-five, to judge by their curved spines, bowed legs, and abundant wrinkles. But the young boys were even more astonishing. . . . They had been hastily dressed in worn uniforms cut for men, and were carrying guns which were often as big as they were. They looked both comic and horrifying, and their eyes were filled with unease, like the eyes of children at the reopening of school. Not one of them could have imagined the impossible ordeal which lay ahead. . . . We noticed some heart-wringing details about these children, who were beginning the first day of their tragedy. Several of them were carrying school satchels their mothers had packed with extra food and clothes, instead of schoolbooks. A few of the boys were trading their saccharine sweets which the ration allowed to children under thirteen.

Poignant though the sight was, this Volkssturm unit seems to have been better equipped than many. In theory there were two categories of Volkssturm: those who had weapons, and their replacements. But just as in England in the summer of 1940, the range of weapons on offer was random and often eccentric, with Italian rifles providing a mainstay.* Eventually, there was a plentiful supply of grenades and the *Panzerfaust*, a hand-held anti-tank weapon which had first appeared in 1942. In the hands of youthful members of the Volkssturm, the Panzerfaust was to prove a highly effective weapon, but many battalion commanders had little relish for the fight in prospect. After the war, the commanding officer of the 42nd Volkssturm Battalion in Berlin recalled:

> I had four hundred men in my battalion, and we were ordered to go into the line in our civilian clothes. I told the local Party leader that I could not accept the responsibility of leading men into battle without uniforms. Just before commitment we were given 180 Danish rifles, but no ammunition. We also had four machine-guns and a hundred Panzerfausts. None of the men had received any

---

* In the Volkssturm the only common issue was an armband in lieu of a uniform. The Wehrmacht had no responsibility for the Volkssturm, which had to be armed and equipped from local resources.

training in firing a machine-gun, and they were all afraid of handling the anti-tank weapons. Although my men were quite ready to
help their country, they refused to go into battle without uniforms
and without training. What can a Volkssturm man do with a rifle
without ammunition? The men went home; that was the only thing
we could do.

On 13 January 1943, as disaster overwhelmed Field Marshal Friedrich
Paulus's Sixth Army at Stalingrad, Hitler issued a decree stating, 'The total
war confronts us with tasks which must be unequivocally mastered'. Two
years later, and with complete disaster staring him in the face, there was
still much that was equivocal about the German war effort. The endemic
corruption bred by the warring fiefdoms within the Nazi Party hierarchy
ensured that successive attempts to mobilize for 'total war' were only
partially successful. As late as January 1945 the Propaganda Minister
Josef Goebbels, who had been appointed Plenipotentiary for Total War
in August 1944, was still scouring the nooks and corners of the Reich for
pockets of remaining manpower. Women of fifty were drafted into war
factories, where they worked a sixty-hour week, to release men for the
Volksgrenadier divisions. Beauticians and U-bahn (underground railway)
ticket collectors were conscripted. The curtain came down at Berlin's
Charlottenburg Opera House and the staff were sent to the Siemens
electrical plant.

The redirection of stage hands and manicurists was a drop in the
ocean. The German war economy survived because of the 12 million foreign workers, including prisoners of war,* in the Reich. The great majority were forced labourers impressed from occupied Europe since
January 1942. Forced labour made up about 40 per cent of the German
work force, and in some war factories the proportion was as high as 90
per cent, a breeding ground for sabotage.

In Germany forced labourers constituted a society within a society, living in their own compounds, eating in their own canteens, publishing
their own newspapers, and even making use of the sixty brothels
thoughtfully provided for the men by their German hosts. The Russian
workers fared the worst, invariably being used as slave labour. A French
worker, André Boudeau, wrote in his diary that the Russian compound
was 'terribly overcrowded, with men, women and children all jammed
together . . . their food, most of the time, inedible'. Boudeau considered

---

* At the synthetic oil plant at Brux, in Czechoslovakia, for example, there were at
least 4,000 British POWs among a multi-national workforce of about 45,000. The
British POWs christened the plant's three big chimneys Churchill, Roosevelt and
Stalin.

himself lucky as on Sunday the chief guard allowed his French charges into the fields 'to pick a potato or two'.

Most Germans had little or no contact with this submerged world. When they did, it often came as something of a shock. In November 1944, Ursula von Kardorff, a young journalist, sought shelter from an air raid in Berlin's Friedrichstrasse rail station, only to stumble into an alien environment:

> The Friedrichstrasse U-bahn [subway], with its broad stairways, which lead to a kind of underworld, is supposed to be bomb-proof. It is all rather as I imagine Shanghai to be. Ragged, romantic-looking characters in padded jackets, with high, Slav cheekbones, mixed with fair-haired Danes and Norwegians, smartly turned-out Frenchwomen, Poles casting looks of hatred at everybody, fragile, chilly Italians – a mingling of races such as can never before have been seen in any German city. The people down there are almost all foreigners and one hardly hears a word of German spoken. Most of them are conscripted workers in armaments factories. All the same they do not strike one as being depressed. Many of them talk loudly and cheerfully, laugh, sing, swap their possessions and do a little trading and live in accordance with their own customs. . . . They say that foreign workers are very well organized indeed. It seems that there are agents among them, officers sent in by the various resistance movements, who are well supplied with arms and have wireless transmitters. Otherwise how could the *Soldatensender**** be so up to date with its news? . . . There are twelve million foreign workers in Germany – an army in itself. Some people call it the Trojan Horse of the war.

Ursula von Kardorff's vision of the Berlin sub-world created by Hitler's New Order anticipates the teeming, seedy city of the future created by Ridley Scott in the feature film *Blade Runner*. Berlin, battered by Allied bombs, was full of surreal sights which nowadays conjure images of another, earlier dystopia, George Orwell's *1984*. On 20 April 1944, Hitler's birthday, Ursula von Kardorff wrote in her diary:

> So-called 'Führer weather' again, simply wonderful. The city is half empty, as everybody has gone out into the country in overcrowded trains. The streets have been brightened up in rather hectic fashion. Red flags wave from every empty window-frame. Some bold spirit has even clambered up the frontage of the Bristol [Hotel],

---

* Allied 'black' propaganda radio stations broadcasting from England.

probably with the help of a fire ladder, and hung up an enormous flag. People were buried under those ruins and their knocking could be heard until they stifled to death. The heaps of rubble are gaily decorated with little paper flags and streamers bear the words, 'Führer! Command! We'll follow!' or 'Our walls are breaking but not our hearts'.

The war had strangely transformed areas seemingly untouched by the conflict. Whole forests sparkled with the 'Window' anti-radar tinsel,* thousands of tons of which had been dropped over Germany by Allied bombers, festooning trees with an eerie Christmas glitter. By the turn of the year the trains from Berlin were no longer carrying picnickers into the countryside. Hans-Georg von Studnitz wrote in his diary:

At the main Berlin railway stations scenes occur such as have not been experienced since the days of the mass air raids in the late autumn and winter of 1943–44. When I took Mariette [his wife] to the station yesterday about midnight to catch the train to Hanover, we saw people fighting their way into the compartments and trampling over anyone who got in their way. . . . Thousands of men on leave are squatting in the railway stations. What they are doing here, when the situation at the front is so desperate, no one knows.

The game was up, and Hitler knew it. Characteristically, his nerve did not falter. In the past his powers of decision had often become jellified at precisely the moment that success seemed within his grasp. He was always at his best when defying disaster, as before Moscow in December 1941. The Führer never fully recovered from the shock of Stalingrad, but now he drew on his dwindling reserves of willpower. On 28 December 1944, in his snowbound headquarters near Bad Nauheim, the Adlerhorst, he addressed the commanding generals of the divisions preparing to launch the abortive thrust in northern Alsace, Operation Nordwind. He admitted that the Ardennes offensive had broken down and that Germany was now fighting for survival. Hitler continued:

'Never in my life have I accepted the idea of surrender, and I am one of those men who have worked their way up from nothing. Our present situation, therefore, is nothing new to me. Once upon a

---

* Window consisted of foil strips cut to half the wavelength of German radar pulses. Dropped in quantity it cluttered radar screens with false returns. It was first employed, with great success, in the raids on Hamburg in July 1943. The Americans called it 'Chaff'.

time my own situation was entirely different, and far worse. I say this only so that you can grasp why I pursue my goal with such fanaticism and why nothing can wear me down. No matter how much I might be tormented by worries, even if my health were shaken by them – that would still have not the slightest effect on my decision to fight on. . . .'

Hitler went on to cite the 'miracle of the House of Brandenburg' when Frederick the Great, defeated in the Seven Years War, regained by the Peace of Hubertusburg all the territory he had lost after the coalition against him fell apart. Hundreds of thousands of soldiers and civilians were to die while the Führer waited for another miracle.

Since the failure at Kursk in July 1943, Hitler had been the prisoner of events rather than their master. As his strategic horizons shrank ever smaller, his will alone was all that mattered. Armies and battles did not figure in this crackpot equation. Military and economic weakness was irrelevant so long as the Führer himself did not weaken. But although Hitler's psychological powers to galvanize those around him still burned with fitful brilliance, his physical powers were fading fast. His back was bent and his gait shuffling. His face was drawn, his hair grey and his moustache flecked with white. His hands trembled uncontrollably over the maps at his 'midday' situation conferences – which now rarely began before 5pm – setting up a terrible rustling which those surrounding him did their best to ignore. He was no longer able to write, and his signature on official documents had to be forged by a trusted civil servant. Admiral Assmann, a regular participant in the war conferences, noted that the Führer's 'handclasp was weak and soft, all his movements were those of a senile man'.

On 30 January 1945, twelve years after his appointment as Chancellor of the Reich, Hitler delivered his last speech on the radio. He touched on familiar themes, invoking the menace of an 'Asian tidal wave' and, in curiously flat tones, appealed to the German spirit of resistance. He signed off with a weary rallying cry: 'However grave the crisis may be at the moment, in the end it will be mastered by our unalterable will, by our readiness for sacrifice, and by our abilties. We will overcome this emergency also.'

A more realistic assessment of events had been delivered a month earlier when, on 5 January, the German writer Ernst Jünger had confided in his diary, 'Hopelessness is the only positive aspect of this situation'.

At the Muhldorff concentration camp near Dachau in southern Germany there was still hope of salvation. Many of the inmates had convinced themselves that New Year's Day would mark the end of the war. One of them, a Hungarian Jew called Moshe Sandberg, recalled the atmosphere in the camp, a terrible mixture of hope, despair and dread:

> The first day passed, the second, third and fourth, on and on endlessly. We wondered how many had gone by and how many still remained until 1 January 1945, the date we had decided would be the final one, by which time the war would surely end with the victory of the Allied powers, and whoever was lucky enough to see it would be able to leave this Hell. It was difficult to keep count of the days, the date we wanted approaching so infinitely slowly. Work hours seemed to get longer and the hours of sleep shorter. At last came the awaited day, but it did not bring deliverance. The disappointment was bitter. What would become of us? We could not endure much longer. Some of our colleagues were already dead and most of the others looked like shadows of themselves and it was a wonder that their legs could carry them. The few who still kept up their spirits had set January 15 as the latest date for the war to end, then they extended it for a fortnight, and then later and so on, but the last date I do not remember.
>
> With each new estimate the number of those who believed in it fell, while that of those who were apathetic about any guess rose. They stopped believing and hoping. Only two things remained in their thoughts: hunger and the beatings. How to get a little more food and how to get a little less beating. In a month or two we had turned into real camp denizens, indistinguishable from the veterans. The same way of thought, the same miserable appearance. Now we could understand why they had laughed at us when we expressed our hopes and speculated about the 'last date'. The remark 'The war will never end' became clear to us. Death was the time of our deliverance.

CHAPTER 3

Sympathy for the Devil

'God is on your side? Is He a Conservative? The Devil's on my side, he's a good Communist.'

Josef Stalin in conversation with Winston Churchill,
Tehran, November 1943

THE SOVIET LEADER, Josef Stalin, celebrated the arrival of 1945 in more sprightly fashion than the beleaguered Führer. On New Year's Eve he invited the members of the Politburo and a number of senior generals to a party at his *dacha* (country house or cottage) at Kuntsevo, outside Moscow.

At midnight, after a lavish buffet accompanied by a great deal of strenuous drinking, Stalin proposed a toast to the Soviet armed forces. Then his old crony Marshal Semyon Budenny* serenaded the company on an accordion, treating them to a medley of folk songs, waltzes and polkas, after which he broke into a Cossack dance when Stalin put on a gramophone record.

Present at the party was the Deputy Chief of the Soviet General Staff, Colonel-General S.M. Shtemenko. He recalled the mood in which the partygoers returned to Moscow:

> It was about three in the morning when we returned from Kuntsevo. This first celebration of the New Year in an informal

---

* An officer of monumental incompetence, Budenny had presided over the loss of half of the active strength of the Red Army when commanding the armies in the Ukraine and Bessarabia in 1941. He survived execution principally because he was one of Stalin's favourite drinking companions, and thereafter was kept away from any post of serious responsibility. In January 1943, Budenny was appointed Commander of Cavalry.

atmosphere had set us thinking. Everything seemed to indicate
that the end of the war was near. We could breathe more freely
these days although we knew, if anyone did, that in a few weeks a
new offensive would begin and much hard fighting lay ahead. . . .
Moscow still retained its wartime appearance. We drove along the
dark, deserted streets past freezing houses with closely curtained
windows and an occasional timid gleam showing through a chink.

Shtemenko was one of a new breed of Soviet officers who had proved
themselves in the cauldron of war and now led a resurgent Red Army.
This was a very different organization from the one which had come
close to disintegration in the campaigns of 1941 and 1942. Nowhere was
this more apparent than in the Soviet tank arm. By the end of 1941 all of
the Red Army's large tank units, caught by *Barbarossa* (the codename for
the German invasion of Russia in June 1941) in the process of reorgani-
zation into divisions, had been destroyed or disbanded and replaced by
brigades, regiments and battalions used in an infantry-support role. Tank
and mechanized corps reappeared in the summer of 1942, only to be
chewed up in the fierce battles in the south. Soviet tactical rigidity and
superior German battlefield reflexes continued to tip the balance of
power in favour of the Wehrmacht, but out of these campaigns emerged
a sufficient number of able corps commanders to sustain the painful
progress towards the creation of tank armies as the principal exploitation
forces of the Red Army's fronts.

The first tank armies began to appear in the early summer of 1943 and
were to play a crucial role in the destruction of the German panzer arm at
Kursk in July. In the huge armoured clash at Prokhorovka on 12 July, Fifth
Guards Tank Army, commanded by General Pavel Rotmistrov, one of the
Red Army's most accomplished exponents of armoured warfare, denied
II SS Panzer Corps the breakthrough which would have carried Fourth
Panzer Army into open country and on to the encirclement of the huge
Soviet concentration in the Kursk salient. For the first time on the Eastern
Front, the Red Army had not buckled at the first impact of Hitler's elite
armoured formations. Rather it was the Ostheer (Eastern Army) which had
given way and then been driven back to the line of the Dnieper.

The price was savage. In the high summer of 1943 the Soviet tank
armies were relatively weak in artillery and their component infantry
units had not been successfully integrated with the armoured forces. At
Prokhorovka, Rotmistrov's two tank corps lost 400 tanks, half his armoured
strength, but the panzers committed to the Kursk offensive (codenamed
Zitadelle) had been mauled beyond immediate repair. After the war,
Guderian reflected sadly on their fate:

The armoured formations, reformed and re-equipped with much effort, had lost heavily in both men and equipment and would now be unemployable for a long time to come. It was problematical whether they could be rehabilitated in time to defend the Eastern Front; as for being able to use them in defence of the Western Front against the Allied landings that threatened next spring, this was even more questionable. Needless to say, the Russians exploited their victory to the full. There were to be no more periods of quiet on the Eastern Front. From now on the enemy was in undisputed possession of the initiative.

By the end of 1944 the Soviet tank army was a powerful, well-balanced force, usually containing two or three corps of tanks and a single corps of mechanized infantry, representing an establishment of up to 50,000 troops, 900 tanks (three tank corps) and 850 artillery pieces and mortars. The mechanized infantry travelled on American-supplied Dodge trucks, their main task as the end of the war approached being that of dealing with pockets of Panzerfaust-armed German infantry in broken terrain. The principal constituent part of the tank army, the tank corps, was capable of operating independently, with one brigade of mechanized infantry supporting three brigades of tanks. Each tank corps fielded some 12,000 men, 220 tanks, forty assault guns, 150 towed artillery pieces and eight *Katyusha* multi-barrelled rocket launchers, the 'Stalin organs' so dreaded by German troops.* Individual tank brigades were often attached to rifle divisions and corps, or held as a personal reserve by a tank army commander, poised to plug a gap or exploit a breakthrough. Brigades were also combined with infantry and artillery to operate ahead of their parent armies and corps as 'forward detachments', probing the weak spots in enemy defences and engaging them until the arrival of the main body. Artillery observers travelled with the forward detachments in radio-equipped tanks, ready to call down fire ahead of the spearhead's advance.

The basic weapon of the tank army was the T-34, the best all-round tank of the war, which since the autumn of 1943 had been armed with an 85mm gun. Over 11,000 T-34/85s were produced in 1944, and such was the overall excellence of this rugged, fast and highly manoeuvrable tank that it remained in production until the mid-1950s. The T-34 was supported by the IS-2 (Josef Stalin) heavy tank, an impressive beast which

---

* The *Katyusha* (Little Kate) rocket launcher, mounted on a heavy truck, fired volleys of up to forty-eight fin-stabilized rockets with a range of up to three and a half miles. A Katyusha division was capable of firing a barrage of nearly 4,000 projectiles (230 tons of high-explosive) with devastating effect.

made its combat debut in February 1944 and whose 122mm gun was capable of penetrating 185mm of armour at 1,000 yards. As more IS-2s became available, they were formed into heavy brigades, each consisting of three regiments. The IS-2 was a match for the German MkV Panther, and the 88-mm gun of the MkVI Tiger could only penetrate its armour by closing to a range of less than 2,000 yards.

In stark contrast to the multiplicity of vehicles fielded by German armoured divisions – often as many as twelve different types of armoured vehicle and twenty types of other vehicle – the Soviet mechanized formations relied on just two, the T-34 and the Dodge truck, of which 440,000 were supplied by the Americans during the war. US Lend-Lease enabled Stalin's war factories to concentrate almost exclusively on the production of battlefield equipment. Stalin himself told Churchill that he wanted trucks more than tanks. The German commander General Fridolin Senger und Etterlin, who had led 17th Panzer Division in the abortive attempt to relieve Stalingrad in the winter of 1942, commented that the Russians

> had these principles to pick up the best type of machine wherever they could get it; to have only a very few types; to contruct the type as simply as possible; and then to produce these types in large quantities. . . . The Russian tank maintenance was also good. The bigger repairs were not carried out as fast as in the German Army, but their normal maintenance service was very efficient, and they had plenty of well-trained mechanics. Indeed, we came increasingly to employ Russian mechanics in our own tank maintenance companies.

Even at the end of the war experienced German armoured units were capable of shooting up large Soviet tank formations which heavily outnumbered them. The moment fighting became fluid, mulish Russian adherence to orders often exposed them to heavy losses. German tank aces like Hyazinth von Strachwitz, who finished the war as Commander (Armour), Army Group North, regularly claimed bags of up to fifty enemy tanks in engagements against Russian armour. But these tactical successes were achieved against a background of strategic defeat.

Like the tank arm, Russian artillery underwent a revolution during the war, the most significant feature of which was the creation of an extremely powerful Artillery Reserve controlled by Stavka.* This gave the

---

* The Stavka of the Soviet high command, the highest organ of field direction of the armed forces of the Soviet Union. It drew up battle plans and, through its adjunct, the general staff, directly organized the preparation and execution of strategic operations.

Soviet high command considerable operational flexibility and, aided by Hitler's insistence on holding on to every foot of occupied soil, enabled Stavka to concentrate colossal numbers of guns at key points to deliver systematic massed blows. The density of 300 guns a kilometre achieved at Stalingrad was to be more than doubled by the spring of 1945 to as many as 670 guns a kilometre. The lengthy preparation required to bring these masses of artillery into action, and the difficulty of moving forward quickly to consolidate gains, led in late 1942 to the creation of sixteen 'artillery breakthrough' divisions, each of 356 guns, over twice the normal establishment of 168. In the spring of 1943 artillery breakthrough corps were formed, and anti-tank regiments were also brigaded for breakthrough operations.

The Red Army's most effective anti-tank gun was the characteristically robust 76mm. Its high muzzle-velocity meant that there was a very short interval between the noise of the gun being fired and the detonation of the shell, prompting the Germans to dub it *Ratsch-boom* (crash-bang). Another highly effective tank destroyer was the SU-152 assault gun, mounted on a KV-1 heavy tank chassis and armed with a powerful 152mm howitzer mounted forward in a heavily armoured superstructure.

No soldier was better equipped for anti-tank fighting than the Red Army infantryman. His RPG-43 anti-tank grenade, firing a hollow-charge projectile from a short steel tube, much like the German Panzerfaust, was capable of knocking out a medium tank. In full battle order the Red Army soldier carried 60 pounds of equipment and ammunition in summer and 77 pounds in winter. Even when burdened with his own weapons and ammunition, he was often required to carry artillery ammunition to the forward areas. Independent of season and environment, expert at infiltrating enemy lines, capable of sustaining himself on a fraction of the supplies considered necessary by Western armies, the Red Army man was a formidable if volatile opponent. The German armoured commander Major-General F.W. von Mellenthin noted the Russian tendency to panic when an attack was launched against them from an unexpected angle:

> There is no way of telling what the Russian will do next; he will tumble from one extreme to another. . . . His qualities are as unusual and many-sided as those of his vast and rambling country. He is patient and enduring beyond imagination, incredibly brave and courageous – yet, at times, he can be a contemptible coward. There were occasions when Russian units, which had driven back

German attacks with ferocious courage, suddenly fled in panic
before a small assault group. Battalions lost their nerve when
the first shot was fired and yet the same battalions fought with
fanatical stubbornness on the following day.

To the end of the war there was an extraordinary contrast between the
ruthlessly modernized elite Guards divisions – bristling with tanks,
artillery and rocket launchers – and the seemingly inexhaustible mass of
infantry which came in their wake, evoking images of the Dark Ages
hordes. General Hasso von Manteuffel, one of Germany's finest panzer
commanders, painted a vivid picture of the Red Army on the move:

Behind the tank spearheads rolls on a vast horde, largely mounted
on horses. The soldier carries a sack on his back, with dry crusts
of bread and raw vegetables collected on the march from the
fields and villages. The horses eat the straw from the roofs – they
get very little else. The Russians are accustomed to carry on for as
long as three weeks in this primitive way, when advancing. You
can't stop them, like an ordinary army, by cutting their communications, for you rarely find any supply columns to strike.

As the experienced General von Tippelskirch observed, against such
an army one needs forces 'with masterly leadership, first-class training,
high morale and excellent nerves'.
Dominating the Soviet war effort was the figure of Stalin. In the opening days of Barbarossa, he had come close to a complete nervous collapse. When he regained his grip, his characteristic reaction was to
consolidate control of the war in his hands. The overall direction of the
political, military and economic aspects of the war was undertaken by
the State Defence Committee, or GKO, a cabinet consisting of members
of the Politburo. GKO administered military matters through the Stavka of
the Soviet high command, effectively Stalin's personal staff. In turn Stavka
devised battle plans and through its adjunct, the General Staff, directly
organized the preparation and execution of strategic operations. Stalin
saw Stavka as a kind of 'military Politburo' of top commanders, later
augmented by technicians, who could present him with options and supporting facts for discussion. At the end of this process Stalin would make
the final decision, although as the war progressed this usually reflected
Stavka's conclusions. Stalin remained supreme, but by encouraging a
degree of collective initiative within Stavka, and establishing a framework
in which individuals could present radical ideas, he ensured that he got
the best out of the outstanding military professionals who emerged during the course of the war.

Stavka representatives also made frequent visits to the Red Army fronts and, in accordance with the strategic plan, organized on-the-spot operations, exercising control over Stavka orders and co-ordinating the actions of different fronts. By the summer of 1943 what had begun as an *ad hoc* system, thrown up amid impending military disaster, had evolved into a highly flexible instrument of command, headed by a hard core of able staff officers and battle-hardened field commanders who had proved their worth without undermining Stalin's final authority over the Soviet armed forces.

At the head of the staff and battlefield chains of command were, respectively, Marshal A.M. Vasilevsky, Chief of the General Staff and Second Deputy Defence Commissar, and Marshal Georgi K. Zhukov, First Deputy Defence Commissar and, in January 1945, commander of the First Belorussian Front. Zhukov possessed an authority which far transcended his nominal level of command. In effect he came as close as Stalin would allow to being Commander-in-Chief of the Red Army.

Burly and businesslike, with a broad, handsome face, Zhukov had earned a formidable reputation for 'persistence', a Soviet military euphemism for ruthlessness on the field of battle. This quality was leavened with a gruff human touch and, by Soviet standards at least, an economical expenditure of the forces under his command. Nevertheless, woe betide the commanders who failed to match Zhukov's exacting standards. In 1944, during Operation *Bagration*,* which saw the destruction of the German Army Group Centre, Zhukov was at the front watching an attack on the German lines. Suddenly he lowered his binoculars and barked to his companions, Marshal Konstantin Rokossovsky and General Pavel Batov, 'The corps commander and the commander of 44th Rifle Division – penal battalion!' Frantic pleading by Rokossovsky and Batov saved the corps commander's skin, but not that of the general commanding 44th Rifle Division. He was stripped of his rank on the spot and sent to lead a suicide attack on the German lines in which he was killed almost instantly. Having served Zhukov's harsh disciplinary purposes, he was posthumously created a Hero of the Soviet Union.

Zhukov came of peasant stock and had been conscripted into the Tsarist army at the beginning of the First World War. He joined the Bolshevik revolution in 1917, serving as a Red Army cavalry commander during the civil war (1917–21) and the invasion of Poland (1919–20).

---

* A major Soviet offensive against German Army Group Centre launched in June 1944. When the offensive ran down, it had nearly reached the Vistula, tearing a 250-mile gap in the German line, advancing 450 miles in a few weeks and destroying the equivalent of twenty-five enemy divisions.

Zhukov subsequently became a specialist in armoured warfare, teaching the subject at the Frunze military academy. In the early 1930s, during the military honeymoon between Hitler and Stalin, he studied military science in Germany. Most important of all, Zhukov escaped the purges which destroyed the Red Army's officer corps in the late 1930s. In August 1939 he was responsible for inflicting a heavy defeat on the Japanese at Khalkin Gol, in Mongolia, at a time when the Red Army's morale and prestige were at a very low ebb. And at the important high command war games, held in January 1941 with a view to modernizing the army's approach to mechanized war, Zhukov's 'Western Force' defeated General Pavlov's 'Eastern Force' in a prophetic projection of some of the elements in Barbarossa.* This led directly to Zhukov's appointment as Chief of Staff in January 1941. He never flinched from disagreeing with Stalin, always a dangerous way of dealing with the dictator, but such was Stalin's respect for Zhukov that throughout the war he relied on him to resolve the most difficult military situations. In July 1941 Zhukov was dismissed by Stalin for advocating a withdrawal from Kiev, but in the following September he was given control of forces in the field, directing the holding operation which denied Leningrad to the Germans. A month later he was ordered to co-ordinate the defence of Moscow, launching a successful counter-offensive with fresh Siberian divisions in December. In August 1942 he was appointed Deputy Commissar for Defence, subsequently co-ordinating the defence of Stalingrad before launching Operation Uranus, planned with Vasilevsky and his fellow Stavka member, the artillery expert Marshal Voronov, which encircled the German Sixth Army. Seven months later Zhukov presided over the defence of the Kursk salient, inflicting an even heavier defeat on the Ostheer before co-ordinating a massive Soviet counter-offensive and controlling the advance of the Red Army's fronts across the Ukraine. In the spring of 1944 he assumed personal command of First Ukrainian Front after the death of General N.F. Vatutin at the hands of anti-Soviet partisans. He then planned Operation Bagration, during the final stages of which he took command of the First Belorussian Front.

Zhukov was Stalin's battle-winner, a master manipulator of the Red Army's strategic reserve, who in concert with Vasilevsky was able to restrain Stalin from the wilder flights of impetuosity to which he was prone, notably at Kursk when he was champing at the bit to launch a premature, and almost certainly fatal, strike out of the salient. Zhukov and Vasilevsky prevailed, and the German panzer arm was picked apart in the

---

* Poor Pavlov fared no better when the real thing happened in June 1941. Then the commander of West Front, he was dismissed and shot.

killing ground which Zhukov and Voronov had prepared for it.

Stalin's genius was organizational rather than operational. His greatest wartime achievement was the mobilization of manpower and massive resources which, in the final count, the Ostheer could not match. His task was made easier by the great quantities of Lend-Lease material which the Soviet Union received from the United States. The German occupation of large tracts of the Soviet Union had gouged great chunks out of the latter's productive capacity in spite of Stalin's retention of industrial bases in the Moscow-Upper Volga region, the Urals, and western Siberia. Even in 1945 the Soviet Union's overall figures for the production of coal and steel had not returned to the levels of 1940. In 1944, in spite of the attentions of Allied bombers, Germany's coal output exceeded that of the Soviet Union by 162 million tons, and that of steel by 23 million tons. Nevertheless, Soviet armaments production far surpassed that of Germany. This was made possible by Lend-Lease. Stalin was dismissive of the tanks and many of the aircraft shipped to the Soviet Union by his Western allies, but the almost limitless outpouring of US aid which met his war-industrial needs ensured Soviet survival. By May 1945 the Americans had shipped 16.4 million tons of supplies to the Soviet Union, touching every aspect of the Russian war effort: 2,000 locomotives and 540,000 tons of rails, with which the Russians laid a greater length of track than they had between 1928 and 1939; $150 million-worth of machine tools and, by the summer of 1943, nearly 1 million tons of steel; three-quarters of the Soviet Union's copper requirements; high-grade petroleum for aviation fuel; and 13 million winter boots with which the Red Army marched from Stalingrad to Berlin.

Food, too, was desperately needed as the land lost to the Germans in 1941 produced nearly 40 per cent of the Soviet Union's cereals and cattle. The mobilization of tractors for the towing of artillery had contributed to a fall in agricultural output in those areas still in Soviet hands. American agriculture, fast recovering its strength after the ravages of the Depression of 1929–34, provided the Soviet Union with 5 million tons of food, enough to give each Red Army soldier half a pound of concentrated rations for every day of the war. To meet a specific request, 12,000 tons of butter were shipped to the Soviet Union for troops convalescing in military hospitals.

Having virtually destroyed the Soviet officer corps in the purges of the 1930s, Stalin had the good sense to restore its authority as his confidence grew after Stalingrad. Revolutionary egalitarianism was replaced by military orthodoxy. Saluting was reintroduced and the distinctive gold and silver epaulettes of Tsarist days – the *pogon* – were restored. New decorations, the Orders of Suvorov, Kutuzov and Alexander Nevsky, not only invoked the pre-revolutionary past but also were exclusive to officers.

Red Army discipline, for men and officers, as Zhukov demonstrated with the commander of 44th Rifle Division, remained extremely harsh. Fear of punishment played a large part in the Red Army's continuing tactical inflexibility up to army level. After the war the American General Omar Bradley commented that a US lieutenant was granted greater authority on the Elbe than a Soviet divisional commander. Front commanders could, on occasion, exercise personal initiative, but at lower levels armies, corps and divisions were the pawns of Stavka, bound by plans and instructions from higher commands. In the background lurked the ever-present threat of the *strafblats*, the penal battalions introduced in the autumn of 1942. At a post-war dinner in Berlin, General Eisenhower described to Zhukov the various specialized armoured vehicles the Americans used to clear minefields. After a pause the Marshal of the Soviet Union replied that the best way he knew of clearing a minefield was to march a penal battalion over it.

On the morning of New Year's Day 1945, Colonel-General Guderian was again in conference with Hitler, informing him that General Gille's IV SS Panzer Corps, transferred from Army Group Centre to Army Group South, was now ready to relieve Budapest, where forward detachments of Marshal Malinovsky's Second Ukrainian Front were already probing the outer suburbs of Buda on the eastern bank of the Danube.

According to Guderian, 'Hitler expected great results from this attack. I was sceptical since very little time had been allowed for its preparation and neither the troops nor their commanders possessed the same drive as in the old days.' Back in Zossen, Guderian decided to visit Hungary and Galicia to consult with the various commanders-in-chief on the spot. First on his list was the headquarters, at Esterhaza in Hungary, of Army Group South, commanded by General Wöhler. Arriving on 5 January, Guderian discovered that Gille's offensive was faltering after making a promising start. IV SS Panzer Corps had detrained at Komarno, fifty miles north-west of Budapest and the principal German base in the sector, and had gone straight on to the attack at 10.30pm on 1 January. Driving southeast, it had slammed into the exposed left flank of the Soviet Fourth Guards Army. Attacking on a narrow front and strongly supported by the Luftwaffe, the arrival of the panzers sent a shiver of apprehension running through Stavka as they threatened to join hands with German forces counter-attacking from Budapest. Stavka immediately ordered Malinovsky to mount an attack on Komarno with Seventh Guards Army and Sixth Guards Tank Army, taking IV SS Panzer Corps in the rear. At the same time another threat from the west developed in the shape of the three divisions of III Panzer Corps attacking north-east from Mòr in an attempt to link up with the German forces fighting north of Bicske, thirty miles due west of Budapest. III Panzer Corps was thrown back with heavy losses while hard fighting continued on IV SS Panzer Corps' front until 11 January, when it withdrew by train, apparently heading west.

Leaving Hungary, Guderian ruefully reflected that 'We had neither commanders or troops of the 1940 quality any more. . . .' The next stage of his tour of the Eastern Front took him to the Cracow headquarters of Colonel-General Harpe, commander of Army Group A, whose five armies held a sector which ran for more than 400 miles due south from Warsaw along the middle Vistula to the Carpathians and Czechoslovakia. Discussing Gehlen's prediction of an imminent Russian offensive, Harpe requested that immediately before the anticipated attack he evacuate the German positions on the Vistula and withdraw to a shorter and more easily defensible line twelve miles to the west. Harpe and his Chief of Staff, Lieutenant-General von Xylander, had drawn up a plan, code-named Operation *Schlittenfahrt* (Sleighride), which concluded that their present deployments could expect to hold up for a maximum of six days before being broken and then threatened with encirclement. A with-drawal would shorten their line by some seventy miles, cushion the bulk of their forces against the initial Soviet bombardment, which would now fall on thinly held or abandoned defences, and enable them to create a mobile reserve of four armoured divisions, grouped in pairs and capable of mounting a pincer attack on the Russian break-in.

Guderian was well aware that this eminently realistic attempt to give Army Group A a fighting chance of survival would cut no ice with the Führer, but nevertheless agreed to present the Sleighride proposal at his next meeting with Hitler. A similar point of view to that of Harpe was expressed by Colonel-General Reinhardt, commander of Army Group Centre, whose three armies covered East Prussia and northern Poland as far as Warsaw. Over the telephone, Reinhardt proposed giving up his line on the River Narev in northern Poland and withdrawing to the borders of East Prussia.

At the eleventh hour Guderian steeled himself for another confronta-tion with the Führer. Later he wrote:

> My intention was to persuade him that he make the Eastern Front the point of our main defensive effort, that he free forces for this purpose from the Western Front, and that he agree to the wishes of the army group commanders concerning the withdrawal of the

front line, since there was no other way of creating a reserve in time.

The meeting was held at the Adlerhorst on 9 January. Guderian was accompanied by the Chief of Staff of the Inspectorate of Armoured Troops, General Thomale. When Hitler was shown Gehlen's carefully prepared report, complete with maps and diagrams showing the relative distributions of strength, he flew into a rage, denouncing its author as a madman who should be consigned to a lunatic asylum forthwith. Guderian, who also possessed a fiery temper, replied that if Hitler wanted Gehlen – 'one of my very best general staff officers' – locked up in a madhouse, then the Führer might as well certify the Army's Chief of Staff. The storm blew over but as Guderian recalled, with heavy understatement, 'the conference was from a military point of view unsuccessful. Harpe's and Reinhardt's proposals were turned down, with the now customary and odious remarks about generals for whom operations meant nothing more than retreat to the next rearward position. It was altogether most unsatisfying.'

At the end of the conference Hitler tried to smooth things over with a piece of disingenuous flattery. He told Guderian, 'The Eastern Front has never possessed such strong reserves as now. That is your doing. I thank you for it.' Guderian brushed aside these blandishments, replying, 'The Eastern Front is like a house of cards. If the front is broken through at one point all the rest will collapse, for twelve and a half divisions are far too small a reserve for an extended front.' Privately Guderian believed that the conference had demonstrated, once and for all, that for Hitler and his OKW stooges, Keitel and Jodl, 'ostrich politics was . . . combined with ostrich strategy'.

Returning to Zossen, Guderian concluded that the Austrian Hitler was incapable of grasping the threat to East Prussia, 'our immediate homeland . . . which had been won at such cost and which had remained attached to the ideals of Christian, Western culture through so many centuries of effort, where lay the bones of our ancestors.' All that he could do was wait for the blow to fall.

Meanwhile, at the Adlerhorst, Hitler was still worrying at Gehlen's report like a terrier with a rat. The monologue unreeled in a nightmarish loop: the Russians could not possibly have as many tanks and guns as Guderian had claimed – they were not 'made of artillery'; Army Group A's plan to hold back a mobile reserve was 'downright dangerous'. The Führer was whistling in the dark to keep his spirits up. No one dared interrupt him. But others had to live with the consequences of his decisions. On 10 January, as a cruel wind slashed across the Polish plain, Lieutenant-General Xylander told General Harpe, 'The Führer has rejected everything – Kurland,* reinforcements from the West, and Sleighride. The front line stays where it is, and the situation remains the same. The Führer does not believe the Soviets will attack.' Three days earlier Army Group A had detected fresh Soviet units moving into the front in the west face of their Baranov bridgehead on the Vistula. In the Pulawy and Magnuszew bridgeheads the Red Army was bringing up more of the artillery which Hitler had tried to convince himself it did not possess. The final deployments were under way.

Since 17 August 1944, when the town of Schwirwindt, in East Prussia, had been captured by the Red Army, Russian troops had stood on German soil. Conquered by the Teutonic Knights in the thirteenth century, East Prussia came to represent a particular, albeit romanticized, aspect of German-ness. It was from East Prussia that the *Junker* class of aristocratic landowners had sprung, embodying the virtues of loyalty and an austere life carved out of a harsh land. The military vein running through Prussian history was of singular importance. The Prussian military genius Frederick the Great had been the driving force behind the transformation of 'limited war' into 'total war'. Throughout the war, as Hitler moved from one Führer headquarters to another, the one constant decorative feature which accompanied him was a large portrait of the Prussian king by Anton Graff. As darkness closed around the Third Reich, Hitler spent an increasing amount of time closeted with the Graff portrait, in silent communion with the man he claimed as his military mentor. Frederick had been a master of the 'strategy of survival', a brilliant handler of limited resources against numerically and materially superior enemies, and a firm believer in the principle that 'wars are decided by battles'. For Hitler, whose use of his own resources had been prodigal, the last battle was about to begin.

The Russians had a score to settle in East Prussia. Early in January 1945 the soldiers of the Third Belorussian Front, commanded by the brilliant young General Ivan Chernyakhovsky, were told:

> Comrades! You have reached the borders of East Prussia, and you will now tread on that ground which gave birth to those fascist monsters who devastated our cities and homes, and slaughtered our sons and daughters, our brothers and sisters, our wives and mothers. The most inveterate of those brigands and Nazis sprang from East Prussia. For many years now they have held power in Germany, directing this nation in its foreign aggression and its genocide of other peoples.

---

* The withdrawal by sea of the divisions trapped in the Kurland peninsula.

No quarter was to be given in the Red storm which was threatening to burst over Germany's eastern marches.

At the beginning of January 1945 the battle line on the Eastern Front ran from Memel, on the Baltic coast of Lithuania, to Zagreb in Yugoslavia. The great Soviet summer offensive of 1944 had halted at the gates of Warsaw. Throughout the autumn and winter of 1944 there was savage fighting for Budapest, but to the north the front remained relatively quiescent. In the late summer the Red Army had established three bridgeheads on the western bank of the Vistula in central Poland. The southernmost and most substantial bridgehead was at Sandomierz (Baranov) in the sector of Marshal Konev's First Ukrainian Front. The smaller Pulawy and Magnuszew bridgeheads, in the sector of Zhukov's First Belorussian Front, lay some seventy miles to the north at the junction of the Vistula and the Pilica, twenty-five miles from Warsaw. These bridgeheads were to provide the springboards for the Red Army's winter campaign, the drive to Berlin.

Soviet planning for the final stages of the war had begun during the course of 1944's summer and autumn campaigns. In its original form it envisaged the capture of Berlin in forty-five days of offensive operations conducted to a depth of 500 miles in two successive stages unbroken by any operational pause. The first stage, lasting fifteen days, would carry the Red Army to a line running south from Marienburg through Poznan to Breslau; the second, to which thirty days were allotted, would encompass the capture of Berlin and bring Soviet forces up to the line of the Elbe.

The plan entailed two major blows, related but separated geographically by the course of the Vistula west of Warsaw, where the river sweeps in a long north-easterly loop before turning north again towards Danzig. The main blow was to be opened between Warsaw and the Carpathians by the First Belorussian and First Ukrainian Fronts, supported on the left by Fourth Ukrainian Front. Zhukov was to break out of the Pulawy bridgehead towards Lodz and out of the Magnuszew bridgehead towards Kutno, encircling Warsaw on his right flank. Konev's drive from the Baranov bridgehead was to be aimed westward towards Radomsko, while his right-flank spearhead swung north-west to join Zhukov's left flank in the destruction of German forces in the Kielce-Radom area. As Konev's central spearhead thrust west towards Czestochowa, the forces on his left were to attack south-west towards Cracow and the industrial heartland of Upper Silesia. Having attained their initial objectives, both fronts were to advance abreast and north-west to the Oder.

North of the Vistula bend, Marshal Rokossovsky's Second Belorussian Front was to burst out of its own bridgeheads and drive north-west to the

Baltic coast, isolating East Prussia and clearing the line of the Lower Vistula. On Rokossovsky's right, Chernyakhovsky's Third Belorussian Front was given the task of attacking westward towards the fortress city of Königsberg, cutting Third Panzer Army adrift from its parent body, Army Group Centre, and destroying Fourth Army in the area of the Masurian Lakes, where in September 1914 General Rennenkampf's Russian First Army had been cut up by Hindenburg and Ludendorff.

Detailed planning extended only to the first phase of the drive on Berlin. It took place against a background of almost feverish manoeuvring within the Soviet high command. Although much hard fighting lay ahead, the military outcome of the war was now certain. For Stalin the fight for survival had become a race to secure the maximum political and territorial advantage from the imminent collapse of Nazi Germany. The future balance of the forces within the Soviet Union was also absorbing Stalin's attention – the relationship between the Party and the Army, and that between the Politburo and the brilliant commanders who had masterminded the military campaigning since Stalingrad. Among the commanders a determined jockeying for pre-eminence had developed, a phenomenon which Stalin did little to discourage. In the final analysis they were men of his own making and there for the breaking, too, if the occasion demanded it. Whether commanding, or descending on, a front, a man like Zhukov wielded formidable power, but it was held only at Stalin's pleasure. When it suited him, the distance between the Supreme Commander and his deputies could yawn as wide as the gulf between a marshal and a private.

On 7 November 1944 the leading players in the planned winter offensive, Marshals Zhukov, Vasilevsky, Rokossovsky, Konev, Tolbukhin and General Chernyakhovsky, travelled to Moscow to consult with Stalin and the General Staff. A provisional date of 20 January 1945 was set for launching the last great offensive of the war.

No sooner had his commanders returned to their fronts than Stalin had second thoughts. At this stage in the planning First Belorussian Front was commanded by Marshal Konstantin Rokossovsky, a soldier who had been imprisoned by Stalin during the purges of the 1930s and about whom the Soviet dictator still harboured political doubts. It was clear that First Belorussian Front would spearhead the final drive on Berlin, but Rokossovsky would not lead it. The prize of taking Berlin, the 'Lair of the Fascist Beast', was to be given to Zhukov, the man with the sharpest elbows in the power struggle taking place within the the Soviet high command. Stalin telephoned Rokossovsky and told him that he was to be replaced as commander of First Belorussian Front by Zhukov. Rokossovsky was to take over from General Zakharov as commander of

Second Belorussian Front, covering the right flank of the central thrust on Berlin. Somewhat put out, Rokossovsky later recalled:

> The decision was very unexpected. I had just been at Supreme Headquarters discussing plans for the operation of the First Belorussian Front towards Berlin. Our proposals had been accepted without comment, and now I was getting a new assignment. I could not help asking the Supreme Commander-in-Chief, 'Why am I being penalized?' Stalin answered that his deputy, Marshal Zhukov, was being named commander of the First Belorussian Front and I would learn the other necessary information at Supreme Headquarters.

Zhukov assumed command of First Belorussian Front on 19 November, and the exchange of commands was accompanied by Stalin's announcement that he would personally co-ordinate the four fronts tasked with the assault on Germany. The planning was now moving into its second stage, at the level of the individual fronts, where significant adjustments were made. At the end of November Zhukov persuaded Stalin to agree to shift the direction of his front's advance from due west to north-west along a Lodz-Poznan axis, enabling him to skirt a heavily fortified region. In turn Konev's front was allotted Breslau rather than Kalisz as its principal objective. Beyond Breslau lay the industrial region of Silesia, where Albert Speer had concentrated clusters of German armaments factories out of the range of British and American heavy bombers. When Konev had presented his operational proposals to Stalin at the end of November, he had been left in no doubt about the importance of this region. Stalin had silently traced the outline of the great industrial basin on the map before uttering the single word, 'Gold'. At all costs Konev had to liberate this priceless economic asset without destroying it.

The scale of the preparations for the coming offensive was massive. Along a front of nearly 400 miles, Stavka proposed to launch four major breakthrough operations aimed at Königsberg (Chernyakhovsky), Danzig (Rokossovsky), Poznan (Zhukov) and Breslau (Konev), with thirty field armies, five tank armies and four air armies,* supported by independent mobile operational groups and artillery breakthrough divisions. Between them, Zhukov and Konev's fronts mustered 163 rifle divisions, 32,143 guns and heavy mortars, nearly 6,500 tanks and 4,772 aircraft. Under their com-

---

* As a rule each front was supported by one air army. The front and air army commanders jointly worked out operational plans, with the former deciding the priority of missions and, with the advice of the air army commander, developing an overall plan for missions flown in support of ground operations.

mand were some 2.25 million men, including approximately one-third of all Red Army infantry formations and just over 40 per cent of the Soviet armour deployed on the Eastern Front.

First Ukrainian Front's Baranov bridgehead, forty-five miles wide and nearly forty deep, bulged at the seams with about 90 per cent of Konev's front: five armies (Thirteenth, Fifty-Second, Fifty-Eighth Guards in the first echelon and Twenty-First and Fifty-Ninth in the second) and two tank armies (Fourth Guards and Third Guards). Konev planned to make his breakthrough on a twenty-five mile front and exploit along two axes in particular: in the south, General Pavel Rybalko's Third Guards Tank Army, operating in Fifty-Second Army's sector, was to drive into the Silesian industrial heartland; in the north, General D.D. Lelyushenko's Fourth Tank Army, in Thirteenth Army's area of operations, was to co-operate with Zhukov's left flank in the elimination of German forces in the Kielce-Radom sector.

Zhukov's two bridgeheads were smaller and less manageable than that at Baranov. The Pulawy bridgehead, on First Belorussian Front's left, contained two armies, Sixty-Ninth and Thirty-Third, supported by two tank corps, IX and XI, rather than two tank armies. Zhukov had concentrated his main strength inside and around the larger of his bridgeheads, at Magnuszew. It was a tight squeeze, with about 400,000 men and nearly 2,000 tanks packed into a pocket fifteen miles deep and eight miles wide. Fifth Shock and Eighth Guards Armies were poised to make the breakthrough, supported by part of a third army, Sixty-First, which was deployed astride the Vistula. Two tank armies, Lieutenant-General M.E. Katukov's First Guards and General Bogdanov's Second Guards, were drawn up on the eastern bank of the Vistula, ready to exploit the breakthrough. On the left flank, First Guards Tank Army was tasked with advancing west-north-west on the Lodz-Poznan axis; on the right, Second Guards Tank Army was to drive south of Warsaw, advancing parallel with the Vistula in a north-westerly direction to Bromberg, where the river turns north-east.

To feed, fuel and arm the forces massing in and around the Vistula bridgeheads stretched the logistical services of fronts and armies to the limit. The shattered railway system running from the Vistula eastward through Poland was repaired, and the track altered to accommodate the wider Russian gauge. The rail bridge over the Vistula at Sandomierz, directly behind the Baranov bridgehead, was rebuilt. Over 2,500 trainloads trundled in to swell Konev's and Zhukov's supply dumps. Thousands of Lend-Lease trucks, the backbone of the Soviet logistics system, drove along dirt roads to deliver nearly 1 million tons of supplies to First Belorussian Front, including a daily requirement of 1,150 tons of bread, 1,500 tons of vegetables, 220 tons of meat and 44 tons of sugar. But ammunition was the principal priority, and Zhukov's men had to endure two meatless days out of every seven.

In December, the waters of the Vistula rose and the ice began to break up, threatening the bridges built by First Belorussian Front's engineers with ice floes both on the surface and beneath it. General V.I. Chuikov, commander of Eighth Guards Army* and the heroic defender of Stalingrad, recalled the threat this posed to the build-up in the Magnuszew bridgehead:

> The Vistula is a treacherous river. It carries ice not only on the surface, but along the bottom too. Ramming the bridge piles the floes form invisible dams, and then the force of the current builds up and washes away the banks and the river-bed around the piles. The engineers and road-building units had to use all their resources. Three companies of demolition men and one road-building battalion were assigned to each bridge, and special emergency teams were formed. Lorries, tractors and a battery of 120mm mortars to demolish the larger ice floes were placed at the disposal of each crossing-area commandant. Our men worked round the clock and managed to keep the crossing points intact, ensuring an uninterrupted flow of transport to the opposite bank.

Chuikov is also revealing about the long-range reconnaissance which preceded the breakout from the bridgeheads. He noted:

> We knew exactly what enemy units were manning the first line of defence. But that was not enough. It was essential to find out what enemy forces were in the second echelon and in the entire depth of the defence zone. Our scouts had to infiltrate the enemy lines and capture identification prisoners, question them and thus check the information obtained by observation.

Colonel Gladki, chief of Eighth Guards Army's intelligence, devised a plan for reconnaissance in depth. A number of reconnaissance groups, operating up to thirty miles behind the front line, kept German troop movements under constant surveillance. Most of them had infiltrated the German lines on foot, and contact with them was maintained by radio and by Polikarpov Po-2 light aircraft flying in at night.

According to Chuikov:

---

* Chuikov commanded Sixty-Second Army at Stalingrad. Redesignated Eighth Guards Army, the formation remained under his command for the rest of the war.

The first two scouts, Sergeant Pyotr Bachek and Private Vassily Bychkov, with whom I had talked on many occasions, went behind the enemy lines in early October. They crossed the front in an area south of Cecylówka, and entered the woods some eight miles south-west of Warka. They were to find out what enemy units were stationed there, and to take note of all the defence installations they spotted on the way. The mission was to be completed in three nights and two days.

The scouts were successful. They reported that no enemy units were stationed in the woods, and Chuikov decided to put a permanent reconnaissance group in the area. A base was set up in the heart of the forest and observation posts were arranged on its fringes to follow troop movements along the neighbouring roads.

This permanent reconnaissance group consisted of seven men, with Lieutenant Ivan Kistayev, an experienced scout, in command. The men made their way into the woods secretly, concealed themselves effectively and functioned for over two months, transmitting to Army HQ valuable information obtained by direct observation and from captured enemy soldiers. They pinpointed the positions of enemy artillery, six-barrelled mortars* and panzer units. Also they watched the everyday routine of the enemy forces, and found out when the soldiers had their regular meals and how they rested, when the men in the outposts were relieved, and the like. All this had to be taken into account in delivering a surprise blow.

The delivery of a 'surprise blow' presented Stavka and the front commanders with a knotty problem. At the end of 1944 the contraction of the Eastern Front produced an increased concentration of Soviet and German troops in the front line, making it extremely difficult for the Soviets either to conceal their intentions from the enemy or to mislead the Germans as to where the main blows would fall. The heavy fighting in Hungary might distract the Germans, but only as to the scale of offensives further to the north, which necessarily would have to be launched from the bridgeheads on the Vistula or from the area south of the Vistula to the Carpathian Mountains.

During the course of the war the Red Army had developed the science of military deception to something approaching an art form. The battle

---

* The multi-barrelled *Nebelwerfer* ('smoke thrower') had originally been intended for use in connection with smokescreens and gas warfare, but the latter was never implemented and Nebelwerfers were increasingly put to use firing explosive projectiles. A Nebelwerfer battery could saturate an area 2,200 yards long by 110 yards deep with 108 rockets in the space of 10 seconds.

of Kursk marked a watershed in this process, for it was in the lengthy preparation for this titanic clash that deception (*maskirovka*) measures were incorporated into the strategic plan for the defence of the salient, and for the counter-offensive that was launched out of it when the German armour had ground to a halt. For the coming offensive Soviet planners devised a *maskirovka* plan of which the main aim was to conceal the scale of the operations, rather than the location, timing or intent of the attack.

Immense care was taken to mask the build-up in the Vistula bridge-heads. Throughout December, planning for the fronts proceeded on a strict 'need to know' basis among a limited number of senior officers. It was not until late in the month that the planning circle was widened to include a select number of staff officers. No written orders were prepared, and all instructions were given orally. A corps commander in First Guards Tank Army, then training near Lublin, recalled:

> The First Belorussian Front directive, which specified the mission of First Guards Tank Army, was revealed to a limited circle of the command staff: the members of the military council, the assistant commanders, and the chief of the operations section. It was forbidden to type documents of the operational plan, and orders for preparing troops for the offensive were given orally. It was prohibited to conduct telephone conversations on matters pertaining to offensive operations; and radio stations, as before, were silent. Brigades received their orders five days before the offensive.

Active and passive measures were taken to blur the enemy's assessment of the size and whereabouts of the Soviet concentrations. Phantom formations appeared on the left and right flanks of First Belorussian Front, where Zhukov hoped to attract German reconnaissance and reserves. Near Joselow, thirty-five miles south of the Pulawy bridgehead, he positioned 1,000 dummy tanks, self-propelled guns and other vehicles, 'animated' by a number of genuine tanks, to simulate a significant armoured concentration. Rail, road and radio traffic in the sector was stepped up, the last using real unit call-signs and frequencies. Engineers were kept busy building bridges and airstrips, while aircraft droned to and fro overhead. Meanwhile, in Zhukov's chosen attack sectors, strict *maskirovka* discipline was enforced as the build-up gathered pace. Incoming transport was camouflaged to resemble loads of hay or building materials. Tanks and artillery were unloaded under cover of darkness and camouflaged by day. Tell-tale tank tracks were erased, and empty rail wagons were dispersed in the front's rear area. All engineering work connected with the offensive was done at night.

Formations from the Stavka reserve moved into the sector in staggered sequence amid the tightest security. At the end of November First Guards Army travelled 200 miles by rail and road from its refitting base near Lvov to a concentration area twenty miles north-east of Lublin, where it remained concealed in a forest before being ordered to a new assembly area on the eastern bank of the Vistula. All movement was by night, with tanks and artillery carried by rail and the rest of the army using numerous roads, all of which avoided population centres, and resting up by day in woods and forests.

It took a month to move Third Shock Army by train from Second Baltic Front to its new assembly area east of Warsaw. Twenty-three trains, heavily camouflaged and moving at night under radio silence, were used to transfer the Army's three rifle corps. A total of 117 trains were needed to complete this regrouping, the last unit detraining thirty miles east of Warsaw on 10 January, four days before the offensive began. The depth of this manoeuvre ensured that it passed undetected by German intelligence.

Inside the Magnuszew bridgehead, the build-up could not escape closer German scrutiny. Eighth Guards Army, for example, concentrated eight rifle divisions in a sector less than seven miles wide. The ever inventive Chuikov described how he attempted to distract the attention of German intelligence from his preparations:

> ... I suggested implementation of a plan of gradually concentrating forces and weaponry in jumping-off positions. The movement of troops and equipment occurred only at night and in a proportion which could be masked by morning. In the daytime forces, located in trenches in view of the enemy, had to carry on 'household' work intensively: the enemy thought that we were preparing not for an offensive but for a firm defence, in accordance with the use of troops and equipment resources. We tried to use widely loudspeaker broadcasting stations: even music sounded over our positions, entertaining our soldiers and lulling the attentiveness of the enemy.

As Konev occupied only one bridgehead, his *maskirovka* measures were, if anything, even more complex than those initiated by Zhukov. Konev's intention was to persuade the German high command that he was planning to launch a major assault from the left flank of the Baranov bridgehead. Another dummy tank army took shape in this sector, the

skilful emplacement of 600 wooden tanks and self-propelled guns suggesting a south-westerly drive towards Cracow. A network of new roads
appeared to service this phantom formation, and at the beginning
of January billeting parties toured the area, warning the local population
of the arrival of fresh units and of the dangers of the imminent offensive.
Roving batteries of guns and heavy mortars adjusted fire on enemy
positions from fake gun emplacements, all the while ensuring that every
calibre of weapon was fired. Night reconnaissance raids were mounted
to simulate final attack preparations. These measures prompted the commander of Army Group A, Colonel-General Harpe, to shift two German
infantry divisions, 344th and 359th, south into the Tarnow sector while
Konev was busily slipping armour, infantry and artillery across the Vistula
by night into the sector directly opposite Kielce.

Inside the Baranov bridgehead, *maskirovka* measures included the
building of earthworks and trenches to conceal movement from German
observation posts, which were able to peer for up to five miles beyond
the Soviet front line. Where the terrain afforded little or no cover, engineers employed camouflage masking techniques to hide road and other
movements. By the eve of the offensive, they had erected some fifty miles
of camouflaged vertical masking and dug a hundred miles of communications trenches. There were few forests in the bridgehead, but such
cover as they did provide was artificially extended by the building of
huge screens made of vegetation, running out of wooded areas. Special
patrols ensured that the troops did not cut down precious timber and
thus further denude a predominantly open area. More than a hundred
miles of cross-country roads were carved through the forests, and on
their edges the engineers raised over 150 miles of woodland screening.
Careful traffic control at night enabled a staggered insertion into the
salient of up to two rifle divisions, moving in battalion columns, every
night.

German intelligence was significantly influenced by the *maskirovka*
campaign. OKH had long expected an attack on the central sector of the
front from the Niemen River to the Carpathians, but successive false alarms
had induced an increasingly querulous note in German intelligence
assessments. Konev's deception plan exerted a strong gravitational pull,
tugging Gehlen towards an estimate that the main blow would be
launched south-west from the Baranov bridgehead, striking towards
Katowice and Cracow. The OKH intelligence chief was not taken in by
Zhukov's deception but nevertheless agonized that

> on the one hand all reports from agents designate the western and
> north-western part of the Baranov bridgehead as the area of

special importance, but on the other hand all other evidence (air reconnaissance, artillery reconnaissance, interrogation of POWs) points to the northern front, leaving us for the time being with the question as to whether this is due to extremely good camouflage measures on the western and northern parts of the bridgehead or due to agents' reports not being fully exploited.

Gehlen toyed with a number of appreciations of Soviet intentions, including the notion that Zhukov and Konev might launch a limited offensive on the Vistula to establish a larger, continuous lodgement on the west bank of the river. These uneasy musings were accompanied by a serious underestimate of the forces massing to break out of the Vistula bridgeheads. OKH completely failed to detect the redeployment from the Stavka reserve of Sixty-First, Third Shock, Thirty-Third, Fifty-Second, Twenty-First and Fifty-Ninth Armies, continuing to believe that they remained in their former sectors, in some cases hundreds of miles away, or were deep in the Russian rear. Other armies were identified, but their concentration areas were often only dimly apprehended. Those armies German intelligence correctly identified and positioned – Sixth Army, for example, on the northern shoulder of the Baranov bridgehead – were in all probability meant to be detected as part of the overall *maskirovka* plan. By this stage in the war the Soviets were extremely skilful at revealing only what they wanted the enemy, and their Western allies, to know at any particular time.

According to David Glantz, the undisputed expert in this field, the net effect of the German intelligence failure in the winter of 1944–5 was fatal: 'In all three bridgeheads the Germans assessed [that] they faced odds of about 3:1 or 3.5:1. Actually the Soviets created an operational superiority of between 5:1 and 7:1 in the bridgeheads. When Soviet concentration occurred, that translated into Soviet tactical superiorities of between 8:1 and 16:1.'

Throughout December 1944, OKH had been living in a fool's paradise. There was a strange reluctance to anticipate a major Soviet offensive, born in part of Hitler's conviction that the front would remain quiet while Stalin continued to wrangle with the Western Allies over the status of the puppet Polish government which he had established in Lublin. As long as Roosevelt and Churchill refused to recognize the Lublin Poles as the *de jure* government of Poland, OKH took the political view that Stalin would exact revenge by holding back and allowing his allies to soak up heavy punishment in the Ardennes.

In fact, the reasons for the Soviet delay were not hard to discern. Stalin declined to go on to the attack in conditions of heavy mud and poor visibility, which would have taken the edge off Soviet artillery armoured and mechanized superiority. He was waiting for the rivers and canals to freeze over and the ground to become as hard as iron under a thin covering of snow, good going for the T-34s which would allow them to forge across the flat, open plains of western Poland to Silesia and Brandenburg in Germany. As early as 14 December, Stalin had told Averell Harriman, the US Ambassador in Moscow, that he was waiting for a spell of fine weather before ordering any major action. OKH might have taken its eye off the ball, but at the front the German army groups took a less sanguine view of the threat they faced; their war diaries noted the fact that the Red Army's preparations were over and it was now waiting for a spell of clear and frosty weather.

On 6 January Churchill had sent a personal message to Stalin, asking whether the Western Allies could count on an offensive on the Vistula during that month, the fighting in the Ardennes being 'very heavy'. The next day Stalin replied that preparations would go ahead 'at a rapid rate' and 'regardless of weather'. The Soviet offensive would be launched no later than the second half of January. On 8 January Marshal Konev was telephoned by General A.I. Antonov, the Chief of the General Staff, who informed him that because of the 'difficult position' of the Allies in the Ardennes* the Soviet attack would begin as soon as possible. First Ukrainian Front would attack on 12 January. Then, in familiar fashion, a series of rolling blows would be delivered along the Eastern Front, by Third Belorussian Front on the 13th and First and Second Belorussian Fronts on the 14th. By 15 January the entire Eastern Front would be ablaze.

Hitler was still in the West, at the Adlerhorst. On 9 January, after his strained meeting with Guderian, an army adjutant handed the Führer the first documentary indication that the Red Army offensive was soon to begin: 'Over the last few days there have been continuous heavy movements into the Baranov bridgehead . . . the impression there is that they are going to start soon after all.'

Danger signals were now coming in thick and fast. 'Ice bridges'† were being laid and minefields cleared. Intercepted Russian radio traffic revealed that heavy reinforcements were being moved up. Prisoners confirmed that the offensive would begin between 11 and 16 January.

In the Soviet bridgeheads the front commanders had given their army commanders their orders personally early in January. Tank corps and

---

* The exchange had an artificial flavour. By 8 January the British and Americans had already gone on the offensive and, within a week, would eliminate the 'bulge' in the Ardennes.
†Rail tracks and planked causeways laid across frozen rivers.

regimental commanders had received their orders four or five days before the attack, and battalion commanders were briefed forty-eight hours later. On Konev's front platoon commanders were given their orders on 11 January; the soldiers would have to wait for just a few hours before the preliminary artillery bombardment was unleashed.

On the night of 11/12 January the loudspeakers continued to blare in the Baranov bridgehead as thousands of tanks, assault guns and towed artillery pieces were moved into position. Konev had set up his command post in a small house on the edge of a wood. To the west lay the German front line, obscured by fog, low cloud and flurries of snow. The ground was hard, but at times visibility was close to zero, eliminating the possibility of close support by the Red Army Air Force's formidable Ilyushin Il-2 Shturmovik ground-attack aircraft, the 'flying artillery' which accounted for about a quarter of all Soviet combat missions flown on the Eastern Front.

Inside the bridgehead the artillery was ranged wheel to wheel in concentrations of up to 300 guns per kilometre of front. At 4.35am, while Hitler slumbered fitfully at the Adlerhorst, Konev's artillery attack began, obliterating the German front line, churning the frozen earth, collapsing command posts and bunkers and tossing maimed men and mangled machines through the smoke of the barrage. At 5am Soviet reconnaissance battalions, stiffened by the desperate men of the *strafblats*, stormed the first line of enemy trenches and then pushed forward to identify the strongpoints between the first and second lines which had survived the initial, pulverizing bombardment. Then they went to ground as the Russian gunners readied themselves for a second, heavier storm of fire.

The Germans who had survived the first bombardment had been so shaken up that they assumed that Konev's reconnaissance in force was his main attack. Thus, at 10am, they were wholly unprepared for a second 107-minute bombardment which worked its way back and forth across the full depth of the German defences. The commander of the Soviet Fourth Tank Army, General Lelyushenko, recalled:

> The recent silence gave way to a general thundering, booming, crackling and whistling. Shells and mortar bombs fell on an area tens of kilometres wide and deep, from where there arose plumes of smoke, fire and dust compounded with snow. The ground quivered, and the very earth of the battlefield was blackened.

Under the huge pall of dust and smoke which loomed over the the German lines the headquarters of Fourth Panzer Army was blown apart.

The German mobile reserves – deployed close to the main battle line, the *Hauptkampflinie*, on Hitler's orders – were broken up. Entire units fled, panic-stricken, to the rear.

The main Russian infantry attack went in later that morning. Rifle battalions, supported by tanks and self-propelled guns, pushed down 'fire lanes' left open by the artillery. At 2pm the T-34s of Fourth Tank Army, discernible, in their white winter camouflage, only by movement, began to move off. Each of the army's two corps, XI and VI Guards Mechanized, was reinforced with a regiment of Josef Stalin heavy tanks mounting 122mm guns. Within two hours Fourth Tank Army had advanced twelve miles on a front of twenty-five miles towards Kielce, facing the northern tip of the Baranov bridgehead, crashing through the forested terrain, criss-crossed with river valleys, which Harpe, the commander of Army Group A, had considered 'untankable'.

At the moment Lelyushenko's tanks were roaring off their start lines, Hitler was taking lunch at the Adlerhorst with two of his secretaries, the young and recently widowed Traudl Junge and the elderly Johanna Wolf. As Fourth Panzer Army fell apart, the Führer was regaling his female companions with a mildly scatological story of how, in happier days, he had been trapped in his car by adoring crowds while his bladder threatened to burst. These meandering monologues, increasingly taxing for those who had to endure them, provided Hitler with a brief respite from reality. As Frau Junge later observed, '. . . those who, like us, knew him well, recognized that he had recourse to such small talk as a kind of anaesthetic to distract him from the losses of territory, equipment and human life of which every hour brought fresh report.'

Meanwhile disaster threatened to overtake the German forces in the path of Konev's drive north-westwards from the Baranov bridgehead. It was not until late in the afternoon that Fourth Panzer Army's tactical reserve, 16th and 17th Panzer Divisions of General Walther Nehring's XXIV Panzer Corps, were committed to the battle and then only with orders to close up to the 'hinge' of Kielce. It was too late. Soviet tanks were already streaming past 16th and 17th Panzers' assembly areas, shooting up entire battalions on the move. The battered remnants of the German armoured reserve fell back towards Kielce, harried all the way. On the morning of the 13th, 17th Panzer's divisional headquarters was overrun and its commander, Colonel Brux, taken prisoner.

That day Lelyushenko's tanks and Colonel-General N.P. Pukhov's Thirteenth Army continued to drive towards the River Nida on a broad front, while Third Guards Tank Army and Fifth Guards and Fifty-Second Armies beat off German counter-attacks against the western face of the rapidly expanding salient that threatened to engulf Kielce. To the south,

Sixtieth Army was moving on Cracow, supported on its right flank by Fifty-Ninth Army and IV Guards Tank Corps.

The colossal tumour swelling inside the German battle line consumed the right flank of Fourth Panzer Army, annihilating LXVIII Panzer Corps in the south and gnawing away at XXIV Panzer Corps in the centre, where Nehring's divisions were conducting a desperate fighting retreat along the roads leading north. The capture of Kielce secured Konev's right flank, spilling his armour into open country, where it placed General Hermann Recknagel's XLII Corps in imminent danger of encirclement. The corps headquarters was shot up by Soviet tanks and the rest of Recknagel's command abandoned their heavy equipment and withdrew northward on foot, where on 18 January they linked up with the survivors of XXIV Panzer Corps.

As darkness fell on the evening of 17 January, Konev's left flank was encircling Cracow. Rybalko's tanks and Fifth Guards Army had out-flanked the city to the north, while Fifty-Ninth and Sixtieth Armies closed on the city itself, which was evacuated by the German garrison without a fight on the evening of 19 January. The way now lay open for Konev's infantry armies to secure the industrial treasure trove Stalin sought in Silesia.

On the night of 13 January all the formations of First Belorussian Front were placed on full alert. Preparations for the offensive were complete. Chuikov later wrote:

> Over 10,000 guns emplaced in the two bridgeheads were aimed at the enemy fortifications. Two hundred and fifty guns per kilometre of frontage was our guarantee of a successful breakthrough ... the powerful loudspeakers still transmitted music and songs. The enemy had to be led to believe that nothing was in the offing.

Engineer battalions had cleared passages through the minefields First Belorussian Front had laid in front of its positions, and were now engaged in the dangerous business of removing the mines in front of the forward trenches of German Ninth Army. Until midnight the stars shone brightly in a clear, frosty sky, but then a mist began to settle over the front. Towards morning it thickened, and by 7am, when the field kitchens were giving the assault troops a hot breakfast, visibility had been reduced to a few yards.

Tension had tightened as the small hours dragged past. At his command post in the centre of the bridgehead, General Berzarin, command-ing Fifth Shock Army, chain smoked and compulsively consulted his watch as dawn approached. One of his staff recalled:

Those final hours before the attack were wearisome and anxious. Everything seemed to have been prepared, calculated and checked, and yet we were uneasy in ourselves. Our eyes were drawn involuntarily to the map, which was streaked with arrows and crossed by the dark blue markings which indicated the enemy defensive positions – and there were seven of them between the Vistula and the Oder. . . .

When Zhukov bustled into Berzarin's command post, he brusquely dispelled the tension. Visibly pleased with Berzarin's report, he reassured the general and his staff that he had a 200 per cent guarantee of success.

At 8.25am First Belorussian Front's artillery received the order to load. Four minutes later the 'Ready' command was given, and at 8.30am the ground shivered under the feet of the Russian assault troops as the artillery commanders gave the order to fire.

In most sectors the bombardment lasted for a short and stunning twenty-five minutes, raking the German lines up to a depth of five miles. Then 'forward battalions' raced through the 800 passages cleared through the German minefields to seize the first and second lines of enemy trenches. The preliminary bombardment had thrown the German command and observation posts into utter confusion, compounded by the heavy mist which hugged the battlefield. When the sun came up resistance began to stiffen. The German tactical reserve, 19th and 25th Panzer Divisions, was ordered to counter-attack at 7.45am. They left their start lines nearly three hours later, but this relatively prompt response was vitiated by the decision to launch them in separate and diverging counter-blows, 19th Panzer against Sixty-Ninth Army attacking out of the Pulawy bridgehead, and 25th Panzer against Fifth Shock Army on the northern flank of the Magnuszew bridgehead.

The weather prevented the Red Army Air Force from flying a single sortie on Zhukov's front, and the task of breaking up the German reserves therefore fell on the artillery. But much of it was toiling through the mist to new positions and was unable to join the battle. Meanwhile Zhukov held back his tank armies, which were champing at the bit to exploit the breakthrough, while the rifle divisions of Eighth Guards and Fifth Shock Armies ground their way through the German positions.

The lower Pilica, thinly covered with ice broken in parts by fast-flowing water and straddled by German artillery fire, was crossed near Warka by XXVI Rifle Corps, which seized a tank-bearing bridge that the enemy had mined but not blown, the Warka garrison having taken to its heels in the direction of Warsaw. By the evening of the 14th, T-34s of Bogdanov's Second Guards Tank Army were pouring over the bridge to swing north-west towards Sochaczew, a rail and road junction thirty miles west of Warsaw whose capture would block the German retreat.

On Bogdanov's left, First Guards Tank Army was held back for agonizing hours until Zhukov rasped out the agreed signal for its release, 'Get the ball rolling!'. It drove towards Lodz, crossing the Pilica on the night of the 15th. Leading the advance was 44 Tank Brigade of XI Guards Tank Corps, commanded by the energetic Colonel I.I. Gusakovsky, who had sent his mechanized infantry scrambling across the ice on foot. Getting tanks and assault guns to the other side was more problematic, as the ice would not bear their weight. Fortunately for Gusakovsky, his engineers discovered a ford and twenty-six tanks and six assault guns plunged into the black water. Six tanks and two of the assault guns spluttered to a halt, but the rest emerged on the west bank, their engines stuttering and roaring, huge chunks of ice piled around their turrets, to join 45 Tank Brigade in beating off a counter-attack by 25th Panzer Division.

At dawn on the 15th, Eighth Guards Army had delivered a powerful forty-minute artillery barrage before moving up on the third German defence line, the Warka-Radom railway. At midday Chuikov launched an attack on the railway, but was still denied air support by the clammy mist which hung over the battlefield. Driving up to the front line, Chuikov encountered General Vaingrub, the commander of his mechanized and armoured forces, who was directing the battle for the railway line and co-ordinating the assault conducted by a tank group and XXIX Rifle Corps:

> Taking cover in the station buildings and the adjoining forest the enemy was putting up a stiff resistance. His anti-tank artillery and machine-guns blocked the way of our units. Behind the fully deployed infantry regiments and General Vaingrub's tanks were the vanguard columns of the First Guards Tank Army. They were waiting for our troops to clear the breach. We had to dislodge the Germans from the railway line. Then the tanks would gain freedom of manoeuvre and split the enemy's front. A powerful artillery strike followed by a concerted attack by infantry and tanks would tip the scales in our favour. The sun was already setting. We had but an hour of daylight to demolish the enemy strongpoint. Fortunately a column of vehicles came into sight at the edge of the wood south-east of Czarny Lug. Taking a closer look, we saw that they were Katyusha multiple rocket launchers. A whole brigade of new rocket launchers – 36 of them, combat-loaded and ready to fire. I immediately gave the brigade commander an assignment, and 20 minutes later such a powerful salvo was delivered that

hours after it the enemy troops were still reeling from shock. Our units attacked. In another twenty minutes they crushed the weakening resistance and crossed the railway line. The vanguard of First Guards Tank Army followed in their wake. The penetration of the enemy's defences to their entire depth was accomplished. The Eighth Guards Army had fulfilled its first combat assignment on schedule and, along with First Guards Tank Army, gained freedom of manoeuvre. At such moments exhaustion is forgotten and none of the things that vexed and irritated you a short while ago matters any more. That's the joy of victory!

By nightfall on 15 January, Konev and Zhukov had torn through Army Group A's tactical defence zone. The three gaping holes they had punched in the enemy's line were now being joined to form a continuous lodgement on the west bank of the Vistula stretching for 300 miles. Tanks and mechanized infantry were moving at speed across open country up to seventy miles from their start lines. On Zhukov's right flank, north of Warsaw, Forty-Seventh Army was clearing the reach between the Vistula and the western Bug, threatening the Polish capital.

Army Group A, sundered by these hammer blows into dozens of disconnected shards, was fighting for survival. On 17 January, Chuikov was watching 120th Regiment of 39th Guards Rifle Division, with an attached artillery battalion, crossing the Pilica. Suddenly a column of about twenty tanks appeared on the southern bank, pulling out of the village of Gramiaca and heading towards the crossing. To Chuikov's amazement they had German crosses on their sides. The tanks were cold meat for the Russian artillerymen, who quickly readied their guns and opened fire at a range of about 300 yards, setting about half the panzers ablaze. Returning fire, the surviving German tanks fell back on the village, only to run into the fire of another of 39th Guards Rifle Division's regiments which had entered it. All but two of the panzers were knocked out. The surviving German tankmen told their captors that they were from 25th Panzer Division. After three days of fighting they had lost contact with their headquarters and had been trying to fight their way to safety on the northern bank of the Pilica. Unluckily for them, they had driven straight into a fire-trap.

Chuikov crossed the Pilica and drove past long columns of the second echelon of 79th Guards Division marching towards Sadkowice. Shortly afterwards he found himself outside a distillery on the outskirts of the village of Strykow:

It struck us that the villagers and distillery workers were behaving strangely, hiding behind walls and nervously peering in all directions. Then we saw a column of Germans half a kilometre away deploying for action. It was hard to explain their presence behind our lines. But there was no time to investigate. Their machine-guns were already hammering. Under fire we sped back to Sheikin's* regiment. His men were deployed in a skirmish line and the machine-gunners were returning the fire. Then the regiment thrust forward and cut off the enemy's avenue of escape to the south-west. It so happened that First Guards Tank Army was refuelling in a nearby wood. The tankmen immediately opened fire, forcing the Germans to down arms and surrender. About 1,500 German officers and men were taken prisoner. They were from different units, out of contact with their command, and were fleeing to the west. They had lost their bearings and were retreating without authorization.

The surrounding countryside was full of German troops hiding in woods, haystacks and cattle sheds. Falling back from the Vistula, they had sought refuge in what they believed to be the rear areas of their divisions, only to find themselves in the Red Army's rear areas, amid its supply trains, field kitchens and quartermaster services. Chuikov watched one column of about eighty German prisoners being led away by a Red Army sergeant and three soldiers:

> They were a miserable lot, trudging along and shivering with cold in their *ersatz*-wool greatcoats. Only the two officers at the head of the column preserved a soldierly bearing. We were afraid that the crowd would fall on the Germans and were ready to prevent a lynching. But the Poles kept their distance, only shaking their fists and shouting curses, '*Psia krew, Psia krew*', 'Dog's blood'.

---

* Colonel Sheikin, commander of 220th Regiment of 79th Guards Division.

CHAPTER 4

Clutching at Straws

'I'm going to attack the Russians where they least expect it! The Sixth Panzer Army is off to Budapest! If we start an offensive in Hungary, the Russians will have to go too.'

Adolf Hitler, 16 January 1945

AT 3PM ON 15 January Hitler interfered for the first time in the defensive battle boiling up on the Eastern Front. Ignoring Guderian's protests, the Führer ordered the transfer of two divisions of General D. von Saucken's Grossdeutschland Panzer Corps, Hermann Göring Parachute Division and Brandenburger Panzergrenadier Division, from East Prussia to Kielce. Guderian was appalled. It was obvious to everyone but the Führer that the rickety railway communications connecting East Prussia with Poland were unequal to delivering Grossdeutschland's divisions in time to block the Soviet drive on Poznan. Moreover, it was little short of madness to strip Army Group Centre of its last significant operational reserve in the Baltic sector at precisely the moment when it was coming under mounting pressure from Rokossovsky's Second Belorussian Front, which had gone on the offensive at 10am on 14 January.

Guderian dug in his heels, and while the argument ran back and forth on the telephone line between Zossen and the Führer's headquarters, Grossdeutschland's divisions sat stranded in railway sidings, a fate which was to overtake many formations in the weeks to come as the Führer robbed Peter on one front to pay Paul on another. Inevitably, Hitler got his way, but as Grossdeutschland moved south with painful slowness it was hit in the left flank by First Belorussian Front, and was forced to detrain near Lodz in piecemeal fashion under heavy shellfire.

Grim sights had greeted Grossdeutschland as it rattled south. The stations on the way were packed with ethnic German refugees fleeing the Russian advance. From his command post in a textile mill on the outskirts of Lodz, Saucken, a veteran East Prussian cavalryman, could see the T-34s of First Guards Tank Army nosing over the horizon, white puffs of snow indicating the fall of shells. Saucken was keenly aware of the exposed position into which Grossdeutschland had been deposited. There was nothing for it but to throw out a screen south and east of Lodz to cover the remnants of Ninth Army, all the while watching Grossdeutschland's rear as First Guards Tank Army, sweeping down from the north, threatened the corps with encirclement.

On 13 January, at the last military conference held at the Adlerhorst, Hitler had instructed his commanders in the west, Field Marshals Rundstedt and Model, to hold off the Western Allies for as long as possible. At 6pm he was driven to the station to board his special train, where he held another conference. Hardly had it begun than Guderian telephoned requesting that 'everything be thrown into the Eastern Front'. When business was concluded, the Führer's train moved off to Berlin.

Snow was falling as the train pulled into Grunewald station at 9.30am on 16 January, masking for the moment the German capital's most savage wounds. The Führer was driven to the Reich Chancellery, scene of so many pre-war political triumphs, where he was now to take up residence. The new Chancellery had been designed as the starting point for the rebuilding of Berlin. Now, pounded and pockmarked by bomb blasts, it loomed like a great grey hulk in a sea of devastation. Snowfall had smoothed out the craters and piles of rubble in the garden but the Chancellery's boarded-up windows stared sightlessly out on to a desolate landscape. Snow also lay on a large rectangular concrete slab in the garden, rising several feet above ground level and marking the site of the deep shelter designed for Hitler by Albert Speer.

Berlin had never been a centre of Nazi strength. Before Hitler came to power in 1933 it had been a Communist stronghold. Throughout the war Hitler had spent little time in the German capital – like a medieval king, he had moved from one purpose-built headquarters to another. Their crumbling concrete hulks still litter Europe, from Soissons in France to Rastenburg in East Prussia, now part of Poland.

The Rastenburg headquarters, codenamed *Wolfsschanze* (Wolf's Lair) and set in the gloomy, dripping pine forests of the Masurian Lakes, had been Hitler's home for most of the mid-war years. He had left its blockhouses and belts of barbed wire and mines for the last time in November 1944. Now that his 'skirmishing in the Vosges', as Guderian acidly put it, was over, the Chancellery and then the bunker in its garden were to be the last of the Führer headquarters.

Berliners were unaware of Hitler's return. They were now fighting a losing battle to maintain a semblance of normal life in a city slowly bleeding to death. Hans-Georg von Studnitz noted in his diary: 'Every now and then the electric current is cut off. In houses which have coal grates the gas supply has been discontinued. The use of sun-ray lamps has been forbidden. . . . Postal services have ceased to function.'

The day Hitler returned to Berlin, Guderian attended a military conference held in the Führer's study in the Chancellery, overlooking the rubble-strewn garden. After an encouraging start, when Hitler announced his decision to go on to the defensive on the Western Front to allow the transfer of forces to the East, the meeting quickly ran into trouble. Anticipating Hitler's belated recognition of reality, Guderian had prepared a plan for the eventual employment of these reinforcements in an attack on the flanks of the Russian advance. To his astonishment, however, he was informed by Jodl that the most important strategic element in the formations awaiting transfer to the East, Sixth SS Panzer Army, was to go to Hungary, to relieve Budapest and safeguard the Hungarian oilfields and refineries. In vain Guderian protested that Sixth SS Panzer Army had to be brought to bear in the battle for the Oder, where two army groups faced destruction, rather than the secondary theatre in Hungary. Hitler stood fast, declaring, 'I'm going to attack the Russians where they least expect it! The Sixth Panzer Army is off to Budapest! If we start an offensive in Hungary, the Russians will have to go too.' Oil remained uppermost in his mind as he chided Guderian, 'If you don't get any more fuel your tanks won't be able to move and the aeroplanes won't be able to fly. You must see that. But my generals know nothing about the economics of the war.' What Hitler seemed to know little of was the Wehrmacht's galloping debility and the imperviousness of Stavka to subsidiary manoeuvres. Nor did he appreciate that shunting an entire panzer army halfway across Europe along poor rail communications, rather than straight to Berlin, must in any event keep it out of action for several weeks.

The meeting went from bad to worse. When Hitler began to rave about the idiotic siting of the major defensive line on the Vistula, the stenographic record was produced to demonstrate that the decision had been his own. Next came the location of the reserves; according to Guderian, Hitler thought that they had been held 'too far back from the front, while the generals held exactly contrary views and blamed Hitler for having insisted that they be too far forward'. Casting around for a scapegoat to take the blame for the débâcle, Hitler lit on the hapless Harpe, who was now to be replaced as commander of Army Group A by the diehard Nazi Colonel-General Ferdinand Schörner, then in command of Army Group

North which, on Hitler's orders, was bottled up in the Kurland peninsula where, as Guderian ironically observed, 'there were no more laurels to be won'.

While Hitler clutched at straws, the Red Army was rapidly outrunning the timetable originally laid down by Stavka for the Vistula-Oder operation. Rifle divisions were covering twenty miles a day, and the mechanized and armoured divisions were advancing up to fifty. The speed and size of the breakthrough caused Stavka to redefine Zhukov's and Konev's objectives. On 17 January Konev was ordered to make his main effort in the direction of Breslau, crossing the Oder south of Leszno no later than 30 January and establishing bridgeheads on the western bank. Zhukov's primary objective was Poznan and the establishment of a line running north-east from that city to Bydgoszcz (Bromberg) by 4 February.

However, the development of the Russian offensive quickly overtook Stavka's calculations. By the morning of 17 July elements of Forty-Seventh, Sixty-First and First Polish Armies were moving through the streets of Warsaw while its token force of German defenders – including an 'ear' battalion composed entirely of men with hearing disorders – pulled out as best they could.

By mid-afternoon on the 17th Warsaw was finally free of its German occupiers and tormentors. The first Red Army men into the city picked their way through a scene of total devastation. After the suppression of the Warsaw uprising in October 1944 the Germans had laid waste what remained of the city, piling destruction on destruction with no military aim, but driven simply by the terrible nihilism which had characterized Nazi rule in Poland. Russian troops entered a silent city whose pre-war population of 1.3 million had been reduced to about 160,000 famished survivors.

Two days after the liberation of Warsaw, Konev personally directed the liberation of Cracow. The ancient city passed into Russian hands virtually intact, the German garrison having withdrawn in such haste that there was no time to set off the demolition charges placed by its engineers. In a village outside Cracow the war came to an end for a young Jewess, nineteen-year-old Janina Bauman, who had escaped from the Warsaw Ghetto in 1943 and was now living on a farm. Writing after the war, she remembered:

> After a sleepless night echoing with cannon-fire, heavy with great expectations, we saw in the faint light of the wintry dawn the weird, grey hunched outlines of the first Russian soldiers. Stealthily, they scuttled, one by one past our window, their guns at the ready. By noon the sounds of heavy battle subsided and were

replaced by a steady rumble of heavy vehicles coming from afar.
Just before dusk I went out to fetch some wood. In the semi-dark
shed, crammed with logs and tools, something stirred. I sensed a
human presence. I pushed the door wide open to let in more light.
Only then did I notice a flap of field-grey military coat sticking out
from between two logs. Calmly, I locked the shed and ran back to
the cottage. In the kitchen, Mrs Pietrzyk, tired and worn after the
restless night, was busy cooking. Gasping for breath, I told her
what I had seen. But she was not surprised: she already knew.
Staring full in my face with her ancient, all-knowing eyes, she said,
as if quoting from a holy book, 'Whoever comes under my roof
seeking shelter, no matter who he is, no matter what he believes
in, he will be safe with me'. In a flash I understood. Shocked, I
watched her fill a tin bowl with hot dumplings and pour pork fat
over it. 'Hold it child', she screeched in her usual way. 'Take it to
him.' As if mesmerized, I blindly obeyed and went back to the
shed. It seemed as deserted as before, even the field-grey flap had
disappeared. I stood benumbed, the hot dish burning my fingers
and filling the air with a strong smell of food. There was a brief
commotion behind the pile of logs and an unkempt head suddenly popped out. I saw the pale face of the German, a boy rather
than a man, staring at me in terror. He grabbed the steaming bowl
from my hands and fell on the food with unspeakable greed. He
was still trembling from hunger and fear. For a long while I
watched him blankly. I felt no pity, no hatred, no joy.

On the same day units of Third Guards Tank Army crossed the German
border east of Breslau. One hundred miles to the north-east, on Zhukov's
front, Eighth Guards Army took the industrial city of Lodz before the
Germans could destroy anything, or even evacuate the valuable lathes
and other equipment packed up for shipment to the Reich. North of
Lodz, Zhukov's armour was fanning out across western Poland.
Objectives which Stavka had anticipated reaching at the end of the first
phase of the Vistula-Oder operation, after twelve days' fighting, were
being reached and left behind within a week.

On 22 and 23 January Zhukov's front advanced up to ninety miles. On
the evening of the 23rd IX Tank Corps took Bydgoszcz, opening the road
to the German border, which lay only forty miles away. In his memoirs
Zhukov wrote that Stavka had delayed making a decision about further
operations in Poland until the establishment of the Poznan-Bydgoszcz
line. But, as he recalled,

> in the course of the operation the troops of First Belorussian Front
> significantly overfulfilled the Stavka timetable, and by 23 January

the front's right wing had already seized Bydgoszcz and had developed the offensive towards Schneidemuhl and Deutsch-Krone (Walcz). On January 25 the centre of the front surrounded the powerful forces at Poznan, and the left wing, closely co-ordinated with the First Ukrainian Front, advanced to the region of Jarocin.

Simultaneously, on First Ukrainian Front's left, the southern flank of the Soviet breakthrough, Konev had launched a skilfully handled envelopment of the Silesian industrial heartland, turning Rybalko's Third Guards Tank Army through 90 degrees to bring it sweeping south along the line of the Oder and so seal off the rear of the region in the area of Katowice. While Rybalko executed this difficult manoeuvre, demonstrating the new dash and flexibility of the Soviet tank arm, Konev's infantry (Sixtieth, Fifty-Ninth and Twenty-First Armies) attacked frontally from the north, east and south, forcing the German garrisons out into open country where they could be cut up without imperilling the industrial plant coveted by Stalin. By 27 January Rybalko was in a position to close off the German escape routes but, mindful of his instructions, the normally ruthless Konev left them a 'golden bridge' over which to withdraw. The opportunity was seized by the new commander of Army Group A, Colonel-General Schörner, whose fanatical devotion to Hitler did not blind him to the military hopelessness of the situation in Upper Silesia. It was not until the evacuation of the German Seventeeth Army was well under way that Schörner informed Hitler by telephone that he was withdrawing to make a stand on the Oder. Generals had been shot for less but the Führer's regard for Schörner, and his own disintegrating nerve, produced the mildest of replies – 'Yes, Schörner, if that's what you think. You are doing well.'

Konev was doing better. From a hilltop the commander of First Ukrainian Front watched with Rybalko as the latter's tanks deployed in almost parade-ground fashion towards Ratibor on the upper Oder, their turrets draped in improvized winter camouflage – bolts of white tulle pillaged from a Silesian textile warehouse. In the distance were the smoking chimneys of war factories which, until this moment, had been producing nearly 100 million tons of coal and 2.4 million tons of steel a year for the German war effort. One of Katowice's most important factories produced the 88mm gun which had accounted for so many Soviet tanks on the Eastern Front.

While Konev secured the industrial prize of Silesia, the soldiers of First Belorussian and First Ukrainian Fronts uncovered another form of industry as they overran the labour and extermination camps which dotted central and southern Poland. As the Red Army drew nearer, the Germans began to evacuate the areas which remained under their control and to step up the killing. At Chelmno, on Zhukov's front north of Lodz, the SS set about murdering the special *Kommando* which had been formed to dismantle the camp's crematoria. There had originally been a hundred men in the Kommando but their numbers had already been whittled down to about forty by a reign of casual terror. To amuse themselves, the SS guards had lined the men up, placed bottles on their heads and then enjoyed target practice, whooping with delight when the bullets missed their mark and another man slumped out of the line, shot through the head. On 17 January the shooting became more systematic, in batches of five. Only two men survived, one of them shot through the neck and rescued by the arrival of the Russians.

In the Auschwitz-Birkenau complex in southern Poland, an area which contained numerous camps and factories, about 60,000 Jews and non-Jews remained, many of them barely alive. On 18 January the order was given to evacuate the survivors by foot to railheads from which they could be dispersed into camps all over Germany. Thousands who were too enfeebled to march were shot on the spot; others who stumbled or fell out of line on the march suffered the same fate. No one was allowed to turn his head while the ragged columns trudged forward through the snow, the terrible sound of shuffling feet punctuated by single gunshots as another straggler was executed. One of the marchers, a Jewish girl called Raiz Kibel, remembered the agony of the death marches:

> In a frost, half-barefoot, or entirely barefoot, with light rags upon their emaciated and exhausted bodies, tens of thousands of human creatures drag themselves along in the snow. Only the great, strong striving for life, and the light of imminent liberation, kept them on their feet. But woe is to them whose physical strength abandons them. They are shot on the spot. In such a way were thousands who had endured camp life up to the last minute murdered, a moment before liberation. Even today I still cannot understand with what sort of strength and how I was able to endure the 'death march' and drag myself to Ravensbruck* camp, and from there, after resting a week or two, to Neustadt, where I was liberated by the Red Army.

---

* Ravensbruck was a concentration camp in Mecklenburg, established in 1934 and used exclusively for the imprisonment of female political prisoners. Hideous medical experiments were carried out on many women there, and it was also the place of execution for female Allied agents.

When one column stopped at Blechhammer, the site of a synthetic oil plant manned by slave labour, the SS guards went on the rampage, setting fire to the huts in which the marchers were sheltering and spraying those who ran out with machine-gun fire. Several Jews survived by jumping into a midden, where they remained chest-deep in excrement until the SS men moved off. Thousands who survived the march froze to death in open cattle trucks as they were transported to the Reich. One such truck, padlocked and full of freezing and starving Jews, was stranded in a siding at Brünnlitz when, on 29 January, it was discovered by Oscar Schindler, that ambiguous wartime saint. Using a combination of bluff and sleight of hand, Schindler managed to have the rail wagon, marked 'property of the SS', transferred to the siding of his own armaments factory in Brünnlitz. When he unlocked the wagon he discovered that sixteen of its hundred occupants had frozen to death. Helped by his wife Emilia, he freed, fed and guarded the survivors, evacuees from Birkenau, all of whom were emaciated to the point of death.

At Birkenau, one of Auschwitz's subsidiary camps, the SS had dynamited what was left of the crematoria and shot 200 of the camp's 4,200 sick women. Most of the camp's storehouses were set ablaze, but when the Russians overran the camp on 27 January six storehouses remained intact, crammed with the remnants of unspeakable tragedy: nearly 840,000 women's dresses, 348,000 suits for men and 38,000 pairs of men's shoes. Among those still alive at Birkenau was Otto Frank, the father of Anne Frank. A long journey via Odessa and Marseilles was eventually to take him back to Amsterdam, and to a rendezvous with the diary kept by his daughter.

On the same day Soviet troops liberated the main camp at Auschwitz, where they found 648 corpses and some 1,800 survivors – they liberated 7,600 survivors in all, most of them at Birkenau. At least 2 million Jews had died in this terrible place and another 2 million Russian prisoners of war, Polish political prisoners, gypsies, and non-Jews from all over Occupied Europe. Marshal Konev did not tarry to see what the Red Army had found: 'I simply made up my mind not to see it. The combat operations were in full swing, and to command them was such a strain that I had neither the time nor the justification for abandoning myself to my own emotions. During the war I did not belong to myself.'

By now, with the Oder in their sights, the strain of co-ordinating Konev's and Zhukov's advances, both within and between each front, was beginning to unravel Stavka's plans. At midday on 25 January Stalin telephoned Zhukov. After Zhukov had briefed Stalin on the situation, he was asked about his next moves. Zhukov replied that

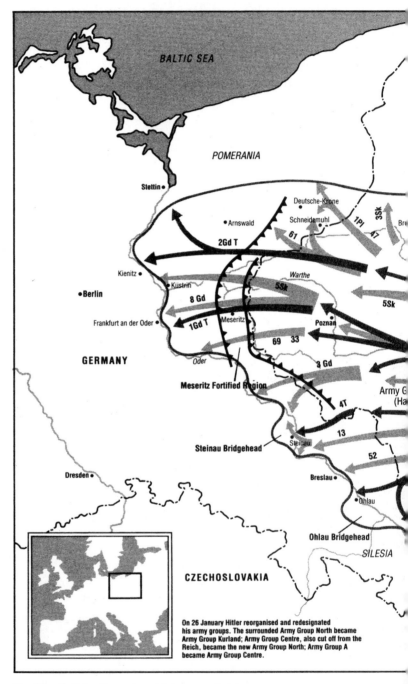

The Vistula-Oder Operation, 12 January–2 February, which drove through weste
Poland into the Reich and struck south at the industrial region of Silesia.

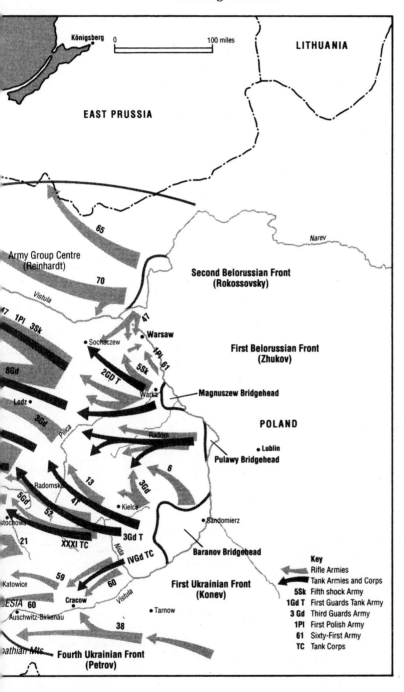

since the enemy was demoralized and unable to put up serious resistance, we would continue our drive towards the Oder River and attempt to seize a bridgehead at Küstrin. The right wing of our front would advance to the north and north-west against the enemy forces in eastern Pomerania, which did not seem to pose any threat to us.

Stalin, however, pointed out that when Zhukov reached the Oder his right flank would be separated from Second Belorussian Front by as much as a hundred miles: 'You cannot do that. You must wait until the Second Belorussian Front completes its operations in East Prussia and regroups its forces on the Vistula.' When Zhukov asked how long these operations would take, Stalin gave him an estimate of up to fifteen days, reminding the commander of First Belorussian Front that he could expect no support on his left flank while Konev was mopping up enemy resistance around Oppeln and Katowice.

Undeterred, Zhukov urged Stalin not to halt his offensive, as this would only give the enemy a breathing space in which to reinforce the fortified zone around Meseritz, which stretched westward from the old Polish border along the swampy River Obra. After Zhukov had requested another army to secure his right flank, the conversation came to an end, with Stalin promising 'to think about it, but I had no further word from him that day'.

In spite of Stalin's earlier reassurances, Zhukov was steeling himself for an all-out race to Berlin against Konev. On 26 January he submitted a plan to Stavka, proposing that his front continue its offensive without a pause to take Berlin on the run. According to General Sergei M. Shtemenko, the Deputy Chief of the General Staff, Zhukov intended to take

four days to move up his troops, particularly the artillery and the rear services, to replenish his supplies, to get his mechanized units into order, to put the Third Shock Army and First Polish Army into the first echelon, and on 1–2 February to renew the offensive with all his forces. His first objective was to force the Oder on the march, following up with a swift blow at Berlin, directing the chief force of his attack on the German capital from the north-east, the north and north-west. To achieve this, Second Guards Tank Army would strike from the north-west and First Guards Tank Army from the north-east.

Within twenty-four hours Stavka had received a proposal from Konev to press ahead on his front, launching an offensive on 5–6 February which would carry First Ukrainian Front to the Elbe in three weeks while his right wing, co-operating with Zhukov's left, took Berlin. The rival marshals were planning to go hell-for-leather for Berlin, upsetting the original plan which had allocated the prize of the German capital to Zhukov alone.

The problem of reconciling the two plans produced an uneasy compromise. Stavka approved both of them while retaining the demarcation line between the fronts, which bent Konev's line of advance south of Berlin towards Guben and Brandenburg. As Shtemenko admitted after the war:

> The General Staff knew that this was absurd – on the one hand approving Marshal Konev's plan for his right wing to attack Berlin and on the other establishing a demarcation line that would prevent him carrying out his plan. We had to find some way out of this situation, and we believed that either the situation itself would provide its own needed correction or that we would be able to correct this stupidity in some way in the course of the operation, particularly as we were some distance from Berlin. But, as the evolution of events disclosed, it proved impossible to carry out the attack on Berlin in so short a time.

This was not immediately evident. On 26 January one of First Guards Tank Army's patrols reached the Meseritz Line, a potentially formidable obstacle which had been stripped of much of its equipment and was patchily manned by Volkssturm units. Armed with this information, Zhukov was back on the telephone to Stalin, requesting permission to press on to the Oder and establish a bridgehead on its western bank. It took several calls to secure Stalin's permission for this plan to go ahead. To shield his main striking force (First and Second Guards Tank Armies and Fifth Shock, Eighth Guards and Thirty-Third and Sixty-Ninth Armies) from German counter-attacks launched from East Prussia, Zhukov proposed to swing Third Shock, First Polish, Forty-Seventh and Sixty-First Armies to the north and north-west. In addition, parts of Eighth Guards and Sixty-Ninth Armies were detached to take Poznan, declared a 'fortress city' by Hitler. Here Zhukov made a serious miscalculation, believing the city to be garrisoned by no more than 20,000 troops. In fact Poznan's uniquely strong defences were held by over 60,000 men, and the fight for the city was to last until 23 February.

Zhukov's offensive developed rapidly at first. First Guards Tank Army, once again spearheaded by XI Guards Tank Corps, sliced through the Meseritz defences at such speed that by 1 February its forward

detachments were briefly threatened with encirclement by counter-
attacks launched by the German tactical reserve. Under a sky hidden by
low, scudding clouds – an indication that damp weather was blowing in
from the Baltic, heralding a thaw – First Guards Tank Army, Sixty-Ninth
and Thirty-Third Armies broke through to the Oder to establish a succession of small lodgements on the far bank. On Zhukov's right, Fifth
Shock Army skirted the northern edge of the swampy Warthe depression
to reach and cross the Oder and capture the small town of Kienitz, whose
cafés and streets were full of drinking and strolling German officers and
men. German radio was blaring out bulletins that the front was holding
up on the Bzura, west of Warsaw, and here was the Red Army, only fifty
miles from Berlin. Kienitz's dumbfounded station master approached
Colonel K.F. Esipenko, the commander of Fifth Shock Army's forward
detachment,* to enquire whether the Berlin train would be allowed to
leave. Esipenko rose to the occasion. 'I regret, Station Master, but that is
impossible. The passenger service to Berlin will undergo a short interruption – let's say until the end of the war.'

On the night of 2–3 February, Fifth Shock Army's 301st Rifle Division
made an assault crossing of the icebound Oder in the teeth of fierce
German opposition. In the centre of Zhukov's front Eighth Guards Army
was also involved in an opposed crossing. At 10am on 2 February
Colonel-General Chuikov arrived at the observation post of General
Glazunov, housed in a ruined fort near Zibice, south of Küstrin.
Glazunov's IV Guards Rifle Corps was deployed along a dike between
Küstrin and Goreyca, poised to cross the Oder. Chuikov swept a tele-
scope across

> a wide river . . . lined with dikes. Our troops were concentrated on
> the eastern bank. A highly responsible and difficult hour had
> arrived. The ice on the river was so brittle that even the infantry-
> men, let alone heavy equipment and tanks, could move across it
> only at great peril. We had no organic crossing facilities. And yet
> the troops, under cover of artillery fire, began to make their way to
> the far bank, carrying poles, planks and bundles of brushwood.
> On the way they laid planking and improvized footbridges. Here
> and there they managed to get anti-tank guns to the opposite bank
> by putting then on improvized skis.

At this point the Luftwaffe intervened. Luftflotte 6, reinforced with

---

* The forward detachment consisted of 220 Independent Tank Brigade, 89th
Independent Heavy Tank Regiment and 106th Rifle Regiment.

some 800 aircraft transferred from the West, was now able to establish air uperiority over critical areas of the front. The Red Army Air Force was, for the moment, desperately short of fuel, the result of the rapid Soviet advance, which had also left most of its bases 300 miles to the rear. In contrast, the Luftwaffe had only short distances to fly to the combat zone, where its aircraft could remain for sustained periods. As Chuikov watched his infantry struggling over the Oder, formations of Focke-Wulf FW190 fighter-bombers roared in to strafe and bomb the crossing points. Chuikov could only watch helplessly. There was no air cover and he was impatiently awaiting the arrival of General Seredin's 16th Anti-Aircraft Artillery Division, which had succumbed to the shortage of fuel and was still twenty-four hours' march away. The FW190s flashed back and forth over Chuikov's infantry, 'flying so low that at times it seemed that their propellers would touch the heads of our men'.

Chuikov was forced to call off the crossing until nightfall. When it was resumed the going was still hard, as the ice had been holed in so many places by German bombs. In the meantime Chuikov gained a glimpse of the confusion reigning on 'the other side of the hill'. His scouts, reconnoitring the Seelow-Küstrin highway, had returned with two captured German staff officers, who confirmed that OKH had little or no idea of the situation on the Berlin axis. On 3 February Seredin's anti-aircraft guns arrived and soon saw off a renewed attempt by the Luftwaffe to interfere with the crossing of the Oder. The 35th, 47th and 79th Guards Rifle Divisions crossed with practically no losses and transferred their artillery observation posts to the opposite bank. The bridgeheads were then linked to form a single lodgement, although the bulk of Chuikov's armour and artillery remained on the eastern bank. The high-capacity pontoon bridges needed to bring them over were still in the deep rear.

The Germans still clung to significant bridgeheads of their own on the eastern bank of the Oder, at Frankfurt and Küstrin, but these could not disguise the stark fact that along the rest of the Oder front their defences were stretched to breaking point. In contrast, Zhukov and Konev had reached the middle Oder along almost its entire length and had gained footholds at numerous points on its western bank which they were now busily expanding. Yet there was to be no attempt to rush Berlin. On 2 February Stavka declared a formal end to the Vistula-Oder operation. The final assault on Berlin would not be made until mid-April.

In the post-war years the delay between the closing of the Vistula-Oder operation and the drive on Berlin was the focus of an increasingly bitter dispute between the participants and Soviet military historians. In great

measure it provided a mirror image of the 'broad' or 'narrow' front arguments which racked relations between Eisenhower and his British and
American subordinates on the Western Front as the war drew to a close.
Inevitably, it was also coloured by the changing political fortunes of
the main protagonists in the years of de-Stalinization and the period
which followed the fall of Khrushchev in 1964, when the row erupted
with full fury. That same year open war broke out between Zhukov and
Chuikov when the latter wrote a series of articles accusing his former
commander of wasting a golden opportunity to take Berlin on the run
and, in the process, secure an even greater slice of Europe for the Soviet
Union. Chuikov argued that having covered over 300 miles in just over
two weeks, Zhukov should have taken the last fifty to Berlin at the gallop.
It was Chuikov's view that 'Berlin could have been taken even in
February'.

It is clear from the plan he presented to Stavka on 26 January that
Zhukov initially shared Chuikov's enthusiasm to go flat-out for Berlin. But
doubts soon began to edge in. On 31 January Zhukov informed Stavka
of his mounting alarm at the gap which had opened up between his right
flank and the left wing of Rokossovsky's Second Belorussian Front. The
sixty-mile gap, screened only by cavalry, presented the German forces
concentrating in eastern Pomerania with an opportunity to take First
Belorussian Front in the flank and rear. A week earlier, during his telephone conversation with Stalin, Zhukov had discounted the threat from
this quarter, but now it loomed larger by the hour. However, it was just
one of the problems caused by the success of the Vistula-Oder operation.
As Chuikov himself had discovered when crossing the Oder, fuel and
ammunition were running short as the front's supply bases remained
on the Vistula. The fuel shortage had enabled the Luftwaffe, seemingly
on its last legs, to seize air superiority over critical areas on the Oder
front, and the arrival of a thaw made the construction of viable Russian
airfields nearer the front all but impossible. Both Zhukov's and Konev's
fronts had also sustained significant casualties during the last three
weeks. Several of Eighth Guards Army's rifle divisions had been reduced
to 4,000 men, and in Zhukov's two tank armies many brigades fielded as
few as fifteen tanks against an establishment of sixty-five. After the war
Zhukov argued with some force that at the beginning of February neither
his nor Konev's front was capable of executing an assault on Berlin. Of
the eight combined-arms armies and two tank armies which had originally been on Zhukov's Berlin axis, only four understrength armies
remained: Fifth Shock, Eighth Guards, Thirty-Third and Sixty-Ninth.
Eighth Guards and Sixty-Ninth had also given up two of their corps for
the siege of Poznan, and the rest of Zhukov's front had been swung

towards eastern Pomerania to confront the threat apparently building up on his flank.

Writing after the war, Zhukov observed that 'to exaggerate the capabilities of one's forces is just as dangerous as to underestimate the strength of the enemy'. In this context he cited the catastrophe which overtook the Red Army outside Warsaw in 1920, an indirect thrust at Stalin who had been a strong supporter of that ill-fated drive. More fresh and painful in Zhukov's mind would have been the mauling that Vatutin's South-Western Front had received in February 1943 at the hands of Field Marshal Erich von Manstein, when the overextended Soviet counter-offensive launched after Stalingrad was destroyed by Manstein's masterfully handled 'backhand' riposte.

The part played by Stalin in the delaying of the final assault on Berlin remains unclear. The Yalta Conference was approaching and it is possible that the Soviet leader wanted to hold back from this major decision until the Allied deliberations were over and he had gained the measure of his Western partners' intentions. A striking feature of this phase of the war is that while Hitler's behaviour and conduct of operations grew increasingly wild and unrealistic, Stalin was becoming ever more cautious. A more shadowy role has been attributed to General V.D. Sokolovsky, a 'political' general *par excellence*, whom Stalin had appointed Deputy Commander of First Belorussian Front to act as his eyes and ears. It has been suggested that it was Sokolovsky who planted the seeds of doubt in Zhukov's mind.

Hindsight might indicate that Zhukov's fears for his right flank were exaggerated, but at the time his reservations about the drive to Berlin were fully justified. Moreover, the relatively slow progress made by Second Belorussian Front when it was unleashed against the German forces in eastern Pomerania in February 1945 tends to support Zhukov's position.

In Berlin, successive convulsions had followed the fall of Warsaw, which had been evacuated against Hitler's orders, and the collapse of the front in Poland. Hitler's contempt for the German officer corps knew no bounds. In a towering rage, he shrieked at Guderian, 'I'm out for the General Staff's blood! This General Staff clique has got to be stamped out'. Convinced that his field commanders were withdrawing because of cowardice or failure of nerve, Hitler issued an order that no commander of any formation, from divisional level upwards, was to attack, counter-attack, or withdraw, without first notifying his intentions through the normal military channels to the high command, in sufficient time to enable the Führer to intervene. As Albert Seaton has observed, 'Hitler was now ready to conduct his war games from Berlin, like a champion chess player facing opponents on a dozen or more boards, the master of every move.'

The Führer's daily conferences were now taking ever more surreal turns. On 20 January he demanded that work begin on a long-range jet bomber, an indication that, for the moment at least, Hitler was casting himself as a twentieth-century Frederick the Great, planning for a Seven Years' War while the enemy was at the gates. Worse was to follow the next day when, at a conference with Guderian and Jodl, Hitler announced that the Reichsführer SS, Heinrich Himmler, was to take over command of a new Army Group Vistula to plug the huge gap which had opened up between Army Group Centre, fighting in East Prussia, and Schörner's Army Group A. Himmler was also to assume responsibility for organizing the 'national defence on German soil behind the entire Eastern Front'.

Guderian suggested that such a task would be more appropriately undertaken by Field Marshal Maximilian von Weichs, who had conducted the withdrawal of Army Group F from the southern Balkans, not an operation likely to stir Hitler's heart. Weichs's candidacy was brushed aside after Jodl had pointedly made a sneering reference to the Field Marshal's religious faith, a quality calculated to set the Führer's teeth on edge. Hitler brought the argument to an end by telling Guderian that Himmler had 'given a good account of himself on the upper Rhine'. Moreover, as commander of the Home Army, Himmler had a ready source of reinforcements to hand when bolstering his front. Only Himmler, Hitler declared, would provide the necessary ruthlessness which was so singularly lacking in worn-out generals like Weichs.

On Army Group Centre's front ruthlessness was not enough. On 13 January Colonel-General Reinhardt's command came under attack by Chernyakhovsky's Third Belorussian Front. At 6am, after an intensive artillery preparation, the Russian assault battalions advanced through the dense mist which lay over East Prussia's eastern frontier. Third Belorussian Front's objectives were the destruction of the German forces in the Tilsit-Insterburg sector and the reduction of the city of Königsberg, the 'citadel of East Prussia'. On the 14th Rokossovsky's Second Belorussian Front opened its offensive along the line of the River Narew. The main blow was delivered northwards, on Rokossovsky's right flank, by four infantry armies (Seventeenth, Sixty-Fifth, Second Shock and Forty-Eighth) and one tank army (Fifth Guards Tank, the heroes of Kursk). On Rokossovsky's left Forty-Ninth and Fifteenth Armies were to advance through the Masurian Lakes to join hands with Third Belorussian Front. The two fronts were then to conduct parallel power drives aimed at the Baltic coast, a plan which was to be quickly dislocated.

For the Russians, the going proved tough on both fronts. Rokossovsky was well supplied with armour and artillery but was weak in infantry, in spite of a last-minute reinforcement of 120,000 men of whom 10,000 were liberated prisoners of war, 39,000 released from field hospitals and 20,000 combed from from the rear services and supply units. Thousands more were local conscripts pressed into the Red Army – not the most dependable of troops. After two days of hard pounding, in which the Soviet Third Army was severely handled by the Grossdeutschland panzer units shortly to be transferred to Kielce, Rokossovsky broke through at Ciechanov, an important road junction thirty miles west of the Narev. With the clearing skies allowing Russian ground-attack aircraft to range over the battlefield, Fifth Guards Tank Army raced through the breach.

Alert to the danger of deep envelopment, Reinhardt pleaded with Hitler to be allowed to withdraw to a shorter defensive line. OKH's only response was the transfer of the greater part of Grossdeutschland Panzer Corps to central Poland. On the third day of his offensive, Rokossovsky had broken through Army Group Centre's defences on a sixty-mile front to a depth of up to fifty miles. On 18 January Seventeenth Army took the ancient fortress town of Modlin and on the following day another Hitler-designated fortress, Mlawa, fell into Russian hands. General Weiss's Second Army, in the direct path of Rokossovsky's drive, was in danger of disintegrating.

On 13 January the opening of Chernyakhovsky's offensive had been heard by a Major Baumann, a gunner returning to his battery with Third Panzer Army, which was guarding the northern and eastern approaches to Königsberg. As his train trundled through East Prussia, Baumann noticed an almost imperceptible vibration in the air. When the train pulled out of Königsberg station, eighty miles from the front line, he could hear a soft but insistent rumbling, the sound of a continuous Soviet barrage being laid down between Gumbinnen and Schlossberg.

At the front, Chernyakhovsky's artillery preparation proved more deafening than destructive. Dense fog blinded Third Belorussian Front's gunners, whose shells fell on untenanted positions, their German defenders having withdrawn to duck the enemy's first heavy punch. When the Russians advanced they ran into strong defences and fierce counter-attacks which threatened to stop their offensive in its tracks, albeit at the cost of committing 5th Panzer Division, the sole German operational reserve. In Chernyakhovsky's centre a slogging match developed as Soviet Fifth Army battered its way through the prepared German defences at Pilkallen. It was not until 18 January that Pilkallen fell, and on the 19th Tilsit, thirty miles to the north-east, was taken. Russian tanks were now rumbling along the well-metalled roads to Königsberg and closing on Insterburg, forty miles due north of Tilsit.

Chernyakhovsky now displayed a flash of flexibility all too rare even among the Red Army's front commanders. Eleventh Guards Army was one of his second-echelon formations, tasked with eliminating German defences north of the Masurian Lakes. With the fog lifting and the German front crumbling, Chernyakhovsky shifted Eleventh Guards Army north, to the junction of Fifth and Thirty-Ninth Armies, where the latter was making some progress in the sector north of Schlossberg. Reinforced by I and II Guards Tank Corps, Eleventh Guards went into action on the line of the River Inster, driving south-west to turn the heavily fortified 'Insterburg Gap' while Fifth Army bypassed Insterburg to the east and Thirty-Eighth Army took Gumbinnen.

Powerful Russian forces were now pouring through the fifty-mile gap between the Niemen and Pregel Rivers. Volkssturm and Volksgrenadier units fled to the rear in disorder as the Russians began to leapfrog the river lines barring the way to Königsberg. On the night of 21–22 January the city had been abandoned by its Gauleiter, Erich Koch, one of the vilest of Nazi apparatchiks, who as Reichskommissar of the Ukraine had singlehandedly turned an initially friendly population into implacable enemies of Germany.

During the first week of Chernyakhovsky's offensive Stavka had become increasingly concerned at the relatively slow progress he was making and the casualties he was taking. (Third Belorussian Front sustained 80 per cent of all Soviet casualties during the East Prussian campaign.) On 20 January it ordered Rokossovsky to turn three infantry armies – Third, Forty-Eighth and Second Shock – plus Fifth Guards Tank Army to the north and north-east against German Fourth Army. The Soviet formations were to drive north towards the Frisches Haff lagoon on the Baltic coast east of Danzig.

The change of direction had the immediate effect of unhinging Stavka's original operational orders at precisely the moment at which Chernyakhovsky's breakthrough made the subsequent order redundant. As it was, Rokossovsky's initial assignment, close co-operation with Zhukov's right wing, was heavily compromised by his orders to surround German forces in East Prussia. Thus from 20 January, Zhukov was deprived of effective support on his Pomeranian flank as Rokossovsky now had only two armies, Seventeeth and Sixty-Fifth, available for the purpose.

Rokossovsky's tanks and lorried infantry thrust deep into the under-belly of East Prussia on a hundred-mile front, exposing its central region to the full weight of the Red Army. On Rokossovsky's right III Guards Cavalry Corps crashed into Allenstein on 22 January while German troops were still unloading tanks and artillery from railway cars. Having staved in the frontal defences around Allenstein, Rokossovsky inserted Fifth Guards Tank Army, brought up at speed from the deep rear, where it had remained undetected by the Germans. On 23 January leading elements of its XXIX Tank Corps outflanked Elbing to the east. It fell to the 3rd Battalion of its 31 Tank Brigade, commanded by Captain Dyachenko, to be the first to break into Elbing. Dyachenko had approached from the east, hiding his seven tanks and battalion of infantry by mingling with the columns of refugees streaming towards Elbing. His small force then raced into the city, headlights blazing in the winter gloom of the late afternoon. At first his T-34s were mistaken for a German training unit by the crowds of shoppers, who only that day had been assured by their *Oberburgemeister* that the front had been stabilized. They were abruptly disabused as Dyachenko's tanks began to fire at targets of opportunity. When they recovered their balance the city's scratch garrison forced Dyachenko to withdraw, leaving four gutted tanks behind him. He pressed on to the Frisches Haff, which his force reached at midnight, only a few hours before the main body of Fifth Guards Tank Army broke through to the sandy shores of the Baltic east of Elbing. East Prussia was now cut off from the rest of the Reich, trapping Third Panzer Army, Fourth Army, and six infantry and two motorized divisions of Second Army.

Rokossovsky's eruption into East Prussia triggered a torrent of refugees, who poured westward in search of safety from the Red Army columns. In a matter of days 800 years of German resettlement in the East came to an end as millions of East Prussians abandoned their homes, farms and villages in a desperate trek towards the German interior or the Baltic coast. In the winter of 1944 the German commanders in East Prussia, anticipating that such an exodus would play havoc with their operations, had urged that forward areas be cleared of their German populations before the Russian blow fell. Hitler had denounced these proposals as yet another demonstration of defeatism, and his Gauleiters were ordered to ensure that the population stayed put. Police permits were required for journeys of any length. The result was military disaster and human tragedy on a colossal scale. In East Prussia, Army Group Centre held powers of requisition and command over the civilian population up to a depth of only six miles in the combat zone, barely enough room for a division. Behind this line, operations and even deployments were constantly under threat from interference by the Nazi Party and the state administrative machine.

When the German front collapsed in East Prussia, the pretensions of Nazi Party placemen were thrown to the winds. The population which lay in the path of the Russian advance was under no illusion about the treatment they would receive at the hands of the Red Army. Atrocities had been committed in the tracts of German land seized by the Russians in the autumn of 1944. In October the Germans had recaptured the town of Nemmersdorff to discover that its entire population had been massacred, and that hundreds of them had been horribly mutilated. Fearful of a similar fate, the East Prussians took to the winter roads. The Wehrmacht calculated that by the end of January there were as many as 3.5 million German civilians on the move in the East.

Tens of thousands of them had been trapped in the pocket around Memel, the Baltic port which had been 'ceded' to Germany by Lithuania on 23 March 1939, the last peaceful German conquest before the outbreak of war. Since October 1944 its garrison, the German XXVIII Corps, had been under siege by Marshal Bagramyan's First Baltic Front. The chaotic conditions inside the pocket, 'a half circle about fifteen miles across backing on the Baltic, whose cold grey swells rolled in under a thick blanket of fog', were described by one of its defenders, Guy Sajer, a young man from Alsace who had joined the German Army and was serving with Grossdeutschland Panzer Corps:

> The ruins of Memel could neither hold nor shelter the large segment of the Prussian population which had sought refuge there. The population, to which we could give only the most rudimentary help, paralysed our movements and our already precarious system of defence. Within the half circle we were defending, ringing with the thunder of explosions which covered every sort of shriek and scream, former elite troops, units of the Volkssturm, amputees re-engaged by the services organizing the defence of the town, women, children, infants and invalids were crucified on the frozen earth beneath a ceiling of fog lit by the gleam of fires, or beneath the blizzards which emptied their snows over this semifinal act of the war. The food ration was so meagre that the occasional distributions which were supposed to feed five people for a day would not now be considered enough for a schoolchild's lunch. Appeals for order and observation of the restrictions rang incessantly through the fog, which in part veiled the scene. Ships of every kind were leaving by day and by night, loaded with as many people as they could carry. Long files of refugees, whom the authorities vainly tried to register, moved towards the piers, creating targets for Russian pilots which were impossible to miss. The bombs opened hideous gaps in the screaming crowds, which died

in fragments beneath these blows, but remained in line in hopes of getting on the next ship. These people were exhorted to patience, reminded of the rationing, and told to fast while they waited for deliverance. Old people killed themselves, and mothers of families, who would hand their children over to another woman, begging her to feed them with the ration card she herself was giving up. A gun taken from a dead soldier would accomplish these jobs. Heroism and despair were closely intertwined. The authorities tried to keep up the spirits of the crowd by speaking of the future, but at that time and place everything had lost its importance.

A month later another Frenchman, Christian de la Mazière, serving with the Charlemagne Division of the Waffen-SS, caught up with a column of refugees in Pomerania, on the road to Belgard:

The roads were crowded with thousands of refugees and I recalled France in 1940. It's incredible, I said to myself, everything repeats itself. They had fled from the battle zone but were being inexorably overtaken: two or three days' start and then events, which were running more swiftly than their wretched convoy of horses and handcarts, caught up with them. They were all those who had managed to escape from East Prussia and the annexed territories, old people, women and children, and like us they were heading for Belgard. Some hoped to reach the port of Kolberg on the Baltic and board a ship there; others were trying to go westward to Stettin. What struck me about this interminable and dogged procession was its silence, a heavy oppressive one. The only sounds were occasional cries to the horses: these people did not talk any more, not even with one another, but tramped along with a fixed stare, some of them with babies in their arms. They ate little, although their carts were piled high with provisions, for they had taken all they could from their farms before fleeing. But they had neither the inclination nor, above all, the time to prepare meals. We moved along beside them with scarcely any exchange of words – a smile for a kid, a caress, a piece of chocolate when we had one. Our column and theirs flowed side by side like two streams of liquid that did not mix. One idea, however, obsessed us all: not to be caught, to save our skins. We were like those animals that flee together in one body when the forest is on fire.

By mid-February almost two-thirds of the population of East Prussia had fled. Among them was Guderian's wife, who had been driven away from their estate in the Warthegau only thirty minutes before the first shells began to fall in the area. Guderian recalled: 'She had to stay until the last possible moment since her earlier departure would have been a signal for the civilian population to flee. She was under constant supervision by the Party.' The next day she was at the OKH headquarters at Zossen, fifteen miles south of Berlin, where she shared her husband's quarters.

Others were less fortunate. Many of the refugees attempted to escape by sea from the port of Pillau, on the Samland peninsula, from which over 450,000 were evacuated. Nearly 1 million sought refuge in Danzig, thousands of them trudging over the frozen waters of the Frisches Haff to reach it. The packed ships which left these ports were cold meat for Russian submarines operating in the Baltic, and had the Red Banner Fleet shown only a modicum of efficiency they would have exacted a far greater toll than the twenty-four ships sunk by May 1945.

Nevertheless, there was tragedy enough. On the bitterly cold morning of 30 January the liner *Wilhelm Gustloff* sailed from the Polish port of Gdynia (which Hitler had renamed Gothenburg) with 8,000 refugees crammed on board. Many of them had used babies as passports, carrying them on to the ship and then throwing them down to the quay for waiting relatives to use. With no warships to escort her, and only twelve lifeboats hanging from her davits, the *Wilhelm Gustloff* steamed slowly out into the Baltic, a sitting duck for marauding Soviet submarines. At 11.08pm on the 31st, one of them, the *S13*, found her. Its commander put three torpedoes, bearing the slogans 'For the Motherland', 'For the Soviet People' and 'For Leningrad', into her port side. Within a minute the refugee ship was sinking. Thousands of tons of ice-laden Baltic water stove in the liner's bulkheads and watertight doors, capsizing her and drowning 2,000 refugees on the lower promenade deck. Sixteen-year-old Eva Luck, trapped with her family in the ship's ballroom, watched in horror as a grand piano crashed around like a giant pinball, crushing those in its path to pulp. Another teenager, Gertrud Agensons, emerging from her cabin thigh-deep in water, watched the body of a dead girl float past, followed by a neatly piled tray of sandwiches. Just over an hour after being holed by the *S13's* torpedoes, the *Wilhelm Gustloff*, siren wailing eerily across the Baltic, sank beneath the boiling sea. German warships searching the area plucked about 960 people from the waves, many of whom later died of exposure. At least 7,000 people perished in the *Wilhelm Gustloff* disaster, five times more than went down with the *Titanic*.

Along the entire Soviet front, the scale of the German collapse and the speed of the Russian advance led to a serious breakdown in the Red Army's discipline. Its men were now taking a terrible revenge for the crimes committed on Russian soil by the German occupiers. Nazi ideology had ensured that the war in the east was fought with unparalleled savagery. It had been Hitler's aim not only to destroy the 'Jewish-Bolshevist' government of the Soviet Union, but also to enslave huge numbers of its Slav and Asiatic 'human material' and expel the remainder to a wasteland beyond the battlements of German imperium. Slaughter, both casual and organized, had been the order of the day, as Soviet soldiers and civilians had been massacred by the Wehrmacht and the *Einsatzgruppen* (action groups), SS units which roamed the rear areas executing Jews and other non-Aryan elements in the occupied zones. For those civilians who escaped execution, there remained the ever-present threat of being uprooted by anti-partisan sweeps or deported as slave labour to the Reich. This brutality was repaid in kind by the Red Army. The German survivors of Stalingrad marched into a captivity every bit as grim as that endured by the long columns of Russians who were marched westward after the great encirclements of 1941. Of the 108,000 men captured at Stalingrad, only about 5,000 survived the war.

By the beginning of 1945 there were few Red Army men, of any rank, who did not have a score to settle with the Germans. Stalin himself had lost his son, Yakov, a pilot who had fallen into enemy hands. Colonel-General Rybalko, the commander of Third Guards Tank Army, on Konev's front, had lost his daughter, who had disappeared in the Ukraine in 1942. In a single regiment of his army there were 158 men who had lost close relations, killed or tortured to death by the Germans; 56 whose families had been deported as forced labour; and nearly 450 who had lost their homes. In Silesia a Soviet officer, Captain Mikhail Koriakov, came across a herd of cattle being driven to the Soviet rear. As Koriakov explained:

> Special detachments of soldiers gathered in these animals. They were of prime importance to the Red Army because for a long time Russia had been so impoverished that it could not feed its soldiers and had to depend on American food supplies and Polish grain. . . . [Suddenly another officer] unsheathed a knife, walked up to a cow, and struck her a death blow at the base of the skull. The cow's legs folded under her, and she fell, while the rest of the herd, bellowing madly, stampeded and ran away. The officer wiped the sharp edge on his boots and said: 'My father wrote to me that the Germans had taken a cow from us. Now we are even. . . .'

In Silesia, Soviet rage had been fuelled by the discovery of extermination camps large and small, and by the inflammatory propaganda

written by Ilya Ehrenburg and circulated among the troops.* German
civilians were killed with no more compunction than the cow Koriakov
had seen slaughtered. He recalled:

> The population of Kreuzberg had deserted the town. Only one
> deaf, old man remained behind. The officers of the reserve regi-
> ment spent their entire time arguing whether they should burn the
> town or kill the old man. Later I learned that the old man was mur-
> dered. In another town I saw the body of a woman; she was lying
> across a bed, her legs spread; her skirt was around her shoulders
> and a long triangular bayonet was stuck in her stomach, pinning
> her body to the slats.

Koriakov was all too familiar with the standing joke in the Red Army
of 1945: the first echelon got the watches so prized by Russian soldiers;
the second got the women; and the third scavenged for what was left.

> An infantryman entering an enemy town has no time for girls; he
> had to keep moving in pursuit of the enemy; the men in the first
> wave barely had enough time to collect the watches and jewellery.
> The second wave supporting the advance was in less of a hurry;
> the men had the time to go in for girls. The men in the third wave
> never found any jewellery or untouched girls, but they combed the
> town and packed suitcases with clothes and dresses.

Koriakov saw tanks so crammed with loot that the crew could barely
move inside and would have been unable to go into action. 'I heard a
story about the members of one tank crew who were so drunk that they
took their tank into the front line, opened fire on Russian units, destroyed
gun emplacements and crushed one gun under their tracks.'
On 27 January, Konev issued a series of draconian orders designed to
restore discipline and accompanied by a long list of officers who had
been despatched to the *strafblats*. A stickler for detail, Konev also
banned the wearing of looted top hats and the carrying of umbrellas.[†]
Tales of Russian barbarity spread back from the front to the Reich. Vera

---

* Ehrenburg's basic theme – 'Kill the Germans' – eventually earned him an official
rebuke. In April 1945, in an editorial in the Soviet military newspaper *Red Star*, he
was taken to task for exaggerating: '. . . we are not fighting against the German people, only against the Hitlers of this world'. Ehrenburg, protected by Stalin, continued
to pour out vitriol directed against the German people.
† During the Peninsular campaign (1809–14) the Duke of Wellington also stopped
officers sheltering under umbrellas and parasols, considering the effect decidedly
unmilitary. Montgomery, however, often sported an umbrella.

Bockmann, an Australian woman of Silesian descent who had married a German seaman and settled in Berlin, recalled:

> The approach of the Russians was viewed with dread as the rumour-mongers predicted that they would rape all the women and take away the children. Others were by no means pessimistic about the Russians. In our street there was a family who had fled from Silesia and were actually picked up by a Russian tank. The soldiers had shared their food with them and after having linked with the refugees, bade them a hearty farewell. This was the sort of stuff that I wanted to hear, but very adverse stories came from equally reliable sources. Best not to believe any of it.

Those nearer the front believed every word they heard. The Russian rampage stiffened the resolve of the Volksgrenadier and Volkssturm defenders of Germany as they prepared to fight the last battle of the European war.

CHAPTER 5

Thunderclap

'I do not personally regard the whole of the remaining cities of Germany as worth the bones of one British Grenadier.'
Air Chief Marshal Sir Arthur Harris, Air Officer Commanding-in-Chief, RAF Bomber Command

ON 3 FEBRUARY 1945, Berlin was hit by a heavy daylight raid flown by US Eighth Air Force. Two days later Hans-Georg von Studnitz wrote in his diary:

Last Saturday's . . . attack, directed against the centre of the city, the government district and the railway stations, was the ultimate apocalypse, as far as Berlin is concerned. The attack began at 10.45am and ended at 12.30. The Adlon* shelter is a foot deep in water that has leaked through the roof from the melting snow above. Many people have had to wade about underground for two hours in icy water. Under the heavy explosions the massive shelter swayed and shivered like the cellar of an ordinary house. Finally all the lights went out, and we felt as if we had been buried alive. In the Foreign Ministry, one wing of the Minister's suite and house No.73 were hit. We saw the Foreign Minister† and the Japanese Ambassador wandering about among the ruins surrounded by a crowd of people and being greeted with the Nazi salute by those in uniform. Ribbentrop was wearing uniform, while Oshima was wearing a leather jacket and a deerstalker. Gigantic clouds of smoke hang over the whole city.

---

* The Adlon Hotel
† Joachim von Ribbentrop.

Over 1,000 miles away, on the southern coast of the Crimean peninsula, diplomatic exchanges of a very different kind were about to begin. Arrangements for the second wartime summit between the 'Big Three' – Stalin, Roosevelt and Churchill – had been agreed by the Soviet and American leaders, an indication that Britain was now the junior partner in the Grand Alliance. Only after Stalin had insisted on Yalta as the site for the conference, pleading that the pressure of military operations would not permit him to travel abroad, was Churchill invited to attend.

The outlines of the post-war world were now beginning to take shape. By the end of January 1945 the Americans and British had liberated large parts of Western Europe, Italy and Greece, and had installed sympathetic regimes in countries formerly occupied by the Nazis. In Eastern Europe the Red Army had liberated Romania, Bulgaria and Poland and, in similar if more ruthless fashion, installed regimes which remained under Russian control. Hungary looked likely to go the same way, but Yugoslavia, where Tito's partisans had liberated the country with little outside help, seemed set to retain a substantial measure of independence. Stalin had a straightforward view of these developments, delivered in a speech in July 1944: 'Everyone imposes his own system as far as his army can reach. It cannot be otherwise.'*

Before their rendezvous with Stalin in the Crimea, Churchill, Roosevelt and the Combined Chiefs of Staff met in Malta on 1 February. It was not an encouraging curtain-raiser to the Yalta Conference. Five years of war had sapped Churchill's stamina and powers of concentration. On 19 January his Deputy Prime Minister, the Labour Party leader Clement Attlee, had written to him, chiding him for his increasing lack of attention to detail. When papers came before the Cabinet,

> it is very exceptional for you to have read them. More and more often you have not even read the note prepared for your guidance.

---

* When Churchill met Stalin in Moscow in October 1944, they struck a deal redolent of the old imperial concept of 'spheres of influence'. The Soviet Union would have 90 per cent influence in Romania, 10 per cent influence in Greece, 75 per cent in Bulgaria and 50 per cent in Yugoslavia, with the remaining percentages controlled by Britain. Churchill scrawled these figures on a piece of paper and passed it to Stalin, who simply ticked it and passed it back. Churchill said that that the paper should be burned, as it might be thought 'rather cynical if it seemed we had disposed of these issues . . . in such an offhand manner'. To this Stalin replied, 'No, you keep it'. Stalin was happy to keep his side of the bargain when it came to Greece, and did not intervene on the side of the Communist forces in the six-week Greek civil war in the winter of 1944–5, though he was less restrained when fighting resumed in 1946.

Often half an hour is wasted in explaining what could have been grasped by two or three minutes of reading of the document. Not infrequently a phrase catches your eye which gives rise to a disquisition on an interesting point only slightly connected with the subject matter. The result is long delays and increasingly long Cabinets imposed on Ministers who have already done a full day's work and will have more to deal with before they go to bed.

Roosevelt, who in November 1944 had beaten the Republican candidate Wendell Wilkie to secure an unprecedented fourth term as US President, was now in steep physical decline. He was so wasted as to appear almost transparent. When Churchill's personal physician, Lord Moran, saw the President, he gave him only a few months to live, a term that was to be shortened by the strain of the journey to Yalta. Roosevelt was in no state to pay anything more than cursory attention to the brief-ings prepared for him. The British Foreign Secretary, Anthony Eden, was fearful that too little had been done to ready the ailing Roosevelt and the increasingly dyspeptic Churchill for a crucial encounter with a 'bear who would certainly know his own mind'.

Shortly before midnight on Friday 2 February, the first aircraft in a long convoy bearing 700 Allied officers and officials took off from Luqa in Malta, bound for Saki airfield in the Crimea. They were followed in the small hours by Roosevelt and Churchill, flying in separate Douglas C-54 Skymaster transports, blacked out and maintaining radio silence. The Skymasters and their Lockheed P-38 Lightning escorts touched down at Saki just after midnight on the 3 February. After the reception ceremonies, Churchill and Roosevelt were driven the seventy miles to Yalta over bruisingly bumpy roads and past the litter of wrecked weaponry left in the wake of the German retreat from the Crimea ten months before. Meanwhile, Stalin made the journey to Yalta in more comfortable style in his special train.

By all accounts Churchill was in a foul mood. After an hour of lurching over rutted roads he turned to his daughter, Sarah Oliver,* and said, 'Christ, five more hours of this', before comforting himself by reciting from memory long passages from Byron's *Don Juan*. His mood brightened somewhat on arrival in Yalta. Its backdrop of low mountains, sloping down to the Black Sea through cypress groves, vineyards, orange groves and tobacco plantations, painted a picture light years away from the dreary greys of ration-bound Britain. The British delegation was

---

* Sarah Churchill had married the Viennese-born comedian Vic Oliver.

housed in the Vorontzov Palace, a combination of Scottish baronial and *Arabian Nights* fantasy built in 1837. Thousands of Red Army engineers had been at work around Yalta, demonstrating that when the chips were down Stalin was as good a capitalist as his allies. The palace blazed with log fires and was hung with rich tapestries and masterpieces from Moscow and Leningrad. Throughout the conference Churchill guzzled champagne and caviare. When Joan Bright, the Cabinet Secretariat official in charge of 'housekeeping', casually remarked over lunch that she had never tasted Chicken Kiev, a butler shimmered in within the hour to serve her the real thing.

Taking a sanguine view of Soviet sanitary habits, the British Military Mission in Moscow had advised the delegation to take 'plenty of flea powder and toilet paper'. Churchill, at least, was housed in some comfort, with sole access to one of only two bathrooms in the palace. Conditions were crowded for everyone else. The British were amused to discover that in the Livadia Palace, where the Americans were quartered and the conference's plenary sessions were held, they were sleeping eight generals to a room. General George Marshall, Chairman of the Joint Chiefs of Staff, and Fleet Admiral Ernest King were bedded down in the Tsarina's suite, Marshall in her bedroom and King in her boudoir, which had a garden window reputedly used by Rasputin.

During the conference, Churchill telegraphed Attlee:

> This place has turned out very well so far, in spite of our gloomy warnings and forebodings. It is a sheltered strip of austere Riviera with winding cornice roads, and the villas and palaces more or less undamaged of an extinct imperialism and nobility. In these we squat on furniture carried from Moscow and with plumbing and road-making done regardless of cost in a few days by our hosts, whose prodigality exceeds belief. All the Chiefs of Staff have taken a holiday to see the battlefield at Balaclava. We are not stressing this in our contacts with our friends.

The stresses and strains on the Grand Alliance revolved around the major items on the agenda at Yalta: the future of Poland; the post-war dismemberment of Germany; the terms of Soviet entry into the war against Japan; and the structure of the evolving United Nations organization.

Poland's post-war boundaries had been crudely mapped out at the Tehran Conference in November-December 1943. Stalin was to be ceded a slice of eastern Poland up to 185 miles wide, an area traditionally claimed by Russia. Poland was to be compensated with a tranche cut from Germany's eastern boundary extending to the Oder and Neisse

Rivers. At Yalta the first argument was over the proposal for the German-Polish border. Had Poland been allotted territory up to the eastern branch of the Neisse – as Churchill and Roosevelt believed – or to the western branch, sixty miles closer to Germany, which was Stalin's interpretation? A decision was put off until an eventual European peace conference, which never met.

There was little common ground between Stalin and the Western Allies over the political future of Poland. The Americans submitted a 'Declaration on Liberated Europe', a well-meaning but woolly document, among the provisions of which was the right of all peoples to choose the form of government under which they wanted to live. Poland's prospects of democratic government had already been extinguished. Stalin was determined that in Poland, an age-old invasion route into Russia, any future government would be a 'friend of the Soviet Union'. In 1943 the Polish government-in-exile in London had demanded a Red Cross inquiry into the massacre of more than 10,000 Polish soldiers and civilians whose bodies had been uncovered by the Germans in the forest of Katyn, near Smolensk.* The Soviet Union had immediately broken off relations with the London Poles and had set up a puppet Polish government in Moscow, which moved to Lublin in 1944 and was subsequently installed in Warsaw. At Yalta the London Poles were abandoned by Roosevelt and Churchill. Stalin made one small concession, suggesting that the Lublin government be widened to include a few London Poles, but in all other respects he got his way. The promised 'free elections' in Poland would be monitored by his own stooges, the Lublin Poles, with only minimal outside monitoring. At the plenary session of the Yalta Conference on 8 February, Churchill had undermined all his own and Roosevelt's arguments by suddenly declaring, 'I do not care much about the Poles myself', a disarming display of frankness, perhaps, but a fairly ill-advised negotiating stance. In truth, however, Roosevelt and Churchill had no hand to play over Poland and were obliged to recognize the Soviet Union's power to determine matters there on the ground. They came away clutching the face-saving formula of 'free elections', but could have been under no illusions that such a concept was anything other than entirely alien to Stalin.

As well as settling boundaries – and recognizing realities – in Eastern Europe, the Allies had to decide what to do with Germany itself. As early as 1943 the British had been working on a plan, codenamed 'Rankin C', for a three-way post-war division of Germany and joint occupation of Berlin. Better a divided Germany than the prospect of an energetic

---

* It is now established beyond a doubt that the Poles were killed by the Red Army during the Soviet occupation of eastern Poland, 1939–41.

nation of 80 million people at the heart of Europe rising again as a Fourth Reich. The British plan gave Stalin control of almost 40 per cent of Germany's post-war area, 36 per cent of its population and 33 per cent of its resources. Since Rankin C had first been mooted, however, another plan for post-war Germany had come and gone. At the Quebec Conference in September 1944, Henry Morgenthau, Roosevelt's Secretary of the Treasury, presented a proposal under which Germany would have been stripped of her industry and converted into an agricultural economy. This provided the Nazi propaganda chief Josef Goebbels with a weapon with which to rally his countrymen, not least because Morgenthau was Jewish. Although the plan had received initial support from Churchill, it was eventually shelved by Roosevelt.

At Yalta, the Allies formally agreed to the zones outlined in Rankin C, with the addition of a small French zone in the Saarland, carved out of the British and American sectors. Churchill had argued that France should be restored as a counterweight to Germany, not least because an indefinite American presence on the continent of Europe could not be guaranteed. Berlin was to be divided into four sectors and was to house the Allied Control Council for supervising the occupying powers. Stalin gave informal guarantees of access by air, road, canal and rail through the Soviet zone to the sectors of Berlin occupied by the Western Powers. Austria was to be divided in similar fashion, with Vienna providing the headquarters for a four-power commission.

Like Henry Morgenthau, Stalin had his own designs on German industry. Ivan Maisky, formerly the Soviet Ambassador in London and now Deputy Commissar for Foreign Affairs, presented a plan which proposed the reduction of German industry to one-fifth of its present size, with all arms factories and synthetic oil plants to be dismantled within two years. To this was added ten years' reparations payments, to be followed by the establishment of a tripartite international control commission which would take command of the entire German economy. Stalin also demanded additional monetary compensation of $10 billion, a figure he had cooked up with Roosevelt. Churchill woke up at this point, recalling that reparations imposed on Germany after the First World War had played no small part in hastening the Second, and suggesting that Germany would be hard pressed to meet just the Soviet demands. After much blustering he agreed that the matter should be remitted to a reparations commission, to be established in Moscow.

Roosevelt attempted to act as a conciliator throughout the Yalta Conference. He was convinced that he could 'do business' with Stalin, and reserved most of his suspicions for Churchill's occasional outbursts of crusty imperialism. In order to secure Soviet entry into the war against

Japan, and agreement on the new United Nations organization, particularly the thorny question of the veto on resolutions exercised by members of the Security Council, Roosevelt was prepared to make substantial
concessions to Stalin. The Soviets were to have their way in Poland and
were to gain substantial territories in the Far East. In a deal made without consulting Churchill, Roosevelt agreed to the Russian recovery of the
Czarist territories lost to Japan in the Russo-Japanese War of 1904–5, plus
the Kurile Islands and the island of South Sakhalin. Churchill was presented with the resulting document on the last day of the conference
and had no alternative but to sign it, a brutal reminder of Britain's dimin-
ished status at the top table.

Throughout the conference the mood of the 'Big Three' had yawed
dizzily between petulance and bouts of bogus bonhomie. At dinner on
4 February, Roosevelt felt sufficiently relaxed to tell Stalin that in
the West he was commonly known as 'Uncle Joe', a remark which nearly
sent the Soviet leader stalking from the room in a rage, apparently
stung to the quick by the vulgarity of the nickname. Churchill contrived
to draw him back to the table with a toast. These personal tensions
underlined the political strains on the alliance which, nevertheless,
held together. Stalin emerged triumphant. Where Churchill was long-
winded and Roosevelt vague, Stalin remained incisive, playing a
strong hand with masterly skill. As the delegates assembled for farewell photographs on the sunlit terrace of the Livadia Palace, Stalin was
in fine fettle, barking out the only four English phrases he knew:
'So what?', 'What the hell goes on around here?', 'The toilet is over
there' and 'You said it'. In contrast, Churchill had subsided into the black
mood in which he had arrived, grumpily referring to the joint communiqué as 'this bloody thing'. Writing much later, however, he put Yalta
into wistful perspective: 'We had the world at our feet. Twenty-five million
men were marching at our orders by land and sea. We seemed to be
friends.'

General Sir Hastings Ismay, Churchill's personal Chief of Staff, considered that Yalta had been 'from the military point of view unnecessary
... [and] from the political point of view depressing'. There was, however, one Allied military decision which was heavily influenced by the
Yalta Conference, and whose effects still reverberate today. It was to turn
the spotlight on a part of Germany which had remained remarkably unaf-
fected by the war, the baroque city of Dresden.

Since the summer of 1944 RAF Bomber Command had been flying regularly by daylight. On 27 August 1944, 216 Handley Page Halifaxes of 4
Group and fourteen De Havilland Mosquitoes and thirteen Avro

Lancasters of 8 Group raided the Meerbeck oil refinery in the first major daylight operation by Bomber Command since 12 August 1941, when fifty-four Bristol Blenheims had bombed power stations near Cologne. On the outward flight escort was provided by nine squadrons of Supermarine Spitfires, and the withdrawal was covered by a further seven squadrons. The heavy bombers did not fly in tight formation, like the Liberators and Flying Fortresses of US Eighth Air Force, but in loose 'gaggles'. There was intense flak over Meerbeck, but there were no losses. Production at the Meerbeck plant was not resumed until October.

In the last eight months of the war Bomber Command reached the peak of its strength, with an average daily availability of 1,600 aircraft, of which approximately 1,100 were four-engined Lancasters. The cream of Britain's scientific establishment had been absorbed in the development of the advanced technology employed in the strategic bombing offensive, while the industrial resources devoted to the production of heavy bombers was, at a conservative estimate, equal to that allotted to the production of equipment for the Army.

By night, Bomber Command's target-marking techniques had reached new levels of sophistication. In the summer of 1944, 5 Group developed the system of 'offset' marking in which each aircraft of the Main Force approached the aiming point – already illuminated by flares and incendiaries dropped by bombers of the Pathfinder Force – on one of several different pre-instructed headings. Although the Main Force bombers aimed for the same single marking point, the different angles of approach and timed overshoots provided a number of aiming points for the price of one successful marking attack by the Pathfinders. Over Königsberg on 29 August 1944, there were three approach lines. In the attack on Bremerhaven on 18 September there were five, a method perfectly adapted to bombing an elongated port stretching for eight miles along the eastern shore of the Weser estuary. The Bremerhaven raid was carried out by 200 aircraft which dropped 863 tons of bombs, including 420,000 thermite incendiaries. Photo-reconnaissance revealed that of a total built-up area of 375 acres, 297 acres had been destroyed. These techniques were further refined in a raid on Darmstadt on 11 September. After the target had been marked by 627 Squadron's Mosquitoes, 234 heavy bombers approached the aiming point – an old army parade-ground one mile west of the city centre – along seven lines of approach, at varying heights and with each aircraft timing its overshoot by between three and twelve seconds. This ensured that the destruction was spread in an unfolding V-shape across the city. The Germans called it *der Todesfächer*, 'the Death Fan'. Destruction in the centre of Darmstadt was 78 per cent, and 70,000 of the city's population of 115,000 were made homeless. In the Old City only five buildings remained standing after the raid. Some 8,500 people perished in the forty-five minute raid, about 90 per cent of them from asphyxiation or burning. A similar technique was used in the attack on Brunswick on 14 October. A firestorm was started in an area of the city which contained six giant bunkers and two air-raid shelters housing over 20,000 people. They were saved by a 'water alley' driven through the blazing streets by high-pressure fire hoses and screened on each side by overlapping jets of water. Nevertheless the city had suffered such terrible damage that although the raid had been made by only 200 aircraft of one group, the Brunswick authorities estimated that at least 1,000 bombers must have carried out the bombing. Within forty minutes over one-third of the population of 200,000 had been made homeless and nearly half the built-up area of the city laid waste.

These crushing raids were the prelude to Operation Thunderclap, the triple blow delivered to the city of Dresden between 13 and 15 February 1945 by Bomber Command and US Eighth Air Force. The Saxon city of Dresden, which lies 110 miles south of Berlin, was the largest German city to have escaped the attentions of Allied bombers. Its first experience of air attack was delayed until 7 October 1944, when a force of thirty US Eighth Air Force bombers was diverted to Dresden's industrial outskirts as a secondary target during an attack on the oil refinery at Ruhland. The raid killed 435, including a number of Allied prisoners of war employed in work detachments in the city's light industrial plants and railway yards, and was such a local sensation that coach-owners ran special excursions to the bomb-damaged streets. Even when 133 Eighth Air Force aircraft made a second and far heavier raid on the the city's marshalling yards on 16 January 1945, Dresdeners remained convinced that their city, whose beautiful baroque centre was unscathed by war, would escape the fate which had overtaken Cologne, Hamburg and Darmstadt. Dresden was famed for its cultural institutions and the elegant porcelain made in nearby Meissen, but it possessed no war industries of strategic significance. The city's two largest plants employed a total of 5,000 workers in the manufacture of electronic components for the AEG radar sets made in Berlin. In the winter of 1944 the war seemed a long way off. A British prisoner of war, captured at Anzio in December 1944, wrote in his diary: 'The Germans here are the best I have ever come across. The Commandant is a gentleman, and we are allowed an extraordinary amount of liberty in the town. The Feldwebel [sergeant] has already taken me to see the centre of the town. Unquestionably it is beautiful. I would like to see more of it.'

In the autumn of 1943, following the firestorm raised by Bomber

Command raids on Hamburg, the authorities in Dresden made some desultory efforts to beef up the city's civil defence measures. As so often happened in Nazi Germany, the implementation of even the most basic measures was bedevilled by the overlapping jurisdictions of mutually antagonistic fiefdoms – Göring's Luftwaffe, Goebbels's Propaganda Ministry and Himmler's SS – each of which had assumed responsibility for different aspects of civil defence. Eventually a number of 'safe' open spaces in the city were selected and signposted. The population was encouraged to take elementary fire precautions – clearing their lofts of inflammable material and coating the beams with white fire-resistant fluid. Sandbags, water buckets and small handpumps were placed inside houses and apartments, the sand to douse incendiary bombs and the water to combat small fires. Trenches were dug in parks and open spaces. In a pointedly perfunctory gesture, six static water tanks were placed in public places to provide Dresden's fire brigade with a reservoir on which to draw if the mains were destroyed by air attack.*

As in the majority of German cities, most of the citizens of Dresden were apartment dwellers. Relatively few had access to the kind of small back gardens in which Londoners sank their Anderson shelters in the winter of 1939–40. Nevertheless, their apartment blocks contained spacious cellars whose dividing walls were knocked through and then lightly bricked up, so enabling shelterers trapped by a fire above them to break down the partition and seek safety in the adjoining basement. In this fashion they could proceed along a line of cellars to the end of their street, emerging in an area free of smoke and flames. If a firestorm took hold, however, such calculations became academic; the shelterers would surface in a sea of flame to be asphyxiated or roasted alive. Escape from a firestorm could only have been provided by an extensive network of tunnels driven under the centre of Dresden to channel the population to the open spaces around the Elbe.

Dresden's seemingly charmed survival in the middle of a continent seared from end to end by war only served to encourage official complacency. Rumours circulated that the Allies had spared Dresden because it was to be the new capital of Germany after the war, or because a relation of Winston Churchill was held as a prisoner of war there. In December 1944 Colonel Hugo Eichhorn, the commander of a regiment of SS Pioneers, was consulted by Dresden's mayor, SS Gruppenführer Nieland, about the provision of air-raid bunkers in the city. According to Eichhorn, 'the gentlemen in the town hall felt the time had come to do something for the population of Dresden'. By then it was

---

* Dortmund, in the Ruhr, had 134 similar water tanks

too late. In the entire city there was only one concrete bunker suitable for use as a bomb shelter, and this was reserved for the use of Dresden's Gauleiter, Martin Mutschmann.*

Nor were Dresden's air defences in any better shape. By mid-January 1945 they had been dismantled, the batteries of 88mm guns transferred to tank-killing duties on the Eastern Front or sent to defend the battered industries in the Ruhr. By mid-January only their concrete pads remained, and a few forlorn papier mâché dummies.

By then the tide of war had engulfed the city. The Red Army's eruption from the Vistula bridgeheads had triggered a stampede for safety by 5 million Germans, flinging them on to the snowbound roads on carts and on foot, often with little more than the clothes they stood up in. It was as if the suppressed knowledge of what the Wehrmacht had done in the East had bobbed to the surface like a bloated corpse, long submerged, seizing the panic-stricken population with an overmastering urge to escape the Russian columns, which by the end of the month had advanced to within ninety miles of Dresden. Tens of thousands died on this terrible journey, frozen in ditches or crushed under the tracks of T-34s. For those who survived, Dresden was one of the principal places of refuge. By the end of January the city's population of 630,000 had swollen to 1.6 million. Few of the refugees, mostly country people who had never heard an air-raid siren, had access to any form of shelter.

The refugees who reached Dresden by train fared little better than those who walked. They were packed into cattle trucks with only a little straw on the floor, arriving frozen, foul with lice and starving. Many children died from hunger and cold. Their grandparents simply gave up the ghost. Eva Beyer was a seventeen-year-old Red Cross worker receiving refugees at Dresden's central station, the Hauptbahnhof:

> There were so many refugees from Silesia and Warthegan. My task was to give them soup, bread, coffee and milk. What I saw there of suffering and misery can hardly be described. There were women, old men and children in a condition which was not human any more. After my first day of duty I couldn't eat for two days afterwards and I had nightmares, for I had never seen anything like that in my whole life, or thought that things like that were possible. As I walked along the train to distribute food, a woman came and

---

* In true Gauleiter fashion, Mutschmann was reported to be building, at considerable public expense and with SS labour, an elaborate bunker in his garden and another in a wooded area outside the city. He was clearly a man who did not believe in taking chances.

begged me for milk for her child. I asked her where her child was, and she unfolded her apron and showed me the child. I wasn't a doctor but I could see that the child was dead; it was stiff and blue and must have been dead for several days. When I told her that her baby was in heaven and wouldn't need any more milk, she replied: 'No, my baby is only sleeping. Please give me milk for my baby.' When we tried to take the baby away from her, so that we might bury it, she turned wild and screamed: 'My child is not dead – it's only hungry. . . .' Once in mid-January I was on duty and the train which drew in had been bombed on the way. What I saw there was worse than horror. Not only were the people squeezed together in a goods train, but they had to suffer hunger and thirst and the bombs, too. There were so many injured on that train that we didn't know where to start. The screams and cries for help were almost unbearable . . . I bent down to a woman who had a baby at her breast, to see if I could help, for she was smeared with blood. She was dead but the child was still alive. Beside her lay an old man. He was her father. He called: 'Annie, come and help me.' His arm was torn to pieces. When we told him that Annie was dead, he broke down completely and sat crying: 'What is going to happen to us? My son-in-law in the war, my daughter dead, a two-months-old baby and an eight-year-old boy.' The old man clung to me asking: 'What can we do next? We have lost our homes, our possessions. Oh God, what have we done that we are being punished like this? Can there really be a God who allows such things?'

Allied prisoners of war marching westward, away from the advancing Russians, suffered equally nighmarish experiences. Jack Meyers, a British artilleryman who had been captured in the Western Desert in June 1942, joined the exodus when Stalag VIIIB, near Breslau, was evacuated. He eventually arrived in Dresden's marshalling yards in a cattle truck:

It was closed, unheated, unventilated, with only a bucket at one end for sanitation. There were not three fit people in that truck. I personally was not really conscious most of the time. We'd not had too much to eat for a long while. And for the last few days we'd not been fed or watered at all. Even the biggest lead-swingers were really sick now.* It was freezing cold, no food, people dying. We didn't dehydrate because we could suck the snow and ice which entered the truck, although it was enclosed. We stacked the dead

---

* Meyers, who was suffering from a septic foot, had been loaded on to a train in a railway siding in Görlitz.

at one end, with a bit of no man's land in the middle near the
doors. There were about eighty in all, of mixed nationalities, and I
suppose about twenty or thirty died. The rest huddled together for
warmth.

Refugees and Allied *realpolitik* now combined to destroy Dresden. As
the war drew to a close, with most of Germany lying in ruins, the Allied
bombing chiefs cast around for remaining targets against which to
despatch the huge forces at their disposal. By the autumn of 1944, however, the British and Americans were at odds with each other over the
most effective method of continuing the combined bombing offensive.
General Carl 'Tooey' Spaatz, in overall command of the US Strategic Air
Forces in Europe, urged a concentrated attack on oil targets. He was vigorously opposed by Air Chief Marshal Sir Arthur Harris, chief of RAF
Bomber Command since 1942, who had never wavered from the belief
that the systematic destruction of the urban areas of Germany would, by
itself, bring an end to the war. In spite of a persuasive body of evidence
to the contrary, Harris was convinced that there were no key weaknesses
in the German war economy. He referred contemptuously to raids on oil
and transport-linked targets as mere 'panaceas'. Harris had been dragged
kicking and screaming into the oil offensive which, between July and
September of 1944, had crippled German oil production,* but as winter
set in he returned to his principal preoccupation – the progressive
destruction of Germany's cities. On 1 November 1944 he wrote to the
Chief of the Air Staff, Air Chief Marshal Sir Charles Portal:

> In the past eighteen months Bomber Command has virtually
> destroyed 45 out of the leading 60 German cities. In spite of the
> invasion diversions† we have so far managed to keep up and even
> extend our iverage of two and a half cities devastated a month. . . .
> There are not many industrial centres of population now left
> intact. Are we going to abandon this vast task, which the Germans
> themselves have long admitted to be their worst headache, just as
> it nears completion?

One plan for finishing Harris's 'vast task', hatched in the autumn of
1944, was 'Thunderclap', designed to inflict four days and nights of fright-
fulness on Berlin with an Anglo-American assault which would drop
25,000 tons of bombs on the city. Thunderclap's supporters believed that

---

* Even so, between July and September 1944 only 11 per cent of Bomber Command's
sorties had been devoted to oil targets.
† The Transportation Plan, again opposed by Harris, in which Allied bombers hit rail
networks in France and western Germany.

The Allied Supreme Command during the preparations for D-Day. Seated (*left to right*): Air Chief Marshal Tedder, General Eisenhower and General Montgomery. Standing (*left to right*): General Bradley, Admiral Sir Bertram Ramsay, the naval C-in-C for Overlord, Air Chief Marshal Sir Trafford Leigh-Mallory, commander of the Allied Expeditionary Air Force, and Lieutenant-General Walter Bedell Smith, Eisenhower's highly efficient Chief of Staff. Both Ramsay and Leigh-Mallory died in air crashes before the war was won, Leigh-Mallory in November 1944 while on his way to take up his new post as Allied Air C-in-C, South-East Asia Command, and Ramsay in January 1945 on a flight to meet Montgomery in Brussels.

Left: A terrible harvest –
burning the bodies of
civilians killed in the
Dresden air raids,
February 1945.

Below left: A half-track of
US Ninth Army rattles past
the corpse of a German
officer towards Cologne in
early March 1945.

Right: Two contrasting
representatives of the
German officer corps.
Above: Colonel-General
Heinz Guderian, whose
eight months (from July
1944) as Chief of the Army
General Staff were marked
by a series of blazing rows
with Hitler. *Below:* Field
Marshal Ferdinand
Schörner, pictured here
(*centre*) in the Balkans in
1941 wearing the Pour-le-
Mérite he won during the
First World War. A diehard
Nazi, Schörner was
appointed the wartime
German Army's last
Commander-in-Chief in
Hitler's testament.

Above left: Present and correct – Colonel-General (later Marshal) Konev inspecting troops of the Thirty-First Army on the Kalinin Front in 1941. On his left is the Army's commander, Major-General V. S. Polenov.

Left: The redoubtable General Chuikov (*centre*), commanding Eighth Guards Army, at an observation post during the Vistula-Oder Operation.

Above: Tanks of Konev's First Ukrainian Front roll through a Silesian town on the way to Berlin.

Right: A relaxed Stalin and Churchill share an informal moment at the Yalta Conference, February 1945.

Left: Soviet artillery prepares for the assault on Berlin.

Below left: American troops take a stroll through the dragon's teeth defences of the West Wall (popularly known as the Siegfried Line), near Aachen. On 21 October 1944, Aachen became the first German city to be captured by the Allies.

Right: Weary German prisoners watch as American troops cross the bridge over the Rhine at Remagen, which was seized by units of General Hodges's First Army on 7 March 1945.

Below: All quiet on the Western Front. US soldiers crossing the Rhine on 25 March 1945, two days after the mounting of Operation Plunder.

Left: The face of defeat. An exhausted panzergrenadier, his cheek brushing the cold metal of his Panzerfaust.

Below: 'Germany is *kaput*! Might as well loot.' The contents of a train are picked over by Russian and Polish slave labourers near Leipzig, April 1945.

the operation would crush civilian morale and bring Germany to its knees. The war could be won by the exercise of air power alone, the cherished belief of air strategists from 1917. Harris's Directorate of Bomber Operations produced some rough calculations on the effects of Thunderclap:

> If we assume that the daytime population of the area attacked is 300,000, we may expect 200,000 casualties. 50 per cent of these or 110,000 may expect to be killed. It is suggested that such an attack, resulting in so many deaths, the great proportion of which will be key personnel, cannot but have a shattering effect on political and civilian morale all over Germany. . . .

Combined with ground operations, this might lead to a formal German surrender. Thunderclap reached the planning stage at Supreme Headquarters Allied Expeditionary Force (SHAEF) before being shelved. It had been opposed by Spaatz, the architect of the oil plan, but even he was beginning to move in the same direction. In October, he floated a proposal 'to beat up the insides of Germany enough by air action to cause her to collapse next spring, particularly if the Russians continue pressure against the eastern area'. Spaatz's proposal emphasized the destruction of targets requiring precision bombing rather than the area bombing to which Harris devoted the greater part of his resources. The Americans were careful to distance themselves from area bombing – SHAEF's Psychological Warfare Division had stigmatized Thunderclap as 'terroristic' – but even Spaatz was happy to commit his aircraft to the bombing of cities if some convenient pretext could be invoked, such as the radar-assisted blind bombing of 'transportation centres'. With an average circular error of two miles on missions guided by radar, however, blind bombing was area bombing in all but name.

In Allied deliberations, Dresden did not figure on the target list. It might have survived the war unscathed had it not been for Winston Churchill's desire to strengthen his hand when dealing with Stalin at Yalta, the last great Allied conference of the war, which began on 4 February 1945. Yalta, which determined the shape of post-war Europe, also decided the fate of Dresden.

As Churchill prepared to leave for Yalta, he pondered what evidence he could offer 'Uncle Joe' of Western support for the great offensives in the East. The Joint Intelligence Committee of the British War Cabinet was considering the same problem. On 25 January it produced two papers. The first proposed that heavy bombers should support the Russians, particularly in interdicting the movement of German armoured formations from the West to the Eastern Front. The second paper re-examined Thunderclap,* casting doubt on the likelihood of a four-day assault on Berlin producing a collapse in German morale. It then moved on to consider the role heavy bombers could play in triggering the uncontrollable movement of huge numbers of refugees back and forth across the Reich, fleeing from one shattered city to the next and creating the chaos generated by the lava flow of fugitives in the East as the Russians raced towards the Oder. The collision of these great masses of tortured humanity, one struggling westward, the other eastward, would place an intolerable strain on the enemy's military movements and communications.

Portal was also sceptical about the Berlin option, preferring to concentrate on targets associated with oil and jet fighter production, but he nevertheless conceded that the Allies could commit their 'available effort' to 'one big attack on Berlin and attacks on Dresden, Leipzig, Chemnitz and any other cities where a severe blitz will not only create confusion in the evacuation from the east but will also hamper the movement of troops from the west.' Harris, telephoned on the 25th by Air Vice-Marshal Norman Bottomley, Deputy Chief of the Air Staff, was reluctant to relinquish another chance to level Berlin, over which his bombers had been defeated in the winter of 1943–4,† but also suggested that the assault on the German capital should be augmented by simultaneous operations against Chemnitz, Leipzig and Dresden which, equally with Berlin, would share the task of housing evacuees from the east and, again equally with Berlin, were focal points in the German system of communications behind the Eastern Front. Dresden, with its helpless refugee population, was moving up the target list.

At this point Churchill intervened. On 25 January he telephoned the Air Minister, Sir Archibald Sinclair, demanding to know what plans Bomber Command had for 'basting [sic] the Germans in their retreat from Breslau'. Portal informed Sinclair of the proposal to attack Berlin, Dresden, Leipzig and Chemnitz, highlighting the refugees as a potential

---

* Thunderclap had been revived by Air Commodore S.O. Bufton, the Director of Bomber Operations who, in a minute to Air Vice-Marshal N.H. Bottomley, Deputy Chief of the Air Staff, also suggested that it should include simultaneous attacks on Breslau and Munich as well as on Berlin: 'If the operation were launched at a time when there was still no obvious slackening in the momentum of the Russian drive, it might well have the appearance of a close co-ordination in planning between the Russians and ourselves. Such a deduction on the part of the enemy would greatly increase the moral effect of both operations.'

† Between November 1943 and March 1944 Bomber Command lost 592 bombers in sixteen heavy raids on Berlin, which Harris had threatened to 'wreck from end to end'. This represented a loss rate of 6.5 per cent.

target. But when Sinclair reported back to Churchill, he took a significantly different line, suggesting the use of the Tactical Air Force to harry retreating German military formations rather than refugees. This operation, Sinclair argued, was best suited to the Tactical Air Force rather than heavy bombers at a time 'when cloud often makes it impossible to bomb from a high level. It would be extremely difficult for our heavy bombers to interfere with these enemy movements by direct attacks on their lines of retreat.'

Sinclair received a terse reply from the Prime Minister:

> I did not ask you last night about plans for harrying the German retreat from Breslau. On the contrary, I asked whether Berlin, and no doubt other large cities in East Germany, should not now be considered especially attractive targets. I am glad that this is 'under examination'. Pray report to me tomorrow what is going to be done.

Sinclair did his master's bidding. The next day, 27 January, Harris was given the go-ahead to mount the operations he had proposed to Bottomley on the 25th. On the same day Sinclair informed Churchill that 'subject to the overriding claims of attacks on enemy oil production and other approved target systems within the current directive' the available effort would be thrown against Berlin, Dresden, Chemnitz and Leipzig, 'or against other cities where severe bombing would not only destroy communications vital to the evacuation from the East but would also hamper the movements of troops from the West.' As soon as the moon waned and weather conditions were favourable, Harris would dispatch his bombers. It was most unlikely, however, that conditions would favour the operation until about 4 February, the day on which the Yalta Conference was scheduled to begin.

In the late afternoon of 4 February, at the first plenary session in Yalta, the Chief of the Soviet General Staff, General A.I. Antonov, reported on the military situation and provided the Soviet assessment. During the presentation he called for British and American air attacks against Berlin and Leipzig to disrupt the German reinforcement of the Eastern Front. Antonov returned to this theme on the following day when the Anglo-American Combined Chiefs of Staff and the Soviet General Staff met to discuss military policy and co-ordination. At no time did Antonov mention Dresden, and at one point suggested a bomb line, to mark the limit of Allied strategic bombing, which would have passed through Dresden. It is unlikely that the Russians would have welcomed the total destruction of a city which lay within their agreed zone of occupation. Their Western allies, however, were now straining at the leash to provide Stalin with a salutary demonstration of strategic air power.

On 3 February the Americans had fulfilled the first part of this mission, sending nearly 1,000 Eighth Air Force bombers to Berlin. Meanwhile, at Yalta misgivings surfaced about the true nature of Thunderclap. General Lawrence Kuter, the representative at the conference of General H.H. 'Hap' Arnold, the chief of the US Army Air Forces, asked Spaatz whether the Allies' stated intention of coming to the aid of the Russian offensive in the East was not a cover for the indiscriminate bombing of population centres. Spaatz came up with a smoothly disingenuous reply. He assured Kuter that there would be no indiscriminate bombing; the attacks were aimed at transportation targets at the request of the Russians who, it seemed, were highly appreciative of the effort about to be put in by Bomber Command and the USAAF.

On 7 February Stalin was informed, via the US Military Mission in Moscow, that US Eighth Air Force was to attack communications targets in East Germany. The principal order of priority, in a now familiar litany, was Berlin, Leipzig, Dresden and Chemnitz. On 12 February, Spaatz signalled the Military Mission that Eighth Air Force would attack the 'marshalling yards' at Dresden on the 13th. Bomber Command's attack would follow hard on Eighth Air Force's heels on the night of the 13/14th.*

Bomber Command now sent its briefing notes to the groups involved in Thunderclap. Little was known about the city's defences and the staff planners even lacked a standard map of the area. The notes were as disingenuous as Spaatz had been with Kuter:.

> Dresden, the seventh-largest city in Germany . . . is also by far the largest unbombed built-up area the enemy has got . . . At one time well known for its china, Dresden has developed into an industrial city of first-class importance and . . . is of major value for controlling the defence of that part of the front now threatened by Marshal Konev's breakthrough. . . . The intentions of the attack are to hit the enemy where he will feel it most . . . to prevent the use of the city in the way of further advance, and incidentally to show the Russians when they arrive just what Bomber Command can do.

Bomber Command's plan for Thunderclap was simple, and designed to cause the maximum amount of destruction in the centre of Dresden. The

---

* Eighth Air Force's operation on 13 February was aborted because of bad weather, and then postponed by one day to follow the assault by Bomber Command.

city was to be attacked by two separate waves of Lancasters. The first attack, codenamed 'Plate-rack'*, beginning at 10.15pm on the night of the 13th and lasting for approximately seven minutes, would be followed by a second, heavier blow, codenamed 'Press-on', delivered three hours later, which would last for half an hour. The technology and operational expertise harnessed by Bomber Command, and the collapse of the German air defences, now ensured the concentration of the maximum number of aircraft over the target for the minimum amount of time. The first attack would engage Dresden's civil defence systems, which would then be overwhelmed by the second strike, leaving huge fires to rage uncontrolled through the close-packed, combustible streets of the old city. German night-fighters would be lured away by 'spoof' raids executed by small groups of high-flying Mosquitoes, and by an attack by 368 Halifax bombers on the Böhlen oil refinery a hundred miles west of Dresden. The path of the bomber stream was swept by Allied night-fighters, while within the stream the electronic counter-measures aircraft of 100 Group played havoc with the shredded remnants of the Reich's radar defences. Anticipating the rough treatment crews might receive if they came down behind Russian lines, Bomber Command issued them with Perspex envelopes containing large Union flags which bore the embroidered legend 'I am an Englishman', an interesting safety precaution but an inaccurate description of the many nationalities, including Canadians, Australians and New Zealanders, flying in the raid.

When the crews were told that they were flying to Dresden, their reaction was not ecstatic. Aircraft commanders and navigators exchanged sombre glances as the sheets on the briefing maps were pulled aside to reveal the long ribbon running into the heart of Germany. In a Lancaster equipped with exceptionally large fuel tanks containing 2,154 gallons, such a deep penetration into Germany meant ten hours in the air. Rear gunners winced at the prospect of the long, lonely vigil they would keep in their turrets, tugging icicles from their oxygen masks and blinking their eyes to keep the lashes from freezing in the intense cold.

The aim of the raid varied from group to group and squadron to squadron, to a great extent depending on the creative abilities of the briefing officers. In 1 Group, flying in the second wave, crews were told that the aiming point was the city's marshalling yards and great stress was laid on Dresden's importance as a transport centre. In 6 (Canadian) Group, also flying in the second wave, crews were informed that Dresden was 'an important industrial area producing electric motors, precision instruments, chemicals and munitions'. On one station crews were told that

---

* A derisive reference to Dresden china.

their mission was to destroy a Gestapo headquarters in the middle of the city – a precision task usually reserved for the Mosquitoes of such elite units as 487 Squadron. Another squadron's briefing included the fanciful information that there was a poison gas plant in Dresden.

In only a few briefings was there any mention of refugees. When the target was revealed Peter Goldie, a rear gunner in 75 (New Zealand) Squadron, immediately thought of Dresden china: 'They started to explain to us why we were going to Dresden. I think that there was a hint it was Churchill's instruction to destroy the city. But they never really told us what was there. They just said, "Go in there and firebomb the city". We walked back from the briefing, talking together. I couldn't understand why this raid.' Others wondered why, if the bombing of Dresden was so important to the Russians, they didn't undertake it themselves. However, for the majority of aircrew involved, Dresden was just another raid. No one could foresee that the results of their night's work would still reverberate today.

By 5.30pm on 13 February the first squadrons of Bomber Command's 5 Group had taken off from their stations in the Midlands. Thirty minutes later the entire first wave of 244 Lancasters was airborne, circling their airfields before setting course for their first route markers, and Dresden.

The weather section at Bomber Command's headquarters in High Wycombe had predicted with an unusual degree of accuracy that on the night of the 13th a dense bank of cloud looming over Central Europe would clear over Dresden for about five hours. This was the window of opportunity for Plate-rack and Press-on. At 10.05pm the Mosquito of 5 Group's low-level marker leader flashed across Dresden's rooftops at 300mph to place his red target indicators within 100 yards of the aiming point, the Dresden Friedrichstadt Sportplatz. The sky was eerily free of probing searchlights or flak tracer, as the marker leader flew over the Hauptbahnhof, whose staircases and passageways were now clogged with the abandoned possessions of refugees from the East. As he lost altitude for his marking run, the marker leader glanced down at 'a large number of black-and-white half-timbered buildings; it reminded me of Shropshire and Herefordshire and Ludlow. They seemed to be lining the river which had a number of rather gracefully spanned bridges over it; the buildings were a very striking feature of the city's architecture.'

At one-second intervals a flash camera in the Mosquito's bomb bay took pictures of the city below: the railway station; the Dresden-Friedrichstadt Krankenhaus, the biggest hospital complex in East Germany; the hospital's railway sidings, where a train was unloading casualties from the front line; a locomotive puffing along the track by Dresden's Japanese Palace Gardens. The last moments of a doomed city.

By 10.09 the marking was complete and the stadium ringed by the red fires of the target indicators, 1,000-pound bombs whose distinctive pyrotechnics were easy to recognize and difficult for the Germans either to imitate or extinguish. There was no panic among Dresdeners as the target-marking Mosquitoes buzzed busily to and fro a thousand feet overhead. They had lived through 171 false air-raid alarms, and this was surely the 172nd. Now the first intimations of disaster arrived. When a raid threatened a German city, radio broadcasts were interrupted by the sinister tones of a ticking clock. The ticks were replaced by a warning when the target was identified. In the brief moment between the target-marking and the arrival of Plate-rack the ticking was interrupted by the tense voice of an announcer:

> *Achtung, Achtung, Achtung*! The first waves of the large enemy bomber formation have changed course and are now approaching the city boundaries. There is going to be an attack. The population is instructed to proceed at once to the basements and cellars. The police have instructions to arrest all those who remain in the open. . . .

It was Shrove Tuesday, and in Germany in happier days a time of carnival when children donned fancy dress and adults took the day off. Even now many children were wearing their carnival clothes. In the building in Dresden's New Town which housed the Circus Sarrasani, the clowns' demonstration of donkey-riding was interrupted by an announcement ordering the audience to take shelter in the basement. In the Hauptbahnhof a train which was on the point of pulling out ground to a halt when someone pulled the communication cord. Passengers stumbled out on to the blacked-out platform seeking shelter in subways and storerooms already packed with refugees and thousands of would-be travellers. Many people chose to stay on the train to secure their seats. Most of them would die in the second raid.

Eva Beyer had watched the colourful overture to the raid from her bathroom window. At about 10pm she saw a strange green light glowing over a bend in the Elbe. This was the primary green marker dropped by 83 Squadron to guide the marker leader. Eva stayed at the window as the sky was lit up by 'Christmas tree' flares. Then she rushed through the building, hustling her own and the other five families living there into the basement. 'I got down under an arch and waited for what was to come. I crouched on my knees with my face buried in my arms, and my heart doing overtime out of fear.'

By now Plate-rack's Master Bomber, circling Dresden in a Mosquito and responsible for orchestrating the raid over the target, had realized that the city was undefended. He ordered the Main Force bombers down to a lower altitude, enabling them to achieve an even greater concentration on the area marked for attack.

Each of the Main Force Lancasters flew in on a different heading, fanning out across the centre of the city in a wedge 2,400 yards deep, their bombs cascading into an area of about 1.3 square miles. From the bombers the scene below resembled a gigantic fireworks display.

The cheese-shaped sector under attack glowed and twinkled with red, green and white target indicators. Bright, quick flashes marked the point of impact of smaller high-explosive bombs while the 4,000-pound and 8,000-pound bombs exploded more slowly, spreading quivering white concussion ripples around them as they detonated before subsiding into a dull red flame. The entire area was carpeted with the bright pinpoints of igniting incendiaries. A sudden blue flash flared through the night as a stray stick of bombs, falling outside the target area, blew up an electricity plant.

It was different on the ground. The 4,000-pound and 8,000-pound bombs smashed roofs and blew in windows while the incendiaries set individual buildings ablaze. Floors collapsed and huge tongues of flame burst through the shattered roofs, turning houses and apartment blocks into giant Roman candles. As the last Lancasters of Plate-rack flew away from the stricken city, the fires were coalescing, heating the air above and setting up a violent updraught, which in turn sucked in air from all sides into the centre of the fire area. As the firestorm took hold, this colossal suction created hurricane-force winds. During the worst night of the Blitz in London, 29 December 1940, the fires had spread as fast as a man could walk. In Dresden they were eating their way through the city as fast as a man could run.

When Press-on's Master Bomber arrived over Dresden at 1.30am to direct the second attack, he found a firestorm raging through the city, engulfing eleven square miles and covering its eastern sector in a pall of smoke which made it impossible to identify the aiming point, the railway marshalling yards. After a conference with his deputy, the Master Bomber directed the target markers to drop their indicators on either side of the area already burning, thus concentrating the bombing while spreading the damage.

The second blow, delivered by 529 Lancasters carrying 75 per cent incendiary bombloads (an inappropriate ratio for the destruction of rail track), took Dresden completely by surprise. The city's telephone system had been knocked out by Plate-rack and the civil defence had not grasped the extent of the fires raised in its centre. The unfolding tragedy was all too clear from the air. An aircraft log-book entry made over the city at the height of the second attack reads: 'Dresden. Clear over target, practically the whole town in flames.'

Inside the firestorm temperatures rose to 1,000 degrees centigrade. Fifty-foot jets of flame belched across streets and squares. Furniture piled outside burst into flames and was then tossed, blazing, through the streets by howling winds. Trees were uprooted or snapped like matchsticks. People caught in the open crawled on hands and knees gulping the air near the ground, but unaware whether their agonizing progress was carrying them away from the flames or further into the firestorm. Others clung to railings, only to be seized by the suction and whirled, in a maelstrom of debris, into the inferno. Dead and dying lay where they fell in the melting, glutinous asphalt of the streets, their clothes burnt away, their bodies shrivelled like mummies'. The corpses of children lay like fried eels on Dresden's pavements. In the Altmarkt Square hundreds tried to escape the heat in the water tanks, but drowned in eight feet of water as fires raged all round them.

The Hauptbahnhof had been spared in the first attack, and during the three-hour gap between the raids more refugee trains, including two containing hundreds of children, had been run into the station. At 1.30am, as Press-on's Master Bomber was conferring with his deputy, the Hauptbahnhof was illuminated by brilliant white chandelier flares. Then thousands of incendiaries smashed through the station's glass roof, setting piles of baggage ablaze and sending dense clouds of smoke and fumes down the tunnels and passageways where thousands sheltered. They were asphyxiated where they sat, slumped against the walls, seemingly in a deep slumber from which they would never wake.

Hugo Eichhorn's SS Pioneers formed many of the improvised rescue teams which went into action during the first raid. For most of the night they were confined to operating on the periphery of the firestorm. When Eichhorn and his men were able to break into cellar shelters they discovered

> the most gruesome sights. Young girls of the Frauenarbeitsdienst,* indeed whole groups of people, dead in cellars without surface wounds, their lungs torn by blast, and other cellars full of water and drowned people. Many cellars had their exits blocked by rubble, so the people had suffocated. I was struck by the fact that whatever cellar we broke into, death in some form or other had visited before us. And in and around the main railway station we found nothing but dead, maimed or burnt people.

---

* Women's Labour Service.

When the last of Press-on's Lancasters arrived over Dresden, it was clear to the pilot that

> the city was doomed. There was a sea of fire covering in my estimation some 40 square miles. The heat striking up from the furnace below could be felt in my cockpit. The sky was vivid in hues of scarlet and white, and the light inside the aircraft was that of an eerie autumn sunset. We were so aghast at the awesome blaze that although alone over the city we flew around in a stand-off position for many minutes before turning for home, quite subdued in our imagination of the horror that must be below. We could still see the glare of the holocaust thirty minutes after leaving.*

No German night-fighters rose to meet the bombers. On the night of the 13th there were only twenty-seven operating over the Reich. During the second raid the night-fighter crews stationed at Klotzsche airfield, less than five miles south of the city, remained impotent spectators. They sat in the cockpits of their eighteen Me110s, tanks fuelled and cannon armed, but no orders came to scramble. Wave after wave of Lancasters passed overhead while the airfield's flarepath lights were switched on and off, not to enable the fighters to take off but in anticipation of the arrival of a flight of transport aircraft from Breslau. The telephone lines through Dresden had been cut, and the station commander could not raise 1st Fighter Division's headquarters at Doberitz on short-wave radio, which had been most efficiently jammed by Bomber Command's 100 Group. Of the nearly 800 aircraft despatched to Dresden, only five were lost, a 'chop rate' of just 0.5 per cent in what had been Bomber Command's deepest penetration into Germany.

In Dresden, surreal images were superimposed on the suffering as the casualties continued to mount. During the first raid a trapped rescue party, breaking out into the open through several cellars, emerged near the Circus Sarrasani building where the party's commander saw 'a terrified group of dappled horses with brightly coloured trappings standing in a circle close to each other'. It was their last performance. The circus's Arabs died in the second raid. Later their carcasses were dragged down to the banks of the Elbe, where they were feasted upon by a flock of vultures which had escaped from Dresden's zoo.

The zoo itself had been plastered with high-explosive and incendi-

---

* An Air Ministry communiqué, issued immediately after the raid, stated that the flames could be seen 'nearly 200 miles from the target'.

aries, killing and maiming many animals and sending terrified survivors, including reindeer and buffalo, careering out of their mangled cages and into the streets. Under the bombs, the keepers went about the grim task of shooting the carnivores, lest they too ran free. At the height of the second raid a young man working at a Red Cross post near the zoo was hurled against a tree by bomb blast and knocked unconscious. He woke up with what seemed like someone clinging tightly to him. As he came round he realized he was being hugged by a great ape which was whimpering gently to itself. The young man fainted dead away with shock and pain. When he came to, the ape had let go and was no longer moving.

Dawn broke to reveal a three-mile-high column of dirty brown smoke hanging over Dresden. It was Ash Wednesday, and as if to underline the point with the grimmest of irony a fine, sooty shower of charred paper and shredded debris was falling over the city and the surrounding countryside. A heavy rainstorm followed the firestorm, miring thousands of charred bodies in a sea of slime. Amid the dull boom of collapsing buildings, rescue parties picked their way through the smouldering ruins. Terrible sights greeted them. The commander of a Speer Transport Company based in Dresden described the scene when he and his men entered Lindenau Square, near the main railway station:

> In the middle of the square lay an old man, with two dead horses. Hundreds of corpses, completely naked, were scattered around him. . . . Next to the tram shelter was a public lavatory of corrugated iron. At the entrance to this was a woman, about thirty years old, completely nude, lying face down on a fur coat; not far away lay her identity card, which showed her to be from Berlin. A few yards further on lay two young boys aged about eight and ten clinging to each other; their faces were buried in the ground. They too were stark naked. Their legs were stiff and twisted in the air. . . .

Eva Beyer, separated from and searching for her family* in the area near the zoo, clambered over mountains of rubble where there had once been streets: 'When I kicked a charred piece of wood and it slid to one side, I saw it was a human being. I got such a fright I screamed.' In Seidnitzer Square a static water tank, smaller and more shallow than that

---

* Eva Beyer was not reunited with her family until August 1945. She came to England in 1959, married an Englishman and settled in a Hampshire village where one of her neighbours was a former Bomber Command rear gunner who had flown on the Dresden raid.

in the Altmarkt, was ringed with about 250 corpses still sitting stiffly upright, frozen in the moment of death. Here and there was a gap where one of the dying had toppled into the tank.

Dresden's agony was not over. Just after noon on the 14th its citizens came under attack again, this time from 316 Boeing B-17 Fortresses of Eighth Air Force. The B-17s' bombs caused little damage, but low-level strafing by their long-range North American P-51 Mustang escorts caused heavy casualties among the bombed-out civilians massed along the banks of the Elbe and confined, like sitting ducks, in the Grosser Garten, once the most beautiful park in Dresden. Allied prisoners of war who were marched into Dresden to help with the rescue work also came under fire, as did the columns of relief trucks converging on the city.

That night Bomber Command's Lancasters were flying again, this time against Chemnitz, an industrial city thirty miles west of Dresden. As part of a complex plan of feints and diversions, 244 Lancasters of 5 Group attacked the Deutsche Petroleum refineries at Rositz, near Leipzig. Their course took them fifty miles north-west of Dresden, and the aircrew could see the fires still burning on the horizon as they flew in to their new target. On the 15th, 200 B-17s returned to Dresden, but their bombs, delivered through heavy cloud, were hardly noticed by the stunned population. That morning the dome of the city's great church, the Frauenkirche, had collapsed with a great roar, brought down when the German Air Ministry's film archives, stored in the basement, ignited and exploded in a ball of flame.

The stench of death hung over Dresden for weeks afterwards. Even a month after the firestorm some cellars in the Old Town were too hot to enter. For several days after Bomber Command's double blow thousands of corpses lay in the streets where they had fallen. In many cases only the sickly green pallor of their faces indicated that they were no longer alive. Hans Voigt, a schoolmaster appointed head of the Abteilung Tote (Dead Persons' Department), the bleakly named agency created to iden-tify the dead, recalled the task:

> Never would I have thought death would come to so many people in so many different ways. . . . Never had I expected to see people interred in that state: burnt, cremated, torn and crushed to death; sometimes the victims looked like ordinary people apparently peacefully sleeping; the faces of others were racked with pain, the bodies stripped almost naked by the tornado; there were wretched refugees from the East clad only in rags, and people from the Opera in all their finery; here the victim was a shapeless slab, there a layer of ashes shovelled into a zinc tub.

The German rescue and salvage teams assigned the task of recovering and disposing of the dead were sustained by a generous ration of cigarettes and hard liquor – about thirty bottles of cognac per gang – a reward not extended to the Ukrainian slave labourers and Allied prisoners of war who worked alongside them and who were often assigned the most harrowing tasks. In one basement all that remained of up to 300 shelterers, blown apart by a high-explosive bomb which burst through the ceiling, was a sludge of blood, flesh and bones a foot deep. German soldiers who refused to carry out the more gruesome recovery operations were shot on the spot. Their bodies were then tossed on the carts already loaded with the corpses of air-raid victims. Looters received the same summary treatment.

For a week the carts lumbered out of Dresden to mass burial grounds in the pine forests on the northern outskirts of the city. But the normal methods of disposal could not keep pace with the daily discovery of thousands of bodies buried or half-hidden under the wreckage and rubble. To prevent the spread of epidemics, and particularly typhus, Dresden's authorities took drastic measures. The centre of the city was cordoned off and the Altmarkt became a vast dump for the dead. Steel girders, salvaged from a burnt-out department store, were laid across sandstone blocks to create 25-foot-long grills on which up to 500 bodies were piled, and then trampled down by soldiers.* Patches of colour marked the presence in this terrible human sandwich of dead children in their Carnival outfits. The square was then cleared of troops and fires lit under the grills. An eyewitness to these mass cremations recalled that 'thin and elderly victims took longer to catch fire than the fat and young ones'. Their ashes were shovelled into waiting carts and trucks and buried in large pits dug in one of Dresden's cemeteries. Secretly taken photographs of Dresden's funeral pyres survive today, an eerie echo of the Middle Ages when Jews were burnt at the stake in the Altmarkt.

Thousands more mutilated, charred and crushed corpses were bulldozed into mass graves. The Abteilung Tote's attempts to identify all the dead were defeated by the sheer scale of the tragedy. The agency used a number of methods, the most macabre of which was the recovery of wedding rings, from both men and women, by cutting them off victims' fingers with bolt-croppers. By the end of the war the Abteilung Tote had

---

* Many of these troops were Russian prisoners of war recruited into a renegade army commanded by General Andrey Vlasov, who had been captured by the Germans near Sebastopol in May 1942 when he was commanding Second Shock Army.

accumulated approximately 15,000 rings, many of them engraved with names and the dates of engagements and weddings. Eventually, about 40,000 of the dead were identified, but the toll was much higher. In Hamburg, a city with a smaller population and far more effective civil defences, at least 45,000 died in the firestorm raid. In the worst-hit areas of Dresden, 24,866 of 28,410 buildings were destroyed, and 400,000 of the city's inhabitants were made homeless. Hans Voigt's estimate of the dead was about 135,000, a figure supported by the controversial English historian David Irving. The true number of deaths will never be known. As the inscription over the mass grave in one of Dresden's main cemeteries laments, 'How many died? Who knows the number?'

The destruction of Dresden was followed by a second, propaganda, battle from which the Allies emerged badly mauled. On 15 February, in the immediate aftermath of the Bomber Command raids, the British Ministry of Information was at great pains to treat the operation as a routine affair aimed at an important industrial centre 'the size of Sheffield'. As the day wore on, the BBC's news bulletins increasingly emphasized the importance of the raid in aiding the advancing Red Army. Then, on 16 February, the cat was let out of the bag by an unwary air commodore at SHAEF, who referred to 'terror raids' and Allied plans to 'bomb large population centres and then to prevent relief supplies from reaching and refugees from leaving them'. The Associated Press correspondent jumped on the story, and on the following day a dispatch from his agency reported that the Allied air chiefs had made the 'long-awaited decision to adopt deliberate terror bombing of the great German population centres as a ruthless expedient to hasten Hitler's doom'. The dispatch was incorrect only in suggesting that such indiscriminate bombing was a new policy; Bomber Command had been vigorously pursuing area bombing since February 1942.* The dispatch achieved wide circulation in America but was immediately censored in Britain. This did not, however, prevent Lord Haw-Haw† commenting on the controversy in his broadcast on the German radio the following evening:

* Between February 1942 and April 1945, 75 per cent of the total tonnage of bombs dropped on Germany by Bomber Command fell on area targets.
† Lord Haw-Haw was William Joyce, a former member of the British Union of Fascists, who had offered his services to Germany at the beginning of the war. His broadcasts became legendary, as did his undeserved reputation for seeming omniscience about Allied plans and the pseudo-upper-class drawl which earned him the mocking 'Haw-Haw' nickname. He was captured by the British in 1945, tried for treason and sentenced to death. His defence had been that he was an American citizen, having been born in New York to an English mother and Irish father. Unfortunately for Joyce, he had a British passport, and this was enough to send him to the gallows.

Eisenhower's headquarters have now issued a stupid and impudent denial of the obvious truth that the bombing of German towns has a terrorist motive. Churchill's spokesmen, both in the press and on the radio, have actually gloried in the air attack on Berlin and Dresden. . . . Various British journalists have written as if the murdering of German refugees were a first-class military achievement. . . . One BBC announcer prattled, 'There is no China in Dresden today'. That was, perhaps, meant to be a joke: but in what sort of taste?

Goebbels's propaganda machine, still in good working order, moved into action, awarding General Spaatz the 'Order of the White Feather' for his attacks on 'non-combatant refugees' and, on 23 March, deliberately leaking a denial that the final death toll in Dresden was 250,000, a Machiavellian method of increasing the death toll in the mind of a public which fed on rumours, and of galvanizing Germans into a last-ditch stand against their invaders.

Undeterred, the Americans launched a third daylight attack on Dresden on 2 March. The target was the marshalling yards, but they suffered little damage. However, the bombers did succeed in sinking a hospital ship on the Elbe which was packed with survivors of the earlier raids. Four days later, on 6 March, the fate of Dresden was raised in the House of Commons by Richard Stokes, the Labour MP for Ipswich. Stokes quoted freely from the Associated Press report and also from the *Manchester Guardian* newspaper of 5 March, which had commented:

Tens of thousands who lived in Dresden are now burned under its ruins. Even an attempt at identification of the victims is hopeless. What happened on that evening of February 15th [*sic*]? There were 1,000,000 people in Dresden, including 600,000 bombed-out evacuees and refugees from the East. The raging fires which spread irresistibly in the narrow streets killed a great many from sheer lack of oxygen.

Stokes received a rough ride in the House, but launched a powerful attack on area bombing, arguing that 'there is no case whatever under any conditions, in my view, for terror bombing. . . .'

Queasy feelings about Thunderclap now reached all the way to the top. On 28 March Churchill minuted the Chiefs of Staff: 'It seems to me that the moment has come when the question of bombing of German cities simply for the sake of increasing the terror, *though under other pretexts* [author's italics], should be reviewed. . . . The destruction of Dresden remains a serious query against the conduct of Allied bombing. . . .'

Amid the growing controversy surrounding area bombing, Churchill's note appears nothing less than a calculated attempt to distance himself from a policy which the War Cabinet had endorsed since 1942, and to shift the blame for its consequences on to the shoulders of his bomber chiefs. It produced an immediate and angry response from Portal which persuaded the Prime Minister to withdraw the note and, on 1 April, to resubmit a more circumspectly worded memorandum which made no reference to 'terror bombing' or to Dresden:

> It seems to me that the moment has come when the question of the so-called 'area bombing' of German cities should be reviewed from the point of view of our own interests. If we come into control of an entirely ruined land, there will be a great shortage of accommodation for ourselves and our Allies: and we shall be unable to get housing materials out of Germany for our own needs because some temporary provision would have to be made for the Germans themselves. We must see to it that attacks do not do more harm to ourselves in the long run than they do to the enemy's immediate war effort. Pray let me have your views.

Harris's views, delivered to Bottomley on 29 March, were characteristically robust and unrepentant:

> The feeling, such as there is, over Dresden, could be easily explained by any psychiatrist. It is connected with German bands and Dresden shepherdesses. Actually Dresden was a mass of munition works, an intact government centre and a key transportation point to the East. It is now none of those things. . . .
>
> Attacks on cities, like any other act of war are intolerable unless they are strategically justified. But they are strategically justified in so far as they tend to shorten the war and so preserve the lives of Allied soldiers. To my mind we have absolutely no right to give them up unless it is certain that they will not have this effect. I do not personally regard the whole of the remaining cities of Germany as worth the bones of one British Grenadier. . . .

Harris was being less than honest. The centre of Dresden had been utterly destroyed – leaving about eleven truckloads, or 56 cubic yards, of rubble for each of its citizens – but its war factories and marshalling yards remained largely intact.* Nor were any of its vital bridges collapsed by Allied bombs.

---

* Only the Zeiss optical works, situated three miles from the city centre, was severely damaged. During his post-war interrogation, Albert Speer indicated that Dresden's industrial recovery was swift.

Harris himself was not the villain of Dresden. The decision to mount the raids, and those on Berlin, Leipzig and Chemnitz, was taken by the combined US, Russian and British Chiefs of Staff, fully supported by Roosevelt, Stalin and Churchill. It was Harris's duty to execute their orders. Nor was Harris the architect of area bombing, a policy already in place when, in 1942, he became C-in-C of Bomber Command. However, he was by temperament and conviction the man best qualified to see this policy through to the bitter end. It was not until 16 April 1945 that the Chiefs of Staff called a halt to area bombing.

By then Churchill's fears about coming into a ruined land had already been realized. For every ton of bombs dropped by the Luftwaffe on Britain, Germany had received 315 tons. The greater part of the devastation caused by this Allied bombardment was achieved after the point at which Germany's defeat had become inevitable. Seventy-five per cent of US Eighth Air Force's bombs fell on Germany after D-Day, when the Luftwaffe, although still dangerous, was being bludgeoned into a corner from which there was no escape.

As the war neared its end, Bomber Command was able to deploy all the professionalism and techniques it had acquired since 1939. On 14 March the great Bielefeld railway viaduct linking Hamm and Hannover was destroyed by fourteen specially modified Lancasters of 617 Squadron carrying the 22,000-pound 'Grand Slam' bomb designed by Barnes Wallis. Ten days later, immediately before Field Marshal Sir Bernard Montgomery's 21st Army Group began its crossing of the Rhine, 200 heavy bombers dropped 1,092 tons of high-explosive on German troop concentrations. On 9 April the pocket battleship *Admiral Scheer* was capsized in Kiel harbour. On 21/22 March, in the climax of 8 Group's 'Light Night Striking Force' campaign against Berlin, 139 Mosquito sorties were flown against the German capital. By then Mosquito losses had fallen to one for every 2,000 sorties. In the last four months of the war Bomber Command flew 67,487 sorties for the loss of 608 aircraft. It is an indication of the scale of strategic operations that although these losses represented nearly twice the Command's front-line strength in 1939, they were considered a small price to pay for the defeat of Nazi Germany.

In one final spasm, the Luftwaffe caught Bomber Command unawares. On the night of 1 March the latter's main targets were the synthetic oil plant at Kamen and the Dortmund-Ems Canal at Ladbergen. As the Main Force streamed homewards, more than a hundred German night-fighters launched Operation *Gisella*, the first big intruder strike against Bomber Command's bases in England since the summer of 1941. Two waves of Junkers Ju88s and Heinkel He219s attacked airfields in Suffolk, Norfolk, Lincolnshire and Yorkshire, and the aircraft returning to them from Germany. There were also aircraft from a number of Operational Training Units in the air that night, and they were caught cold by the night-fighters. Twenty-seven were shot down and eight badly damaged.

With Gisella the Luftwaffe had all but shot its bolt in the west. Two weeks later, on 17 March, a similar operation was flown by eighteen Ju88s. But there were no heavy bomber raids planned for that night, and the intruders succeeded only in shooting down a single training aircraft. It was the Luftwaffe's last offensive action over Britain.

CHAPTER 6

One More River

'The Germans are very good soldiers and will recover quickly if allowed to do so. All risks are justified – I intend to get a bridge-head over the Rhine before they have time to recover.'
General Sir Bernard Montgomery, 26 August 1944

IN THE EAST the Red Army had reached the Oder. From August 1944 the overriding aim of the Western Allies had been to reach and cross the Rhine, which rises in Switzerland and flows 830 miles to the North Sea. It was a formidable barrier, wide, fast-flowing and flanked for much of its length by cliffs and steep hills. The crossing of it was to provoke an inter-nal war between the generals led by the Supreme Allied Commander, the American General Dwight D. Eisenhower, almost as bitter as the one they were waging against their German enemy.

By the end of August 1944, the Allies had surged out of the Normandy bridgehead which had been established on D-Day, 6 June, and were standing on the Seine from Troyes, a hundred miles south of Paris, to the sea. Paris had been liberated on 25 August and four days later the last German troops slipped across the Seine, leaving behind them in Normandy 2,200 destroyed or abandoned armoured vehicles and 210,000 prisoners. German casualties in the fighting had been 240,000 men killed and wounded. Three months of fighting in Normandy had cost the German Army in the West, the Westheer, twice as many men as had Stalingrad. On 20 August 50,000 men had been trapped in the Falaise Pocket, sealed off in the north by Lieutenant-General Henry Crerar's Canadian First Army and in the south by General George Patton's US Third Army. Two days after the Allied jaws had snapped shut, Eisenhower toured the battlefield, encountering 'scenes that could only be described by Dante. It was literally possible to walk for hundreds of yards at a time stepping over nothing but dead and decayed flesh'. Allied aircrew flying low over these scenes of carnage wrinkled their noses in disgust at the rising stench of corpses putrefying in the late summer heat.

One casualty of the Falaise battle had been Field Marshal Günther von Kluge, who had replaced Field Marshal von Rundstedt as Commander-in-Chief West in July. On 15 August, while he was in the front line near Avranches, his wireless tender was knocked out, cutting off communications with his headquarters for several hours. At Rastenburg, where Kluge was already a marked man, suspected of complicity in the bomb plot against Hitler of July 1944, it was assumed that he was trying to negotiate with the Allies. On the 17th he was relieved of his command and received the dreaded order to return to Germany. Kluge preferred to commit suicide.

The collapse of the German front now opened up a fundamental disagreement over strategy within the Allied camp. Four Allied armies were champing at the bit: Canadian First and British Second, which made up 21st Army Group, commanded by General Sir Bernard Montgomery; and US First and Third Armies, which comprised the newly formed 12th Army Group commanded by General Omar Bradley. Eisenhower, who on 1 September took over operational command of land forces from Montgomery (whose consolation prize was a field marshal's baton), favoured a broad advance into Germany on all fronts, which would allow Patton's Third Army to maintain its drive to the Saar on the right flank, and enable Montgomery's 21st Army Group to seize the vital Channel supply ports and overrun the enemy's V-1 flying bomb and V-2 rocket sites on the left. Montgomery and Patton had other ideas.

As the German front disintegrated, the hard-driving Patton had pursued the enemy to the Meuse, which he had crossed at Verdun and Commercy at the end of August, having captured two bridges before the Germans could blow them. Patton believed that he was now in a position not only to destroy the command structure of the disorganized forces he was pursuing but also to 'bounce' the Rhine. On 21 August he had written in his diary:

> We have at this time the greatest chance to win the war ever presented. If they will let me move on with three corps . . . we can be in Germany in ten days. There are plenty of roads and railways to support the operations. It can be done with three armoured and six infantry divisions. . . . It is such a sure thing that I fear these blind moles don't see it.

Patton was straining at the leash to cross the Rhine in the area of Worms: 'The faster we do it, the less lives and munitions it will take. No one realizes the terrible value of the "unforgiving minute" except me.' Had Patton but known it, he would have found ready confirmation of his views in the German high command. On 4 September Hitler had reinstated Rundstedt as Commander-in-Chief West. According to the latter's new Chief of Staff, General Siegfried Westphal:

> The overall situation in the West was serious in the extreme. A heavy defeat anywhere along the front, which was so full of gaps it did not deserve the name, might lead to a catastrophe, if the enemy were to exploit his opportunity skilfully. A particular source of danger was that not a single bridge across the Rhine had been prepared for demolition, an omission which took weeks to repair. ... Until the middle of October the enemy could have broken through at any point he liked, with ease, and would have been able to cross the Rhine and thrust deep into Germany almost unhindered.

Along the entire front on 7 September the Westheer could scrape together only one hundred serviceable tanks. South of the Ardennes, 2nd Panzer Division fielded just three tanks. In contrast, Eisenhower had at his disposal an establishment of nearly 6,000 medium and 1,700 light tanks, a figure which was constantly topped up. At the beginning of September, of the forty-eight German infantry divisions in the West, only thirteen were considered fit for offensive operations, nine were reorganizing, twelve were partially fit, and fourteen were deemed to be next to useless. Along a 400-mile front this amounted to an effective strength of little more than twenty-five divisions. Luftwaffe Kommando West, the successor to Luftflotte 3 which had flown in the Battle of Britain, could put up about 570 aircraft. Allied air strength in Britain and France now stood at 14,000 aircraft, nearly 9,000 of them American.

On the northern flank of the Allied advance, Patton's arch-rival, Montgomery, also had his eyes fixed firmly on the Rhine. On the surface the two men were a study in opposites: Monty was prim, teetotal and schoolmasterly, a stringy, birdlike man, exhorting his men to 'hit the enemy for six'. Cricketing metaphors were not Patton's style. He was the embodiment of all-American aggression, sporting an ivory-handled Colt .45 in his holster and firmly of the belief that you grabbed the enemy by the nose 'the better to kick him in the pants'. Both men had developed a hearty dislike for each other after their race to Messina in the campaign for Sicily in July-August 1943. But they had more in common

than they would have cared to admit. Both were instinctive showmen –
Patton's revolver was matched by Monty's cap badges – who concealed
complex characters beneath an all-too-evident egotism. They prompted
mixed emotions in the men they led, some of them less than compli-
mentary. Patton's nickname of 'Old Blood and Guts' was often said to
stand for 'our blood, *his* guts'. In any coalition they were highly combustible elements.

On 3 September, amid ecstatic scenes of rejoicing, the British liberated
Brussels, and on the following day entered Antwerp. By mid-September
the whole of Belgium and Luxembourg, and a small slice of Holland,
were in Allied hands. The German border had been crossed near
Aachen on the 11th by advanced elements of General Courtney Hodges's
US First Army. On the same day the vanguard of the Franco-American
force which had landed in Provence a month earlier joined hands with
Patton's army near Dijon. By the end of the second week in September
there was a continuous battle front in Northern Europe running from the
banks of the River Scheldt in Belgium to the headwaters of the Rhine at
Basle on the Swiss frontier.

Like Patton, Montgomery believed that a more sharply defined strategy
and clear-cut allocation of supplies would lead to a breach in the West
Wall, the fortified German defensive line (popularly known as the
Siegfried Line) which ran along the Dutch and French borders from near
München-Gladbach to the Swiss border near Freiburg. Naturally Monty,
now demoted to the command of one British and one Canadian army
but still the most senior Allied fighting general in north-west Europe, considered that any such allocation should be entirely in his favour. He
maintained that the way to defeat the enemy in the shortest possible time
was by halting the Allied effort on the right and concentrating all
resources on a single drive through Belgium into the Ruhr and on to
Berlin.

It was Eisenhower's thankless task to balance the demands of his
increasingly shrill subordinates within the overall political restraints of a
coalition war. The protégé of General George Marshall, the US Army's
Chief of Staff, Eisenhower was not a fighting general, a fact which constantly chafed with the combative Montgomery, who was of the opinion
that 'If we want the war to end within any reasonable period you will
have to get Eisenhower's hand taken off the land battle. I regret to say that
in my opinion he just doesn't know what he is doing.'* In contrast to
Montgomery, Eisenhower's skills were essentially diplomatic, oiled by

---

* In a letter to Field Marshal Sir Alan Brooke, Chief of the Imperial General Staff,
October 1944.

an ability to weld a co-ordinated team from a collection of powerful individuals with often conflicting views and clashing personalities. Eisenhower's personality was fundamentally sunny and benign – in later years, as US President, he achieved an almost papal authority – but he could be quick-tempered and ruthless with those he considered incompetent. He exercised monumental patience with Montgomery, though much of the time the two men were conversing in completely different military languages, blind to each other's virtues and faults. After the war Eisenhower insisted that Montgomery had wanted to advance on Berlin with a slim 'pencil-like' thrust. This was never Montgomery's style. The new Field Marshal envisaged a a massive forty-division push which in some respects resembled a reverse version of the Schlieffen Plan of 1914, the great wheeling German movement through the Low Countries aimed at turning the French line. Political considerations meant that Montgomery could never be given absolute priority at all times over Eisenhower's American subordinates,* but in August-September 1944 the Supreme Commander was also constrained by the supply problems caused by the speed of the Allied advance. Patton was so far ahead of his planned objectives and timetable that, having left the SHAEF planners far behind, he was relying on a Michelin road map. The Allies had arrived at a point which, when planning the invasion, they had not expected to reach until May 1945. Supply was now the factor dictating Eisenhower's options in the allocation of resources. The Allied air campaign in the run-up to D-Day had been so successful in destroying the French rail system that when the Allies broke out of the Normandy bridgehead the means to sustain their advance could be provided only by truck and road, and this was not enough to meet the daily divisional requirement of 700 tons of ammunition, equipment and rations. As Eisenhower later observed, 'the life blood of supply was running perilously thin through the forward extremities of the Army.' For the moment, he could maintain momentum only by giving scarce resources to one commander and withholding them from another.

Patton was the loser. With the Rhine only seventy-five miles away, and Third Army restricted to a fraction of its fuel requirements, Eisenhower turned off the tap. The fuel shortage was compounded by a confusion of competing options. An airborne invasion of Belgium had been planned but never executed, resulting in a week-long interruption of air supplies and the loss of 1.5 million tons of fuel, enough to get all the Allied armies to the Rhine. This might not have mattered had the Allies captured the

---

* By April 1945 there were fifty-five American divisions in Europe and thirteen British and Canadian, plus nine American-equipped and one British-equipped.

ports along the Channel coast, slashing the distance the trucks would have to travel to the front, but on Hitler's orders the German Army Group B had left garrisons to hold Le Havre, Boulogne, Calais, Dunkirk and the mouth of the River Scheldt. Le Havre was captured on 12 September and Calais at the end of the month, but Dunkirk held out until the end of the war. Even more critically, the defences of the Scheldt estuary were still in German hands at the beginning of November.

Although Montgomery was to be the beneficiary of the fuel crisis, he had himself largely contributed to it. British XXX Corps, commanded by Lieutenant-General Sir Brian Horrocks, had seized the port of Antwerp with all its harbour facilities intact, but Montgomery, his attention focused to the east on the Rhine, had failed to push north over the Albert Canal to clear the northern bank of the Scheldt estuary. This enabled the German Fifteenth Army, which had been shunted into a pocket on the southern bank of the Scheldt, to pull back to Walcheren and Beveland on the northern bank, leaving a bridgehead behind. In a remarkable improvised operation between 4 and 23 September, the Germans ferried 86,000 men, 616 guns, 6,200 vehicles and a similar number of horses across the estuary and into positions which denied the Allies the use of Antwerp, and which also presented a threat to Montgomery's left flank as he prepared for a drive on the Rhine. Horrocks later wrote that Montgomery's pause

> was a tragedy because, as we now know, on . . . 4 September the only troops available to bar our passage northwards consisted of one German division, the 719th, composed entirely of elderly gentlemen who hitherto had been guarding the north coast of Holland and had never heard a shot fired in anger. . . . This meagre force was strung out on a fifty-mile front along the [Albert] Canal.

Antwerp was not opened to Allied shipping until 29 November.

By 4 September, Montgomery had finalized what he believed was a plan to clinch the priority argument in his favour. In Operation 'Market Garden',* the three divisions of Allied First Airborne Army were to seize the bridges on the Eindhoven-Arnhem road, establishing a sixty-mile corridor along which British Second Army would race to outflank the West Wall. This would be the preliminary to the mounting of 'a really powerful and full-blooded thrust towards Berlin. . . .'

---

* Market was the airborne phase of the operation, Garden the ground phase. The bridges to be seized were, in the direction of advance, those over the Wilhelmina Canal, the Willems Canal, the River Maas, the River Waal, and the Lower Rhine at Arnhem.

Eisenhower gave the go-ahead for Market Garden after a stormy meeting in Brussels on 10 September during which Montgomery was forced to apologize after demanding that priority meant absolute priority, even if it halted the southern armies in their tracks. However, the concessions which Eisenhower had made – the allocation of First Airborne Army, fuel priority and control of US First Army on the British right flank – reinforced Montgomery's conviction that the Supreme Commander had chosen the northern axis as the route into Germany. He had never come to terms with having to yield operational command of the land forces to Eisenhower and by insisting on the primacy of the northern axis, to which all else was to be subordinated, he was seeking to regain control by other means.

US First Army's commander, Bradley, was deeply hostile to Montgomery's ambitions. His self-effacing manner and slow Missouri drawl cloaked a tetchy temperament and, as he himself later admitted, a naive approach to the inevitably blurred lines between the Allies' military strategy and their political aims. On the relationship between Eisenhower and Montgomery, Bradley sourly commented: 'The force of Monty's personality seemed to mesmerize Ike and befuddle his thinking. I think in this instance Ike succumbed to Monty in part to stroke his ego and keep peace in the family.' But it was a family whose thought processes were not always clear to each other. Eisenhower saw the priority accorded to Montgomery as a purely temporary measure in response to specific strategic needs and political pressures. Market Garden fitted the pattern as an essentially *ad hoc* operation to exploit what appeared to be a vulnerable sector in the enemy's line and as a useful way of employing First Airborne Army. Montgomery was unable, or unwilling, to grasp that Market Garden was merely part of the pack Eisenhower constantly shuffled in pursuit of his 'broad front' strategy, rather than the overture to a triumphant British descent on Berlin. Eisenhower's own evasively emollient style only served to exacerbate the problem.

Incandescent with rage, Patton wrote in his diary: 'To hell with Monty. I must get so involved with my own operations that they can't stop me.' Then Eisenhower had second thoughts. He had received intelligence reports of two German armoured divisions (9th and 10th of II SS Panzer Corps) in the Arnhem area. He told his Chief of Staff, General Walter Bedell Smith, 'I cannot tell Monty how to deploy his troops. You must fly to 21st Army Group immediately and argue it out with Monty. I cannot order Monty to call Market Garden off when I have already given him the green light.' Smith dutifully flew off, Montgomery poured scorn on his fears, and Eisenhower did nothing more to halt the operation, which was launched on 17 September.

The first part of Montgomery's plan was successful. US 101st Airborne
Division, dropped between Veghel and Eindhoven, captured the two
southern bridges, and XXX Corps raced to link up with US 82nd Airborne
at Grave and Nijmegen. But at Arnhem, the most northerly target, British
1st Airborne Division ran into trouble. Dropped eight miles from their
objective, because of the RAF's unfounded fears of heavy anti-aircraft
concentrations around Arnhem, they found their way blocked by the
German armoured formations whose presence had been discounted.
The two divisions were refitting in the area after the mauling they had
received in Normandy. Between them they mustered only a company of
tanks and a handful of armoured cars and halftracks, but even the shell
of an armoured division packed a heavier punch than 1st Airborne. Of
the two bridges at Arnhem, one was blown as the British airborne troops
closed on the town. Only one battalion managed to reach the other, the
road bridge, where it was cut off. Private James Sims has described the
fighting which had boiled up around the bridge by 19 September:

> The Germans withdrew a short distance and began to mortar and
> shell our positions systematically. . . . The very air seemed to wail
> and sigh with the number of projectiles passing through it. The
> enemy had also brought up some self-propelled artillery, heavy
> stuff, and against this we were virtually helpless. One by one the
> houses held by the paratroopers were set alight. There was noth-
> ing to fight the fires with, even if we had been able to. The airborne
> soldiers kept on firing from the blazing buildings even with the
> roof fallen in; then they moved to the second floor; then to the
> first, and finally the basement. Only when this was alight did they
> evacuate the building and take over another. As each hour passed
> we were driven into a smaller and smaller area. Casualties began
> to mount rapidly. Our food and water were practically gone, but
> worst of all the ammunition was running short. . . .

The rest of 1st Airborne was forced back into a bridgehead near
Oosterbeek and awaited relief. The two bridges at Nijmegen were taken
on 20 September by 82nd Airborne and XXX Corps, but when they tried
to push on to Arnhem, along a single road surrounded by waterlogged
fields, they were shelled heavily on both sides. As General Horrocks
remarked to 82nd Airborne's commander, Major-General James M. Gavin,
'Jim, never try to fight an entire Corps off one road'. Gavin recalled:

> As General Horrocks tried to force the XXX Corps armoured
> vehicles and trucks bumper to bumper and track to track up the
> two-lane road, he found himself under harassing attacks time and

again. We did not know it at the time but the German general opposing us, General Student,* had in his hands a complete copy of our attack order within an hour of the landings on D-Day [that is, D-day for Market Garden, 17 September]. It had been taken from a wrecked glider. It told him exactly what roads we were to use and what troops were given what specific missions. He at once organized counter-attacks that cut the road at several places. So, not only was Horrocks frustrated by the overwhelming logistics problems that he had on his hands, but in addition he had to fight a series of battles along the tenuous, threadlike route that led from Belgium up to Nijmegen, and the initiative was now with the Germans.

The weather broke up, air support and supply broke down. The Polish Parachute Brigade was sacrificed in a vain attempt to break the German ring. On 24 September the British were ordered to withdraw. Some men improvised boats in which to cross the Rhine, others swam back to the southern bank or clambered aboard the collapsible wooden and canvas assault boats brought up by XXX Corps. Just over 2,000 men succeeded in escaping; 1,000 had been killed in the course of the battle, and 6,000 were taken prisoner. The 1st Airborne Division had ceased to exist. Years later Captain Jan Lorys of the Polish Parachute Brigade reflected:

> For many years a feeling of frustration, a feeling that we didn't really manage to beat the Germans, was to haunt many of us. . . . We were so full of vigour. The whole Western Front was marching forward, but instead of going forward, we were stopped. We did what we could. . . . It was the brigade's first operation, its first battle, the soldiers behaved very well and we did make an impact on the battle. We secured and held the south side of the river and by doing so we enabled the remnants of the 1st Airborne to be evacuated from the north. We were sorry that we didn't win the battle, but we are still proud.

Even after Market Garden had irretrievably broken down, Montgomery was highly economical with the truth in his dealings with Eisenhower. It was not until 8 October that a situation report from 21st Army Group left the Supreme Commander in no doubt that the chance of a breakthrough had disappeared. Eisenhower had been given a brief glimpse of the possibility of bringing the war to a speedy end, but Market Garden had

---

* General Kurt Student was the leading German exponent of airborne warfare. In 1940 his glider-borne forces had captured the Belgian fortress of Eben Emael and in the following year he directed the airborne invasion of Crete.

created nothing more than an awkward salient. Moreover, the problem of the Scheldt estuary remained. Without the port of Antwerp, any renewed drive for the Rhine, on a broad or narrow front, would be next to impossible. Eisenhower, who had convinced himself that the simultaneous execution of Market Garden and the clearing of the Scheldt were well within the capacity of 21st Army Group, was furious. Montgomery declined to be coaxed into clearing the Scheldt, so he had to be bullied into action by a telephone call from Bedell Smith threatening to cut off his supplies. The Breskens pocket, on the southern bank, was eliminated by 21 October. It was not until 8 November that the coastal batteries on the northern bank had been silenced and the last pockets of resistance eliminated by Allied commandos moving across the watery wilderness of Walcheren in Buffalo amphibious landing craft.

The Allied stop-go strategy gave the Germans a crucial breathing space. With defeat staring it in the face, the German Army was able to exploit its remarkable ability to recover and regroup. A scarecrow army of 135,000 cadets, line-of-communications troops and convalescents were set to work rebuilding the West Wall, much of which had been stripped in 1943 to bolster the Atlantic Wall. Reichsmarschall Hermann Göring roused himself from the drug-sodden lethargy into which he had subsided to reveal the existence of six parachute regiments and a further 10,000 men from redundant Luftwaffe aircrew and groundcrew. They formed a new army, First Parachute, commanded by General Student, and were inserted along the line of the Albert Canal. A similar stiffening of the defences was taking place in Patton's sector, where First Army, under the command of a tough veteran of the Eastern Front, General Otto von Knobelsdorff, underwent a rapid transformation. At the end of August one of its corps commanders had estimated that First Army consisted of no more than nine battalions of infantry, two batteries of artillery and ten tanks. By mid-September it had been strengthened by the arrival from Italy of 3rd and 15th Panzergrenadier Divisions and the badly mauled 17th SS Panzergrenadier Division. They were joined by two Volksgrenadier divisions and several battalions of police. Nevertheless, to Major-General F.W. von Mellenthin, who arrived from the Eastern Front on 20 September to take up the post of Chief of Staff with Army Group G,* the overall weakness of the Westheer was alarming:

---

* Army Group G, facing US Third Army and from 20 September commanded by General Hermann Balck, consisted of: First Army in the Metz–Château-Salins area; Fifth Panzer Army, commanded by General Hasso von Manteuffel, covering the northern Vosges between Lunéville and Epinal; and Nineteenth Army, commanded by General Wiese, covering the southern Vosges and the Belfort Gap.

Those of us who had come from the Russian front, where the German formations were still in tolerable fighting order, were shocked at the condition of our Western armies. The losses in material had been colossal; for example, Nineteenth Army had possessed 1,480 guns and lost 1,316 in the withdrawal from southern France. The troops under our command provided an extraordinary miscellany – we had Luftwaffe personnel, police, old men and boys, special battalions composed of men with stomach troubles or men with ear ailments. Even well-equipped units from Germany had received virtually no training and came straight from the parade-ground to the battlefield. Some panzer brigades had never even done any squadron training, which explains our enormous loss in tanks.

The autumn campaign of 1944 was marked by atrocious weather, the wettest on record, which turned the ground into a quagmire. The open country of northern France and Belgium lay behind the Allies, who were now confronted with a hostile landscape in which dense, dripping woods gave way to ranges of steep hills defended by an enemy fighting on his own soil. Allied casualties were to mount steadily, not only from enemy action but also increasingly from trench foot, influenza and physical exhaustion.

On the American front, south of 21st Army Group, Bradley's 12th Army Group was now confronted with the West Wall. It had originally been conceived by the German Army as a series of earth redoubts facing the French Maginot Line, its object merely to slow and disrupt any attack rather than offer a solid resistance. In 1938 Hitler had ordered the construction of a series of permanent fortifications, although very little work was done on these.* Before the invasion of Normandy the Wall's most prominent feature had been a deep belt of concrete 'dragon's teeth' tank obstacles covered by pillboxes. As the Allies approached the German frontier, a 'good deal of digging', as Montgomery put it, had strengthened the Wall with deeply echeloned trench systems covered by minefields and barbed wire. These static defences were the spine of an elaborate defensive belt which ran through villages, farmhouses and woods. In this belt skilfully positioned and protected machine-guns, mortars and artillery were ranged on key approaches and road junctions, and the 88mm guns of dug-in MkVI Tiger heavy tanks were sited to make the best possible use of the terrain.

---

* The permanent fortifications featured prominently in German propaganda films of 1938–9, but the latter in fact consisted of footage of the Czech defences on the eastern German border which had been taken over by Germany in 1938.

With Montgomery turning his attention to the clearing of the Scheldt, Eisenhower reverted to his 'broad front' strategy. Bradley was allotted two objectives: US First Army was to clean up the area around the ancient city of Aachen, and US Third Army was to advance on the industrial region of the Saarland and then the Rhine. At the southern end of the line, the newly created US 6th Army Group, commanded by General Jacob Devers, was to attack through the mountainous Vosges region towards Strasbourg.

It was at Aachen that Charlemagne had been crowned Holy Roman Emperor in AD 800 and it was here that he had been buried. The city was protected by two strong defensive lines: the Scharnhorst Line along the frontier; and the thicker Schell Line which covered the 'Stolberg Corridor', along which Major-General Lawton 'Lightning Joe' Collins of First Army's VII Corps intended to drive into the Reich. It might have fallen without a fight. The local Nazi Party chiefs had ordered the evacuation of the civilian population and the defence of the city 'to the last round and the last man'. They had then prudently removed themselves to the safety of Julich.

The senior German officer on the spot, General Count von Schwerin, commander of 116th Panzer Division, planned to fight north of Aachen, which was to become an open city. With the artillery of US 1st Division, the 'Big Red One', firing into the outskirts of the city, Schwerin hastily scribbled a note in English, to be given to the first US officer to enter Aachen: 'I stopped the absurd evacuation of this town; therefore I am responsible for the fate of its inhabitants and I ask you in the case of an occupation by your troops to take care of the unfortunate population in a humane way. I am the last German Commanding Officer in the Sector of Aachen.'

The note was discovered, Schwerin himself narrowly escaped interrogation and execution by the Gestapo,* and Aachen did not fall to American troops until 21 October, after three weeks of house-to-house fighting which left the city in ruins. It was the first German city to be seized by the Allies. General Clarence Huebner, the commander of US 1st Division, attended mass in the great cathedral. Eisenhower paid a visit and fell flat on his backside in the mud as he was about to address the troops. A BBC reporter, Robert Reid, described the scene in Charlemagne's cathedral:

> It was an eerie experience wandering through the historic old place. I walked through the cloisters. Three chickens fluttered

---

* Rundstedt saved Schwerin's skin by transferring him to Italy, where he commanded a corps.

through the shattered windows and began pecking the dirt in search of food. Two American doughboys, who'd just finished a meal of bread and cheese threw them some crumbs.... I haven't seen many towns like this before. But this is Germany. Late this afternoon I watched a group of German prisoners being led through the wreckage. They were silent, bent and sick-looking. Maybe they saw more in that terrible scene than the wreckage of Aachen. They were taking with them into captivity a preview of the wreckage of Hitler's Germany.

With Aachen in American hands, US First Army pushed north-east up the Stolberg Corridor, a narrow strip of open country bounded on the left by a straggle of industrial suburbs and on the right by the sinister dark mass of the Hürtgen Forest, fifty square miles of dense pine forest, cut with steep gorges and packed with pillboxes and mines, which in the next three months was to consume five American infantry divisions.

Hodges planned to anchor the right wing of First Army on the high ground around Schmidt in the south-east corner of the forest. This plateau was the site of seven dams controlling the headwaters of the River Roer, which meandered across First Army's front before it joined the Maas at Roermond. Dominating this strategic complex was the Schwammenauel dam, an immense structure of concrete and earth 188 feet high, 1,000 feet thick at the base, and with a 40-foot-wide road running along the top. American planners had given little or no thought to the significance of the dams, which if opened would flood the Rhine valley, or to the near certainty that such significant installations would be strongly defended. The clearing of the forest looked very neat on staff officers' maps, but on the ground the Hürtgen was to become a living hell for the men who fought there.

In late September, Hodges committed 9th Infantry Division, an experienced formation which had been in action since February 1943, when its artillery had helped to stop Rommel's panzers after they had broken through the Kasserine Pass in Tunisia. The terrain into which it now plunged was reminiscent of the Argonne Forest between Champagne and Lorraine where Hodges himself had fought in the autumn of 1918: steep wooded heights rising to 1,000 feet covered with tight-packed fir plantations down which fast-flowing streams raced into narrow valleys and precipitous gorges. It was country tailor-made for determined defence. Every firebreak and logging track was covered by concrete pillboxes and bunkers with interlocking fields of fire. Rings of snaggle-tooth concrete stumps kept tanks at bay and everywhere there were mines. The dreaded *Schuhminen* anti-personnel mine, impervious to detectors, was no bigger than an ointment box but when trodden on produced an explosion powerful enough to blow off a man's testicles. The Americans dubbed them 'debollockers', as they did the 'Bouncing Betty', which exploded at waist height, throwing out a mass of metal balls. One survivor of the Hürtgen recalled after the war: 'We called it a 50–50 mine. The name was derived from your chances once you trod on it. If you hit it with your right foot, the rod flew up your right side. If you hit it with your left you'd end up singing tenor.'

Two weeks after entering the forest, 9th Division had advanced 3,000 yards at a cost of over one casualty a yard – 4,500 men killed, missing and wounded. They were replaced by the inexperienced men of 28th Infantry Division, who found a nightmarish landscape awaiting them: rivers of yellow mud clogged with the detritus of battle, bloated bodies, empty ration crates and shell cases, belts of ammunition and unearthed mines. At terrible cost they learned the lessons of survival in the forest. Foxholes were useless if they were not covered with logs and sod. Shells did not explode on the ground, shooting their shrapnel upwards. In the Hürtgen they exploded in the air on impact with the trees. These 'tree bursts' showered all those below them with red-hot shards of razor-sharp metal. Caught in the tree bursts, it was pointless to throw yourself on the ground as this would only expose your entire body to the deadly hail. Survival required standing upright in the shelter of a tree – and strong prayer.

. Two weeks were enough for 28th Division, most of whose rifle companies suffered 50 per cent casualties or more. Men died from exposure in waterlogged foxholes. Frostbite took a heavy toll. Morale plummeted as progress was measured in yards. Tanks were useless in the murk and mire, orderly evacuation of the wounded almost impossible. Most of the time the battle was reduced to the viewpoint of the individual infantryman crawling across the slimy, leaf-choked floor of the forest and peering through the deep green mass ahead. The assault on Schmidt made by 28th Division was one of the US Army's most costly division-strength attacks of the war. One regiment, 112th Infantry, lost 2,093 of its 3,000 men. Overall casualties were 6,184, 45 per cent of the division's strength, although the percentage among rifle companies, at the sharp end, was much higher.

In November 1st, 4th and 8th Infantry Divisions plunged into the forest with armoured support. Like one of the château generals of the First World War, Hodges continued to feed units into the killing ground in the vain hope that the breakthrough could be achieved with just one more push. One of the men of 4th Division's 22nd Infantry Regiment told a correspondent: 'You can't see. You can't get fields of fire. Artillery slashes the trees like a scythe. Everything is tangled. You can scarcely walk. Everything is cold and wet as the mixture of cold rain and sleet keeps falling. Then we attack again and soon there is only a handful of the old men left.'

The 1st Infantry Division was withdrawn after suffering nearly 4,000 battle casualties.* The rest centres in the rear filled up with troops suffering from the condition known as combat fatigue. A US Army chaplain remembered:

> It was time for chow, and hot chow was being served. During the serving an artillery observation plane flew overhead. The effect was amazing and pitiful. One soldier poured a cup of hot coffee over his head. Another turned his mess kit of C rations over his lap. Still a third made an effort to dive into the latrine and had to be forcibly restrained. . . . The wards with shattered and missing legs and arms were bad, but the hospitals with vacant and missing minds were worse.

The peculiar intimacy of the fighting in the Hürtgen produced an unpredictable mixture of savagery and tolerance. One soldier of 4th Division was stranded in no man's land after his foot had been blown off by a mine. Snipers prevented American medics from reaching him and when darkness fell the Germans crawled out to the wounded man, stole his combat jacket and cigarettes, and then booby-trapped him with a spring-loaded explosive charge placed under his back. When help arrived after the man had lain untended for seventy hours, he retained sufficient presence of mind to warn his rescuers, who then dismantled the booby-trap before bearing him off.

In another part of the forest, men of 9th Division's 47th Infantry Regiment had a working arrangement with the Germans opposite them not to attack a certain house whose cellars bulged with cheese and beer. By day American patrols visited the house to supplement their rations, and the Germans did the same at night. This cosy state of affairs continued until a trigger-happy German opened fire on the foraging Americans. Appalled by this unsporting behaviour, the Americans booby-trapped the house and then watched it and their shared 'rations' go up in smoke when the Germans paid their next visit.

Another curious incident occurred in the sector occupied by 951st Field Artillery. One of their roadblock parties heard some rustling in the nearby undergrowth. Lieutenant Keate gave his machine-gunners the

---

* Overall American casualties in three months of fighting in the Hürtgen were 120,000 men.

order to open fire. There was a howl of agony followed by silence. The
Americans

> went out to see what they had got and found a wounded Jerry
> officer and a girl dressed in an American officer's coat. She was a
> slick chick, but a slug had nipped her military career in the bud.
> Questioning disclosed that the German officer had a sketch show-
> ing all our roadblocks and machine-gun posts and the girl was
> supposed to be a come-on. In between times she kept the boys
> from getting homesick. However, a .50-calibre slug has no con-
> science. The officer followed the little girl a little too close to our
> outpost. It only goes to show.

The Hürtgen Forest had not been fully cleared in February 1945 when
General Gavin and 82nd Airborne Division arrived with orders to capture
Schmidt. While reconnoitring the Kall River valley, he encountered the
gruesome evidence of the bitter fighting which had raged in November
for control of the trail running along the valley floor:

> I proceeded down the trail on foot. It was obviously impassable for
> a jeep; it was a shambles of wrecked vehicles and abandoned tanks.
> The first tanks that attempted to go down the trail had evidently slid
> off and thrown their tracks. In some cases the tanks had been off the
> trail and toppled down the gorge among the trees. Between where
> the trail begins at Vossenach and the bottom of the canyon, there
> were four abandoned tank destroyers and five disabled and aban-
> doned tanks. In addition, all along the sides of the trail there were
> many, many dead bodies, cadavers that had just emerged from the
> snow. Their gangrenous, broken and torn bodies were rigid and
> grotesque, some of them with arms skywards, seemingly in suppli-
> cation. They were wearing the red keystone of the 28th Infantry
> Division, the 'Bloody Bucket'.* It had evidently fought through there
> the preceding fall, just before the heavy snows. I continued down the
> trail for about half a mile to the bottom. . . . Nearby were dozens of
> litter [i.e. stretcher] cases, the bodies long dead. Apparently an aid
> station had been established . . . and in the midst of the fighting it
> had been abandoned, many of the men dying on their stretchers. Off
> to the right, about fifty yards, a hard road appeared. Across it were
> about six American anti-tank mines. On this side of the mines were
> three or four American soldiers who had apparently been laying
> the mines and protecting them when they were killed. Beyond the
> American mines, about ten feet away, was a string of German anti-

---

* The keystone earned this morbid accolade during the fighting in the Hürtgen.

tank mines. On the other side of the mines were three or four German dead – a dramatic example of what the fighting must have been like in the Hürtgen. It was savage, bitter and at close quarters.

Gavin could not understand why Hodges had attempted to steamroller his way through the Hürtgen when on his southern flank there was a perfectly good approach road for tanks which bypassed the river valley that had claimed so many American lives. Hodges had simply multiplied the combat effectiveness of the one German division in the forest and nullified the overwhelming superiority he enjoyed in armour and air support. When Gavin asked a corps staff officer 'why in the world' Hodges had attacked through the Hürtgen, he was told that this was a 'no-no' question.

At the end of October a third American army, General William H. Simpson's recently arrived Ninth Army, was inserted between Hodges's northern flank and 21st Army Group. Simpson, lean, lanky and bald as an egg, assumed responsibility for the area from Aachen north to Roermond. In mid-November, he committed his untried 84th Infantry Division in a joint operation with the British 43rd (Wessex) Division to pinch out a German salient jutting westwards around the town of Geilenkirchen. The men of the veteran British division were dismayed by the American preparations. They failed to evacuate the local population, who might well have passed information about the coming attack to their fellow countrymen only 1,000 yards away. The British, on the other hand, had no qualms about sending columns of civilians to the rear and into Holland, balancing their possessions on handcarts and bicycles, just as the refugees fleeing the German Army had done in 1940. The history of the 43rd Division gives a breezy account of its soldiers' attitude towards the villages they occupied:

> There was complete cover both in the houses and the woods for the concentration of reserves. The villages, however, seemed sinister and alien ... even the Gasthauses [inns] seemed funereal. The churches with their bulbous spires lacked dignity. They were dark and forbidding within. Surprising to relate the cowed inhabitants were still in occupation. Within a few hours it was brought home to them that a change in management to their disadvantage had taken place. Battle-hardened soldiers, completely ignoring their existence, removed the doors from their houses to provide head cover for their slits [slit trenches]. Whatever blankets or eiderdowns were wanted were coolly removed. Next day the Military Police appeared and ordered them to go. Bewildered parties of men, women and children, pushing a few possessions on wheelbarrows, moved

painfully back through the rain and sleet to the Dutch border. At long last the Germans were being paid in their own coin. . . . They left behind them their flocks of geese, their crowded pigsties, their cellars full of large supplies of food, the pickled cucumbers, the beans and the fruits which the German housewife knows how to preserve so well. Their attics were stuffed with clothes and footwear. Their rooms were so full of new furniture as to be overcrowded. Rationing scarcely touched them. They were plump and healthy looking. Most houses held their share of French wine and brandy. Many of the big stoves concealed a ham or two. There were ample stores of coal and wood. All this was legitimate booty.

The Americans were also careless about laying mines on their front, and the absence of detailed maps cost the lives of a British brigadier and fourteen of his men before the attack went in.

The British and Americans fought their way through a maze of strongly defended positions in hilly country scarred with slag heaps, furnaces and dotted by dreary industrial towns. As another BBC correspondent, Robert Barr, told his listeners:

It is not a question of taking a township or a village and then push-ing on. It's a question of taking a village and digging in under fire until the villages on either side of you are taken – or until a whole line has been taken and then getting up from your waterlogged fox-hole or from your cellar and crouching forward to the next line of villages with new names and with more cellars and more machine-guns, and more snipers who are prepared to stay and die for the Fatherland.

When it fell, Geilenkirchen had been reduced to a heap of rubble. One American rifle company's report read:

Holes had been punched in roofs and walls for firing ports. By knocking holes between cellar walls, the defenders had created block-long tunnels to connect strongpoints. Household goods – clothing, books, cookware, furniture, children's toys – spilled through the gaps in the walls. Alleyways and streets were blocked with jumbled piles of bricks, roof tiles, charred beams, electric cable and telephone wires. Mud churned up by the bombs and artillery seemed to cover everything. Fires smouldered, and the stench of wet-burned wood and dead horses clung to the city.

When US Ninth Army's offensive slithered to a halt in the snows of December, it had penetrated the West Wall to a depth of up to ten miles at a cost of 1,133 killed, 6,864 wounded and 2,059 missing. Thousands more had fallen victim to pneumonia, trench foot and combat exhaustion. Nor were the men of First Army astride the Rhine; rather they were gazing glumly at the flood-threatening waters of the Roer. On their right a worrying gap had opened up between them and Patton's Third Army. Berlin was still 300 miles away. At Montgomery's headquarters the betting book showed that the smart money was going on the war ending in October 1945.

Patton had also found the going tough in Lorraine against Army Group G, commanded by General Balck. Patton had declared that he would go though the West Wall 'like shit through a goose', but Balck made the best of the defensive possibilities offered by a succession of river lines – the Moselle, Meurthe and Seille – and by the extensive fortifications built in the region between 1870 and 1914. Conducting a skilfully handled withdrawal, Balck denied Patton the city of Metz until 13 December, when its surrounding fortresses were finally cleared. With his heightened sense of military history, Patton felt able to congratulate himself on being the first conqueror to take the city since Attila the Hun.* In private, however, he confessed to the US Secretary for War, Henry L. Stimson: 'I hope that in the final settlement of the war you insist that the Germans retain Lorraine, because I can imagine no greater burden than to be the owner of this nasty country where it rains every day and where the whole wealth of the people consists in assorted manure piles.'

It was not until 15 December that Patton was fully in contact with the lower reaches of the West Wall which ran along the River Saar. The first snows were falling as Third Army's spearheads seized a number of small bridgeheads on the east bank of the river. To Patton's south, the recently formed 6th Army Group, commanded by General Jacob Devers and consisting of US Seventh Army and French First Army, made better progress in pushing the Germans out of Alsace as it fought through the mountainous Vosges country. On 20 November French armoured units drove through the 'Belfort Gap' between the Vosges and the Jura, closing with the upper reaches of the Rhine on the same day. Eighty miles to the north, a Franco-American force achieved a similar breakthrough, cruising through the 'Saverne Gap' to take Strasbourg on 23 November. However, between the American and French Armies bulged a large pocket formed around the city of Colmar. As Eisenhower ordered Devers to turn north along the Rhine's west bank to protect Patton's flank, there remained the danger of an enemy counter-attack out of the Colmar salient.

---

* Patton's history was awry. In October 1870 Marshal Bazaine surrendered Metz to the Prussian army.

Having failed with the 'narrow front' option offered by Market Garden, Eisenhower had achieved only limited gains with with a 'broad front' strategy, of which the two *points d'appui* had been the widely separated and strongly held cities of Aachen and Metz. As the autumn wore on the Americans had become mesmerized by these ancient fortresses. Had they attacked in the thinly held hill country of the Ardennes between them, they would have forced the enemy to relinquish his grip on at least one of these pillars in the line. But the SHAEF planners had ruled out the Ardennes as an invasion route. Bradley had chosen the 'Aachen Gap', a traditional invasion route into Germany and one which was likely to be heavily defended. In September 1944 he had missed an opportunity to outflank the West Wall south of Aachen where, according to Field Marshal Model, the commander of German Army Group B,* a front of about ninety miles between Aachen and Trier was held by only eight battalions. Although hampered by foul weather, difficult terrain and determined German resistance, the Allies had studiously eschewed every opportunity to make their overwhelmingly superior firepower count against an enemy reeling on the ropes. This failing can be traced back to the battle of the Falaise Gap, out of which the escaping Germans were squeezed by the over-deliberate closing of the pincers, rather than being destroyed inside a swift and savage encirclement. In spite of the heavy losses they suffered, the Germans were to strike only one infantry division, 77th, from their order of battle after the fighting at Falaise. Of the remaining twenty-five which had been involved in the battle (nine armoured, two parachute and fifteen infantry), one parachute and ten infantry divisions had been so badly mauled that they were withdrawn from the line and sent to rear areas to reform. The remaining divisions, although effectively reduced to battle groups, absorbed replacements on the move and when called upon fought rearguard actions as they withdrew behind the West Wall or into Holland. In most cases these divisions had preserved their vital cadres of NCOs, junior officers and headquarters staff, the key to rapid rebuilding and reinsertion into the line, in some cases within weeks. The survival of corps headquarters staff was equally important in enabling the Westheer to live to fight another day behind the defences of the West Wall.

The painful progress made by the Allies in the autumn of 1944 induced an attritional psychology redolent of the First World War. A 12th Army Group assessment of 12 December smacked of General Erich von

---

* Model had been appointed Commander-in-Chief West on 17 August, after the death of Kluge. On 5 September he was replaced by Rundstedt, but retained command of Army Group B.

Falkenhayn planning to bleed the French Army white at Verdun in 1916:

> All of the enemy's major capabilities . . . depend on the balance between the rate of attrition imposed by the Allied offensives and the rate of infantry reinforcement. The balance at present is in favour of the Allies and with continuing Allied pressure in the south and in the north, the breaking point may develop suddenly and without warning.

Meanwhile, the dissension within the Allied high command rumbled on. On 10 October Montgomery renewed his campaign to be placed in charge of the land battle. In notably undiplomatic language he suggested that Eisenhower was out of touch with the front and increasingly inclined to fall back on fuzzy political compromise. Eisenhower replied with a letter which reminded Montgomery of his failure to secure the approaches to Antwerp, which was the 'real issue now at hand'. He then informed his unruly subordinate that the front was too long for one man to exercise close 'battle grip' on it, and pointed out that 'it is quite often necessary to make concessions that recognize the existence of inescapable national differences.' He concluded by telling Montgomery that if he remained unhappy, he could refer the matter to higher authority, an invitation to a battle which the British commander could never win, so great was the preponderance of American troops in the European theatre.

Montgomery would not let the matter drop. On 30 November he demanded that one man – himself – should be given full operational control north of the Ardennes. Tacking again, Eisenhower fell back on the familiar tactics of fudge. Monty would have priority in the north, but there would be no halt to the offensive in the south. This did not prevent him from appealing to Churchill through the Chief of the Imperial General Staff, Field Marshal Sir Alan Brooke. At their invitation, Eisenhower met Churchill and Brooke in London on 12 December, when the CIGS strongly criticized what he saw as the Supreme Commander's 'double front' strategy. He taxed Eisenhower with 'violating the principles of the concentration of force', and voiced his concern that he apparently did not propose to cross the Rhine until May 1945. Any further discussion was prevented by Churchill's ruminations on the possibility of floating 'fluvial mines' down the Rhine. The next day Churchill attempted to cheer the despondent Brooke by telling him that he had taken Eisenhower's side only because the Supreme Commander was a guest, a foreigner, and in a minority of one.

In spite of the hard pounding their armies had endured in the efforts to breach the West Wall, the Allied high command still carried the infection of over-confidence from the sweeping victories of the late summer of 1944. As Christmas approached, Montgomery was anticipating a spot of leave. In mid-December he told his troops: 'The enemy is at present fighting a defensive campaign on all fronts: his situation is that he cannot stage major offensive operations.' In playful mood, he demanded the prompt payment by Eisenhower of a £5 bet he had made with him that the war would not be over by Christmas. Eisenhower kept Monty waiting for nine days, by which time there were more important things on the Supreme Commander's mind.

But on 16 December Eisenhower was also in festive mood. He had just received a fifth star, becoming General of the Army, and that evening Bradley arrived at SHAEF headquarters in Versailles to discuss the growing manpower shortage, play bridge, and eat oysters. Roosevelt's press secretary, Steve Early, had sent Eisenhower a bushel, and he had planned a veritable oyster orgy – oysters on the half-shell, followed by oyster stew and then fried oysters. As Bradley arrived, reports were beginning to filter in of enemy activity in the Ardennes. Bradley dismissed these as nothing more than details of localized fighting, but Eisenhower immediately sensed danger, telling the commander of 12th Army Group, 'That's no spoiling attack'.

The hilly, forested Ardennes, held on an eighty-mile front by only six American divisions, was a 'quiet' sector. Soldiers amused themselves by shooting wild boar from spotter aircraft. In October 1944, Captain Charles MacDonald's company, part of 23rd Infantry Regiment, 2nd Infantry Division, moved up into the line:

> As we neared the German border, the road began a steep ascent into the mountains to our front. A big white signboard with glaring letters told us what we were near: 'You are now entering Germany, an enemy country. Be on the alert!' [Suddenly the West Wall came into view:] It looked like a prehistoric monster coiled around the hillsides; the concrete dragon's teeth were like scales on the monster's back – or maybe the headstones in some crazy cemetery.

Routines resembled those on similar sectors in the First World War. By day the men filled sandbags, strung wire and strengthened their foxholes. Officers hid their rank bars to avoid the attention of snipers. The nights were more dangerous, filled with sudden, savage mortar and artillery bombardments and aggressive patrolling in search of prisoners for interrogation by intelligence. The flavour of life in the sector was caught in the diary of Staff Sergeant Henry Giles of 291st Combat

Engineers, based at Steinfort in Luxembourg and working on a bridge across the Our for US 4th Armoured Division. On 1 October he wrote:

> Some of the wildest things can happen. I didn't have the Sgt. of the Guard last night. Think Loftis did. Anyway it was set up and the security posted. Then a work detail had to go out and repair a culvert. They either didn't know the password or had forgotten or something went snafu.* Anyway some kid got excited, thought they were Krauts and started shooting off his rifle. Today we heard practically the entire artillery of the 4th Armoured was alerted. . . . And there's a weird story about one of the artillery crews. Seems they got their own private dame. One of the boys swears it's the truth. Says she visits them every two or three days and they 'queue' up. Asked him why he didn't join the line. He said, much astonished, 'Hell, them artillery boys'd murder you'. He's a sort of mild fellow, quiet type, doesn't talk much and just the way he said it sent us into convulsions.

The Ardennes was not destined to be a quiet sector for much longer. Poring over his maps in the Wolf's Lair, Hitler's gambler's eye had spotted an opportunity for a counterstroke in the West. On 16 September he told Colonel-General Jodl, the OKW Chief of Staff, 'I have made a momentous decision. I shall go over to the offensive . . . out of the Ardennes, with the objective Antwerp.' Here, where he had settled the fate of France in a single afternoon, the Führer planned to repeat the triumphs of 1940. A quick victory was necessary, he argued, before the French began to conscript their manpower. It was as if, in Hitler's mind, the war would last for ever and that after five years he had merely returned to square one, like a Monopoly player passing 'Go', and was readying himself for the second round. Once again German armies would drive through the forests of the Ardennes to the Meuse, then sweep north to seize Antwerp. Cut off from their American allies, the British Second and Canadian First Armies would be encircled and destroyed. The 'artificial' coalition against the Axis would fall apart 'with a tremendous thunderclap' and Germany would turn to deal with the threat from the East.

This was the last occasion on which the Führer still possessed enough chips to double the stakes. It was a bold plan, sweeping in concept and impossible to execute. When it was unveiled to Rundstedt on 24 October, the Commander-in-Chief West was 'staggered. . . . It was obvious to me that the available forces were far too small – in fact no soldier really believed that the aim of reaching Antwerp was really practicable. But

---

* American slang for 'situation normal, all fucked up'.

I knew by now it was useless to protest to Hitler about the *possibility* of anything.'

Even the fanatically loyal General Sepp Dietrich, commander of Sixth SS Panzer Army, one of the two armies earmarked for the operation, was uneasy about his prospects of success. 'All Hitler wants me to do', he complained,

> is to cross a river, capture Brussels and then go on and take Antwerp. And all this in the worst time of the year through the Ardennes when the snow is waist deep and there isn't room to deploy four tanks abreast let alone armoured divisions. When it doesn't get light till eight o'clock and it's dark again at four and with re-formed divisions made up chiefly of kids and sick old men – and at Christmas.

Rundstedt and Field Marshal Model, commander of Army Group B, tried and failed to persuade Hitler to scale down the offensive to a more modest attempt to excise the American forces which had pushed beyond Aachen to the River Roer. But the Führer was seeking what the General Staff referred to as a *ganzer Entschluss* – a total decision. The plans were drawn up in conditions of the greatest secrecy, with Hitler controlling every detail, right down to the daily decisions as to the supply of vehicles and horses to individual divisions. The Führer beavered away, lost in a world where renewed strategic success beckoned. For him, the dreamers were Eisenhower and his lieutenants. 'Perhaps', Hitler mused later, 'they also believed that I might already be dead, or at least suffering from cancer somewhere – unable to drink or live on much longer, which would rule me out as a danger.' This time, Hitler decreed, no German soldier was to set foot in Paris. Special SS squads were formed to execute Nazi Party officials who had surrendered their towns too readily to the Allies. The Führer wandered happily in a fog of detail, dictating orders for the initial artillery bombardment and inspecting plans for tanks adapted to spread grit on icy roads. When Rundstedt received the final orders, the words 'Not To Be Altered' were scrawled across them in Hitler's spidery hand. Thoroughly dispirited, Rundstedt relinquished overall control of operations to Model, and spent the greater part of the offensive reading novels and drinking cognac.

Hidden from Allied air surveillance, a formidable force assembled in the narrow, mist-bound valleys and thick forests of the Eifel, on the German side of the Ardennes. It consisted of two panzer armies, Sixth SS commanded by Sepp Dietrich in the north, and Fifth in the south, led by the diminutive, hard-driving Hasso von Manteuffel, one of the best of

Hitler's younger tank generals. Between them they deployed twenty-eight divisions*, including eight panzer and two panzergrenadier divisions in which were concentrated 1,250 of the 2,600 tanks and assault guns amassed for the Ardennes attack, now codenamed Operation Autumn Mist. Most of the armoured divisions had been brought well up to strength and included 294 of the excellent MkV Panther tanks and 45 MkVI Tigers, but the Volksgrenadier divisions which were to support their armoured spearheads were less impressive formations, their ranks made up with 'ethnic' Germans who owed their nationality to frontier changes. The 62nd Volksgrenadier Division, for example, contained many Czech and Polish conscripts whose sympathies were more likely to lie with the Allies than the army in which they had been impressed. These underlying manpower deficiencies were accompanied by a shortage of fuel. Only a quarter of the minimum requirement was available when Autumn Mist was launched, the greater part of it held east of the Rhine. The leading German attack elements were expected to exploit their breakthrough with captured fuel supplies.

Hitler refused to contemplate defeat. On 12 December, at Rundstedt's headquarters, he took his generals on a geopolitical *tour d'horizon* in which he derided the Allies as 'heterogeneous elements with divergent aims, ultra-capitalist states on the one hand, an ultra-Marxist state on the other'. Britain, he said, was 'a dying empire'; America, its former colony, a nation bent on inheritance.

After several postponements the attack went in at 5.30am on 16 December. After a 20-minute barrage hundreds of searchlights were snapped on, creating 'artificial moonlight'. Moments later German shock troops emerged from the thick winter mists, overwhelming the American divisions on the attack front, 2nd, 99th, 106th and 28th, the last still recovering from its ordeal in the Hürtgen Forest. In the American rear German infiltrators wearing American uniforms cut telephone wires and spread confusion. Imitating his Russian enemy, Hitler held back the bulk of his armour until his infantry had carved their way through the American tactical defence zone.

The 99th Division, on the north of the attack front, fell back under the weight of 3rd Panzergrenadier Division. In 99th's rear were elements of 2nd Division, including Captain MacDonald's 23rd Infantry Regiment. MacDonald realised that something had gone badly awry when hundreds of men from 99th Division streamed back through the trees. They did not stop. Only two of them were persuaded to remain with

---

* In 1940 the German advance through the Ardennes to the Channel had been launched with forty-one divisions.

MacDonald's company to meet the German attack. When it came, he recalled,

> Wave after wave of fanatically screaming German infantry stormed the slight tree-covered rise held by three platoons. A continuous hail of fire exuded from their weapons, answered by volley after volley from the defenders. Germans fell right and left. The few rounds of artillery we did succeed in bringing down caught the attackers in the draw [gully] to our front, and we could hear the screams of pain when the small-arms fire slackened. But still they came on.

Then Tigers appeared, over 60 tons of ponderous metal, grinding through the forest and snapping trees like matchsticks. The line broke and within half an hour MacDonald and his men were in headlong flight. As dusk drew in and he crashed through the trees, MacDonald

> slipped and fell face down in the snow. I cursed my slick over-shoes. I rose and fell again. I found myself not caring if the Germans did fire. My feet were soaked. My clothes were drenched. Perspiration covered my body, and my mouth was dry. I wanted a cigarette. I felt we were like helpless little bugs scurrying blindly about now that some man-monster had lifted the log under which we had been hiding. I wondered if it would not be better to be killed and perhaps that would be an end to everything.

At first there was something like blind panic behind the American lines. At Manderfeld, headquarters of US 14th Cavalry Group and directly in the path of the German drive, staff officers completely lost their nerve. They fled in their vehicles and, in a frantic attempt to dispose of anything which might aid the Germans, simply set the whole town ablaze. Things were no better in 106th Division's sector, covering St Vith where, in October, Marlene Dietrich had entertained the troops. The division's historian later wrote:

> Let's get down to hard facts. Panic, sheer unreasoning panic, flamed that road all day and into the night. Everyone, it seemed, who had any excuse, and many who had none, was going west that day – west from Schoenberg, west from St Vith, too. Jeeps, trucks, tanks, guns and great lumbering Corps Artillery vehicles which took three-quarters of the road – some of them double banking. Now and again vehicles were weaving into a third line, now and again crashing into ditches. All this on a two-lane high-

way. And this was what the US 7th Armoured Division (ordered up from Holland to St Vith) was bucking as it drove – practically the only eastbound element to get from Vielsalm to St Vith.

Scattered bands of American infantry wandered about the wintry forests, fighting the Germans when they collided with them or trying to link up with larger formations. After four days of confused fighting the Americans had pulled themselves together. On the northern shoulder of the German advance General Gerow's V Corps blocked Sixth SS Panzer Army. On 17 December 1st SS Panzer Division had arrived at St Vith, from which a valley road led to the Meuse and Belgium, to find the spearheads of 7th Armoured Division barring its way. The 101st Airborne Division, rushed up by truck from Reims, clung grimly to the vital road centre of Bastogne, forcing Manteuffel to bypass it as he pressed on to the Meuse. The Germans were now running out of time and fuel, and as they fell back the Americans fired their fuel dumps, so denying them to the enemy.

Eisenhower strove to exercise a tight grip on the battle. At a staff conference held at Verdun on 19 December and attended by Bradley, Patton and Devers, the Supreme Commander declared: 'The present situation is to be regarded as one of opportunity for us and not of disaster. There will only be cheerful faces at this conference table.' Patton was ordered to swing three of his divisions through 90 degrees to drive on Bastogne, a manoeuvre which Third Army accomplished in two days. Within seventy-two hours Patton had brought the major part of Third Army, two corps totalling seven divisions, to bear on the southern flank of the 'bulge'. To prevent the expanding German salient from severing Bradley's communications with his troops on the northern side of the bulge, Eisenhower gave Montgomery, still spoiling for a fight over the question of priorities, temporary overall command in the north. With his usual sublime lack of tact, the British commander could not resist the opportunity to 'tweak our Yankee noses', as Bradley tartly put it. One of his own staff officers recalled that Montgomery arrived at the headquarters of the lugubrious General Hodges's US First Army 'like Christ come to cleanse the temple'. Well informed by Ultra* decrypts of the intentions of both Sixth SS and Fifth Panzer Armies, he moved quickly to guard the bridges across the Meuse, towards which the fingers of Dietrich's advance were reaching, with British troops brought down from northern Belgium. The battle was

---

* The British codename for the information on German movements and intentions acquired by intercepting and decrypting the coded signals traffic sent on the Wehrmacht's Enigma electrical coding machines.

now assuming a shape calculated to appeal to Montgomery's cautious instincts. The Germans would punch themselves out trying to batter their way past the nineteen American and British divisions gathered in and around the the rapidly attenuating nose of the salient they had driven into the Ardennes.

Fifth Panzer Army had taken St Vith on 23 December, but two days later Manteuffel's most advanced units were fought to a halt by US 2nd Armoured Division just three miles short of the Meuse. Having run out of petrol, 2nd Panzer Division was subjected to a merciless pounding, losing almost all of the eighty-eight tanks and twenty-eight assault guns with which it had started the battle.

By now the mists which had masked the German concentration and initial assault had cleared and Allied aircraft were ranging over the battlefield. On Christmas Day a Spitfire pilot, Flight Lieutenant Jack Boyle of 411 Squadron based at Heesch airfield, had an encounter with an Me262 jet. Boyle's entire Wing, consisting of five squadrons including 411, had been ordered to provide maximum support in the American sector of the Ardennes around Bastogne, which was now completely surrounded. Boyle had been forced to turn back to act as escort to a fighter with engine trouble:

> I was sorely troubled by this turn of events and grumbled to myself all the way home about bad luck and fickle fate. As we neared the home base at Heesch, we were far too high and in an irritable mood. To get rid of the excess height, I stuck the nose almost straight down in a screaming spiral dive. As my speed shot past 500mph, out of nowhere appeared a German Me262 jet. It only took a second to see to my gun–sight and safety catch and then I was right behind him. My first burst of cannon fire hit his port engine pod and it began streaming dense smoke. He immediately dived for the deck as an evasive tactic, but with only one engine he couldn't outrun me. I scored several more hits before he clipped some tall tree tops and then hit the ground at an almost flat angle. His aircraft disintegrated in stages from nose to tail as it ripped up the turf for several hundred yards until only the tailplane assembly was left and it went cartwheeling along just below me at about my speed. Fire and smoke marked his trail. As I circled, Dutch farmers emerged from their barns and waved up at me. . . . Most of the airmen in the wing had witnessed the whole attack. Because it was noon on Christmas Day they had all been lined up for turkey dinner and at the sound of gunfire they had hit the deck, facing upwards in case there was anything to see. On this day, it was an Me262 jet with a Spit right on his tail.

The breakdown in the Ardennes offensive is chronicled in tersely ironic fashion in the diary kept by an officer of one of Das Reich Division's grenadier battalions, which had been moved up on Sixth SS Panzer Army's front on 23 December. He spent a dispiriting Christmas Day under fire:

> Monday 25 December, 1944. With Panzer support we drive the enemy out of his positions. He withdraws slowly towards Manhay and Grandmenil under the cover of a barrage fired by hundreds of guns. There is absolutely no cover. Our guns in an orgy of spend-thrift recklessness reply with 8 rounds – and then cease fire. We have to save ammunition. But the order to attack has raised our spirits. It is much better than lying about in slit trenches in the cold subject to the enemy's savage bombardments. Some men are brought back suffering from frostbite. There are not enough felt boots to go round. During the evening the enemy is driven out of Manhay and Grandmenil and for tonight at least we have dry billets. We are guarded only by a thin outpost line on the edge of the village. . . . An attack has been ordered for tomorrow. The objective is Mormont. This means that we have to be in position in good time. But the tanks and artillery have almost no fuel or ammunition left.

Bastogne was relieved by US 4th Armoured Division on 26 December. Four days earlier Rundstedt – mindful of the growing threat on the Eastern Front – had begged Hitler to call off the offensive. The Führer ordered his commanders to slog on and, on 1 January, launched a second, abortive attack southwards from the Saar. But by now the game was up. On 29 December, Major-General F.W. von Mellenthin, on his way to take up a new appointment with 9th Panzer Division,* was making his way through the wooded hills north-west of Houffalize, in the centre of the salient: 'The icebound roads glittered in the sunshine and I witnessed the uninterrupted air attacks on our traffic routes and supply dumps. Not a single German plane was in the air, innumerable vehicles were shot up and their blackened wrecks littered the roads.'

On 3 January the Allies went on to the offensive and by the 16th units of US First and Third Armies had linked up at Houffalize, closing the last German escape route from the salient. As men of Third Army's 11th Armoured Division and First Army's 2nd Division moved into the town, General Patton and his driver Sergeant Mims were motoring up to join

---

* Mellenthin had been dismissed as Chief of Staff of Army Group G and removed from the General Staff. Guderian had re-employed him.

them. At one point Patton ordered Mims to stop so that he could investigate what appeared to be a long row of dark twigs projecting above the surface of the snow. On closer inspection they proved to be the toes of soldiers whose boots had been removed after they had been hit, 'a nasty sight', as the normally hard-boiled Patton later told his staff officers. The last spasm of fighting in the Ardennes salient had been fought in a giant refrigerator which turned corpses the colour of claret.

In the month-long offensive Fifth and Sixth SS Panzer Armies had inflicted some 19,000 fatal casualties on US 12th Army Group and had taken 15,000 American prisoners. But the cost to the Westheer had been 100,000 men killed and wounded, and 800 tanks destroyed. These losses could not be made good, while, in contrast, the Americans shipped over seven new divisions, three of them armoured and fully equipped, while the Battle of the Bulge was being fought. The Luftwaffe also entered its death throes in the winter skies of January 1945. It lost 1,000 aircraft in the Ardennes offensive, around 220 of them in Operation *Bodenplatte* (Ground Plate) launched against the Dutch and Belgian airfields of the Allied Tactical Air Force on 1 January. Eight hundred aircraft of almost every type save heavy bombers and spotter planes were assembled for the operation, but poor serviceability meant that only 600 took to the air. Hermann Göring's orders underlined the last-ditch character of Bodenplatte: 'No pilot is to turn back except for damage to the undercarriage: flights are to be continued even with misfiring engines. Failures of auxiliary tanks will not be accepted as an excuse for turning back.' Many of the pilots had received insufficient training to find their targets, and instructors were drafted in from as far away as Prague to act as formation leaders. Bodenplatte achieved surprise and some success, knocking out 140 Allied aircraft, but at the cost of around 220 planes and a similar number of pilots, among them many of the irreplaceable instructors. Allied losses represented just 0.5 per cent of the aircraft available to SHAEF; German losses were nearly 30 per cent of the strike force painfully amassed for the operation at the cost of denuding other fronts of air support.

Hitler had given the Allies a shock, prompting Eisenhower to surround himself with bodyguards and forcing him briefly to contemplate sending black American troops, previously strictly segregated, into action alongside whites in fully integrated units. Even after the elimination of the salient the Führer believed that there had been

> a tremendous easing of the situation . . . the enemy has had to abandon all his plans for attack. He has been obliged to regroup his forces. He has had to throw in again units which were fatigued.

He is severely criticized at home. . . . Already he has had to admit that there is no chance of the war being ended before August, perhaps not before the end of next year.

In reality Autumn Mist had merely caused a hiccup in the Allied preparations to break into Germany, at the expense, to the Germans, of transferring from or denying to the Ostheer the men and material desperately needed on the Eastern Front. In the last two months of 1944, 2,229 tanks and assault guns and eighteen new divisions had been committed to the West, but only 920 tanks and five divisions to the East, where the Ostheer faced 225 Red Army rifle divisions, 22 tank corps and 29 other armoured formations, with only 133 divisions, 30 of which were already threatened with encirclement in the Baltic states.

With the Battle of the Bulge all but won, Montgomery further inflamed relations within the Allied high command by claiming, at a press conference on 7 January, virtually the entire credit for the victory: 'The battle has been most interesting; I think possibly one of the most interesting and tricky . . . I have ever handled.' Churchill was obliged to mollify the outraged Americans with a generous speech in the House of Commons. However, the jolt administered by the Ardennes offensive also enabled Eisenhower to settle on a formula which would place the least pressure on the fault lines within the Allied high command. On 15 January, in a letter to General Marshall, he re-emphasized the importance of strong flanks and a firm defence running right down the Allied line. The defences would provide a springboard for Allied counter-attacks but would also tie down many divisions. Eisenhower's answer was to 'get a good natural line for the defensive portions of our long front. . . . That line ought to be, substantially, the Rhine.'* Thus Eisenhower could continue to reassure Montgomery that the main effort would be placed north of the Ruhr, while allowing Bradley and Patton greater scope in the south than would seem consistent with his support for the British. At the same time a blind eye was turned on Patton's notorious reluctance to assume

---

* Eisenhower's strategy of closing up to the Rhine led to some heated exchanges at the meeting of the Joint Chiefs of Staff which preceded the Yalta Conference in February 1945. The British assumed that it was Eisenhower's intention to clear every foot of the west bank of the Rhine before crossing the river. The British Chiefs of Staff sought an assurance that it was not the Supreme Commander's intention to clear the entire west bank before launching 21st Army Group's thrust in the north. Eisenhower's reassuring reply was a masterpiece of his guarded style: 'I will seize the Rhine crossings in the north immediately this is a feasible operation and without waiting to close to the Rhine throughout its length . . . I will advance across the Rhine in the north . . . as soon as the situation in the south allows me.'

a defensive posture of any kind. Patton had developed his own formula for disobeying orders, which he dubbed the 'rock-soup' method. In his memoirs, Patton claimed that he had based this on a story about a hobo

who went to a house and asked for some boiling water to make rock soup. The lady was interested and gave him the water, in which he placed two white polished stones. He then asked if he might have some potatoes to put in the soup to flavor it a little, and finally ended up with some meat. In other words, in order to attack we first had to pretend to reconnoiter, then reinforce the reconnaissance, and finally put on an attack – all depending on what gasoline and ammunition we could secure.

CHAPTER 7

Over the Rhine

'My dear General, the German is whipped. We've got him. He is all through.'

Churchill to Eisenhower, 23 March 1945

THE ARDENNES OFFENSIVE delayed the Allied drive to the Rhine by some four weeks. Eisenhower still planned to make the principal thrust in the north where the combined British, Canadian and American troops on the Maas and the Roer were close to the Rhine, which they were to cross between Emmerich and Düsseldorf. In the south, Bradley's 12th Army Group was to advance through the Eifel, a region of moorland and forests, to close up with the Rhine between Cologne and Koblenz. Here he would make a second crossing if Montgomery's failed to split the German forces. The double crossing underpinned the Allies' next strategic objective, the encirclement of the Ruhr valley, Germany's industrial heartland. On Bradley's right flank, Devers's 6th Army Group was tasked with clearing the Saar before moving up to the Rhine at Mannerheim.

Having starved the Eastern Front to attack in the West, Hitler now reversed the process. In February, when the British and Americans returned to the offensive, sixteen divisions and quantities of artillery trundled eastward; 1,675 armoured vehicles went to the Ostheer and only 67 to the Westheer. To this bankrupt strategy was added Hitler's obsession with holding ground. When Rundstedt proposed that German forces should be conserved by abandoning the whole of Holland west and south of the Ijssel Sea, Hitler immediately declared that it was to be yet another 'fortress', in which an entire army would be trapped by the end of March. Rundstedt, supported by Westphal, then gingerly attempted to broach the subject of the west bank of the Rhine. According to Westphal, Rundstedt declared

> that the only aim of decisive importance was to maintain coherence on the front and to prevent a breakthrough on a strategic scale. In the face of this necessity, the policy of clinging on to every foot of German soil in the rigid form in which it had been ordered till now, must be abandoned. Moreover, it was now indispensable to make extensive preparations for the organization of the defence on the east bank of the Rhine. Even though rivers no longer presented the same obstacles as in earlier times, the Allies, in their methodical way, were sure to make careful preparations for crossing the Rhine. Staying too long west of the river would increase the danger of the enemy's following closely on the heels of the German troops. Would Hitler preserve his freedom of action?

Hitler would have none of it. The West Wall, he insisted, was still strong enough to beat off any attack. He forbade the surrender of even the smallest outpost without his permission. The Rhine, he argued, was the vital link between the Ruhr and the rest of Germany. Withdrawal to its east bank would 'merely mean moving the catastrophe from one place to another'. As General Walter Warlimont, the former Deputy Chief of OKW's Operations Staff,* reflected, 'Hitler's orders remained as rigid as ever. . . . So in spite of its courage and self-sacrifice, the remnants of the German army were to a great extent expended forward of the Rhine.' Manteuffel put it more bluntly: 'After the Ardennes failure Hitler started a "corporal's war". There were no big plans, only a multitude of piecemeal fights.'

In contrast, the Allies' overwhelming superiority in manpower and material enabled its high command to contemplate expansive operations the scope of which was limited only by the difficulties of the wooded and waterlogged terrain they had to negotiate before reaching the Rhine. Montgomery's plan for the initial phase of his February offensive had two parts, codenamed 'Veritable' and 'Grenade'. In Veritable, Canadian First Army, commanded by Crerar and based in the Nijmegen sector in the eastern Netherlands, was to advance down a narrow corridor between the Maas and Rhine Rivers and through the dense fir plantations of the Reichswald to reach the Ruhr south of Emmerich. US Ninth Army was entrusted with Grenade, a north-eastwards sweep from the

---

* Warlimont had held this post until September 1944, when he went on sick leave as a result of injuries he had received in the July bomb plot against Hitler.

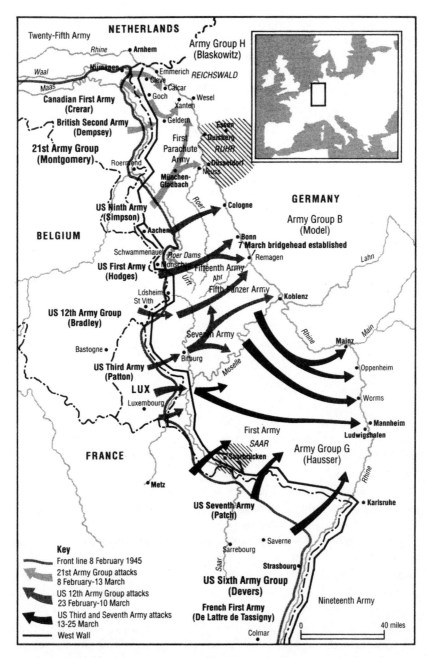

Twenty-Fifth Army
NETHERLANDS
Arnhem
Rhine
Army Group H
(Blaskowitz)
Waal
Nijmegen
Emmerich
REICHSWALD
Maas
Cleve
Calcar
Canadian First Army
(Crerar)
Goch
Wesel
Xanten
British Second Army
(Dempsey)
Geldern
Essen
Duisburg
21st Army Group
(Montgomery)
Roermond
First
Parachute
Army
RUHR
Düsseldorf
München-Gladbach
Neuss
Roer
GERMANY
US Ninth Army
(Simpson)
Cologne
Army Group B
(Model)
BELGIUM
Aachen
Bonn
7 March bridgehead established
Schwammenauel
Roer Dams
Remagen
US First Army
(Hodges)
Monschau
Fifteenth Army
Lahn
Urft
Ahr
Lösheim
St Vith
Fifth Panzer Army
Koblenz
US 12th Army Group
(Bradley)
Seventh Army
Rhine
Main
Bastogne
Bitburg
Mainz
US Third Army
(Patton)
Moselle
Oppenheim
LUX
Luxembourg
Worms
First Army
Mannheim
SAAR
Ludwigshafen
FRANCE
Saarbrücken
Army Group G
(Hausser)
Metz
Rhine
US Seventh Army
(Patch)
Karlsruhe
Saverne

Key
Front line 8 February 1945
21st Army Group attacks
8 February-13 March
US 12th Army Group attacks
23 February-10 March
US Third and Seventh Army attacks
13-25 March
West Wall

Sarrebourg
Saar
Strasbourg
US Sixth Army Group
(Devers)
French First Army
(De Lattre de Tassigny)
Nineteenth Army
Colmar

0   40 miles

As the Allies broke through the West Wall and headed for the Rhine, German troops were, for the first time, fighting on their own soil. Operation Veritable (21st Army Group's drive to the Rhine) drew important German reserves from other sectors and thinned out defences on the Roer.

Roer towards Düsseldorf to link up with Canadian First Army opposite Wesel, the point at which Montgomery proposed to cross the Rhine.

The Reichswald was like a stopper in a long-necked bottle. On either side of the great forest lay the flooded polder land around the Maas and the Rhine. Through it ran the northern end of the West Wall, which ran south from the Nijmegen-Cleve road, over the high ground in the centre of the forest, to the heavily fortified town of Goch, whence it continued southwards along a slight lip overlooking the valley of the Maas to Roermond. The approaches to the Reichswald were covered by a belt of defences about 2,000 yards deep, fronted by an anti-tank ditch and a series of strongpoints built into the villages and farms which dotted the landscape. Seven miles to the east of the Reichswald was a third defensive line, dubbed the 'Hochwald layback' by the British after the wooded hills through which it ran.

Reflecting on the Battle of the Reichswald, General Horrocks, whose XXX Corps had been transferred from British Second Army to spearhead the attack, wrote:

> There was no room for manoeuvre and no scope for cleverness. I had to blast my way through three defensive systems, the centre of which was the Siegfried Line. . . . After the initial attacks this was a battle in which generalship played no part at all; it developed into a slogging match in the mud between regimental officers, NCOs and men.

In the build-up to Veritable, Montgomery had tried a little *maskirovka* of his own, in an attempt to persuade General Johannes Blaskowitz, commanding German Army Group H in the Netherlands, that the attack was to be launched across the Maas and Roer Rivers further south. Montgomery had held XXX Corps well back and had forbidden any British officers from the assault divisions to visit the front without first donning distinctive Canadian battledress. Deep German patrols found evidence only of the presence of 2nd Canadian Division. On the maps at Rundstedt's headquarters, XXX Corps was labelled 'whereabouts unknown'. Dummy guns were placed in Montgomery's front line in anticipation of their being detected by German analysis of aerial reconnaissance photographs.

As the weather conditions swung between snow and thaw, infinite pains were taken to whitewash tanks one day and smear them with mud the next. Ammunition* was stored in unrecognizable groupings simulat-

---

* The ammunition accumulated for the offensive was the equivalent of the bomb drop of 25,000 medium bombers. Stacked in a line 5 feet high, it would have stretched for thirty miles.

ing hedgerows, kitchen gardens and irregular patches of scrub. All British aircraft were warned off the area. On 5 February Rundstedt's chief intelligence officer informed senior staff officers of Army Group H:

> Allied activities west of the Reichswald are intended to deceive us regarding the real centre of the coming attack. It is possible that a subsidiary offensive by the Canadians in the Reichswald area might be launched to draw our reserves but the appreciation that the main British attack will come from the big bend in the Maas [at Venlo] is being maintained.

The German high command had nibbled the bait, but the canny General Alfried Schlemm, whose First Parachute Army covered the Reichswald, was convinced that the main blow would fall there, on his northern flank. In spite of Montgomery's deception measures, the evidence of the build-up was mounting steadily. Blaskowitz, however, remained sceptical, calling on the support of Schlemm's predecessor, General Student, who maintained that the next big attack would be an American crossing from Roermond with a supporting British attack from Venlo. Blaskowitz told Schlemm, 'There is no evidence of large enemy concentrations in the Nijmegen area.' Unimpressed, Schlemm continued with his own covert preparations to meet the Allied attack.

On 30 January Alexander McKee wrote of Montgomery's preparations: 'It's a typical Monty set-up. Bags of guns crammed on to a narrow front, all your force at one point and bash in. Unsubtle but usually successful. Jerry knows you're coming, but he can't do very much because the gigantic bomber formations we will wield will sweep it like a broom.' Within a week Montgomery's concentration was complete. Half a million men were hidden behind the front. The assault would be made by 50,000 men and 1,000 armoured vehicles. As Brigadier Hubert Essame, commander of 43rd (Wessex) Division's 214 Brigade, later wrote, 'The tension could be felt – the kind of feeling which runs through the crowd before the Derby.' Seasoned soldiers, the 'poor bloody infantry', took a less sporting view of the coming offensive. One of the men of 6th Battalion Royal Welch Fusiliers remembers:

> According to intelligence reports, the Reichswald was not as strongly fortified or defended as the more open country to the north and south. The Germans were said to regard it as being too dense, the going too rough for an attack to be marched through it. We couldn't quite believe this, the Germans themselves having twice attacked through so-called 'impassable' territory in the

Ardennes; we therefore took the information with a pinch or two of salt, regarding it as being a possible morale-booster. In our briefing group we were shown the latest air photographs of the enemy's zone. On these, defences had been outlined: flooded parts, roads and trails showed up well. The forest itself, of course, was just a mass of trees with no indication as to what lay beneath them. We – pessimistically as ever – believed the worst.

The bombers predicted by Alexander McKee came on the night of 7 February, thundering over the rain-sodden start lines to plaster Cleve to the north of the Reichswald and Goch to the south with 2,000 tons of high-explosive. At 5am on the 8th Veritable opened with a massive artillery bombardment from over 1,000 guns on the seven-mile front occupied by the single German division defending the Reichswald, 84th Infantry. The history of one of the British armoured regiments involved in the operation, the 4th/7th Royal Dragoons, records:

It was a fantastic scene, never to be forgotten. One moment silence and the next moment a terrific ear-splitting din, with every pitch of noise imaginable. Little bangs, big bangs, sharp cracks, the rattle of machine-guns and the ripple of Bofors intermingled with the periodic swoosh of a rocket battery. The night was lit by flashes of every colour and the tracer of the Bofors guns weaving fairy patterns in the sky as they streamed off towards the target.

At 7.30am the barrage abruptly ceased and the German artillery responded, only to be hit minutes later with crushing counter-battery fire. RAF Mosquito light bombers swept across the smoke-shrouded landscape to bomb the German lines only 1,000 yards away from the forward British positions. At 10.30am the order to advance was drowned by the roar of tank engines as the first wave moved forward behind a screen of mine-exploding flail tanks. Ahead of them the ground was churned by a creeping barrage programmed to advance one hundred yards every four minutes; at twelve-minute intervals all guns fired a round of yellow smoke and increased their range by another 300 yards.

In the centre, the leading brigades of 15th (Scottish) and 53rd (Welsh) Divisions advanced towards Groesbeek, where the ground was littered with the skeletons of the gliders used by US 82nd Airborne Division during Market Garden the previous September. On the right 51st (Highland) Division broke into the solid, forbidding mass of the Reichswald, so thick it seemed to Lieutenant John Foley, the commander of a troop of Churchill tanks, that the tree trunks looked as if they had been 'carved from granite'. Foley later recalled:

Dead on the dot of ten-thirty we emerged from our wood and headed for the Reichswald. In front of us the Black Watch moved purposefully forward, little groups of men hurrying over the ground, while others spreadeagled themselves behind what cover they could find and fired their rifles and Bren guns calmly and methodically.

So far there was little sign of enemy resistance. Foley's tank clattered past a Black Watch company commander puffing away at his pipe. 'With his little cane and red hackle at the side of his cap, he might well have been taking a Sunday morning stroll down Aldershot High Street, except vicious little spurts of dust were cracking about his heels.' As Foley's tank rolled on he suddenly heard a noise 'like a small boy dragging a stick along some iron railings,' and a line of sparks flashed off the side of his tank, 'Avenger'. 'They've woken up!' Foley shouted to his crew, and slipped down inside his turret as, all around him, the Black Watch 'melted into the landscape'.

It took nearly a week to clear the Reichswald. Schlemm, his instinct confirmed, began to feed in reinforcements* while torrential rain turned the floor of the forest into a quagmire in which men and machines slewed about in a sea of mud. The lanes and logging tracks cut through the forest, often in long straight lines, provided German machine-gunners and anti-tank gunners with deadly fields of fire. A sergeant in the Welch Regiment came under fire while picking his way along a sunken lane in the dark, dripping interior of the Reichswald:

On either side of the lane were muddy banks topped with masses of dead and soaking bracken. It was pouring with rain and the soil was washing down the banks in muddy little landslips of earth and stones. Suddenly a machine-gun opened up on us from somewhere in the trees and thick undergrowth. One of my men fell and I scrambled from the bank. We were like rats in a barrel in that bloody lane. I jumped for the top of the bank, pulling at the bracken to try and heave myself up into cover at the top. But the ferns pulled out at the roots and I got showered with mud. I sprawled down the bank again, which probably saved me because the German stopped shooting at me, probably thought he'd hit me. For God knows how long I lay in the mud and shivered with fright and cold while the machine-gun rattled on. Then some of our boys came up and hit it with a captured panzerfaust.

---

* By 14 February Canadian First Army was faced by one panzer, one panzergrenadier, four parachute and three infantry divisions.

Mud, minefields and monsoon-like rain were the leitmotivs of the
Battle of the Reichswald. Numerous enemy strongpoints were dealt with
by 79th Armoured Division's Crocodiles, fearsome flame-throwing
Churchill tanks which belched a jet of blazing liquid that clung to everything it touched up to a range of 120 yards. Fighting for the high ground
at Materborn, on the northern edge of the forest, 6th Royal Scots Fusiliers
called up a Crocodile to take out some troublesome pillboxes. A member of the Crocodile's crew recalled:

> We had been ordered to put pressure on the approach and to con-
> centrate on the pillboxes and emplacements. There was a terrify-
> ing fight going on with the mass of armour advancing on a broad
> front, explosions everywhere and the infantry pressing on behind
> the tanks. We headed for a concrete emplacement from which a
> couple of machine-guns were playing havoc with the infantry. As
> we turned right to attack, a self-propelled gun fired at us but
> missed, its shell exploding some feet behind us. Before it could fire
> again it was in turn hit and seemed disabled. We rattled on and the
> order was given: 'Flame gun, fire'. There was a roaring noise as
> the yellow jet shot straight out, then bubbled along the ground and
> flickered over the bunker. The undergrowth burst into flame
> and clouds of smoke blotted out our view. The Croc slewed again
> and we could see a German soldier writhing in the flames.

The rain fell, the waters rose and the few usable roads were submerged, creating acute congestion in the rear. When 43rd Division was
moved up to join the attack on Cleve, it ran straight into one of the worst
traffic jams of the war, in which 15th Division's transport was mingled
with a wide selection of vehicles of Canadian First Army. On either side
of the road tanks, flail tanks, Crocodiles and wheeled vehicles lay inert
in the mud. Brigadier Essame has described the scene which confronted
Major-General Ivor Thomas, commander of 43rd Division:

> Behind him stood a vast motionless traffic jam: the road was
> flooded and the water was rising rapidly. Through this confusion
> Major-General Barber of the 15th Scottish [Division] was endeav-
> ouring to pass his 227th Brigade to complete the task of capturing
> the Materborn heights and the town of Cleve. The meeting
> between the two commanders lacked cordiality. Major-General
> Barber, who was about seven feet tall, could personally contem-
> plate the rising water with greater equanimity than Major-General
> Thomas, who was more in the jockey class. In the early dawn, after
> an exchange of argument notable more for its forceful expression

than urbanity, it was eventually agreed that the 43rd Wessex Division should clear the road to enable the 15th Scottish reserve brigade to struggle and work its way round the south of the town. A day of nightmare traffic congestion ensued. It is not surprising, therefore, that the 15th Scottish's plan for capturing Cleve on this day had to be abandoned. By nightfall the axis of both divisions at Kranenburg was three feet deep in water.

By 13 February the Reichswald had been cleared. The 15th Division had mopped up Cleve after forty-eight hours of house-to-house fighting which, according to one participant, resembled a mass shoot-out in a Wild West movie. The division's task had not been helped by the lunar landscape left behind after Bomber Command's attack on the town on the night of 7 February. The roads through Cleve were now impassable. The town was handed over to 3rd Canadian Division, which had crossed the flooded land to the north of the Kranenburg-Cleve road in Buffalo amphibious landing craft, while 15th Division joined 51st Division in the attack on Goch, the anchor at the northern end of the West Wall. The defenders held out until the morning of 22 February, by which time Canadian First Army had established a line twenty miles long between the Maas and the Rhine and, with its southern supply route clear from the Maas, was poised to advance across open country to a line running from Geldern to Xanten. On 22 February the French-Canadians of 3rd Canadian Division had taken the village of Moyland, which barred the way to Calcar, Horrocks's last objective before XXX Corps took on the Hochwald layback. After four days of bitter fighting, which saw the near destruction of the elite Panzer Lehr Division, thrown in by Schlemm on the night of the 19th, the French-Canadians broke into Moyland, there to be greeted by the aged Baroness Steengracht von Moyland, protesting vigorously that they had ignored the white sheets of surrender which she had hung from the walls of her castle. When the French-Canadian infantrymen informed her that experience had taught them to be extremely wary of white flags of surrender, the Baroness regretfully concluded that such sad failures to abide by honourable conventions of war were the fault of those 'dreadful SS people'. Later that day the British war correspondent R.W. Thompson listened to a young French-Canadian officer playing the Warsaw Concerto* on a grand piano amid the debris of the Baroness's ruined drawing room. As he left for a spot of leave in Brussels, Thompson looked back for the last

---

* Composed by Richard Addinsell for the 1940 romantic movie *Dangerous Moonlight*, starring Anton Walbrook and Sally Gray.

time at 'Moyland Castle with the white flags drooping at its round tower'.

Calcar fell on 23 February, and Horrocks sent a personal message to his troops.

> You have now successfully completed the first part of your task. You have taken approximately 12,000 prisoners and killed large numbers of Germans. You have broken through the Siegfried Line and drawn to yourselves the bulk of German reserves in the West. A strong US offensive was launched over the Roer at 0330 hours this morning against positions, which, thanks to your efforts, are lightly held by the Germans. Our offensive has made the situation more favourable for our Allies and greatly increased their prospects of success. Thank you for what you have done so well. If we continue our efforts for a few more days, the German front is bound to crack.

The American offensive to which Horrocks referred was Grenade, scheduled to begin a day after Veritable but disrupted by US First Army's failure to seize the Roer dams intact. The dams at Schmidt had remained in German hands, defended by 62nd and 272nd Volksgrenadier Divisions, which were well dug in and supported by armour. On 5 February US First Army's 78th Division launched a determined attack against the Schwammenauel dam, supported by the Sherman tanks of US 7th Armoured Division. They ground towards the dam but they lacked the artillery, and the specialist armour employed by the British, to gain their obective. On 8 February Schmidt finally fell to 78th Division's 311th Regiment, and on the following day 9th Infantry Division was moved forward to take the dam, which controlled the headwaters of the Roer.

German engineers had planted explosive charges in the dam's inlet and outlet gates. Their aim was not to blow the dam in one cataclysmic blast, producing a 20-billion gallon deluge which would subside in hours, but rather to ensure, by jamming the inlet and outlet gates, that the Roer, swollen by rain and a sudden thaw, would be flooded for several weeks. Hitler himself had taken the decision, after consulting with the General Staff.

It was almost dark on the evening of 9 February when men of 9th Division broke through to the dam. Among them was Private Tony Sullivan:

> . . . on our right the huge twin outlet pipes ran down the steep hill into near darkness. Our sergeant shouted for us to get on up the hill and we had just grabbed our weapons, which included a light

machine-gun, when there were several sharp bangs – they echoed
and reverberated down the valley and the next moment this enormous jet of water literally soared out in a huge arc and plunged
down the hill. The noise was terrific and further down we could
see our troops scrambling out of its path. We all stood around for
a moment, not sure what to do, and I suppose, thinking it was all
over, but the next moment the German artillery began shelling us
in earnest and we had to take cover.

At midnight the dam's control room was seized by men of 309th
Infantry Regiment. A platoon of combat engineers raced across the top
of the dam to an inspection tunnel, only to find their path blocked by
rubble. With enemy machine-gun fire cracking around them, they slid
200 feet down the face of the dam to reach the outlet gate. They were too
late; millions of gallons of water were rushing out, on their way to flood
the country north of the Reichswald over which US Ninth Army was
about to advance. Its commander, General William H. Simpson, was
forced to stand by, a helpless spectator, while the British fought their way
through the Reichswald.

Grenade was not launched until 23 February when, at 3.30am, XIX and
XIII Corps attacked across the Roer, supported on Simpson's right by First
Army's VII Corps. A swarm of craft carried Simpson's four assault divisions through the raging torrent – motor-powered assault boats butted
through the waves while rubber boats bobbed wildly in the wash set up
by tank landing craft and the shell splashes of fierce German artillery
fire. By dawn divisional engineers, braving a hail of machine-gun and
small-arms fire, battled to extend two temporary bridges over the Roer.
Both were located and destroyed by German artillery, the severed sections whipped away downstream by the current. On the east bank
Simpson's infantry, supported by Republic P-47 Thunderbolt fighter-
bombers, pushed on to Julich which was occupied by nightfall, with the
exception of the town's citadel, a massive moated fortress. By then
infantry and armour were moving over two infantry bridges and a heavy
pontoon bridge laid across the Roer. Schlemm's First Parachute Army
was now being squeezed between Simpson's thrust in the south and
Crerar's imminent drive into the wooded hills of the Hochwald layback
to the north, opposite Wesel. On the Roer, Schlemm's defensive front was
rapidly breaking up, and by 26 February Simpson's bridgehead, fed by
seven heavy bridges and numerous light infantry bridges, had swelled to
a depth of twenty miles and a width of ten. With the weather clearing and
the ground drying, Simpson committed the bulk of his armour. XIII
Corps swung north-east to join hands with Canadian First Army while

XIX Corps rolled towards the Rhine. Watching the deployment of XIX Corps's 2nd Armoured Division from a spotter aircraft, *Time* correspondent Sidney Olsen waxed lyrical about the sight below him:

> First came a long row of throbbing tanks moving like heavy dark beetles over the green cabbage fields of Germany in a wide swath. ... Then a suitable distance behind, came another great echelon of tanks even broader, out of which groups would wheel from their brown mud tracks in green fields to encircle and smash fire at some stubborn strongpoint. Behind this came miles of trucks full of troops, manoeuvring perfectly to mop up bypassed tough spots. Then came the field artillery to pound hard knots into submission. ...

On 1 March XIX Corps' 29th Division took the undefended city of München-Gladbach, twelve miles from the Rhine. On the following day Neuss, on the west bank of the Rhine opposite Düsseldorf, fell to 83rd Division. The Americans had seized the western end of the city's railroad bridge across the Rhine but could not prevent it from being blown by the Germans. That night the division despatched a 'phantom' column of Sherman tanks south to capture the bridge at Oberkassel. Mocked up to resemble panzers and manned by German-speaking men, the Shermans rumbled on their way, past columns of incurious German troops to Oberkassel. They were within sight of the bridge when a lone bicycle-borne German soldier raised the alarm. He paid with his life, cut to shreds by a Sherman's machine-gun, but as the American tanks raced towards the bridge a huge explosion toppled it into the Rhine amid great geysers of water and a rain of debris.

On Simpson's left British XXX Corps was advancing south-east towards Geldern where, on 3 March, 53rd (Welsh) Division joined hands with US 35th Division of XVI Corps. At the moment of contact the American tank crews of 135th Battalion had opened fire on the armour of the 4th/7th Dragoons, mistaking them for an enemy formation. A British officer advanced 300 yards through shell fire, holding a recognition panel aloft, before the Americans stopped firing and greetings and cigarettes were exchanged in the snow.

The greater part of the Hochwald had been cleared by 2 March, after three days of heavy fighting, although pockets of German troops held out for another week. The British and Canadians now turned east towards Wesel, where Schlemm had relocated his headquarters in a shrinking perimeter covering his Rhine crossings. Hitler had issued strict orders that bridges were to be kept open for as long as possible, and none prepared for demolition until the enemy was within twelve miles. The death penalty awaited anyone who surrendered a bridge to the Allies. (Later, after being taken prisoner, Schlemm laconically told his interrogator that, with several bridges in his sector, 'I could see my hopes of a long life rapidly dwindling'.) Schlemm telephoned Rundstedt and told him bluntly: 'If you have a map before you, you will take in the situation at a glance. My divisions are surrounded with the Ruhr at their back. Under these conditions I cannot do anything against the enemy's superior forces. I am asking your authorization to withdraw to the east bank of the Rhine.'

Rundstedt, who had famously observed that the only troops he could move on his own initiative were those standing guard at his door, referred the matter to OKW. The reply was inevitable: Schlemm must hold on at all costs and in the meantime OKW would send staff officers to the front to assess the situation. On 5 March Schlemm blew all the bridges in his sector with the exception of the span at Wesel. Three days later Crerar launched a heavy attack against the village of Xanten, the hinge of the hard-pressed perimeter around Wesel, where German parachute troops, protected by deep minefields, barbed-wire entanglements and anti-tank ditches, put up a fantical resistance against repeated assaults by 29 Brigade of 43rd Division and 4 Brigade of 2nd Canadian Division. Under a storm of fire, engineers laid bridges over the ditches, across which the Crocodiles passed to clear the enemy's forward positions, supported by smaller flame-throwing Wasps* which burnt the parachute troops out of the houses. The village was finally secured by the 4th Somerset Light Infantry who, one German soldier remembered, were 'very dirty but grinning with delight when we gave up'. Brigadier Essame ordered his staff to stand in respectful silence as the exhausted, grime-caked defenders of Xanten were marched past under guard. Essame later observed that this had attracted critical press comment, but he remained unconcerned, 'for the German garrison of Xanten were very gallant men'.

With the net closing around them, the remnants of First Parachute Army fought on. The promised OKW officer, resplendent in immaculate uniform, arrived at Schlemm's headquarters to assess the situation. Schlemm exacted vicarious revenge on the high command by suggesting that they take a short walk to the front line through the heavy fire which was rocking the walls of his command post. White-faced with terror, the staff officer hastily agreed that withdrawal across the Rhine

---

* The Wasp was a flame-throwing Bren-gun carrier with the flame projector in the gunner's compartment.

was the only option and swiftly returned whence he came. At 7am on 10 March the bridge at Wesel dropped into the Rhine. The battle for the West Wall in the north was over. Canadian First Army had paid a high price, suffering 15,734 casualties, the greater part of them British – 770 officers and 9,660 men to the Canadians' losses of 379 officers and 4,925 men. US Ninth's Army's losses were 7,300 men.

A week earlier, Winston Churchill had arrived at Montgomery's head-quarters to inspect the West Wall. Accompanied by Brooke, Montgomery, the American General Simpson and a convoy of press cars, Churchill motored off in a Rolls-Royce to inspect the military feature which had proved so tough a nut to crack. Their trip was enlivened by a surreal episode in which the Prime Minister's car was halted in order to take delivery of his dentures, brought up at speed in a jeep, which Churchill unconcernedly popped into his mouth before waving the driver on. At the West Wall, Churchill was at his most theatrical. Clad in the uniform of a colonel of the 4th Hussars, the regiment he had joined as an eighteen-year-old in February 1895, he walked purposefully towards a row of dragon's teeth, opened his fly, and invited his distinguished com-panions 'to urinate on the great West Wall of Germany'. Turning to the gaggle of photographers aiming their cameras, while he aimed a jet of urine at the concrete, Churchill shouted, 'This is one of the operations connected with this great war which must not be reproduced graphi-cally'. Brooke later recalled, 'I shall never forget the childish grin of inner satisfaction that spread all over his face as he looked down at the critical moment'.

On 7 March, Collins's US VII Corps of Hodges's First Army had reached the Rhine at Cologne, part of Bradley's Operation 'Lumberjack' by which he was bringing 12th Army Group up to the Rhine along the central sector of the Allied line. Here, too, the retreating Germans had destroyed all the bridges across the river. Forty-five miles to the south lay the town of Remagen, where beetling bluffs overlooked the Ludendorff railway bridge spanning the Rhine. At 12.56pm on 7 March the men of A Company, 27th Armoured Infantry Battalion, reached the top of a gorge on the west bank of the Rhine at Remagen to find themselves gazing in astonishment at an intact bridge over the river. Commanded by twenty-two-year-old Lieutenant Karl Timmermann, A Company, travelling in half-tracks supported by four M-26 Pershing tanks, was acting as 'point' for Task Force Engeman, an all-arms formation which was part of Brigadier-General William Hoge's Combat Command B of 9th Armoured Division. The Task Force's orders were to capture Remagen before turning south to link up with other elements of 9th Armoured on the River Ahr, which flows west from the Eifel Mountains. The Task Force's arrival at Remagen was one small part of US First Army's move up to the Rhine before making assault crossings to the north and south. There was no mention of the bridge at Remagen in its orders, partly because a crossing in this sector was not part of Bradley's plan and also because, after the disappointments of the last few days, no one expected it to be standing. Three days earlier the commander of 9th Armoured, Major-General John Leonard, had been told unofficially that if he seized the bridge, his name would 'go down in glory'. He had merely grunted in reply, convinced that the opportunity would not arise.

Timmermann and his men watched as German troops and vehicles, many of the latter horse-drawn, streamed over the bridge in a disorganized mass which even included a herd of cows being driven to the rear.

Lieutenant-Colonel Leonard Engeman, the commander of the Task Force, was quickly on the scene. At this point, his primary objective remained the seizure of Remagen. After making a swift reconnaissance, he decided not to risk his armour in a drive down the narrow, steep-sided road running below his vantage point into the town, a potential death trap. Instead, Timmermann's company was ordered to move down a wooded track to clear the outskirts of the town, after which the four Pershings, under the command of Lieutenant John Grimball, would join them. Timmermann's three platoons were soon skirmishing through the streets of Remagen, dodging from doorway to doorway, dispersing an enemy patrol and capturing the town's rail station. At 2.20pm they were joined by Grimball's tanks, which moved down to the towpath and began to lay down a suppressive fire across the bridge to prevent any sudden enemy movement. German troops could be glimpsed on the east bank of the river, sheltering in the tunnel into which the rail line ran at the base of a basalt cliff.

By 3pm Timmermann and his No.3 Platoon, led by Sergeant Joseph Delisio, had arrived at the town's cemetery, close to the two granite towers at the western end of the Ludendorff Bridge. The Americans had encountered little resistance. The defence of Remagen had not been one of the priorities of Field Marshal Model, the commander of German Army Group B, who considered the mountainous country east of the town unsuited to an armoured drive into Germany. Model's attention was divided between Bonn, twenty-five miles north of Remagen, where his intelligence staff anticipated an American assault crossing, and Koblenz to the south, which was threatened by Patton's Third Army. On 7 March the bridge at Remagen was defended by a rag-tag force consisting of a squad of engineers, sixty members of the Volkssturm, and some Luftwaffe anti-aircraft gunners, whose 20mm flak guns directed a desultory fire at the Americans on the other side of the river. The local commander, Captain Willi Bratge, had been authorized to prepare the bridge for demolition but his bridgemaster, a local man, could only scrape together 600 kilograms (1,300 pounds) of low-grade industrial explosive, which had been strapped to the girders of the central span. The commander of the engineer squad, Captain Karl Friesenhahn, had also used some of the explosive to mine the earth approach ramp to the bridge on the west bank, which he had had built to enable vehicles to drive up on the bridge and cross over on wooden planks laid over the rails.

Acompanying Bratge that day was Major Hans Scheller, the representative of Major-General Hitzfeld, commanding LXVII Corps in the Ahr valley and the senior officer responsible for the bridge at Remagen. Hitzfeld had ordered Scheller to keep the bridge open as long as possible as an escape route for his corps. While Scheller dithered over whether or not to blow the bridge, the American tanks appeared on the towpath. Twenty minutes later, with Friesenhahn agonizedly awaiting orders, Engeman grasped the nettle and issued a precise command to seize the bridge.

Timmermann and his men now faced the daunting prospect of taking an objective which at any moment might explode beneath their feet. Within two minutes their nervous deliberations were cut short by a big explosion as Friesenhahn detonated the charges on the approach ramp. When the smoke lifted, and it became clear that the bridge was still standing, Timmermann ordered his company to cross the bridge. As the men of No.1 Platoon, led by Sergeant Mike Chinchar, scrambled over the rubble-strewn crater in the ramp, there was a second explosion. The bridge rose in the air and then settled again. Scheller had finally ordered the main charges to be blown, but part of the electrical firing mechanism had failed. Under heavy fire from the tanks on the west bank and Task Force Engeman's assault guns and mortars above Remagen, one of Friesenhahn's engineers, Sergeant Faust, ran out to ignite the fuse in the manual firing box on the bridge with a flare pistol. Faust had just regained the safety of the tunnel when the charges went off, whirling huge fragments of debris into the Rhine, but succeeding only in twisting the central span and punching a gaping hole in the flooring. With machine-gun fire from the bridge's eastern towers and from a sunken barge to their right pinging and whining around them, Timmermann's men began to zig-zag their way over the bridge. The machine-guns in the towers were silenced, and the honour of being the first man to set foot on the east bank of the Rhine south of Holland fell to Sergeant Alex Drabik, a squad leader in No.3 Platoon. By 4.05pm some seventy-five men had passed safely across and were taking their first prisoners. Behind them engineers were frantically cutting cables and throwing undetonated charges into the river.

The exit to the tunnel was blocked and at about 4.30pm Bratge surrendered, Scheller having disappeared from the scene. Hoge was ordering reinforcements over the bridge and sending a report of his success up the chain of command with an urgent request for support.

Bradley was at SHAEF headquarters when the news broke, in the middle of an angry meeting with General H.R. 'Pinky' Bull, Eisenhower's Assistant Chief of Staff for Operations, who was attempting to relieve Bradley of four divisions to support 6th Army Group in the south. After Bradley had talked on the telephone to General Hodges, he turned triumphantly to Bull and declared, 'There goes your ball game, Pink. Courtney's [Hodges] gotten across the Rhine on a bridge'. Bull was unimpressed. There was nowhere to go from Remagen and, in any case, 'It just doesn't fit into the plan. Ike's heart is in your sector right now, but his mind is up north.'

The seizure of the bridge at Remagen presented Eisenhower with a dilemma. In addition to the northern crossing of the Rhine planned by Montgomery, SHAEF planners had also decided that Patton's Third Army should make a second crossing between Koblenz and Mainz. However, on 7 March Patton was still fighting his way towards the Rhine. An immediate thrust from Remagen would have been dangerously exposed while Patton and Montgomery were still unready to cross. At first Eisenhower restricted Bradley to the insertion of four divisions at Remagen, but within a few days the order was rescinded and by 22 March – the day before Montgomery crossed the Rhine at Wesel – the Allied 'hole card' in the south consisted of three corps.

When Hitler learned of the events at Remagen, he immediately ordered a counter-attack. But his decision to defend the west bank of the Rhine, and the northward diversion of forces to deal with the British and Canadians, had denuded defences on the east bank. It took two days for 11th Panzergrenadier Division to arrive on the scene, by which time Hodges had moved three divisions over the Rhine and was expanding his bridgehead by the hour. It was left to the Luftwaffe to put in a maximum effort. For nine days fighter-bombers attacked the Remagen bridge, and the three tactical bridges thrown across the Rhine by First Army's engineers, in an attempt to staunch the flow over the river. American air support was limited, as there were no suitable bases sufficiently close to the bridgehead to enable fighters to remain over Remagen for any length of time. The RAF threw in the Hawker Tempests of 122 Wing, fast air-superiority fighters with the range to reach Remagen from airfields in

Holland. For several days the Tempests swept down the narrow gorge at Remagen to counter Luftwaffe bombing and strafing raids. Leading the first of these missions was the French ace Pierre Clostermann:

Our eight Tempests flew up the Rhine, through Cologne, and reached Remagen, where we were greeted by virulent American ack-ack. The Yanks were in such a state of nerves that, even after we had made the usual recognition signals and they had been acknowledged, they continued to let off an occasional burst of Bofors at us. By the third salvo, which didn't miss me by much as I collected some shrapnel in the wing, I felt I didn't particularly want to go on giving these gentlemen target practice. I got my formation to do a 180° turn to make for home, when horrors! – we found ourselves face to face with an absolute armada of seven or eight Arado Ar234s,* escorted by thirty or so Me262s, diving down on that miserable bridge. At full throttle I fell in behind them. Just as I was opening fire on an Arado 234 at over a thousand yards' range, forty long-nosed Ta152s† emerged from the clouds on my left. To hell with it! I warned my formation over the radio and kept straight on. The speed shot up frighteningly – 420mph, 450, 475. I was hurtling down at an angle of about 50°; the seven tons of my plane, pulled by about 3,000hp, had terrific acceleration. The Arado levelled out gently, insensibly, following a trajectory which would bring it down to the level of the Rhine a few hundred yards short of the bridge. I was 800 yards behind, but didn't dare fire. At this speed I felt that firing my guns would certainly wreck my wings. Still behind my Hun, I flew into a frightful barrage of 40mm and heavy MG. I saw the two bombs drop from the Arado quite distinctly. One of them bounced over the bridge and the other hit the bridge road. I passed over the bridge, forty yards to the left, just as it exploded. My plane was whisked up like a wisp of straw and completely thrown off her balance. I instinctively closed the throttle and pulled the stick back. My Tempest shot up like a bullet to 10,000 feet and I found myself upside down right in the clouds, sweating with funk. A violent vibration – my engine cut out, and a shower of mud, oil and ironmongery fell on my face. I dropped like a plummet and then my plane went into a spin. A spin in a Tempest is the most dangerous thing on earth – after one turn, two turns, you get thrown about helplessly, you cannon into the walls of the cockpit in spite of the harness straps. In a complete flap, I

---

* Known as the Blitz, the Arado 234 was the world's first jet-engined bomber, with a top speed of about 460mph.
† An improved version of the Focke-Wulf FW190D piston-engined fighter. It could outrun most Allied fighters, but only about seventy were built.

wrenched the hood release; it came away in my hand. I tried to get up on my seat to bale out, but forgot to unstrap myself and succeeded only in giving myself a terrific bang on the head. When I came out of the cloud I was still in a spin – there was the ground less than 3,000 feet below. I pushed the stick right forward and opened the throttle wide. The engine coughed and suddenly fired again, practically jerking itself out of the fuselage. The spin turned into a spiral; I gently tested the elevators, which responded all right – the fields however were rushing towards my windshield. I levelled out at less than a hundred feet. A close shave. I raised my helmet and felt my hair soaked with sweat.

The Germans resorted to deperate measures at Remagen, trying to destroy the bridges with frogmen and even the V-2, the only time during the war that the rocket was used tactically. The town was bombarded by the Wehrmacht's biggest artillery piece, the 130-ton 'Mörser Karl', which broke down after firing only a few of its 4,400-pound shells. Long-range guns continued to pound the bridgehead, reducing Remagen to ruins and showering the bridges with splinters and cascades of water. On 11 March the rail bridge was closed while engineers attempted to repair its central span, but the weakened structure could not take the strain and at 3pm on 17 March, with a 'deep, sonorous, grinding noise', it collapsed into the river, killing twenty-eight servicemen.

The capture of the bridge at Remagen had struck a powerful psychological blow at German military and civilian morale. Until 7 March most Germans remained convinced that the Rhine was a natural barrier to the Allied advance. Now that those hopes had been dashed, the Führer's 'Flying Special Tribunal West' took its revenge. Scheller and three other officers were court-martialled and executed in the small hours of 13 March. Bratge and Friesenhahn were tried *in absentia*. Bratge was sentenced to death and Friesenhahn was acquitted. It mattered little, as both were prisoners of the Americans.

Another casualty was Rundstedt, who was sacked – for the last time – and replaced as Commander-in-Chief West by Field Marshal Albert Kesselring, the immensely able Commander-in-Chief South who had been conducting a defensive campaign of great resourcefulness in Italy. For the moment at least, Kesselring was undaunted by the task. He greeted his staff with the remark, 'Well gentlemen, I am the new V-3'.

Another military missile, intermittently unguided, was making spectacular progress in the southern sector of the Allied front. In the first week of March, Patton's Third Army had burst through the Eifel, cleared the north bank of the Moselle and, on 10 March, taken Koblenz. The bridges there had been blown, so Patton swung south-east across the

Moselle, turning the West Wall while Lieutenant-General Alexander Patch's US Seventh Army was still slogging through it between Saarbrücken and Karlsruhe, and isolating large numbers of German troops. Patton was now determined not only to elbow Hodges out of the limelight which had fallen on him after the capture of the bridge at Remagen, but also to upstage Montgomery, preparing to cross the Rhine at Wesel, with a demonstration of the 'rock soup' method on a grand scale. Patton, a thoroughgoing Anglophobe, wrote in in his diary: 'It is essential to get [US] First and Third Armies so deeply involved in their present plans that they cannot be moved north to play second fiddle to the British-instilled idea of attacking with 60 divisions in the Ruhr plain.'

In what became known as the Palatinate campaign, Patton had raced to the Rhine on a 100-mile front from Koblenz to Mannheim, killing 37,000 Germans and capturing another 87,000 on the way, cutting through a disintegrating front as only he knew how. Showing scant respect for SHAEF's precise orders, he had nevertheless attained Eisenhower's objective of bringing the entire length of the Allied line up to the Rhine, an obstacle Patton intended to take on the run. On 21 March he wrote in his diary: 'We have put on a great show but I think we will eclipse it when we get across the Rhine.'

On 22 March Patton joined hands with Patch's Seventh Army moving up from the south. The colossal traffic columns stretching back to the rear, including Patton's carefully husbanded bridging trains, reminded one truck driver of 'New York in the rush hour'. That night Patton crossed the Rhine, pinning the German Seventh Army* at Mainz while crossing at Oppenheim, twelve miles to the south, where he launched the assault boats he had been lugging around since the autumn of 1944 from a small harbour hidden from the east bank.

At about 10pm men of the 23rd Infantry Regiment paddled the hundred yards across the Rhine. The first Germans they encountered threw their weapons down and their hands up in panic. Resistance was sporadic and by dawn 5th Division had six battalions across the river. Triumphant, Patton telephoned Bradley on the morning of the 23rd, telling him that he had 'sneaked a division over last night. There are so few Krauts around that they don't know it yet. We'll keep it secret until we know how it goes.' Patton's press liaison officer at 12th Army Group, Lieutenant-Colonel Richard Stillman, was less reticent, announcing, 'Without benefit of aerial bombing, ground smoke, artillery preparations

---

* Seventh Army had just one corps, a collection of middle-aged men and depot troops loosely grouped into four divisions with little or no armoured support.

and airborne assistance, the Third Army at 22.00, Thursday evening, 22 March, crossed the Rhine.'

Opposite Wesel, Montgomery remained unmoved by the dramatic events to the south. The commander of 21st Army Group was not about to forgo the benefits of aerial bombardment and artillery preparation. Monty was not in a mood to be hurried. The date had been fixed for his Rhine crossing, codenamed 'Plunder', and he was not prepared to bring it forward. Simpson's US Ninth Army, which was to support his right flank in Plunder, had reached the Rhine near Düsseldorf three weeks earlier, on 3 March, but Montgomery had remained deaf to Simpson's pleas to be allowed to cross there and then. Monty's grand design was not going to be derailed by a subordinate's desire to demonstrate his own technical expertise in the hazardous business of opposed river crossings.

Plunder had been planned with all of Montgomery's meticulous attention to detail and remorseless accumulation of overwhelming force. He later wrote that he was determined that 'we should deliver our assault, and develop our subsequent operations, with the maximum weight and impetus at our disposal'. By 22 March British Second Army's* roadheads had received 60,000 tons of ammunition and 30,000 tons of engineering stores alone. In the week before the launch of Plunder, movements in Second Army's sector involved over 600 tanks, 4,000 tank transporters and 32,000 wheeled vehicles. The preparations for the crossings absorbed the efforts of nearly 60,000 British and American engineers, hidden during the final phase by a smoke screen fifty miles long.

Three corps made up the assault force: XXX Corps in the north, opposite the town of Rees; XII Corps in the centre, opposite Wesel; and US XVI Corps in the south in the Dinslaken sector. The bridgehead at Wesel was to be secured and expanded eastward by a massive airborne operation, codenamed 'Varsity', mounted by US General Matthew B. Ridgway's XVIII Airborne Corps, consisting of British 6th and US 17th Airborne Divisions. Their task was to seize the Diersfordter Wald, a thick forest on ground rising 65 feet above the level of the Rhine north-east of Wesel. Both divisions were to be landed complete in one airlift lasting three hours. To ensure that the lightly armed airborne troops would not be isolated for too long without armoured support, the link-up with ground units was to be accomplished on the first day of the operation.

While Montgomery imposed himself on the complexities of Plunder, Eisenhower was once again shifting his position on the priority the

---

* While the Battle of the Rhineland was being fought by First Canadian Army, Second Army was holding a quiet sector of the line along the Meuse, enabling its headquarters to concentrate on planning the Rhine crossing.

British commander should be accorded. The Supreme Commander had recently met Bradley in the seclusion of a villa at Cannes, on the French Riviera. Eisenhower had been increasing the strength of 12th Army Group's thrust, but as a secondary attack to Plunder in the north. Now he decided that Bradley should launch a major drive as an alternative in case Montgomery got bogged down. On 21 March, two days before Montgomery's crossing, Bradley was directed to 'establish a firm bridge-head over the Rhine in the Frankfurt area and make an "advance in strength" towards Kassel', where a junction would be made between Hodges's forces moving south from Remagen and Patton's driving north from Frankfurt. Eisenhower pointedly informed General Marshall that this would give him a force south of the Ruhr at least equal in strength to 21st Army Group. Bradley, secure in the knowledge that he would lose none of his divisions to Montgomery, ordered Patton to take the Rhine on the run. Eisenhower's decision to establish a bridgehead in the Frankfurt area had sounded the death knell of Montgomery's plans to make a triumphal entry into Berlin.

On 23 March, a day of blue skies and bright sunshine, Montgomery told the men under his command:

> The enemy probably thinks that he is safe behind this great river obstacle. We all agree that it is a great obstacle, but we will show the enemy that he is far from safe behind it. This great Allied fighting machine, composed of integrated land and air forces, will deal with the problem in no uncertain manner. And having crossed the Rhine, we will crack about in the plains of northern Germany, chasing the enemy from pillar to post.

The Rhine at Wesel is about 500 yards wide, with a broad flood plain on either bank. On the eastern bank the Germans had prepared an elab-orate trench system, protected by barbed-wire entanglements and mine-fields. The houses and hamlets in the hinterland contained numerous anti-tank and machine-gun emplacements. Once again 21st Army Group was facing First Parachute Army, consisting of II Parachute Corps, LXXXVI Corps and LXIII Corps, which were deployed along the river with XLVII Panzer Corps held in reserve. The sector in which British XII Corps was to make the main assault was held by a parachute division (7th) and an infantry division (84th). The combined strength of these two German divisions was fewer than 1,500 men, many of them raw replacements. In contrast, XII Corps had under command one armoured division, two armoured brigades, three infantry divisions, and an infantry and a com-mando brigade. 84th Division could muster only ten field guns and two anti-tank guns. The paratroopers were slightly better off, with twenty-five field guns, four anti-tank guns and four 88mm guns. In all, the Germans had thirty-five field guns and a few mortars to pit against XII Corps's artillery complement of 670 guns used in a ground role, supplemented by a divisional complement of 1,500 mortars. No contest.

At 3.30pm on 23 March, Montgomery gave the order for the launching of Plunder. At 9pm, as the artillery preparation reached a climax, the assault waves of four battalions of 51st (Highland) Division set off across the Rhine opposite Rees. They reached the east bank seven minutes later, meeting little initial resistance until they collided with German paratroopers, who put up a stiff fight. In XII Corps's sector, at 10pm 1 Commando Brigade crossed the river about two miles west of Wesel. Thirty minutes later they formed up outside the town while 200 Lancasters of Bomber Command flew in to plaster it with 1,000 tons of high-explosive, only 1,500 yards from the leading British troops. One of these, Major P.I. Bartholomew of No.6 Commando, wrote in his diary that it seemed as if 'more than mortal powers had been unleashed' as men pressing themselves to the ground were lifted bodily into the air by the impact of the bombs. To an engineer on the western bank the bombing was

> like fireworks. First a rain of golden sparks as the leading aircraft dropped their markers right over an enormous fire that already lit the town like a beacon. Then we heard the main force. It was a terrific sight. All colours of sparks flying everywhere, red, green and yellow and the fantastic commotion as the bombs went down. On our side of the river the ground shook and we could see waves of light shooting up into the smoke. It was like stoking a fire, the dull glow burst into flames and it was like daylight.

At 2am it was 15th (Scottish) Division's turn to cross the river in XII Corps's sector. Opposition was light, for the Germans dug in behind the dykes which controlled the course of the Rhine had been swept by fire from Bofors and machine-guns skilfully sited on a bend in the river by the commander of 44 (Lowland) Brigade, Brigadier Cumming-Bruce, causing carnage in the enemy weapon pits. As the Buffaloes carried 15th Division over the Rhine, the ebullient BBC war correspondent Wynford Vaughan-Thomas described the scene:

> The Buffalo – the driver in charge – a man of the Royal Tank Regiment is receiving the signal – the captain's waving to him and this is where we move. He feels for the edge of the water – we're

guided up right to the very edge by a long line of small green lights
that have been laid to take us to the jumping-off ground. We've
reached the water's edge and we see the Rhine, not running, as we
thought it would be, bright under the moon, but running red;
because right on the opposite side of the village every single house
and haystack you can see is burning, beaten down by the fury of
our barrage. We can't tell whether there's anything coming at our
boys; we hope that all the stuff we hear is going into Germany, the
German positions; but in this thunder of guns and the tracers that
beat around us, it's impossible to tell which way things are coming. . . . We're in – the Buffalo tips its nose down the bank and now
it's opening up full power. Three minutes to go and we're racing
across and side by side with us go racing the other Buffaloes – racing for that hell on the other side. The searchlights cast a white
beam, they go right across the river on one side of us, but ahead
of us is only red water. The current's carrying us down and we're
putting up our nose against it . . . and the tracer is making a path
on either side of us. . . . The Buffalo springs and points its nose
upstream now – we're tussling, fighting the current to get over. . . .
Now the tracer is quiet, drowned by the revving of our engines. . . .
A signal flashes from the shore – the first Buffaloes are off. We've
reached the other side, climbing up into the skirl of the pipes – the
men of Scotland who've piped their men into battle across the
Rhine . . . there was an immense feeling of relief and excitement.
. . . The Commanding Officer gave the signal, the piper lifted his
pipes to his lips, and he blew, and only an agonized wailing came
from his instrument. Again he tried, and again the wail. If ever a
man was near to tears it was our piper. His great moment and now,
as he cried in despair: 'Ma pipes, man, they'll no play.' That was all
right with us because the Germans were not playing either. They
may have been dazzled by the weight of our barrage, they may
have been preparing their resistance farther back; we couldn't tell
in the tiny section of the fighting which surrounded us. All we
knew, as we lowered the ramp and jumped out on the firelit river
meadow, was that we were on the German side of the river at last;
and that, for the enemy, is the fatal thing.

At the same time, in US Ninth Army's sector, 30th Division crossed the
Rhine, followed an hour later by 75th Division. Everything was going to
plan. There was fierce fighting in Wesel, but follow-up formations were
streaming over the Rhine as the ferries swung into action. In England,
meanwhile, the airborne formations were readying themselves. At
4.45am, while the leading battalions of 15th Division were pushing out of
their bridgehead opposite the village of Diesfordter, the men of 1st

Canadian Parachute Battalion were clambering aboard the trucks which would take them to the RAF airfield at Chipping Ongar. By 7.30am the thirty-five American Douglas C-47 transports carrying the 600 Canadians had taken off to join the great air armada which was converging on the airspace over the suburbs of Brussels before heading for the Rhine: 22,000 airborne troops flying in 1,696 transport aircraft and 1,348 gliders, the largest single day's airborne operation of the war.

Over the bridgehead an air umbrella was formed by 900 Allied fighters, while deeper into Germany fighter formations swept the sky clear of the Luftwaffe. At 10am, in sunshine obscured by the great clouds of dust raised by another massive bombardment, the first airborne wave flew in. Churchill and Eisenhower watched the awesome display of Allied air power from a hilltop on the western bank. Churchill turned to the Supreme Commander and said, 'My dear General, the German is whipped. We've got him. He is all through.'

Drawing on the lessons of Arnhem, the plan was to land the airborne troops in tight concentrations to the north and east of the Diesfordter Wald. They would immediately attack designated objectives, including the village of Hamminkeln and the bridges east of the River Issel, which were well within range of supporting artillery fire from the west bank of the river.

Churchill's excited assessment of the Germans' powers of resistance was not immediately evident to the men of XVIII Airborne Corps. The war diary of 1st Canadian Battalion tersely noted that 'flak was fairly heavy over the dropping zone and several aircraft were seen to go down in flames'. The intensity of the anti-aircraft fire forced the transports to cross the dropping zone at speed, scattering units and leaving many men dangling from trees, where they were cut down by German machine-gun fire. Sergeant Derek Glaister of 7th Battalion, Parachute Regiment, had a short battle:

> When we got to the Rhine, it was murder, because Jerry knew we were coming; every farmhouse was occupied by the Germans. They put a lot of smoke down, so instead of coming down to 400 feet, which is the lowest height you can drop from, we had to go up to 1,000 feet. We were also travelling quite fast. I was No.20, last man out, so you can imagine how far off target I was. Miles out. I and ten others came down near a farmhouse which had an 88mm gun just outside it. Just before my feet touched the ground a bullet smashed through my left elbow, so I lay on my stomach and pretended to be dead. I saw nine of the others come down, some into trees. The Germans shot them as they hung there helpless – it was a sickening sight. I was in big trouble: I am left-handed and my left

arm was useless. But when five Germans came towards me I got
hold of my Sten gun in my right hand, and as they got close I fired
and I think I killed them all. Then I made for the farmhouse hoping to get some help, but as I peered round a corner I saw German
rifles poking out of every window. I tried to give myself some cover
by throwing a smoke bomb, but just as I was making for the nearest ditch a German SS officer came up and shot me in the back
from ten yards away with a Luger pistol. Of course I spun round
and fell down, and this officer grabbed my left arm and shoved it
through the straps of my webbing, then he took the water bottle,
flung it in the ditch and looted whatever he could. I was worried
he'd finish me off with my knife, but I had the presence of mind to
lie on it and when he'd gone I got hold of it and threw it in the
ditch. I lay there feeling pretty rough – my left arm was like a great
black pudding by then, all swollen up – and watched those poor
fellows swinging in the trees. Then one of the gliders came over,
but the 88mm cracked it open like an egg and the jeep, gun, blokes
all fell out. Point-blank range – they couldn't miss at fifty feet.

The dropping zones were soon a maelstrom of confused fighting as the
airborne forces descended directly on to positions held by German
troops who had anticipated that such an attack would be launched
before rather than after the Rhine crossings. Troop-carrying Horsa gliders
and the larger Hamilcar glider transports of 6 Airlanding Brigade continued to swoop across the battlefield, careering crazily over the landscape
before coming to rest at drunken angles while men burst out and went
straight into action. Major Todd Sweeney was with the 2nd Battalion,
Oxford and Buckinghamshire Light Infantry, tasked with seizing a bridge
over the Issel, to the east of the forest. They received a warm reception:

> ... the Airlanding Brigade, the artillery and divisional troops,
> which were the third lot to come over, faced an enemy that was by
> this time prepared for them. The German anti-aircraft gunners had
> a marvellous target – big slow-moving gliders going around look-
> ing for their objectives. It didn't matter too much exactly where I
> landed because mine was a headquarters glider. So we went
> zooming down, twisting and turning, but landed all right. We
> opened the door at the front, put the ramps down, got the jeep out
> and then came under the most tremendous fire from a whole lot
> of steel helmets which we could see on the side of a field by a half-
> made-up road. I realized that we had ended up on the wrong side
> of the River Issel which we were supposed to be defending – I was
> between the autobahn and the river with a jeep and a trailer and
> five men and nothing else. I said, 'Forget about the jeep and the

trailer. Take the radio and we'll get across the river.' We made it across and I got the men down into firing positions. Meanwhile the gliders were still coming in all over the place. The whole battalion had flown in together, and that included gliders carrying jeeps full of mortar bombs and petrol. If the jeep and the trailer were hit and set alight the glider became a flying bomb; a lot of them just blew up.

By the early afternoon of 24 March airborne troops were beginning to link up with the ground forces. The 15th (Scottish) Division had secured its bridgehead on the eastern bank, and the carrier platoon of 8th Battalion, Royal Scots, was sent to make contact with 6th Airborne. Sent forward with a patrol, one Canadian paratrooper described the meeting:

We heard the rattle of an armoured vehicle and were prepared for German tanks, but as we cautiously crept forward through the scrubby undergrowth a platoon of Germans suddenly ran towards us. I was towards the rear of the group but the lead troops opened fire. Only minutes after they began cheering, and pushing between them I saw Bren-gun carriers trundling along a track towards us. The sense of relief was overwhelming and certainly I, at least, felt intense relief that we weren't going to be isolated as had been the troops at Arnhem.

In Operation Varsity, 6th Airborne Division had lost 347 men killed and 731 wounded, while US 17th Airborne had lost 359 killed with another 522 wounded. Thirty-five transport aircraft had been destroyed by anti-aircraft fire. Although casualties had been higher than anticipated, the airborne assault had been a success. General Ridgway summed it up: 'The airborne drop in depth destroyed enemy gun and rear defensive positions in one day – positions it might have taken many days to reduce by ground attack. The impact of the airborne divisions at one blow shattered hostile defence and permitted the prompt link-up with ground troops.'

The last German troops were driven out of Wesel on 25 March. By the 28th the bridgehead had been expanded to a depth of twenty miles and a width of thirty-five. That day 17th Airborne Division had driven up the valley of the River Lippe, and on the morning of the 29th they were thirty-five miles beyond the Rhine. The Battle of the Rhine was over and the way to the Elbe lay open. The entire west bank of the Rhine was in Allied hands and three sizeable bridgeheads had been established on its eastern bank. The 21st Army Group was ready to advance on Berlin across the north German plain.

The last great concentration of German troops in the west was Model's Army Group B in the Ruhr valley, the site of Germany's most important coalfield, and the home of the Krupp armaments factories and the Thyssen steelworks. The region's industrial importance had already been much reduced by Allied bombing. By the end of March, Bomber Command and the USAAF had systematically sealed off the Ruhr from the rest of Germany, cutting nearly all the communications running eastward back into the Reich. On the morning of 1 April units of US First and Ninth Armies had met at Lippstadt, completing the encirclement of 320,000 troops. Millions of civilians were trapped with them. They were in a pitiful state. Allied bombing and shell fire had brought public transport to a halt and cut off electricity and gas. Food had almost run out and water could be obtained only from communal taps. Most of the civilian population spent their days huddled in candlelit cellars, venturing out into the ruined streets only when forced to by hunger and thirst.

Now Chief of Staff of Fifth Panzer Army, Major-General Mellenthin was on hand to witness another military disaster, the death throes of Army Group B:

> The greater part of Army Group B was now pent up between the Ruhr and the Sieg, and the circumstances could not have been more depressing. The fog and cold of winter still hung over the land, and the gaunt and broken cities of the Ruhr formed a fitting background to the last act of this tragedy. The great heaps of coal and slag, the shattered buildings, the twisted railway tracks, the ruined bridges, all made their contribution to the gloomy scene. I have seen many battlefields, but none so strange as the great industrial complex of the Ruhr during the final dissolution of Army Group B.

The Army Group's commander, Field Marshal Walther Model, was a tough customer, famously foul-mouthed, and never without a monocle. As Hitler's confidence in the older generation of generals had fallen, Model's star had risen and he had become the Führer's favourite fireman. Now he was in a position which was not amenable to even his harsh skills. Not only was he encirled and rapidly running out of food, fuel and ammunition, but he also had to grapple with the implications of Hitler's 'scorched earth' directive of 19 March to destroy all communications, installations, factories and supplies in the path of the enemy. Hitler had told his Armaments Minister, Albert Speer, 'If the war is to be lost, the nation also will perish'. Before the Allied encirclement, Speer had toured the region, mobilizing his technocrats to defy the order. Model had also played his part. According to Mellenthin:

> Model never digressed from the strict path of military discipline, but as a true servant of Germany he blunted the edge of senseless commands, and sought to minimize unnecessary destruction. . . . Model limited himself to purely military demolitions. The Field Marshal was determined to preserve; no longer did he fight stubbornly for every building and he disregarded the orders issued by the Führer in a last frenzy of destructive mania.

In some towns the Germans surrendered without a fight. In the small town of Brackwede, south of Bielefeld, the Bürgermeister (mayor) ordered the tank barricades to be removed so that the Americans could drive straight through. The day before they arrived he was arrested and shot on the orders of the local Nazi Party chief. But Brackwede was taken without any serious fighting. The defences around the town – two tanks, one of which could not be moved – were abandoned. Local defence units slipped back into civilian clothes. The Americans had a tougher time at Bielefeld, whose defenders held out for the best part of the afternoon before the white flag of surrender was hoisted, the signal for Bielefeld's citizens to plunder the local military supply depots. Elsewhere the Americans met stiffer resistance. On 11 April, in the eastern suburbs of Cologne, young paratroopers of 3rd Parachute Division destroyed thirty Shermans of 13th Armoured Division with their 88mm guns.

Model consulted Mellenthin about whether he should negotiate with the enemy. Mellenthin later wrote:

> We both rejected it on military grounds. After all Field Marshal Model knew no more about the general situation than the simplest company commander in his army group. His ignorance sprang from the 'Führer Command No.1' of 13 January 1940, which laid down that 'no officer of authority must know more than is absolutely necessary for the execution of his particular task.' Model did not know whether political negotiations were going on, and he was fully sensible of the argument that the Western armies must keep on fighting to the last in order to protect the rear of our comrades in the East, who were involved in a desperate struggle to cover the escape of millions of German women and children, then fleeing from the Russian hordes.

Model was caught on the horns of a dilemma. One officer close to him has suggested that the Field Marshal was 'wrestling with himself to find a solution to some inner conflict . . . as a highly qualified officer he saw the hopelessness of further resistance, but on the other hand, he was bound in duty and honour to his superiors and subordinates.'

On 15 April, General Ridgway, whose XVIII Airborne Corps was now fighting as infantry in the pocket, wrote to Model, calling on him to surrender:

> In the light of a soldier's honour, for the reputation of the German officer corps, for the sake of your nation's future, lay down your arms at once. The German lives you will save are surely needed to restore your people to their proper place in society. The German cities you will preserve are irreplaceable necessities for your people's welfare.

Model sent his chief of staff to Ridgway's command post to reject the latter's offer. The chief of staff, a more flexible man than his commander, did not return, choosing instead to become a prisoner of war. Ridgway washed his hands of Model: 'That was that. I could do no more. From now on the blood was on Model's head.'

By now the Ruhr pocket had been sliced into several rapidly shrinking segments. Mass surrenders had begun. The remnants of elite formations, among them Panzer Lehr and 116th Panzer Divisions, were being herded into the POW cages. When the city of Wuppertal surrendered, its 16,000-strong garrison was marched into captivity by two American military policemen. Hard on the heels of the combat troops came 12th Army Group's special investigation unit, T Force, scooping up all the scientists, industrialists and leading Nazis who had been targeted by Allied intelligence, among them Alfried Krupp von Bohlen, the man in charge of the Krupp armaments empire, and Franz von Papen, the last Nazi ambassador to Turkey.

On 15 April, Model issued orders that all the young and old men in his command should be discharged and should immediately return home as civilians. On the 17th, the day the order came into effect, US 8th Infantry Division, which had fought its way across the pocket from north to south, took no fewer than 50,192 prisoners. Twenty-nine German generals and a lonely admiral had given themselves up. From the air, the huge, hastily erected POW compounds looked as if they held an army of ants. The final count was 317,000 prisoners taken at the cost of 10,000 Americans killed, wounded and missing.

Model remained at large, wandering through a lunar landscape protected by a few loyal staff officers. Surrender was unthinkable. As he told one of his companions, 'I simply cannot do it. The Russians have branded me a war criminal, and the Americans would be sure to turn me over to them.' On the morning of 21 April, Field Marshal Walther Model, accompanied by a single officer, walked into a wood somewhere near the smouldering ruins of Duisburg, and shot himself.

CHAPTER 8

The Race to Berlin

'You will see that in none of this do I mention Berlin. So far as I am concerned the place has become nothing but a geographical location. I have never been interested in these. My purpose is to destroy the enemy.'

Signal from General Eisenhower to Field Marshal Montgomery, 30 March 1945

ON 4 FEBRUARY 1945, Ursula von Kardorff wrote in her diary:

I am no longer the only one who wants to leave [Berlin]. No one can bear to be alone any more. People are herding together like deer in a storm. Everyone talks of forged passports, a *laissez-passer*, a bogus duty trip, foreign workers' identity cards and certificates of one kind or another. Everyone has a different plan, each more idiotic than the last. But our plans, bubbles though they are, do at least save us from lethargy. The new offices at Tempelhof are a madhouse. It takes two or three hours just to reach them. We all sit in an enormous room with glass walls, like parrots in the Zoo. We are robots, performing functions that everybody knows to be pointless. For example, we have to get out broadsheets every day filled with horror stories about the Russians and with asinine appeals and exhortations. 'Hold fast', because Goebbels says that were are on the brink of victory. 'We shall win because we must win' is typical of the convincing logic. Today one of the men in the office who is terribly stiff, always wears a tiepin with the old Imperial crown and never lets himself go, stood in the door, livid with rage, shouting 'Even the bloody food is a load of shit!' I couldn't help laughing.

In another part of Berlin Hans-Georg von Studnitz noted: 'The most desired possession is a car with petrol. Unlimited supplies of coffee, spirits are being offered on the black market in exchange for a private car and fuel . . . the newspapers now appear as single sheets with abbreviated headlines and subtitles.' On 22 February Studnitz's diary returned to the subject of the black market:

> While the troops go short of fuel, the petrol black market in Berlin is doing a roaring trade. Thousands of private cars are still cruising about. A litre of 'black' petrol costs forty marks or twenty cigarettes. Twenty litres cost a pound of coffee or a kilo of butter. Tyres can be bought for two or three thousand marks. Small trailers are being offered at twenty thousand marks each, and even an old car cannot be had for less than fifteen or twenty thousand. There is also a brisk trade in false number plates and diplomatic CD plates. A complete set of false papers, consisting of a travel permit, a military pass, an employment card and a Home Guard Z-card costs eighty thousand marks. Recently a soldier was arrested while carrying a suitcase filled with bogus official rubber stamps. They were better cut than the official originals, and the SS department which arrested the man immediately confiscated them for their own use.

While black marketeers turned a tidy profit, each day brought a sharp twist to the downward spiral which Germany was describing. On 1 March Josef Goebbels's diary addressed the problem of food shortages:

> We are already being forced to make extraordinarily severe reductions in the food ration and shall soon be compelled to make even more. The loss of the eastern territories is now making itself most painfully felt. Backe [Berlin's garrison commander] is in no position to draw up even a conservative ration scale since he does not know what is available at the moment or what will be available in the future. We shall very soon be forced to reduce by 25–50 per cent the ration of the most important items, fat and bread. As a result they will fall below the tolerable minimum subsistence level. In some cases the reductions must be made straight away, in others we can allow ourselves until 9 April. One can imagine what the effect on the public will be. Even if we reconquer our eastern territories, we shall not avoid severe shortages. To all our people's miseries hunger will now be added. But, as we know, in this struggle there is nothing for it but to try to hold out bravely.

Goebbels now combined the posts of Gauleiter of Berlin,

Plenipotentiary for Total War, and Minister for Public Enlightenment and Propaganda. In the last capacity he had lost none of his skills, seeming to draw energy from the mounting destruction around him. On 30 January, after Hitler's last radio broadcast to the German people, Goebbels attended the première of his and Nazi Germany's most extravagant wartime propaganda film. Veit Harlan's *Kolberg*, over two years in the making and with a cast of thousands who might have been better employed in the war effort, told the story of the small East Pomeranian port which, in 1807, had withstood a three-month siege by the French. *Kolberg* had an undeniably contemporary relevance. As one of Hitler's staff officers observed, 'The film matches current history so well that its originators – and work began on the film in 1942 – must have had clairvoyant powers.'

Hitler, who in happier times had been an avid watcher of films, did not see *Kolberg*, but it was screened throughout his rapidly shrinking empire and flown into his beleaguered 'fortresses' from the Atlantic coast to Silesia to stiffen the morale of their garrisons. At the beginning of March Kolberg itself was to join the list of cities under siege, islands of resistance in a Soviet sea whose survival had contributed to the slowing down of the Vistula-Oder operation. On the Baltic coast at the base of the Samland peninsula, the city of Königsberg, ancient seat of Prussian kings and ringed by three lines of defence incorporating fifteen major forts, was on the point of being cut off by Bagramyan's First Baltic Front and Chernyakhovsky's Third Belorussian Front. On Zhukov's front the Polish city of Poznan, located at the junction of six railways and seven roads, and defended by an inner citadel and eight massive forts, had been bypassed in January and was now besieged by four divisions of Eighth Guards Army and two divisions of Sixty-Ninth Army.

A hundred miles to the south, on the banks of the Oder, lay the city of Breslau, the capital of Lower Silesia. The city was in the sector of German Army Group A (soon to be redesignated Army Group Centre*) covering Saxony, Sudetenland and Czechoslovakia and commanded by Field Marshal Ferdinand Schörner, whose National Socialist style of leadership was succinctly described by Josef Goebbels:

> Schörner is decidedly a personality as a commander. The details
> he gave me about the methods he uses to raise morale were first-

---

* On 26 January Hitler reorganized and redesignated his army groups. The surrounded Army Group North became Army Group Kurland; Army Group Centre, also cut off from the Reich, became the new Army Group North; Army Group A became Army Group Centre.

rate and demonstrate not only his talents as a commander in the field but also his superb political insight. He is using quite novel modern methods. He is no chairborne map general; most of the days he spends with the fighting troops, with whom he is on terms of confidence, though he is very strict. In particular he has taken a grip on the so-called 'professional stragglers', by which he means men who continually manage to absent themselves in critical situations and vanish to the rear on some pretext or other. His procedure with such types is fairly brutal; he hangs them on the nearest tree with a placard announcing 'I am a deserter and have declined to defend German women and children'. The deterrent effect on other deserters and men who might have it in mind to follow them is obviously considerable.

Breslau lay directly in the path of a renewed offensive launched on 8 February by Konev from his bridgeheads on the Oder at Steinau and Ohlau, with the aim of clearing Silesia west of the Oder. By closing up on the line of the River Neisse in Brandenburg, Konev would bring himself up alongside Zhukov in readiness for the assault on Berlin. Breslau, situated between Konev's bridgeheads, was cut off on 15 February when Sixth Army, striking south-east from Steinau, joined hands with Fifth Guards Army, driving north-west from Ohlau. The encirclement was completed when Third Guards Tank Army positioned itself to the west of the city in a small-scale repeat of its dash behind the flank and rear of the Upper Silesian industrial region. Trapped inside Breslau were 35,000 regular German troops, 15,000 Volkssturm and 80,000 civilians. According to Konev,

> the whole area around the encirclement was seething. The encircled garrison units rushed hither and thither in search of an exit. Sometimes they fought desperately, but more commonly surrendered. An enormous number of cars and horse-drawn carriages packed with people jammed the roads south-west of Breslau; having lost all hope of finding even the smallest gap, they were now reeling back to the city.

By the end of February, Konev's front had reached a sixty-mile stretch of the Neisse running south from its junction with the Oder, about sixty miles south-east of Berlin. In his rear, Breslau, which was a 'fortress' in name only with none of the forts and citadels which characterized the defences of Poznan and Königsberg, was isolated and vainly awaiting relief by Schörner's Army Group Centre.

While Konev was clearing Silesia, Guderian was planning to use Army

Group Vistula, covering the approaches to north Germany, in a counter-stroke against Zhukov's exposed flanks. Plagued by a weak heart and high blood pressure, he summoned up the energy for another painful confrontation with the Führer. Guderian's intention was to slice off the nose of the huge snowplough-shaped salient which Zhukov had driven into eastern Germany as far as Küstrin, by launching a pincer attack executed in the north by Army Group Vistula and in the south by Army Group Centre. Its jaws would close behind Zhukov's spearheads in the area of Küstrin. This bold stroke would require the withdrawal of the German formations in the Balkans, Italy, Norway and the Kurland peninsula. Hitler's refusal to sanction a single evacuation produced another explosive confrontation between the Führer and the OKH Chief of Staff. Guderian insisted that he was 'acting solely in Germany's interests', which produced another violent spasm from Hitler:

> Trembling all down the left side of his body, he jumped to his feet at this and shouted, 'How dare you speak to me like that? Don't you think I'm fighting for Germany? My life has been one long struggle for Germany.' And he proceeded to treat me to an outburst of unusual frenzy until Göring finally took me by the arm and led me into another room, where we soothed our nerves by drinking a cup of coffee together.

When Guderian rejoined the conference and returned to the subject of the evacuation of the Kurland peninsula, Hitler 'stood in front of me shaking his fists, so that my good Chief of Staff, Thomale, felt constrained to seize me by the skirt of my uniform jacket and pull me backwards lest I be the victim of a physical assault.'

Guderian's plan for a double envelopment was abandoned for an altogether more modest blow aimed at Zhukov's right flank from the Arnswald area with the object of defeating the Russians north of the River Warthe, and of retaining Pomerania and links with West Prussia. Guderian realized that time was of the essence, but was well aware that he could expect little help from the inert commander of Army Group Vistula, Heinrich Himmler, who was fearful of committing himself to an operation which would expose his military incompetence. Guderian attempted to give himself some room for manoeuvre by suggesting, at a Führer conference on 13 February, that his personal assistant at OKH, General Walther Wenck, be attached to Himmler's headquarters and placed in charge of the attack. Hitler, incensed by the implication that Himmler was a military duffer, worked himself up into another well-rehearsed rage. Guderian recalled:

And so it went on for two hours. His fists raised, his cheeks flushed with rage, his whole body trembling, the man stood there before me beside himself with rage and fury and having lost all self-control. . . . He was almost screaming, his eyes seemed about to pop out of his head and the veins stood out on his temples. . . . When Hitler turned his back on me and marched towards the fireplace, I glanced at Lenbach's portrait of Bismarck that hung above the mantel. The eyes of that mighty statesman, the Iron Chancellor, seemed to be grimly watching the performance taking place beneath him. From the dimly lit end of the conference hall, a glint of steel from his cuirassier's helmet seemed to reach across to me, and his expression was of one who asks, 'What are you doing with my country?'

Quite suddenly, Hitler's demon left him and, turning to Himmler, he told him that Wenck would arrive at his headquarters that night to take charge of the attack. Sitting down, Hitler called Guderian over: 'Now please continue with the conference. The General Staff has won a battle this day.' Guderian later reflected, 'This was the last battle I was to win, and it came too late'.

Codenamed *Sonnenwende* (Solstice), the attack, launched by Third Panzer Army, made a small dent in Zhukov's front in the sector held by Second Guards Tank and Sixty-First Armies, but ground to a halt on 17 February when Wenck, driving himself back to the front after a conference with Hitler in Berlin, fell asleep at the wheel and crashed into the parapet of a bridge. The badly injured Wenck was replaced by General Hans Krebs, a staff officer with access to Hitler's inner circle, but who lacked the experience or independence of mind to retain the initiative. Although by 19 February Sonnenwende had fizzled out, it nevertheless had a disproportionate effect on the Soviet high command, confirming its growing fears about the weakness of Zhukov's right flank. Zhukov was turned away from Berlin and instructed to clear East Pomerania.

The result was the destruction of Army Group Vistula. Rokossovsky started the ball rolling on 24 February while Zhukov was still reshuffling the forces on his right wing. Zhukov went on to the offensive a week later with a formidable grouping comprising Second Guards Tank, First Guards Tank and Third Shock Armies, driving north to the Baltic, fanning out across East Pomerania and slicing Army Group Vistula into a succession of isolated fragments. On 4 March First Guards Tank Army reached the Baltic at Kolberg, on the boundary between First and Second Belorussian Fronts, cutting off the German Second Army to the east and forcing it to fall back on the fortresses of Gdynia and Danzig. Hitler immediately declared Kolberg, which was packed with refugees, another 'fortress'.

While Rokossovsky turned east to deal with Gdynia and Danzig, four divisions of First Polish Army and a Russian regiment of self-propelled artillery prepared to break into Kolberg. Defending the small port was a motley garrison of Volkssturm battalions and stranded Luftwaffe and naval units, about 2,300 combatants in all, heavily outnumbered by the 50,000 refugees who had sought shelter there. The only artillery available to the town's commander, Colonel Fritz Fullriede, were four broken-down tanks which had to be hauled around by trucks. Their guns were supplemented by those of two German destroyers standing offshore waiting to ferry off refugees.

The German surface fleet had long been in eclipse, but in the Baltic it had redeemed itself. From 11 March the two destroyers and a torpedo boat operated a shuttle service to the port of Swinemunde, in the Stettiner Haff, arriving off Kolberg to bombard its besiegers before taking on board refugees brought out to them by smaller craft, and then returning to Swinemunde to offload the refugees and take on more ammunition. On its first run one of the destroyers, *Z-34*, carrying 920 refugees and wounded soldiers, arrived at Swinemunde as the air-raid sirens were warning of the approach of a large force of American heavy bombers. Captain Hetz immediately cast off and headed for the open sea. One eyewitness recalled: 'There was a deathly hush on the bridge of the craft, and we could already hear the dull drone of a large number of heavy bombers reverberating from above the low-hanging clouds. Vessels of all kinds were fleeing in panic from the harbour. They rushed past us at full speed in an attempt to reach the safety of the sea before the raid began.' *Z-34* was steaming away from the harbour when American B-17s and B-24s flew in to bomb the quayside she had so recently left: 'The paralysing tension gradually relaxed, and while we were repassing the moles on the way out, two refugee children appeared on the deck. They were holding hands and laughing with joy.'

By 16 March the evacuation of the civilian population of Kolberg had been completed* and Katyusha barrages were pulverizing the narrow strip into which the port's defenders had been pushed. On the night of the 18th the last of them slipped away by sea. On 26 March Fullriede received the Knight's Cross of the Iron Cross from Hitler, but Goebbels forbade any mention of the fall of Kolberg in his Ministry's communiqués.

On 20 March Himmler relinquished command of Army Group Vistula. He had conducted the fight for East Pomerania from his luxurious personal train, christened the 'Steiermark' (Styria), without benefit of proper

---

* During the last months of the war the German Navy evacuated some 2 million civilians in the Baltic.

radio communications or decent maps. He seldom rose before 9am and then spent most of the morning under the hands of his Swedish masseur, Felix Kersten, who had become a kind of father-confessor with whom Himmler could discuss many of his ideas and problems in a stress-free atmosphere, something which money could not buy at this stage in the fortunes of the Third Reich. Himmler called Kersten his 'magic Buddha'.

Soothed by the probing hands of the 'Buddha', Himmler managed an hour of work before lunch, which was usually followed by a siesta and then a burst of three hours' application before exhaustion overtook the Reichsführer SS. Whether broken by the strain of commanding an army group – as his military enemies asserted – or defeated by his multifarious responsibilities, the experience proved too much for Himmler, who disappeared into a sanatorium at Hohenlychen, ostensibly because of an attack of angina. Goebbels visited him on 7 March, driving through Mecklenburg, where

> the country is totally undamaged and exudes complete peace. At a casual glance there is nothing to show that there is a war on. . . . [Himmler] has had a bad attack of angina, but is now on the mend. He gives me a slightly frail impression. . . . He uses strong language about Göring and Ribbentrop, whom he regards as the two main sources of error in our general conduct of the war, and in this he is absolutely right. . . . Himmler summarizes the situation correctly when he says that we have little hope of winning the war militarily but instinct tells him that sooner or later some potential opening will emerge to swing it in our favour. Himmler thinks this more likely in the West than the East . . . from the East he expects nothing whatsoever.

By 15 March, Himmler had recovered sufficiently to journey to Berlin, where he was on the receiving end of one of Hitler's increasingly manic tirades about the 'general conduct' of the war. A few days later he gratefully submitted to Guderian's urging that, for the sake of his health, he should give up the command of Army Group Vistula. However, Himmler lacked the nerve to approach Hitler himself and left the matter to Guderian, who eventually persuaded the Führer to appoint Colonel-General Gotthard Heinrici, then commanding Third Panzer Army in the Carpathians, and a grizzled professional with a keen grasp of flexible defensive tactics against the Red Army.

On 22 March, Heinrici arrived at Himmler's field HQ at Prenzlau, where the Reichsführer SS, his mild moonlike face bloated and seedy, received him beneath a vast portrait of Frederick the Great. Himmler, whose gift for prolix exposition almost equalled that of his Führer, then treated

Heinrici to a rambling account of his, Himmler's, handling of the campaign in East Pomerania which convinced the new commander of Army Group Vistula that 'in four months he had failed to grasp the most basic elements of good generalship'. After an hour of waffle, the shorthand writer laid down his pen in despair. Himmler's seemingly interminable monologue was only interrupted by a telephone call from General Theodor Busse, commander of Ninth Army, who reported that the Russians had cut off the German bridgehead at Küstrin. An immensely relieved Himmler passed the receiver to Heinrici, observing, 'You are the one who leads the army group now. Would you kindly give the appropriate orders.'

After Heinrici had instructed Busse to put in an immediate counterattack, Himmler turned to other matters. Ushering Heinrici to a sofa on the far side of the room, out of earshot of the stenographer, he told him in a low voice that he had taken personal steps to negotiate peace with the Western Allies.* The startled Heinrici wondered whether this was some devilish test of his loyalty. The long silence which ensued was broken when an officer entered to announce that the staff of Army Group Vistula were waiting to wish Himmler farewell.

While Himmler's feeble but persistent grip was being slowly prised off Army Group Vistula, the Führer, that ultimate map general, launched his last offensive of the war. The fall of Budapest in mid-February had served only to stoke Hitler's obsession with the Hungarian oilfields at Nagykanisza, fifty miles south-west of Lake Balaton. The plan, codenamed *Frülingserwachen* (Spring's Awakening), was for General Wöhler's Army Group South to trap and destroy Colonel-General F.I. Tolbukhin's Third Ukrainian Front between Lake Balaton and the Danube. Sepp Dietrich's Sixth SS Panzer Army, which had been withdrawn from the Western Front in January, was to launch the major thrust, attacking south-east from the northern end of Lake Balaton to a line on the Danube between Budapest and Baja; south of the lake, Second Panzer Army was to advance directly east, while a supporting attack was to be launched northwards from the Yugoslavian border by Weichs's Army Group E in the direction of Mohacs. Budapest would be retaken, the oilfields retained, and an entire Red Army front struck off the order of battle.

---

* Himmler had been putting out peace feelers in all directions: via Count Folke Bernadotte, Vice-Chairman of the Swedish Red Cross, the World Jewish Congress, and Karl Wolff, his former liaison officer at Hitler's headquarters and later Military Governor of North Italy. Wolff had opened secret talks with Allan Dulles, Roosevelt's envoy in Switzerland and an agent of OSS, about the surrender of the German armies in Italy.

The preparations for Spring Awakening were made in conditions of utmost secrecy. Heid Ruhl, a gunner with Das Reich Division, part of Sixth SS Panzer Army's II SS Corps, recalled: 'For our move to Hungary we were ordered to remove every divisional identification, even the monogram on our shoulder straps.' It was not until the end of February that the headquarters staff of Sixth SS Panzer Army were allowed into the operational area, and not until late in the afternoon of D-day minus 1 that Das Reich's regimental commanders were able to conduct a visual reconnaissance of the ground over which their units were to attack. Dietrich himself was not allowed to enter the area until the last moment before the operation began on 6 March. During the preceding forty-eight hours the panzergrenadiers, burdened by full equipment, struggled through calf-deep mud to their forming-up areas because their unit transports had been instructed to bring them no nearer to the start lines than fifteen miles. When the attack went in, they were in no state to fight. Heid Ruhl remembered that

on 6 March we fired a heavy barrage behind which our grenadiers should have attacked. They did not because they could not and the barrage only served to warn the enemy. At 5am on the following day the grenadiers went in behind another, but this time much shorter, barrage. The marshy ground meant that the armour could not support the attack and they suffered heavy losses.

Spring Awakening was the last hurrah of Hitler's panzer arm. In the vanguard of the attack was Sixth SS Panzer Army, burning to redeem itself after the failure of the Ardennes offensive and equipped with the MkVI Tiger II heavy battle tank – the Royal Tiger, massively armoured and mounting an 88mm gun. At the limit of the German advance more than 600 tanks and self-propelled guns tried to batter their way through the Soviet lines south of Lake Velencze. By 15 March it was all over. Hundreds of tanks were left stranded like beached whales in the waterlogged plains of eastern Hungary. Panzer commanders remarked bitterly that they should have been issued with Hitler's new Schnorkel U-boats rather than the Royal Tigers, which ploughed to a halt, their fuel tanks empty, to be pounded by Soviet artillery and attack aircraft.

The Waffen-SS was now added to the long list of those who had let down the Führer. Hitler ordered Dietrich's officers to be stripped of their decorations and their men of their treasured divisional armbands. Himmler was ordered to the front to ensure that the orders were carried out, but even he bridled at this, telling Hitler, 'I would have to drive to

Lake Balaton to take the crosses of the dead. A German SS man cannot give more than his life to you, my Führer.'

The Red Army counter-offensive swept past the Royal Tigers' gutted hulks, smashed through Hungarian Third Army, covering Dietrich's left flank, and rolled on to Vienna. By 4 April Third Ukrainian Front had sealed the city off on three sides and joined hands with Marshal R.I. Malinovsky's Second Ukrainian Front, whose Forty-Sixth Army was racing down from the north-east towards the Austrian capital. Twenty-five miles south-east of Vienna was Stalag XVIIIB, a mixed prisoner-of-war camp, the majority of whose inmates were Russians, Hungarians, French and Eastern European partisans. A recent arrival was Edgar Randolph, an Australian medical orderly who had been taken prisoner in Crete in 1941. In January 1945, Randolph and many of his comrades were marched west from their POW camp in Silesia, arriving at Stalag XVIIIB just as the Red Army was about to launch its assault on Vienna. Another 'march-out' was staged, which gave Randolph a grandstand view of a Soviet infantry attack:

> On 4 April we woke at 7am or so and moved out of the barracks into a queer hush. Not a sound anywhere – the Germans had taken off. One of the guard towers had been blitzed after sundown by air-craft – the guards up there were dead and the camp gate by the German barracks was unlocked. No one wanted breakfast, so a dozen of us moved past the Russian compounds (they [i.e. the Russian POWs] were sticking close to home) to the north fence. We had a good view for three to four miles over the plain, which was one to two miles wide. At 8am the Russian infantry started across the plain to attack the river on the other side of it. It was an awesome sight and, even now, I get a slight 'sinking' feeling as I visualize it. They came into view round the edge of the ridge against which the Stalag was built. It was very rough indeed for a couple of miles. They were in arrowhead formations of about twenty-man platoons, fifty yards apart, and about the same behind one another. They just kept coming, line after line, and filled the whole plain, the further ones heading for the town of Bruch and the nearer gradually fanning out to cover the ground in front of us. There were literally thousands of men, who just moved at a walk-ing pace inexorably on towards their objective. They made no attempt to take advantage of 'dead ground' – they just kept on going ahead. The Germans in the position on the river opened up and threw everything but the kitchen sink at them, and we could see them dropping in ones, twos and threes as they advanced. As the men dropped, the arrowheads closed up and when they became too few for a formation they just joined on to the nearest

one. They kept on like this till, after about twenty or thirty minutes, the leading lines were 200 yards or so from the trees along the river. The front formation then dropped down and opened their first fire on the Germans. The next lines went through them, dropped and opened fire and so on. Then they reached the river and the sound of the battle intensified if anything. The troops to our front had by this time got halfway across. They then took cover and moved more slowly. Just then a German 30cwt truck, with four or five men in the back, came roaring down the road from the ridge behind us (probably from an observation post on high ground). It rounded the Stalag and went flat-out down the straight towards the bridge, firing as it went, at the Russians, who had not yet reached the road. They got through OK and roared on to the bridge. As the truck raced on to the humpback, the bridge was blown (by their comrades), flinging the truck forty to fifty feet up in the air, to drop apparently down into the river. Shortly afterwards two mounted Russians, each carrying a huge Red flag, galloped through the Stalag gates (opened wide for them by the Russian POWs) and up the roads between the compounds, to show that at last we were free (or were we?).

In Vienna, fierce fighting raged while civilians continued to go shopping or to work. Cafés and bars remained open as if it were peacetime, although it was observed that most of their customers were foreigners waiting for the war to pass them by. As Das Reich Division withdrew from Vienna, westward towards Melk, one of its artillerymen noted that

On the Bisamberg was the Vienna radio station and one can look down from the summit of the mountain and see, to the right, as far as the Czech border while below us on the left there was the Danube and the Korneuburg-Stockerau road which the Russians had already cut. ... From our positions we could see great columns of Russians with their panje* carts marching westwards and saw how the Russian soldiers who had occupied the first houses of the village of Bisamberg forced the villagers, men and women, to do the goose step, backwards and forwards, from ... early in the morning. ... We were without weapons and moved about on the mountain, in and out of the woods, hoping to find a gap through which we could reach our comrades. Finally some Russian soldiers, probably of the third wave, captured us. They took everything we had, including our military documents, and marched us down the mountain to join a group of prisoners already waiting there.

---

* A small farm cart drawn by a single horse.

The loss of Vienna was but one of a catalogue of disasters threatening
to overwhelm the Ostheer. Poznan had fallen on 22 February, after a grim
four-day fight for its dominating citadel, held by a garrison of 12,000 men.
The ferocity of the fighting was graphically described by Colonel-General
Chuikov:

> The citadel was situated on an elevation dominating the city. Its
> forts and ravelins were reinforced with a three-metre layer of earth.
> The approaches to the inner forts and ravelins were protected by
> a wide and deep moat kept under fire from casemates through
> embrasures invisible to attacking troops. The walls of the moat, 5–8
> metres high, were faced with brick and represented an insur-
> mountable obstacle for our tanks. Heavy guns were brought up to
> help them. At a range of 300 metres they opened up on the citadel.
> But even their 203mm shells could not seriously damage the walls,
> and those that hit the layer of earth over the roofs of the forts and
> casemates just ploughed it up. . . . In order to observe the results
> of our bombardment of the citadel and follow the actions of our
> assault groups, we set up our observation post on the top floor of
> the city's theatre close to the battle zone. With me were Corps
> Commander, General Shemenkov, and my second-in-command
> General Dukhanov. We saw a large group of German soldiers with
> white flags appear on the fortress's inner rampart. They threw
> down their weapons and indicated that they were surrendering.
> Realizing this, our troops ceased fire. But then we saw that the
> group on the rampart began to thin out rapidly. The soldiers fell
> and rolled down the slope of the rampart singly or in twos and
> threes. Soon there were none left. My guess was right. The German
> soldiers who had decided to surrender were shot by their own offi-
> cers, who fired from the casemates.

At times the scene resembled a medieval siege. Assault ladders, raked
with fire, were used to cross the citadel's moats and ramparts:

> The assault groups sustained heavy losses. The flanking fire from
> the embrasures of redoubts No.1 and No.2 and the west tower of
> the main entrance was particularly deadly. Our attempts to silence
> them with portable flamethrowers failed. The men could not get
> to the edge of the moat because of enemy fire, and the streams of
> burning liquid expelled from a distance of twenty to twenty-five
> metres produced no effect. It was then decided to use drums
> packed with explosives instead. Under the covering fire of the
> infantry six sappers crawled up to the edge of the moat rolling the
> drums before them, ignited the fuses and sent the drums rumbling

towards the embrasures. When the enemy machine-gunners, stunned by the explosion, slackened their fire, our sappers lowered their assault ladders and launched crossings. . . .

Resistance from the German defenders firing from the dead zone of the lower casemates of the citadel's last redoubt was only overcome when the deperate attackers hurled crates, barrels and logs down at them, blocking their fields of fire. On the evening of 22 February, Chuikov was informed by General Bakanov, commander of the 74th Guards Rifle Division, that the citadel's garrison had surrendered. Fifteen minutes later he met General Mattern, the citadel's commandant, an incredibly stout man who, puffing and snorting,

> squeezed his frame through the door. Regaining his breath, he handed me a note from the fortress commandant, General Konnel,* asking the Soviet commander to take care of the German wounded. 'Where is Konnel?' I asked. 'He shot himself.' When asked how he himself felt, General Mattern shrugged; 'It's all the same to me. I am not a member of the Nazi Party and I would not have shed blood needlessly knowing that resistance was pointless. Hitler is finished.'

In the Samland peninsula, Königsberg's garrison had given the city a stay of execution when on 19 February it launched a counter-attack which reopened the land corridor with the West, enabling at least 100,000 civilians to reach the port of Pillau and the ferries which took them on to a temporary safety. Briefly, peacetime conditions returned to Königsberg: water, gas and electricity were restored; restaurants and cinemas reopened and cattle were driven in from the surrounding countryside.

While the children of Königsberg took advantage of the unseasonably mild weather to play in the city's parks, the Russians were drawing up a detailed plan, overseen by Marshal Vasilevsky, to storm the city. Vasilevsky had assumed command of Third Belorussian Front after the brilliant young Chernyakhovsky had been killed by a shrapnel fragment on 18 February while driving to the command post of Gorbatov's Third Army. His successor had concentrated four armies in the Königsberg sector (Thirty-Ninth, Forty-Third, Fiftieth and Eleventh Guards[†]) and an unprecedented air striking force, much of it drawn from the Stavka reserve, of 870 fighters, 470 attack aircraft and 1,124 bombers under the

---

* Mattern and Konnel exercised joint command at Poznan.
† They were designated the Samland Group and placed under the command of Marshal Bagramyan.

command of Marshal A. Novikov, Commander-in-Chief of the Red Air Force and the man responsible for air operations during the battles of Stalingrad and Kursk, and the Belorussian campaign.

The storming of Königsberg began on 2 April with a massive artillery barrage which reached a climax four days later, smashing German defensive positions, burying entire companies under the rubble, wrecking signals systems and detonating ammunition stores. A huge pall of smoke hung over the inner city of Königsberg, the streets of which were strewn with chunks of masonry, smouldering vehicles, and the carcasses of horses and human beings. Two days later the city was cut off from the rest of the German force fighting in the Samland peninsula, sealing its fate. General Müller, in overall command of the Samland sector, signalled the city's commandant, General Otto Lasch, that on no account should he attempt a mass breakout. Only a handful of units were detailed to create a corridor through which the remaining civilian population could escape. In the small hours of 9 April the evacuation plan dissolved into bloody chaos as a long column of civilians, moving down the Pillau road, was targeted by the enemy's mortar and Katyusha batteries.

Lasch was now in a desperate plight. In the opening phase of the battle foul weather had grounded Novikov's aircraft, but on 7 April the skies cleared, allowing his heavy bombers to fly in under fighter escort to pound Königsberg's remaining pockets of resistance. On the morning of the 10th, with white sheets of surrender already fluttering from the windows of those houses still standing, Lasch decided to end what he later described as 'the senseless sacrifice of further thousands of my soldiers and civilians. . . . I therefore resolved to cease fighting and put an end to the horror.'

Marshal Bagramyan watched as the captured German generals were led into Vasilevsky's command post:

> They came in and stood before us with drooping heads. The fortress commandant looked particularly downcast and wretched. We knew that there was another reason for his gloom, quite apart from the fact that he was a prisoner of war. We had learned from radio monitoring that the imbecile Führer had declared him a traitor for the surrender of the fortress and ordered the arrest of his family. Obviously General Lasch was depressed by this.

There was a surprise in store for Marshal Bagramyan:

> Before he finished his interrogation Vasilevsky asked the prisoners to name the Soviet Army commanders they knew. To our surprise,

Right: Exhausted Russian troops snatch some sleep in the streets of Königsberg, 9 April 1945. Some 42,000 German soldiers were killed in the battle for the city and 92,000 taken prisoner; an estimated 25,000 German civilians also died in the fighting.

Below: Desperate measures – a German woman receives instructions in the use of the Panzerfaust recoilless anti-tank weapon.

Left: End of a nightmare as the concentration camp at Dachau, north of Munich, is liberated by troops of US Seventh Army on 29 April 1945.

Below left: The camp at Belsen burns in May 1945, put to the torch by British troops armed with flamethrowers.

Right: Soviet Il-2 Shturmovik ground-attack aircraft fly over Germany at the end of the war. The Shturmovik was built in greater numbers than any other combat aircraft of the Second World War.

Below: After the bombers had finished – the ruins of Magdeburg.

Above: The last glimpse of the Führer. Hitler decorates the boy defenders of the Third Reich in the Chancellery garden, 20 April 1945, his fifty-sixth birthday.

Left: What now, little man? A German soldier on the steps of the Reichstag after the guns had fallen silent in Berlin.

Above right: Facing the music – General Jodl and Admiral Friedeburg steel themselves to sign the instrument of unconditional surrender at Reims, 7 May 1945.

Right: Zhukov, whose nickname was 'Zhuk' (beetle), adds his signature to the German capitulation document in Berlin, 8 May 1945, Victory in Europe Day.

Left: A column of German prisoners trudges past the Brandenburg Gate, 2 May 1945.

Below left: Washing day in Berlin, July 1945, in the shadow of a wrecked armoured car.

Right: Soviet and American troops fraternize in the streets of Berlin, soon to be the forward flashpoint of the Cold War.

Below: Marshal Rokossovsky leads the Victory Parade in Red Square, Moscow, June 1945.

The long road back.
German women scavenge
for wood in the Tiergarten,
Berlin, among the tree
stumps uprooted by a
company of British
engineers, March 1946.

they knew Voroshilov, Budenny and Timoshenko* only by name, and none of the other commanders, whose troops had trounced their vaunted armies all the way from Moscow and Stalingrad, at all. I could not refrain from asking them whether they did not know such celebrated names as Zhukov, Vasilevsky, Rokossovsky and Konev. They exchanged glances but said nothing. After a moment's silence Lasch said somewhat bashfully that he had not heard of Marshal of the Soviet Union Vasilevsky before his name was mentioned in the ultimatum to the Königsberg garrison. This meant that hardly any of the German generals had access to information collected by the Reich's intelligence services, since we had no doubt that dossiers on Soviet commanders were filed with them. In contrast to the Germans, Soviet generals and officers sought throughout the war to do something more than find out the names and ranks of the commanders whose troops they would have to deal with. Above all, they wanted to know how competent each of them was and how he could be expected to behave in any particular situation.

Although Breslau had been cut off on 15 February, it held out, sustained by air supply and the brutal encouragement of Karl Hanke, Gauleiter of Lower Silesia, until the end of the war. Hanke was a great favourite of Goebbels, who wrote of him on 20 March:

> Hanke sends me an extraordinarily dramatic and instructive report from Breslau. From it one can see that Hanke is absolutely on top of his job. He is representative of today's most energetic National Socialist leader. The fighting thoughout the city has turned Breslau into a veritable heap of ruins. But the people of Breslau, defending their city like a fortress, have turned this to good account and are defending every pile of stones with dogged fury. The Soviets are shedding an extraordinary amount of blood in the battle for Breslau.

Hanke did not belive in half-measures. On 28 January he had executed the Bürgermeister, Dr Spielhagen, for expressing defeatist opinions. After Breslau was cut off, he urged an airlift of crack parachute troops into the city to create a 'Cassino on the Oder'. At the end of March he arranged for eight large-calibre artillery pieces to be flown into Breslau by an equal number of huge Me232 six-engined glider transports, all but one of which were shot down by Russian anti-aircraft fire. When Hanke relocated his headquarters to the cellars beneath Breslau University's library,

---

* All three were back numbers by this stage of the war.

he proposed to blow up the building, and all its books, so that the rubble would provide extra head cover.

For seventy-seven days the 40,000 defenders of Breslau – a mixture of shredded regular formations, elderly members of the Volkssturm and boys of the Hitler Youth – occupied the attention of some thirteen Soviet divisions of Sixth Army, which were handled with a singular lack of the determination and drive shown at Königsberg. Inside the improvised fortress a semblance of normal life was maintained almost to the end. Concerts were held in the lulls between bombardments, and throughout the siege the Aviatik tobacco factory turned out half a million cigarettes a day to ensure that no one went without a smoke. Berlin had already fallen when, on 6 May, with about 80 per cent of the city in ruins, the commandant, Lieutenant-General von Niehoff, surrendered. Niehoff went into a ten-year captivity in the Soviet Union, but the egregious Hanke, who had been designated Reichsführer SS and Chief of Police in Hitler's will, slipped away in a Fieseler Storch aircraft disguised as an SS NCO. His fate remains unknown, although he is thought to have been killed in Czechoslovakia a month later.

The fate of many of Breslau's citizens was more certain. When the Red Army marched in on 7 May,

> rape began almost immediately and there was a viciousness in the acts as if we women were being punished for Breslau having resisted for so long. Let me say that I was young, pretty, plump and fairly inexperienced. A succession of Ivans gave me over the next week or two a lifetime of experience. Luckily very few of their rapes lasted more than a minute. With many it was just a matter of seconds before they collapsed gasping. What kept me sane was that almost from the very first one I felt only a contempt for these bullying and smelly peasants who could not act gently towards a woman, and who had about as much sexual technique as a rabbit. We women were put on rubble-clearing gangs. Unless we worked we were not fed. There was no distribution of rations against coupons. Instead there were soup kitchens. We would be marched at midday to the kitchen to receive our portion of soup and bread. One day something strange happened. There were Red Army troops of whom the ordinary European Russians were terribly afraid. We were working as usual, then we noticed that the guards were very jumpy. We heard singing, loud, strong masculine voices singing Red Army marching songs. But yet there was something not quite right; the rhythm was wrong . . . the voices singing those Russian songs were not singing them in a Western rhythm. The Red Army men who were guarding us told us in very bad

German to run away and hide. The Mongols are coming, they told us. Very bad men. You go. You go quick. This really was a case of a pot calling the kettle black. These were the same men who had come into our town about ten days before and had carried out practices and orgies of unbelievable savagery. Yet they were telling us that this new group of approaching Soviet soldiers were bad. They were terrified that the Mongols would come near the street we were clearing. They were really afraid. It is strange how the mind works. I seldom recall the days when I was young. Yet when I hear a military choir singing, then all those days come back. All the senseless destruction that the Ivans carried out.

On 5 April 1945, a young British officer, Major Peter Earle, set out to drive from Brussels to take up his posting as one of Montgomery's liaison officers* in northern Germany. It was a long and depressing drive, as Earle recorded in his diary:

> Throughout the journey we had driven through driving wind and rain, utterly devastated towns and villages, glum German civilians, homeless and completely wretched, the wrecks of tanks and guns, streams of refugees of all nationalities carrying their bundled possessions, fields littered with broken gliders. I have never seen such endless misery, such appalling destruction and such a wretched people.

As the Third Reich imploded, misery mingled with scenes of surreal abandon. On the road to Frankfurt, the American photo-journalist Margaret Bourke-White encountered a German goods train which had been halted by an air attack the day before. Looters were now at work. Bourke-White later wrote: 'A German hausfrau came running down the railroad tracks towards us. Her arms were so full of pink panties and undershirts that she was scattering a pink trail behind her, and she was laughing and crying at the same time. "Germany is kaput! Might as well loot!" she shouted.' Bourke-White and her driver noted that the crowd swarming over the carcass of the train was an international gathering:

> Sergeant Asch, who speaks many languages, was able to catch shouted phrases as groups rushed past us. Newly freed Belgians, Dutch, Russians, French and Poles, trekking their monotonous way

---

* Montgomery's personal liaison officers, to whom he was devoted, acted as his eyes and ears, setting out by jeep each day to visit the front line and reporting back directly to him.

westward, had been attracted by the crowd, and had rushed in
and started crawling between the legs and over the shoulders of
the plundering Germans. There was no fighting among the looters
– only a passionate clawing towards the freight cars. The crowd
was even gay; they were people of all nationalities laughing and
looting together. The Poles were radiant. One Polish woman, gathering up armloads of skirts and dress goods, looked up at me and
said, 'The Germans stole all this anyway'. And taking up her words
some Polish men, while they hacked away at packing cases, kept
chanting through their handlebar moustaches, 'The Germans stole
all of this; the Germans stole it all'. There was a good deal of truth
in this, for many of the clothes on this train bore French and
Belgian labels.

In Frankfurt, which had been taken by US Third Army at the end of
March, Bourke-White and Sergeant Asch

> had to drive carefully to avoid the twisted figures of the newly
> fallen dead. But it was the living in the devastated streets that first
> caught the eye. Most of them were women, and they were wan-
> dering around dazedly with their arms full of flowers. Rising
> between the skeletons of houses were magnolias and lilacs, filling
> the incongruous ruins with reminders of spring; and it seemed
> that these women, climbing up out of the darkness, where they
> had hidden day and night from the terrible shellings, with their
> first glimpse of daylight were driven irresistibly to the flowers. It
> was a sense of return to life that had impelled them to fill their
> arms with all the pink and purple boughs they could carry.

For most Germans a sense of numbness overrode the sudden windfall
of a looted train, or the simple fact of survival amid the ruins of the
Third Reich. In mid-April the BBC war correspondent Richard Dimbleby
ducked into a small gasthaus to listen to the Corporation's nine o'clock
news on the owner's radio. The hotel family and guests hovered on the
sidelines as Dimbleby twiddled the knobs and tuned in to the familiar,
urbane tones of newsreader Freddie Grisewood:

> As we sat listening to the news about this battle area, I watched the
> reaction of this German family which had been engulfed in the
> fighting a very short time before and could hear it going on now if
> we turned down the set. They were listening quite intently, under-
> standing no English, but catching the German place-names as
> Freddie Grisewood mentioned them. 'Hanover', said the smart
> guest, 'They're near Hanover'. 'Isn't that what he said?' she asked

me. I said it was. And then the Weser was mentioned and that being the local river, everyone heard it. Even the old man stirred himself from his gloomy apprehension. And then it was announced that the Americans were at or near Würzburg. 'Würzburg? Where's Würzburg?' asked one of the daughters. The other got up and fetched a gazetteer from a shelf. She opened it at a map of central and southern Germany and the whole family pored over it, marking the places as they were mentioned. And as I watched them, a thought struck me. This was a recital from London of our success, of the growing and spreading defeat of their country, and yet there was not one sound or sign of regret on their faces, no shock, no despair, no alarm. They just picked up what was said, checked it on the map and noted it just as if they were a bunch of neutrals hearing all about somebody else. And indeed, I believe that that's what many of these front-line German people are. Neutrals in their own country. They seem to have lost the power of passion or sorrow. They show no sympathy for their army, for their government, or for their country. To them the war is something too huge and too catastrophic to understand. Their world is bounded by the difficulties of managing a country hotel – and there's no room in it for things outside.

British and American armour was now 'swanning it', moving at speed down parallel roads and leaving towns to be mopped up by other units while they pressed on into Germany. In between the armoured thrusts, great tracts of countryside to the north and south remained unvisited even by reconnaissance elements. The German line had been utterly broken, and there were no reserves left to launch attacks against the Allied flanks or to nip the heads off their armoured columns. The roads were lined with German troops, pathetically eager to give themselves up to the first Allied soldier to accept their surrender. In the rear long columns of prisoners, often led by their officers, tramped down the roads, dense clouds of steam rising from their greatcoats in the rain, with no one paying them the slightest attention and with none of them trying to escape.

When it flared up, resistance produced the familiar sights, sounds and smells of battle, as Peter Earle noted:

> I was held up yesterday in a column of tanks near Welzen. The woods were ablaze, the noise of tanks, the bark of the ATK* guns, the sweet stench of dead cows and here and there a dead horse, swollen and bloated with its legs jutting stiffly into space like an overturned

---

* Anti-tank.

The Allied advance from the Rhine to link with the Red Army on the Elbe. A high proportion of the German forces surrendered en masse and towns greeted the Allies with white flags. Model's Army Group B was encircled in the Ruhr, where resistance ended on 18 April. US Ninth Army reached the Elbe, near Magdeburg, on 12 April. By then Eisenhower had made the decision not to go for Berlin.

wooden horse. The air filled with smoke and impenetrable dust . . . then nearer the battle, that special silence that means danger and the absence of vehicles; or perhaps tanks deployed along the edges of woods and the savage chatter of gunfire; huddled corpses, shattered lorries and tanks with clothing and litter hanging on the trees as though a Christmas tree decorated by death. German prisoners too present a sorry sight. Their flimsy uniforms, their sullen, angry young faces as they are marched through the dust to a cage.

The roads into the Reich were jammed, almost bumper to bumper, with immense Allied supply columns – tank transporters, petrol trucks, jeeps and bulldozers, all driving with headlights blazing as the great war machine ground eastward. On Bradley's front, 83rd Infantry Division, part of US Ninth Army, presented an extraordinary spectacle. The 'Rag-Tag Circus', as the division became known, sported a weird and wonderful collection of captured and looted German vehicles which proved as confusing to the enemy as it did to Allied air reconnaissance. At one point a German staff car, crammed with senior Wehrmacht officers, mistook one of the 83rd's columns for a German unit and began to weave in and out of the American formation blasting on its horn. When the Americans recovered from their suprise, a burst of machine-gun fire halted the interloper and the Germans were taken prisoner in the middle of what they had taken to be one of their own outfits. Their Mercedes received a quick paint job, and with a US star applied to its dripping sides took its place in the 83rd's advance.

The sudden collapse of German resistance in the West reopened the question of Berlin. In the autumn of 1944 the Western Allies had made the German capital their target. In September, Eisenhower had written, '. . . Clearly Berlin is the main prize. There is no doubt whatsoever in my mind that we should concentrate all our energies and resources on a rapid thrust to Berlin. . . . Simply stated, it is my desire to move on Berlin by the most direct and expeditious route.' By the end of January, however, Berlin had dropped out of Allied calculations as a military target. While the Western Allies had been held up by the Ardennes offensive, the Red Army had forged to within fifty miles of the German capital. The Russians were now so near that it seemed as if they could take the city whenever they decided to make the effort. But for Churchill, Berlin remained a prime political objective. If the Russians took the city, he argued, 'will not their impression that they have been the overwhelming contributor to our common victory be unduly imprinted on their minds and may not this lead to a mood which will raise grave and fundamental difficulties in the future?'

Churchill had become increasingly anxious about the post-war consequences of shaking hands with the Russian bear so far to the west.
Montgomery, too, still saw Berlin as the 'main prize', which had been
promised to him by Eisenhower in September 1944. On 27 March he had
sent a coded message to the Supreme Commander: 'my tactical headquarters move to northwest to Bonninghardt on Tuesday 29 March.
Thereafter . . . my headquarters will move to Wesel-Munster-Wiedenbruck-
Herford-Hanover – then by autobahn to Berlin, I hope.'

He was to be disappointed. On 28 March, Eisenhower gave him new
orders. US Ninth Army, which had been under Montgomery's command
since 20 December, was to be handed back to Bradley, who was to be
responsible for 'mopping up and occupying the Ruhr and with minimum
delay will deliver his main thrust on the axis Erfurt-Leipzig-Dresden to
join hands with the Russians'. The mission of 21st Army Group was to
'cross the Elbe without delay, drive to the Baltic coast at Lübeck and seal
off the Danish peninsula'. The expressionless military language did little
to conceal the fact that this was a stinging slap in the face for
Montgomery, one that concluded, in the most brutal fashion, the long
and bad-tempered tussle over sole command of the land forces in which
the commander of 21st Army Group had been engaged since September
1944.

Eisenhower had decided not to go for Berlin. In doing so he had found
sufficient reason to deny Montgomery his northern thrust while switch-
ing the main effort to the resurgent Bradley in the south. (It was in con-
sultation with Bradley that Eisenhower had lit on the line of the Elbe,
itself ninety miles inside the Soviet occupation zone and a clearly
defined barrier, as the best place to meet the Russians and avoid the
chances of an accidental collision which might flare into a fight.) The
reasons were partly personal – Eisenhower's patience with Montgomery
was now exhausted* – partly political, and partly the result of the broad-
front strategy which had kept the coalition together in uneasy amity. The
Supreme Commander was reluctant to run the risk of sustaining heavy
casualties in racing the Red Army to a city which the Yalta agreements
had already placed deep inside the Soviet post-war zone of occupation.
Nor had the broad-front strategy, and Eisenhower's decision to devote
eighteen front-line divisions to the reduction of the Ruhr, left him well
placed to make a dash for Berlin. By 1 April, over forty Allied divisions
had crossed the Rhine, but only eight were positioned north of the Harz

---

* After the war Eisenhower told the writer Cornelius Ryan: '. . . Montgomery had
become so personal in his efforts to make sure the Americans and me in particular
got no credit, that in fact we had hardly anything to do with the war, that I finally
stopped talking to him.'

Mountains on the direct road to Berlin. South of the Harz there were thirty-one American divisions, many of which were tied down in the double encirclement of the Ruhr, which might have been sealed off by second-line troops and left to wither on the vine. The striking power and logistic capacity were available to Eisenhower, but much of it was in the wrong place and heading in the wrong direction.

In any event, Eisenhower had uncovered another objective, the 'National Redoubt', a last-ditch Alpine stronghold which was being prepared by diehard Nazis. There was, in fact, no National Redoubt, but a belief in its existence had been skilfully fostered by Goebbels, who had established a special unit to produce a stream of stories about this mythical defence system, complete with impregnable strongpoints, underground supply dumps and factories sunk into mountainsides, all defended by 100,000 fanatical troops. The story was taken up by the American press, which painted an alarming picture of a guerrilla war being waged against the Allies after the fall of Berlin. In these stories the non-existent National Redoubt was linked with the real 'Werewolf' organization established by Himmler in the autumn of 1944. Himmler had ordered SS Police General Hans Prützmann to set up a secret army to keep National Socialism alive underground if Germany were occupied. According to one of Himmler's henchmen, Jurgen Stroop, 'soldiers and civilians, SS people and non-Party, youths and girls, even women and children' were to be schooled in sabotage, the liquidation of enemy agents, poisoning food and water supplies and, attacks on transport. By the end of the war, some 5,000 Werewolves had undergone training. Members of the organization were responsible for the assassination in March 1945 of Franz Oppenhof, whom the Allies had appointed Chief Bürgermeister of Aachen, and a host of incidents ranging from sniping to small-scale sabotage, but these were pinpricks scarcely felt during the collapse of the Third Reich. When General Siegfried Westphal, the last Chief of Staff in the West, was captured in May 1945, he contemptuously referred to the Werewolves as a 'rabble of Boy Scouts'.

The British took neither the National Redoubt nor the Werewolves particularly seriously, but a SHAEF intelligence summary of 11 March reached the conclusion that

> the main trend of German defensive policy does seem directed primarily to the safeguarding of the Alpine zone. . . . Air cover shows at least twenty sites of recent underground activity (as well as numerous natural caves) mainly in the regions of Feldkirch, Kufstein, Berchtesgaden and Golling, where ground sources have reported underground accommodation for stores and personnel.

The existence of several reported underground factories has also been confirmed. In addition several new barracks and hutted camps have been seen on air photogaphs, particularly around Innsbruck, Landeck and the Berghof. It thus appears that . . . reports of extensive preparations for the accommodation of the German Maquis-to-be are not unfounded.

It was a scenario worthy of Ernst Stavro Blofeld, and with about as much basis in reality.

A report by US Seventh Army, allegedly based on reliable sources, claimed that Himmler had ordered preparations to be made to receive 100,000 men in the Alpine fortress and that trains had been seen pouring into the area carrying a new type of cannon and equipment for aircraft assembly plants. The report concluded that the National Redoubt would eventually shelter up to 200,000 elite SS troops, 'thoroughly imbued with the Nazi spirit' and prepared to fight to the last man.

In the map room at Eisenhower's headquarters at Reims an intelligence chart labelled 'Reported National Redoubt' began to sprout red symbols, like a measles rash, over what, on the ground, would have been 20,000 square miles of Bavaria, Austria and northern Italy. After the war, Bradley, who had been a firm believer in the National Redoubt, admitted that 'it existed largely in the imagination of a few fanatical Nazis. It grew into so exaggerated a scheme that I am astonished that we could have believed it as innocently as we did. But while it persisted this legend . . . shaped our tactical thinking.'

The National Redoubt was also a useful stick with which to belabour Montgomery. On 21 March Bradley's headquarters had produced a paper, entitled 'Re-Orientation of Strategy', of which the principal thrust was that the plans 'we had brought with us over the beaches' were now obsolete. Objectives had changed and '. . . the metropolitan area [Berlin] can no longer occupy a position of importance . . . all indications suggest that the enemy's political and military directorate is already in process of displacing to the "Redoubt" in lower Bavaria.' With Montgomery deprived of Ninth Army, and priority shifted to Bradley's southern drive, 12th Army Group would be able to split Germany in two, preventing German forces from withdrawing into the Redoubt. Bradley's troops would then mop up any remaining resistance in the Alps.

These arguments, and a cable from General Marshall in Washington warning Eisenhower of the dangers of an indavertent outbreak of fighting between American and Russian troops, exercised a persuasive influence on the Supreme Commander. On 28 March, the day he dished Montgomery, Eisenhower cabled Stalin on his own initiative and without informing the Joint Chiefs of Staff, the British and American governments, or even his deputy, Air Chief Marshal Sir Arthur Tedder: 'My immediate operations are designed to encircle and destroy the enemy defending the Ruhr. . . . I estimate that this phase . . . will end in late April or even earlier, and my task will be to divide the remaining [German] forces by joining with your forces.' Eisenhower's signal also stated that his forces would meet the Russians at Dresden, a clear indication that Berlin was to be left to the Red Army.

Such was the British fury at this decision that Eisenhower was obliged to cable Churchill, promising him that 'if at any moment "Eclipse" [German collapse or surrender] condition should come about anywhere along the front we would rush forward . . . and Berlin would be included in our important targets'. In contrast, Stalin professed himself delighted with Eisenhower's cable, informing him on 1 April that it conformed entirely with Stavka's plans and that 'Berlin has lost its former strategic significance'. The Soviet high command would be committing only secondary forces to the German capital. On the same day Stalin convened a major command conference in the Kremlin attended by his two rival marshals, Zhukov and Konev. He had a simple question for them: 'Well, now, who is going to take Berlin, will we or the Allies?'

CHAPTER 9

The Final Battle

'My dear Kaltenbrunner, do you imagine I could talk to you like that about my plans for the future if I did not believe deep down that we really are going to win the war in the end?'

Adolf Hitler to Ernst Kaltenbrunner

IN BERLIN, Hans-Georg von Studnitz noted an addition to the city's street furniture:

> At the corner of the Kurfürstendamm and Joachimstahler-strasse, next door to the Kanzler *konditorei* [confectioner's shop], a public notice board carries messages from people seeking accommodation or offering things for barter, from language teachers, masseuses, and so on. Recently the new Berlin Commandant, Lieutenant-General von Hauenschild, joined the band of advertisers. His 'insertion' promulgates, in accordance with a Führer directive dated 17 February . . . the execution of an officer deserter and three soldiers who were using false papers. The proclamation ends: 'These sentences were pronounced also in the name of those women whose husbands, brothers and sons are worthily defending their Fatherland'.

For the Luftwaffe, the defence of the Fatherland had been reduced to the desperate expedient of suicide tactics. In March, Hermann Göring had asked for volunteers for 'special and dangerous' operations. About 330 volunteers were assembled at Stendal for training, half of whom were formed into a *Geschwader* (wing) designated Sonderkommando (Special Detachment) Elbe, whose mission was to ram American bombers. Training was 90 per cent political to give the pilots, most of them little more than boys, sufficient nerve to lay down their lives for the Führer. Their orders were to open fire at maximum range and continue firing until they were in a position to ram a bomber, preferably in the fuselage just aft of the wing. Only then could they bale out.

Escorted by Me262 jets, the piston-engined *Rammjäger* went into action on 7 April, their ears ringing with patriotic messages broadcast over their radios. In between bursts of '*Deutschland über Alles*', women's voices exhorted them to 'Remember our dead wives and children buried beneath the ruins of our towns'. When battle was joined over the Dummer and Steinhuder Lakes, American P-51 Mustang escort fighters enjoyed a turkey shoot, accounting for fifty-nine of Sonderkommando Elbe's 120 aircraft. Eight bombers were downed by the Rammjäger, but only fifteen of the German piston-engined fighters returned to base. It was Sonderkomando Elbe's first and last operation against US Eighth Air Force.

As the round-the-clock bombing of Berlin increased in intensity, Hitler spent more and more time in the concrete shelter built in the Chancellery garden. Eventually he moved underground permanently, into what became the thirteenth and last Führer headquarters, part tinny echo of the caves of the Nibelungen, part throwback to the dug-outs in which Corporal Hitler had sheltered during his days as a company runner in the First World War.

The Führerbunker was contained within a complex of shelters, one of which housed the staff of Martin Bormann, the ever-present Head of the Party Chancellery, and another a field hospital and, during the battle for Berlin, the headquarters of SS General Wilhelm Mohnke, the Chancellery's commandant. Buried 55 feet below the Chancellery garden, the main Führer shelter was built in two storeys with exterior walls 6 feet thick and an 8-foot-thick concrete canopy on top of which was piled 30 feet of earth. In the bunker's upper level were the kitchen, staff living quarters and, towards the end, rooms for Goebbels's family. Connected to the upper bunker by a short spiral staircase was the Führerbunker proper, divided into a series of cramped, low-ceilinged rooms grouped on either side of a central passage, decorated with paintings from the Chancellery, which was partitioned off for daily conferences. To the right of the passage, next to the machine room, was Bormann's office with the main telephone switchboard and teleprinter units, from which Hitler had snatched, page by page, the Yalta communiqué. The walls of Bormann's office were covered with maps of Germany and Berlin, each masked with a celluloid sheet on which the progress of enemy bomber formations was marked with chinagraph pencil, a routine which exerted a morbid hold on Hitler. Further down the pasage were rooms occupied by Goebbels and the SS physician Dr Stumpfegger. To the left of the passage was a suite of six sparsely furnished rooms occupied by Hitler. The small living room – 10 feet by 15 – was dominated by Anton Graff's oil painting of Frederick the Great, the one constant item of decor in all of Hitler's headquarters. In the bunker the Führer would spend long lonely hours brooding over the image of the soldier-king. On one occasion his orderly, Sergeant Roschus Misch, accidentally broke into one of these reveries:

> It was very late, and I thought that the Führer had already retired.
> . . . There was Der Chef, gazing at the picture by candlelight. He
> was sitting there, motionless, his chin buried in his hand, as if he
> were in a trance. The king seemed to be staring right back. I had
> barged in, but Hitler took no notice of me. So I tiptoed out. It was
> like stumbling on someone at prayer.

The other feature of the underground complex from which Hitler drew strange comfort was the large scale model of the city of Linz as it was to be rebuilt. The model had been designed and installed in the bunker under the Voss-strasse by the architect Professor Hermann Giesler. Linz, where Hitler had first heard Wagner's *Rienzi* and dedicated himself to politics, would rise from the ruins caused by Allied bombing to replace Budapest as the most majestic city on the Danube. Here there would be a concert hall capable of holding 35,000 people, and a 550-foot-high bell tower at whose base Hitler's parents would be buried. The Führer himself would be the principal patron of the vast art gallery which Giesler had designed. When Hitler took Ernst Kaltenbrunner, his security chief and a native of Linz, to view the model, he told him, 'My dear Kaltenbrunner, do you imagine I could talk to you like this about my plans for the future if I did not believe deep down that we are really going to win the war in the end?'

The airless claustrophobia of the bunker was the final bleak expression of the artificiality and isolation of Hitler's own existence. In the baleful glare of its electric lights night merged into day. The last military conferences often ended at 6am, after which Hitler would slump exhausted on his sofa, seeking relief in plate after plate of cream cakes. In the hours of darkness he would occasionally emerge from the bunker to take his German Shepherd dog Blondi for a short walk through the rubbish-strewn paths of the Chancellery garden, his SS guards hovering at a discreet distance.

In the summer of 1942, Hitler had sat at the centre of a vast communications web stretching from the Atlantic coast to the Caucasus. Now his links with the outside world had dwindled to a switchboard of the size required to run a modest hotel, one radio transmitter, and one radio-telephone link with the OKW headquarters at Zossen, fifteen miles south of Berlin. Keitel and Jodl had pressed Hitler to move his headquarters to Zossen, but Hitler expressed his doubts about the soundness of 'army concrete'. In the bunker, surrounded by sleek SS guards, he remained safe to draft the script for the last act of the Third Reich, with Josef Goebbels as his chief collaborator in the operatic orchestration of the strategy of doom. As the bombs rained down on Berlin, Goebbels threw himself into the task, exulting, 'The bomb terror spares the dwellings of neither rich nor poor; before the labour offices of total war the last class barriers go down'. Chaos had to be embraced as the necessary prelimi-nary to the establishment of a New Order: 'Now the bombs, instead of killing all Europeans only smashed the prison walls which held them captive. . . . In trying to destroy Europe's future, the enemy has only suc-ceeded in smashing its past; and with that, everything old and outworn has gone.'

Those who made the trip to the bunker were left with an indelible impression of its suffocating atmosphere, pregnant with fear and sup-pressed hysteria. Captain Beermann, one of the SS guards, recalled the debilitating effects of long spells spent underground:

> It was like being stranded in a cement submarine, or buried down in some charnel house. People who work in diving bells probably feel less cramped. It was both dark and dusty, for some of the cement was old, some new. In the long hours of the night, it would be deathly silent, except for the hum of the generator. When you came upon flesh-and-blood people their faces seemed blanched in the artificial light. The ventilation could now be warm and sul-try, now cold and clammy. The walls were sometimes grey, some-times bleached orange; some were moist and even mouldy. . . . Then there was the fetid odour of boots, sweaty woollen uniforms, acrid coal-tar disinfectant. Towards the end, when the drainage packed up, it was as pleasant as working in a public urinal.

To all those who saw him, Hitler presented a dreadful physical spec-tacle, like a man risen from the grave. Awash with drugs provided by the 'Reich Injection Master', Professor Theodor Morell; hunched and shak-ing, with faltering voice, foul breath, and glaucous eyes; a crust of spittle and cake crumbs flecking his lips; his jacket blotched with food stains. Major Gerhard Boldt, Krebs's ADC, who saw the Führer for the first time when he attended a briefing in the bunker early in February, recalled:

His head was slightly wobbling. His left arm hung slackly and his hand trembled a good deal. There was an indescribable flickering light in his eye, creating a fearsome and wholly unnatural effect. His face and the parts around his eyes gave the impression of total exhaustion. All his movements were those of a senile man.

In spite of his physical disintegration, Hitler retained the power to excite those who came to see him with the wildest of hopes. In the middle of March the distraught Gauleiter of Danzig, Albert Forster, arrived in the bunker. Forster, a fervent Catholic, still believed in Hitler's divine mission: 'I . . . believe in some kind of miracle. I still believe in Almighty God, who has given us our Führer, and destined him to make Germany free and turn it into a final bulwark of Western culture against the onslaught from the East.' Now, however, Forster was up against it. Over a 1,000 Russian tanks were at the gates of Danzig, he wailed, with only four Tigers left to oppose them. Before the meeting Forster declared that he was determined to present Hitler with 'the whole frightful reality of the situation'. But after a brief audience he emerged 'completely transformed'. The Führer had promised 'new divisions' – Danzig would be saved.* Only Albert Speer had the courage and detachment to conquer the overpowering ties of loyalty and contemplate killing Hitler and bringing the whole grisly charade to an end. He planned to flood the bunker's ventilation system with poison gas, but the quite coincidental covering of the air intake with a tall metal chimney thwarted his scheme.

By 12 April, Field Marshal Montgomery had sufficiently recovered his equilibrium to arrange a photo call featuring himself, a map and his young liaison officers. The target was no longer Berlin, but Montgomery was in chirpy mood, as Peter Earle noted in his diary:

> Monty ordered a photo of his HQ, which he richly enjoyed. 'Now we will look at the camera,' he said, 'now we will look to the right,' and then, 'now we will look to the left.' Then the liaison officers went through to the other side of the house where his caravan stands and there we were photographed with him. He then demanded that we change into our travelling clothes – 'we are all too smart', he said, 'Take off your coat, John,† is that my coat by the way?' We changed and he changed into especially old clothes.

---

* Danzig fell to Second Belorussian Front at the end of March. A few days later Forster suffered a complete nervous collapse.

† John Posten, Montgomery's favourite liasion officer who was killed in an ambush on 21 April. Peter Earle was badly wounded and (briefly) captured in the same incident.

'And now I will be giving you the form,' he said, 'and now I will
point at the map, and now we will look at Hannover, and you will
be writing.' 'And now this will be for the *Illustrated London News*. I
will be pointing at one of you . . . and you will be looking at me
intelligently. I will have a map, which I understand I should have at
my level.' And so it went, Monty directing the whole effort.

Twenty-four hours later, on Lüneburg Heath near Hanover, British 11th
Armoured Division liberated the concentration camp at Belsen. In the
death throes of the Third Reich trainloads of prisoners had converged on
Belsen from all over Germany. The camp, which hitherto had been run
with a semblance of brutal efficiency by its commandant, Josef Kramer,
collapsed under the weight of nearly 30,000 new arrivals. A former
inmate of Auschwitz, Olga Singer, later recalled: 'Auschwitz was no more
than a Purgatory. Hell was endured between the barbed wire fences of
Bergen-Belsen.' In Block 3, the 'maternity block', women of all nations lay
in cages along the walls, two to a cage, their stomachs hideously dis-
tended by a combination of pregnancy and hunger, their moaning
and crying filling the building with a 'constant, deafening cacophony'.
Typhus raged through the camp, and when the British arrived 13,000
corpses littered the camp in grotesque piles.

The first British soldier to enter Belsen was a young intelligence officer, Derrick Sington. When he entered the camp's inner compound,

> It reminded me of the entrance to a zoo. We came in to the smell
> of ordure – like the smell of a monkey house. A sad, blue smoke
> floated like ground mist between the low buildings. I had tried to
> imagine the interior of a concentration camp, but I had not imag-
> ined it like this. Nor had I imagined the strange simian throng who
> crowded the barbed-wire fences surrounding the compounds, and
> the obscene striped penitentiary suits.

The BBC war correspondent Richard Dimbleby filed this report a few
days later:

> I picked my way over corpse after corpse in the gloom, until
> I heard one voice raised above the gentle, undulating moaning. I
> found a girl, she was a living skeleton, impossible to gauge her age
> for she had practically no hair left, and her face was only a yellow
> parchment sheet with two holes in it for eyes. She was stretching
> out her stick of an arm and gasping something, it was 'English,
> English, medicine, medicine', and she was trying to cry but she
> hadn't enough strength. And beyond her down the passage were

the convulsive movements of dying people too weak to raise themselves from the floor. In the shade of some trees lay a great collection of bodies. I walked about them trying to count, there were
perhaps 150 of them flung down on each other, all naked, all so
thin that their yellow skin glistened like stretched rubber on their
bones. Some of the poor starved creatures whose bodies were
there looked so utterly unreal and inhuman that I could have
imagined that they had never lived at all. They were like polished
skeletons, the skeletons that medical students like to play practical
jokes with.

The Americans were making similar discoveries. On 13 April they
liberated the concentration camp at Buchenwald near Erfurt. On the
29th men of 42nd and 45th Divisions of US Seventh Army arrived at the
camp at Dachau, situated in the pleasant countryside outside Munich.
One of the inmates, a Dutch airman, wrote in his diary: '17.28 first
American comes through the entrance. Dachau free!!! Indescribable happiness. Insane howling.' In a railway siding were thirty-nine cattle trucks
packed with the corpses of Poles who had been transported there and
then left, locked inside, without food or water. Unhinged by the spectacle, the Americans gunned down dozens of SS guards, leaving their bodies 'scattered like tenpins bowled over as they sought to flee'.

The camp was encircled by a ten-foot-high electrified wire fence and
a fifteen-foot-wide moat. Some of the prisoners, desperate for freedom,
tried to climb the fence and were electrocuted. SS guards in the watch-
towers opened fire on them, whereupon they were riddled with
machine-gun fire by the Americans below. Their bodies plunged into the
moat accompanied by a terrible roaring of glee from the prisoners
'unlike anything ever heard from human throats'.

After the Allies crossed the Rhine, the Germans had begun to march
thousands of concentration camp prisoners eastwards, their progress
marked by a trail of battered, emaciated corpses. The SS could not contain their mania for killing even when the Americans were on the point
of overhauling them. As a column from Buchenwald was intercepted
near Posing by 90th Infantry Division, the guards began shooting hundreds of prisoners at the rear to form a human roadblock against the
Americans.

Eisenhower had been exposed to the horrors of the camps when, on
12 April, and accompanied by Bradley and Patton, he visited the camp
at Ohrdruf Nord near Gotha. White-faced, the Supreme Commander
inspected the camp's gallows with its noose of piano wire, the rooms
piled high with corpses, many of which bore the marks of cannibalism

caused when their organs had been gouged out by starving prisoners. Patton was violently sick. Later Eisenhower wrote to his wife Mamie that he had 'never dreamed that such cruelty, bestiality and savagery could really exist'.

Eisenhower had much to ponder, for he had already been informed of the death of President Roosevelt that same day. While resting at the clinic for the disabled which he had established at Warm Springs, Georgia, Roosevelt had died of a massive brain haemorrhage. In London, at No. 10 Downing Street, Churchill had sat hunched in his black leather arm-chair for five long minutes before reaching for the telephone and asking for Buckingham Palace. In Moscow, Stalin felt moved to grasp the hand of Averell Harriman and hold it wordlessly. In Berlin a mood of wild exultation reigned in the bunker. Now, surely, the alliance against Germany would collapse, saving Hitler just as Frederick the Great had been saved by the death of Tsarina Elizabeth. Goebbels, who had been reading aloud to the Führer extracts from Thomas Carlyle's *History of Friedrich II of Prussia*, telephoned Hitler in a frenzy of excitement: 'My Führer, I congratulate you. It is written in the stars that the second half of April will be the turning point for us'. An exhilarated Hitler told his orderly Misch that soon the Russians and Americans would be exchanging artillery barrages over the bunker's concrete canopy. The mood soon passed, however. Later Speer recalled: 'Hitler sat exhausted, looking both liberated and dazed, as he slumped in his chair. But I sensed that he was still without hope.'

On Sunday 15 April, Hitler's mistress Eva Braun arrived in the bunker. Since the middle of March she had been living in her private apartments in the Chancellery. One of Hitler's SS guards mordantly observed, 'The angel of death has arrived'. At the same time US Ninth Army's commander, General Simpson, was summoned to 12th Army Group's headquarters at Wiesbaden. There he was told that he was to halt on the Elbe. He returned to break the news to Brigadier-General Sidney Hinds, whose 2nd Armoured Division was already on the river's eastern bank: 'We're not going to Berlin, Sid. This is the end of the war for us'.

The war between the Allied generals in the West had inhibited Eisenhower's strategy. In contrast, Stalin had exploited the rivalry between Konev and Zhukov to dynamic effect. From as early as 1941, he had been grooming Konev, the politician, as a counterweight to the soldier Zhukov. He conferred honours on Zhukov only when he had to, while Konev received them willy-nilly. Thus Stalin maintained a balance between Zhukov, the indispensable 'organizer of victory', and his equally invaluable political antipode.

According to his own account of the meeting held in the Kremlin on

1 April (see p. 197), Konev was the first to reply to Stalin's pointed question about who was to seize the prize of Berlin. Konev had no doubts that the Red Army would write the finale to the Great Patriotic War by beating the British and Americans to the German capital. Smiling, Stalin replied: 'So this is the sort of man you are. How will you be able to get up a strike group for this purpose? Your main forces are on your southern flank, and it would seem that you will have to do a lot of redeployment.'

Konev replied: 'Comrade Stalin, you can rest assured that the front will carry out all necessary measures and that we will regroup for the offensive in proper time.' Zhukov was equally bullish, informing Stalin that First Belorussian Front was now 'saturated' with troops and equipment, aimed directly at Berlin, and was the shortest distance from the city. Stalin then asked both marshals to remain in Moscow to prepare their plans and report back within forty-eight hours, 'so that you can go back to the fronts with fully approved plans in your hands'.

There was much to resolve. Zhukov remained convinced that he could take Berlin with a frontal assault. Konev, still smarting from the earlier Stavka decision to relegate his forces to securing the territory to the south of the city, was determined to win agreement for a co-ordinated assault by both fronts. When they reconvened on 3 April, Stalin broke the deadlock by walking up to the map and drawing a line between the two fronts which ended at Lübben, on the River Spree, about thirty-seven miles south-east of Berlin. He then declared, 'Whoever gets there first will also take Berlin'.

Zhukov's account of the meeting is less dramatic, emphasizing that the offensive on the Berlin axis and the seizure of the city were charged to the troops of First Belorussian Front. It was Konev's task to attack from the Neisse River and destroy the enemy south of Berlin, isolating the principal formations of Army Group Centre from the units defending the city and thus supporting Zhukov's attack. Nevertheless, Zhukov added the rider: '. . . right here in the conference in the Stavka, I.V. Stalin issued instructions to . . . Konev: in the event of stiff enemy resistance on the eastern approaches to Berlin and the possible delay of the First Belorussian Front's offensive, the First Ukrainian Front will be ready to deliver a strike on Berlin from the south.'

As David Glantz has observed, 'the soundless cries of ten million military dead compelled the Soviets to undertake the last great operation of the Great Patriotic War'. It was not a task which Stavka took lightly. Keen students of history, they were well aware of the fate of earlier Russian armies at the gates of Berlin in 1760 and of Warsaw in 1920, when overconfidence had been heavily punished. History would not repeat itself, and the preparations for the assault on Berlin were accordingly thorough and made on a massive scale.

Stalin had been correct about the problems of redeployment. In the three fronts tasked with the Berlin operation, First Belorussian, First Ukrainian and Rokossovsky's Second Belorussian,* twenty-three armies set about regrouping along the Oder, fifteen of them moving a distance of up to 250 miles and three of them up to 500 miles. All these movements had to be accomplished in fifteen days. On Zhukov's front, where the the main attack was to be launched by Forty-Seventh, Third Shock and Eighth Armies, supported by IX Tank Corps, 7 million shells were brought up by rail and road for 8,983 guns, massed at a density of 295 to each attack kilometre. Thousands of bunkers and gun pits were scraped painfully out of the sodden, swampy ground. Bridge building continued at a frantic rate, with twenty-seven engineer battalions keeping damaged bridges open and laying twenty-five new ones across the Oder, linking the Küstrin bridgehead with the eastern bank of the river. Konev, whose front faced an assault crossing of the Oder and Neisse, had concentrated no fewer than 120 engineer and thirteen bridging battalions whose task it was to consolidate footholds on the western bank for the swift passage of armour across the rivers. Four air armies, deploying 7,500 aircraft, were to support the operation. On First Belorussian Front, Sixteenth Air Army had assembled 3,188 aircraft on 165 airfields and was augmented by the 800 long-range bombers of Eighteenth Air Army. Air corps and divisional commanders were ordered to join the staffs of infantry and tank armies the better to co-ordinate ground-air co-operation, with forward air controllers attached to the mobile units. In Rokossovsky's sector, the 1,360 aircraft of First Air Army were of particular importance as the redeployment of his entire front would not allow him to bring up sufficient artillery to support the forcing of the lower reaches of the Oder. Fire support and cover would be supplied by General Vershinin's airborne artillery.

Zhukov was under no illusions about the complex and difficult nature of the Berlin operation:

> In the experience of war we had not yet had the occasion to take such a strongly fortified city as Berlin. Its total area was almost 350 square miles. The city's subway and well-developed underground engineering structures gave the enemy manoeuvring capability. The city and its suburbs were carefully prepared for a stubborn

---

* In Moscow, Rokossovsky had sought and obtained a postponement of the launching of his offensive until 20 April.

defence. Every street, square, alley, house, canal and bridge constituted a part of the overall defence of the city.

Soviet reconnaissance aircraft made six aerial surveys of Berlin and all
its approaches and defence zones. From these surveys, combined with
captured documents and information gleaned from the interrogation of
prisoners, detailed assault maps were compiled and supplied to all commands down to company level. Army engineers constructed a scale
model* of the city and its suburbs for use in planning the final assault.
Army commanders, chiefs of staff, members of military councils, First
Belorussian Front's political commissar, front artillery chiefs and army
and corps commanders attended a conference from 5–7 April for command war games using maps and models. Also present was First
Belorussian's commander of support services, who made a careful study
of the problem of ensuring a steady flow of supplies. Another series of
war games was conducted at all levels from armies downwards between
8 and 14 April.

Zhukov decided to launch his attack two hours before dawn, 'to stun
the enemy and morally overwhelm him'. After conducting experiments
during the war games, he brought up 143 searchlights to illuminate
enemy positions when the assault went in, disorientate the defenders
and facilitate control over his own formations. He also fretted about the
correct moment at which to commit his armour, First and Second Guards
Tank Armies. The terrain facing the Küstrin bridgehead was distinctly
unfriendly to armoured operations. First, there was the ten-mile-wide
Orderbruch valley, heavily mined and criss-crossed with streams, irriga-
tion ditches and canals, and now extensively flooded by waters released
from an artifical lake 200 miles upstream. Beyond the valley lay the men-
acing mass of the Seelow Heights, a horseshoe-shaped escarpment rising
up to 200 feet above the valley. Here the German defences incorporated
a pattern of interlocking strongpoints and natural obstacles, utilizing
woods, villages and stretches of water as well as man-made abatis
(defences built from felled trees) and anti-tank ditches. Recognizing the
potential strength of these positions, Zhukov decided to introduce his
two tank armies only after the Seelow Heights had been seized: 'We did
not expect expect the tank armies to break into open operational areas
after our tactical breakthrough, as they had in the Vistula-Oder and East
Pomeranian operations.'

Above all, there was the problem of Berlin itself. A modern city, with
its large, strong buildings, boulevards and street complexes, waterways

---

* A similar model had been made before the storming of Königsberg.

and canals, can devour an army committed to a house-to-house battle. Stalingrad had shown as much, and Stavka had no desire to repeat the experience. The city would be taken in an all-out power drive in which specially chosen assault groups drawn from veteran infantry units would be supported by armour and massed artillery laying down a red-hot path of destruction all the way to the Reichstag, the 'Lair of the Fascist Beast'. In the assault sections Zhukov intended to step up the artillery concentration to 450 guns per mile of front.

As Goebbels observed, by the second week of April, Hitler's 'Fortress Europe' had been squeezed into a strip of territory running from Norway to Italy in the shape of a huge elongated hour-glass whose waist was pinched to a 100-mile land bridge between the Elbe and the Oder, with Berlin in the narrowest part between the two rivers. On the lower Oder, covering the northern approaches to Berlin, Colonel-General Heinrici's Army Group Vistula comprised Hasso von Manteuffel's Third Panzer Army, facing Second Belorussian Front, and General Busse's Ninth Army, facing First Belorussian Front. Heinrici also had under his command the remnants of Second Army, surrounded in the delta of the Vistula, and Operational Group Steiner, a headquarters under the command of SS General Felix Steiner which had no formations. South of Berlin, in the sector south-east of Lübben and facing First Ukrainian Front, was Fourth Panzer Army, forming part of the left wing of Schörner's Army Group Centre. It was commanded by the one-legged General Fritz Gräser, described by Goebbels as 'rather one of the old school but his attitude is splendid'. Positioned behind Manteuffel and Busse was LVI Panzer Corps, comprising SS Nordland and 18th Panzergrenadier Divisions, as well as fragments of 20th Panzergrenadier and 9th Parachute Divisions and the recently raised Müncheberg Division. The last was little more than a collection of 'shadow' formations trawled from military schools and reinforcement units with no battle experience. Between the Baltic coast and Görlitz, a hundred miles south-east of Berlin, were some fifty field divisions of the German army, five of them armoured, supplemented by a patchwork of makeshift battle groups and about a hundred Volkssturm battalions. They faced a total of 193 Soviet divisions,* but many of these were very run down, averaging between 2,500 and 5,500 men. For the assault on Berlin the Red Army was relying on its massive superiority in artillery, aircraft and armour.

In contrast with the West, where German troops were surrendering en masse, there was a grim determination to fight on in the East, in

---

* This figure, quoted by Chuikov in his memoirs, should be treated with some caution.

spite of an almost universal recognition of the inevitability of defeat. One German officer recalled:

> Even the last soldier was now aware that the war was lost. He was aiming to survive, and the only sense he could see was to protect the front in the East to save as many refugees as possible. He felt bitter to have to fight on German soil for the first time this century and he could not foresee any alternative but to stay with his unit and to stick to his oath of allegiance. He realized that the attempt of 20 July 1944 against Hitler had failed and, despite the obvious facts, he was hoping for a political solution for ending the war, not knowing however which kind of solution. Last but not least the demand for unconditional surrender* left in the light of self-respect no alternative but to continue the hopeless fighting.

The Führer had not made the task of the 'last soldier' any easier. His celebrated intuition told him that the main Soviet drive would be made in the direction of Prague rather than Berlin. On 6 April, confident that the line on the Oder would hold, he had transferred three panzer-grenadier divisions of Army Group Vistula to the south. When Heinrici protested, the Führer returned to his well-worn theme that the Russians were at the end of their tether and their armies were a motley rabble of released prisoners of war and press-ganged peasantry. By now Heinrici, a glum-faced but determined officer, was becoming inured to his Commander-in-Chief's surreal approach to the defence of Berlin. He had first met Hitler a week earlier, on 30 March, two days after Guderian had been dismissed after a final flaming row with the Führer over the failure of five divisions of Ninth Army to roll up Zhukov's bridgehead at Küstrin. Guderian had been replaced by the pliable Krebs, the protégé of General Burgdorf, who had been appointed Jodl's adjutant in January 1945. Heinrici had found the Führer no easier to deal with than had the hyper-tense Guderian. He had asked Hitler to relieve Frankfurt an der Oder of its 'fortress' status, thus releasing two divisions to bolster the line on the Oder. After quietly listening to Heinrici's arguments, Hitler asked Krebs for some papers on the Frankfurt sector, which he studied in silence for some minutes. Then, according to Captain Boldt, who was at the meeting:

> . . . quite without warning, Hitler raised himself on the arms of his chair, got up and began loudly and hysterically to quote key sentences of his well-known fortress order, going on then to deal with the 'fortress' of Frankfurt an der Oder. He abused Heinrici, the

---

* Issued by the Allies after the Casablanca Conference of January 1943.

General Staff, the generals and the officers as a body, claiming that they had never understood or wanted to understand his fortress order for reasons of cowardice and lack of determination. As abruptly as this outburst had begun, so too it was suddenly all over, and Hitler sank back into his chair completely exhausted. Even today I can still see Heinrici's stupefied face. Thunderstruck, he looked questioningly from one bystander to another. But none of the military leaders, chosen as they were by Hitler and constantly in his presence, were prepared to take Heinrici's part against the Führer. Heinrici went on obstinately fighting for his point of view, completely unsupported. Later on in the course of the discussion the question of the fortress commandant for Frankfurt an der Oder came up again. Hitler wanted a Gneisenau*, harking back to the history of the Napoleonic Wars in Germany. Heinrici wanted Colonel Bieler, because he considered him a sound, conscientious officer experienced in combat. When it emerged in the next few days that Hitler did not want Bieler . . . despite Heinrici's keenness to appoint him, and that neither of the two military command staffs was supporting Heinrici's cause, the General offered his resignation. Thereupon Hitler gave way and agreed, without any motivating factors at all, to Heinrici's wishes.

Later Hitler airily promised Heinrici 137,000 men from the SS, Luftwaffe and the Navy. Eventually about 30,000 arrived.

The defences of 'Fortress Berlin' were part and parcel of the same fantasy world. In mid-April the fortifications expert, General Max Pemsel, had taken one look at the city's defences and declared them to be 'utterly futile, ridiculous'. It was not until March that any serious consideration had been given to the defence of Berlin, and by then it was far too late. Under the direction of the city commandant, Lieutenant-General Helmuth Reymann, a makeshift 'obstacle belt' had been thrown up in a broken ring thirty miles outside the capital. On the hastily prepared defence maps, slit trenches and isolated pillboxes were marked as major strongpoints. A second ring was improvised around Berlin's railway system, whose cuttings, culverts and overhead railways would have provided excellent man-made obstacles and a formidable barrier to tanks, had there been enough troops to man them. The last-ditch defence ring – codenamed *Zitadelle* in an unconscious echo of the disaster at Kursk in 1943 – lay at the heart of the city and contained nearly all the government buildings. Radiating from its inner ring were eight wedge-shaped command sectors, designated clockwise from A to H.

---

* A reference to August Neithardt von Gneisenau (1760–1831), the great Prussian Marshal, military reformer and doughty opponent of Napoleon.

Within the command sectors were six huge flak towers, massive concrete ziggurats virtually impervious to bombs and artillery. The largest, at the Berlin Zoo, was 132 feet high with five storeys above ground. Its walls were 6 feet thick and heavy steel doors covered all the apertures. The top floor housed a 100-strong garrison, the floor below a well-equipped hospital for the use of VIPs, and the third had been turned into a warehouse for many of Berlin's art treasures. The lower floors were big enough to hold 15,000 shelterers and a radio studio. With its own water and electricity supply, bulging magazine and well-stocked food stores, the tower was self-sufficient, although almost unbearably noisy when its eight 128mm guns were action.

General Reymann had estimated that 200,000 fully equipped and trained troops would be needed to defend the metropolitan area of Berlin. However, the city did not have its own garrison. Inside the capital the only unit of any operational value was the Berlin Guard Battalion, from which had grown Grossdeutschland Division. Thus far its finest hour had come in the suppression of the July 1944 plot against Hitler. At Reymann's disposal were some 60,000 Volkssturm and a collection of Hitler Youth, engineer, police and anti-aircraft units. Reymann recalled: 'Their weapons came from almost every country that Germany had fought with or against. Besides our own issues there were Italian, Russian, French, Czech, Belgian, Dutch, Norwegian and English guns.' Although a substantial cache of Greek bullets was re-machined to fit the Italian rifles, few of the Volkssturm were issued with more than five rounds per rifle.

During the course of the Vistula-Oder offensive, a typically sardonic Berlin joke had suggested that the conduct of the war would become easier once the front line could be reached by the city's underground system. Now the sight of the flimsy barricades and improvised tank traps thrown up in Berlin's streets prompted the grim jest that it would take the Red Army two hours and fifteen minutes to break through them – two hours laughing their heads off and fifteen minutes smashing them down. Many of Berlin's 100,000 slave labourers had been put to work on the defences. Lance-Corporal Norman Norris, a British POW who was marched through the city at the beginning of April, noted, 'Huge tank traps were now being dug, one at Königswarterhausen by Polish Jews. They looked plaintively at us; the look in their eyes showing that they knew they would eventually be murdered was unforgettable.'

For the approximately 2.5 million people who remained in Berlin,* the struggle continued to maintain the semblance of a normal life in a city

---

* Berlin's pre-war population was 4.3 million.

which had changed utterly since 1939. The bulk of the male population was either under sixteen or over sixty. Twelve thousand policemen stayed at their posts. The mail continued to be delivered up to the last days of the war. Workers rose at dawn to negotiate the masonry-choked streets to their factories, 65 per cent of which were still in some kind of working order. A section of Berlin's zoo remained open to visitors. The Berlin Philharmonic Orchestra's season ran on until the end of March.

Bureaucrats were given shovels and ordered to become navvies for one day a week. With five companions, Hans-Georg von Studnitz found himself shovelling 'debris lying in the Wilhelmstrasse into some trucks and transport it into the courtyard of the Ministry, where others were engaged in strengthening the side-walls of the air-raid shelter. While we were at work, ankle-deep in muck, hundreds of Russian prisoners of war, also engaged in the clearing operation, watched us derisively.'

On 14 April Zhukov sent out a reconnaissance in force to probe the German positions around the Küstrin bridgehead. Chuikov later wrote:

> It began at 07:40 hours after a ten-minute artillery attack. In the zone of the Eighth Guards Army the reconnaissance battalions overran the enemy's forward position and advanced from two to four kilometres. The situation was much the same in the sector of our neighbour on the right, the Fifth Shock Army. The enemy was caught off balance, sustained losses and pulled back to the second line of defence. We captured a number of prisoners from the 20th Motorized and 303rd Infantry Divisions. A corporal of the 303rd Infantry Division said during interrogation: 'Germany will be finished in a fortnight.' 'Why?' he was asked. 'Your . . . offensive isn't the main one,' he replied. 'It's only a reconnaissance. You'll start the real thing in about two or three days. It'll take about a week for you to reach Berlin and another week to capture it. So, Hitler will be kaput in 15–20 days.'

The fighting had been heavy. General Busse observed:

> On the 14th the enemy continued his attack with increased strength the whole extent of the line down to the Lebus. The right wing of XI SS Panzer Corps repulsed all attacks with heavy losses to the enemy. In the other sectors of the Corps the enemy penetrated as far as as the second line. Near Seelow such a crisis arose that the 'Kurmark' Panzergrenadier Division had to be thrown into the fight to stop them [the Russians] getting too far. . . . In CI Corps's sector the enemy advanced more than five kilometres towards Wriezen. The bridgehead in this sector thus achieved a

depth of fifteen kilometres and was fully adequate for the deployment of strong forces. . . . Losses in men and material were high on
both sides, and ours could not be replaced, a serious matter.

On Sunday the 15th, Hitler issued the last of his Führer directives:

Soldiers of the German Eastern Front! For the last time our deadly
enemies the Jewish Bolsheviks have launched their massive forces
to the attack. Their aim is to reduce Germany to ruins and to exter-
minate our people. Many of you soldiers in the East already know
the fate which threatens, above all, German women, girls and children. While the old men and children will be murdered, the
women and girls will be reduced to barrack-room whores. The
remainder will be marched off to Siberia. We have foreseen this
thrust, and since last January have done everything possible to
construct a strong front. The enemy will be greeted by massive
artillery fire. Gaps in our infantry will have been made good by
countless new units. Our front is being strengthened by emergency
units, newly raised units, and by the Volkssturm. This time
the Bolshevik will meet the ancient fate of Asia – he must and
shall bleed to death before the capital of the German Reich.
Whoever fails in his duty at this moment behaves as a traitor to
our people. . . .

That evening the cautious, pragmatic Heinrici asked and received permission to pull back to his second line of defence, leaving only a skele-
ton force in the main line. In the Russian positions the men were
assembled to hear last-minute exhortations from their political officers.
Weaponry continued to move into the bridgehead while great quantities
of bridging equipment arrived on the banks of the Oder. For all the last-
minute activity, an overpoweringly tense quiet descended on the front.
As John Erickson has written: 'the entire front seemed to be creeping forward, rustling, creaking, stepping out of natural cover and from under
camouflage netting, a military monster in the making and coming more
alive with every minute.'

The colours of the Guards formations were brought up to the front line.
In the light of flares, Lenin's face looked down from the Red banner as if
alive, while the men pledged themselves to fulfil their assignments and
the 'revolutionary ideals and cherished aspirations of all honest men on
earth to freedom and happiness for mankind'.

In Berlin there was little thought given to the 'happiness of mankind'.
Goebbels's assistant, Dr Werner Naumann, considered that 'our propaganda as to what the Russians are like, as to what the population can

expect from them in Berlin, has been so successful that we have reduced the Berliners to a state of sheer terror.' Inside the city there was brisk trade in quick-acting cynanide-based 'KCB' pills.

In the small hours of the 16th, Zhukov joined Chuikov in his command post, calmly sipping tea as the minutes ticked away. At 5am Moscow time, 3am Berlin time, with the front still wrapped in darkness, the second-hand on Zhukov's watch completed its sweep and night became day. Three red flares shot up into the sky and the artillery opened up: Katyushas slashed in thousands from their ramps, muzzle flashes split the night, while heavy bombers and Shturmovik ground-attack aircraft roared overhead to bomb and strafe their targets. The Oder valley seemed to be rocking with the force of the barrage. The German front line, now virtually undefended, disappeared, forests were set ablaze and, in a weird atmospheric distortion, a hot debris-laden wind was sent howling back towards Berlin.

After seventeen minutes, a single searchlight beam sliced straight up into the sky, the signal for the other 142 to be switched on, their beams boring into the dense smoke and boiling dust raised by the bombardment. To the north and south of the Küstrin bridgehead, thousands of Red Army infantry scorned to wait for assault-boats or the completion of pontoon bridges. They plunged into the Oder; to a watching Russian officer, they seemed like 'a huge army of ants, floating across the water on leaves and twigs. The Oder was swarming with boatloads of men, rafts full of supplies, log floats supporting guns. Everywhere were the bobbing heads of men as they swam or floated across.'

Within minutes Zhukov lost control of the battle. Not only was his artillery punching thin air but his searchlights were also proving far more troublesome to his own troops than the enemy. The lights failed to penetrate the dense screen of fumes, dust and smoke shrouding the German front line. The assault troops groped blindly forward in the murk, further confused as the searchlights were bewilderingly snapped on and off, while Chuikov, whose command post had been enveloped by the military equivalent of an old-fashioned London 'pea-souper' fog, strove to stay in touch with his formations by radio and messenger.

For the opening thirty minutes of the battle the assault troops pushed forward for about a mile behind a double rolling barrage, meeting little or no resistance. When daylight came, the advance slowed as streams, canals, boggy ground and deep minefields held up their supporting tanks and self-propelled guns. Co-ordination between artillery, infantry and armour broke down just at the moment that the German artillery came to life. The advance was halted at the Haupt Canal, at the foot of the Seelow Heights, which had been swollen by spring floods. The few

bridges across it were subjected to heavy fire from German batteries on
the reverse slopes of the heights, and from well-camouflaged and dug-in
tanks and self-propelled guns. For once, the Germans seemed to be reading another script than that prepared by Zhukov.

On Konev's front, however, everything was going according to plan.
The forty-minute artillery bombardment which began at 6.15am was
accompanied by a colossal smoke screen, laid by aircraft and artillery,
which curled across his front. On a narrow eleven-mile frontage Konev
launched Thirteenth, Third and Fifth Guards Armies across the Neisse,
moving them up to the eastern bank in broad daylight. At 150 sites
engineers waited for the infantry with bridges and ferries. The leading
battalions crossed in boats, towing small assault bridges behind them.
Once the bridges were in position the infantry raced across them while
engineers, standing shoulder-deep in the icy water, fitted prefabricated
wooden sections to speed the passage of more infantry and the 85mm
anti-tank guns needed to bolster the footholds gained on the western
bank. Tanks and self-propelled guns moved across on ferries while Soviet
artillery and ground-attack aircraft suppressed the defenders' fire. By
8am the smoke was clearing to reveal Soviet armour moving out of the
bridgeheads against German positions. An hour later the first 30-ton
bridge was laid across the Neisse, and at 1pm, on Konev's left flank in
Fifth Guards Army's sector, T-34s of XI Mechanized Corps' 62 Guards Tank
Brigade were clattering across a 60-ton bridge followed by anti-tank gun
detachments and lorried infantry. A second brigade was snapping at 62's
heels, 16 Guards Mechanized, and both formations were immediately
ordered to forge on at top speed ahead of the infantry.

On Zhukov's front a colossal traffic jam was forming as Eighth Guards
Army clawed its way up the Seelow Heights. Chuikov's infantry cleared
the first two German lines but stuck fast in front of the third, while the
tanks and self-propelled guns, stranded in the mud behind them,
attempted to fan out in search of an easier way up the escarpment.
Probing up the roads to the town of Seelow, astride the heights, they suffered heavy losses from the German 88s and Panzerfausts waiting for
them round every turn.

Zhukov was incredulous that his attack had been fought to a halt.
Turning to Chuikov, he exploded, 'What the hell do you mean – your
troops are pinned down?' Chuikov, who was no stranger to Zhukov's outbursts, replied, 'Comrade Marshal, whether we are pinned down
temporarily or not, the offensive will almost certainly succeed. But resistance has stiffened for the moment and is holding us up.'

Later, recollecting in tranquillity, Chuikov pinpointed the reasons for
the initial failure: Heinrici's tactic of placing large numbers of infantry,

artillery and armour in his second and third lines and the strong deployment of reserves in the rear; the formidable field defences on the Seelow Heights; and the Soviet failure to appreciate the specific features of the terrain. 'Lack of roads restricted our freedom of manoeuvre and made it impossible to commit large forces during the attack. Finally our troops had to fight through a great number of inhabited localities where practically every house had to be taken by storm.'

At noon Zhukov's patience snapped and he decided to commit both his tank armies before the heights had been taken, and a full twenty-four hours before he had originally deemed it necessary. Chuikov's orders for a renewed infantry assault, preceded by a twenty-minute artillery barrage, were rescinded. Storming out of the command post, scattering startled staff officers to left and right, Zhukov snarled at Lieutenant-General M.E. Katukov, commander of First Guards Tank Army, 'Well, get moving!'

The 1,300 tanks and self-propelled guns of First and Second Guards Tank Armies were to smash their way up the Seelow Heights, First Guards in Chuikov's sector and Second Guards operating with Fifth Shock Army, on Zhukov's right flank. Zhukov watched Katukov's lead tanks move off at about 2.30pm. Soon chaos reigned as the lead formation, 44 Guards Tank Brigade, became hopelessly entangled with Chuikov's infantry and the artillery he had ordered up to support his renewed attack on the heights.

At 3pm Zhukov had a tense telephone conversation with Stalin. He reported that his front had encountered serious resistance on the line of the Seelow Heights, where the enemy defence seemed to be largely intact. Informing Stalin that he had committed both his tank armies, Zhukov estimated that he would breach the German defences by nightfall on the 17th. Stalin listened without interrupting and then said quietly: 'The enemy defence on Konev's front has proved to be weak. He has easily crossed the Neisse and is advancing while scarcely meeting any resistance. Support the attack of your tank armies with bombers. Report in the evening how things are going.'

Only on Chuikov's right, which was not entirely clogged with armour, was any significant progress made. By midnight IV Guards Corps had gained a foothold on the outskirts of Seelow. The attack continued throughout the night, Zhukov's armour blundering up the heights like an army of maddened beasts, slithering and slewing in the mud, sweeping Chuikov's infantry off the roads and exploding in sheets of flame as German artillerymen brought their 155mm guns to bear over open sights.

When Zhukov reported back to Stalin he admitted that there were still 'difficulties' at the approaches to the Seelow Heights and that there was little chance that the line would be taken before nightfall the next day:

> This time Stalin did not speak to me so calmly as he had in the
> daytime. 'You should not have committed the First Guards Tank
> Army to battle in the sector of Eighth Guards Army instead of
> where the Supreme Command had instructed.' Then he added:
> 'Are you certain you'll take the Seelow line tomorrow?' Trying to
> appear calm I answered: 'Tomorrow, 17 April, by the end of the day
> the defence on the Seelow Heights will be breached. I believe that
> the more of his troops the enemy hurls at our forces here, the
> quicker we will subsequently take Berlin, because it is easier to
> defeat the enemy in the open field than in a city.' After some
> exchanges concerning Konev's next moves and the timing of
> Rokossovsky's offensive Stalin said 'Goodbye' rather wryly, and
> instead of continuing, put down the receiver.

The race to Berlin was on, orchestrated from Moscow by Stalin. On the
17th Rybalko's leading tank units had forced a crossing of the Spree,
crashing over a ford without waiting for the engineers to arrive. Fierce
German counter-attacks were beating on Konev's northern and southern
flanks, held, respectively, by Third Guards and Fifth Guards Armies, while
an inviting gap opened up in the centre ahead of Thirteenth Army and
his armour. From a castle near Cottbus, in the centre of the breakthrough
zone, Konev telephoned Stalin, who told him: 'Zhukov is having a difficult time. He is still trying to break through the defences.' A long silence
followed before Stalin asked: 'Is it not possible to transfer Zhukov's
mobile forces and let them move towards Berlin through the gap you
have created on the sector of your front?' Konev replied: 'Comrade Stalin,
this will take much time and will cause great confusion. It is not necessary to transfer tank troops from the First Belorussian Front into the gap
we have created. Events in our sector are developing favourably, our
forces are adequate and we are in a position to turn both our tank armies
towards Berlin.' Konev then moved on to the direction in which his
armies would be turned, suggesting that the orientation point should be
Zossen, the headquarters of the German General Staff. Stalin asked
Konev the scale of the map he was using, to which the latter replied that
it was 1:200,000. After another silence, in which it appeared that Stalin in
Moscow was trying to find Zossen on his map, he answered: 'Very well.
Do you know that the headquarters of the German General Staff is at
Zossen?' Konev said that he was well aware of this. 'Very well,' said Stalin,
'I agree. Turn your tank armies towards Berlin.'

Konev immediately ordered Rybalko to force the Spree in strength that
same night and swing north-westwards to break into the southern out-

skirts of Berlin by the night of 20 April. Simultaneously, Lelyushenko's Fourth Guards Tank Army was to cross the Spree north of Spremberg and strike towards Luckenwalde before turning north to Potsdam and the south-western suburbs of Berlin. Speed was of the essence. Konev told his tank commanders that towns were to be bypassed and frontal attacks avoided: 'I demand a firm understanding that the success of the tank armies depends on boldness of manoeuvre and swiftness of operations.' In the small hours of the 18th, Rybalko and Lelyushenko, confident that Konev's flanks would hold, swung their tank columns north-west.

Zhukov, fuming with rage and still slogging his way towards the crest of the Seelow Heights, from which the road ran all the way to Berlin, piled on the pressure. On the 18th a fresh set of orders went out:

> 1. Step up the pace of advance without delay. If the Berlin opera-tion develops at a slow rate, the troops will become exhausted and expend their ammunition without taking Berlin. 2. All comman-ders shall be at the observation posts of the corps commanders conducting the engagement in the direction of the main effort. No commander may remain in the rear of his troops. 3. All artillery, including large calibres, shall be brought up to the first echelon and kept at a distance of not farther than 2–3 kilometres behind the first echelon engaging the enemy. Artillery fire shall be con-centrated in the breakthrough sectors. It is to be borne in mind that right up to Berlin the enemy will put up desperate resistance, fighting for each house and bush. Therefore, tank crews and infantry must not wait until the artillery wipes out enemy man-power and provides them the luxury of moving ahead across cleared-up areas. 4. Give the enemy no quarter and advance by day and by night, then Berlin will be in our hands very soon.

Zhukov cracked the whip as a huge pall of smoke, raised by bombers and artillery fire, hung over the churned and scarred slopes of the Seelow Heights. Eighth Guards and First Guards Tank Armies blasted their way to the crest, the T-34s swaddled in wire mattresses to take the sting out of the defenders' relentless Panzerfaust fire. It was not until the evening of the 19th that sheer weight of metal told and Zhukov managed to prise open the Oder line on a forty-four mile frontage, two days behind schedule. Four days of savage fighting had carried First Belorussian Front eighteen miles nearer Berlin. On the following day, Hitler's fifty-sixth birthday, Berlin's outer north-eastern perimeter was breached. Shortly before 2pm the long-range guns of Third Shock Army opened fire directly on the city. Their shells plummeted into the fires started by the last great Allied bombing raid of the European war. To the north, the assault forces of Rokossovsky's Second Belorussian Front went on to the offensive on the lower Oder.

The Führer's birthday was marked by a special issue of stamps and a rather more practical extra allocation of food rations to Berlin's civilian population: a pound of bacon or sausages, half a pound of rice or oatmeal, half a pound of dried lentils, peas or beans, one can of vegetables, two pounds of sugar, about an ounce of coffee, a small package of coffee substitute and some fats. These were to last eight days and were given the ironic nickname of *Himmelsfahrtrationen*, 'Ascension Day rations'.

That afternoon there was a birthday reception at the Chancellery, where the Nazi paladins – Speer, Bormann, Goebbels, Göring and Ribbentrop – gathered for the last time. The Chancellery's great halls and marble corridors were gutted and abandoned, the floors strewn with litter; cracked walls were propped up with timbers, windows boarded with card; watery spring sunlight shafted in through the gaping holes in the roof. But the Court of Honour, in front of the old Chancellery building, was still standing, and it was here that newsreel cameras caught Hitler's ertswhile cronies congratulating the Führer. Hitler's physical disintegration was now almost complete. One witness, Captain Peter Hartmann, noted that

> those of us who had known him in the earlier years before the war, when he was a human dynamo often bursting with restless energy, noted, from about 1942 on, that he seemed to be ageing at least five full years for every calendar year. Near the very end, on the day he celebrated his last birthday, he seemed closer to seventy than fifty-six. He looked what I would call physically senile. The man was living on nerves, dubious medicaments, and driving willpower. Sometimes even the willpower seemed to slacken. Then suddenly it would flash again with the old drive and fury.

Bent and trembling, Hitler, accompanied by Himmler, Goebbels and Göring, inspected a line of troops drawn up for him in the Chancellery garden – men of the SS Frundsberg Division, a detachment from the beleaguered Army Group Kurland, and a platoon of Hitler Youth. The cameras whirred as Hitler tweaked the cheeks of the boy defenders of the Third Reich.

Then Hitler and his party descended into the bunker, where he received Grand Admiral Karl Dönitz, C-in-C of the Navy, Field Marshal Wilhelm Keitel, head of OKW, and Keitel's Chief of Staff, Jodl, individually in his small conference room, before emerging into the corridor for the daily situation meeting. Dönitz's adjutant saw an old man, 'broken, washed-up, stooped, feeble and irritable'. Hitler resisted urgings that he leave Berlin for the south, agreeing only to the establishment of both a northern and a southern command in case Germany was split in two. Then his confederates took their leave. The fat folds in Göring's face glistened with sweat as he announced that he had 'extremely urgent tasks in south Germany'. Hitler merely stared vacantly beyond him. This was also the last meeting between Hitler and Himmler, after which the Reichsführer SS drove back to his headquarters at Ziethen Castle in Schleswig-Holstein to continue his secret negotiations with a representative of the World Jewish Congress, Norbert Masur, to whom he promised to release the Jewish women held in the concentration camp at Ravensbruck.*

After the leave-takings, Hitler retired to his room with Eva Braun. Shortly afterwards she emerged, seemingly vivacious and wearing a magnificent dress of silver-blue brocade. She was determined to celebrate, and according to one of Hitler's secretaries, Traudl Junge,

> . . . she took everyone she met with her up into the old living room on the first floor of the Führer's apartment, which was still standing. The beautiful furniture was all down in the bunker, but the large round table was still there and it had been laid out in festive manner once more. Even the Reichsleiter Bormann had left Hitler's side and abandoned his command post. Fat Theo Morell, Hitler's personal physician, had come out of the safety of his bunker, despite the continual rumble of artillery. Someone had brought a gramophone, but only one record – a popular pre-war hit called 'Red Roses Bring You Happiness'. It is a very catchy tune and everyone started dancing. We drank champagne and laughed loudly, but it was very hollow kind of laughter. I joined in but there was a big lump in my throat. Suddenly a sharp explosion shook the building, making the windows tremble; then the telephone rang and someone hurried to take the call and write down the message; someone else received some important reports. . . . The muffled roar of the artillery seemed to become louder than the laughter and the music. . . .

In the north, the British were on the outskirts of Bremen and Hamburg; in the south the French were on the Upper Danube; Vienna was in

---

* On 22 April 15,000 women were released from Ravensbruck and taken to freedom in a fleet of buses of the Danish and Swedish Red Cross, leaving behind some 2,000 sick women with those who had volunteered to stay to look after them.

Russian hands, while in Italy the city of Bologna had fallen to II Polish Corps and US 34th Division; in the heartland of the Reich, Patton was driving south through Bavaria. On the approaches to Berlin, the German defences had been cracked open. After the war General Karl Weidling, commanding LVI Panzer Corps, declared that 20 April was 'the most difficult day for my corps and very likely for all the German units. They had suffered terrible losses in previous battles, were extremely exhausted and unable to withstand the great onslaught of the superior Russian troops.'

On the morning of 21 April, Colonel-General Krebs held the last conference at Zossen, whose forested, camouflaged compounds contained the nerve centres of the German high command: OKH headquarters, codenamed 'Maybach I'; and 'Maybach II', OKW headquarters, with its huge subterranean communications room, 'Exchange 500', the biggest telephone, teletype and military radio exchange in Germany, the equivalent of a seven-storey building underground. Halfway through the meeting a mud-spattered junior officer arrived with the news that the Russians were at Baruth, only ten miles to the south. Krebs immediately telephoned Hitler to request the transfer of his headquarters, but the Führer refused. Captain Gerhard Boldt, who was at the conference, remembered: 'There was only one thought written on the faces of all the officers . . . a Russian prisoner-of-war camp.'

It was not until about 1pm that Hitler gave Krebs permission to relocate in the Luftwaffe barracks at Potsdam-Eiche. An hour later Boldt was part of the long convoy which roared through the gates of 'Maybach II' in the direction of Potsdam. The convoy drove down the main highway along which

> hundreds of thousands of people were on the move, many with horses and carts, others with bicycles, hand-barrows or prams, most of them on foot, all heading west, anywhere to escape the enemy. Tank barricades on the exit routes of the towns and villages only let a trickle through at a time. Here and there above us, on the huge barricades built of wood and stone children were playing, unsuspecting and ignorant of the danger. They waved to us, wearing paper helmets and brandishing wooden swords. Winding our way through the stream of refugees, we pressed on to Potsdam. A motorcyclist coming in the opposite direction reported that the centre of Berlin was already under artillery fire from the Russians. The first deaths had already been reported in the Dorotheenstrasse, in the centre of the city.

Konev's tank brigades had hung back from taking Zossen, but later that day VI Tank Corps arrived at the abandoned headquarters. In

Exchange 500, guarded by four fat and drunken soldiers who immediately threw their hands in the air, telephones rang and teleprinters spewed out frantic messages from disintegrating fronts. On the consoles the departing Germans had placed hastily written notices in schoolboy Russian: 'Do not damage these installations'.

From the Führerbunker came a ceaseless stream of orders – irrational, contradictory, none of them capable of fulfilment. Manteuffel, whose Third Panzer Army was now all that was left of Army Group Vistula, observed: 'I have no doubt that on Hitler's maps there is a little flag saying 7th Panzer Division, even though it got here without a single tank, truck, piece of artillery or even a machine-gun. We have an army of ghosts.'

On the 21st, General Karl Koller, the elderly Luftwaffe Chief of Staff, who had stayed in Berlin after Göring's departure, spent most of the day in a gruelling telephone marathon. His somewhat less than broad shoulders had perforce to bear the brunt of Hitler's rage against the Luftwaffe. Koller's diary recorded his ordeal:

> In the evening between 8.30 and 9 he is again on the telephone. 'The Reichsmarschall [Göring] is maintaining a private army in Karinhall.* Dissolve it at once and ... place it under SS Obergruppenführer Steiner', and he hangs up. I am still considering what this is supposed to mean when Hitler calls again: 'Every available Luftwaffe man in the area between Berlin and the coast as far as Stettin and Hamburg is to be thrown into the attack I have ordered in the north-east of Berlin', and there is no answer to my question of where the attack is supposed to take place; he has already hung up.

The attack which so puzzled Koller never took place. Operational Group Steiner, another of the flags on Hitler's map, had been ordered to sweep down from Eberswalde, north of Berlin, on to Zhukov's right flank. But Operational Group Steiner did not exist. In the confusion which had followed Hitler's orders, units of Zhukov's Second Guards Tank, Third Shock and Forty-Seventh Armies broke through to the northern outskirts of the city. The units following them were regrouped for siege warfare. Chuikov, the

---

* Göring's vast estate at Birkenheim which contained, among other things a private zoo. Heinrici, who visited Göring on 8 April, recalled that the castle's reception hall was like 'a church so large that one's eye automatically travelled up to the roof beams'. Göring evacuated the estate on 20 April, sending his art treasures south, and personally pressing the plunger which blew the castle to smithereens before driving off to attend Hitler's birthday party.

defender of Stalingrad, knew exactly what was necessary. He later wrote:

> An urban battle is governed by its own laws. . . . It is a fire combat
> in which not only automatic weapons but powerful artillery sys-
> tems and tank guns are involved at close quarters, hitting targets a
> few dozen metres away. The enemy, hidden in basements and
> buildings, opens machine-gun fire and hurls grenades as soon as
> you appear. . . . An advance through a city develops in fits and
> starts as troops dash from one captured building to another. But
> these actions take place on a broad front, on every street. For the
> defenders the main task is to hold tactically important buildings
> and blocks. The loss of a single building is tantamount to the loss
> of a strongpoint or position.

Chuikov formed assault groups, each made up from a company of
infantry, supported by anti-tank guns and troops of tanks or self-propelled
guns, engineer platoons and flame-throwers. The assault groups
remained in constant touch with their armour, which in the confines of
the city was highly vulnerable to Panzerfaust fire, informing tank commanders in what building and on which floor, in which attic or in what
cellar, the enemy was lurking. Chuikov was also keenly aware of the danger of bypassed enemy pockets popping up in his rear:

> In a street battle the enemy is often liable to turn up where
> he is least expected. The retreating enemy left groups of saboteurs
> behind our lines. Hiding in the cellars while the forward, and
> sometimes even the rearward, units had passed, they struck sud-
> denly, aiming to create panic in the rear and thus paralyse and
> slow up the forward troops. To deal with these groups of saboteurs
> we formed special rearward security detachments.

Overhead, heavy artillery and rockets laid down a crushing fire to prepare the way for the next jump forward, while medical teams stood close
to the rear to deal not only with the heavy casualties from shot and shell
but also those who had fallen between storeys or had been buried under
debris.

On 22 April crisis point was reached in the bunker. Berlin was now cut
off on three sides and Soviet tanks had been reported probing round to
the west of the city. At the midday briefing Hitler suddenly lost his self-
control, turning blue in the face and raging against the cowardice,
incompetence and treachery of the assembled military. Finally he
blurted out that the war was lost – the unmentionable had at last been
admitted. Keitel and Jodl were free to leave and conduct operations as

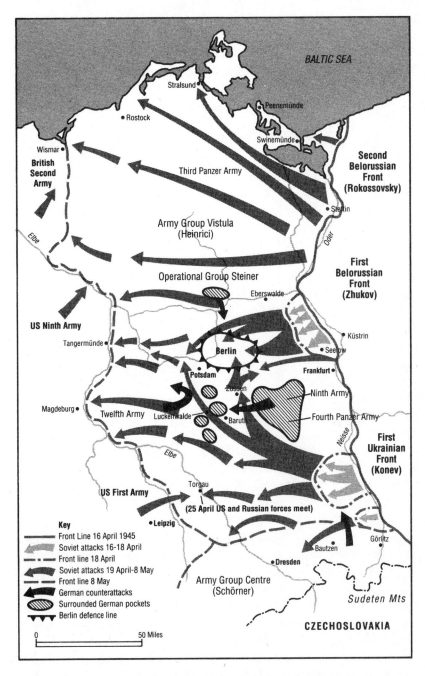

With the Western Allies on the Elbe, Zhukov's First Belorussian and Konev's First Ukrainian Front made the final assault on Berlin while Rokossovsky's Second Belorussian Front overran Army Group Vistula.

best they could. Hitler declared that he would never leave Berlin. As he was in no physical condition to fight, and could never contemplate capture and exhibition in a 'Moscow zoo', he would commit suicide. Any negotiating with the enemy that remained to be done was to be left to Göring.

Slowly Hitler got a grip on himself. In his deep, mellifluous baritone Goebbels calmed him and agreed to remain in the bunker with his family. When, on the following day, two of Hitler's secretaries pleaded to be allowed to stay with him, his eyes misted over and he said with a sigh, 'Ah, if only my generals were as brave as my women'. Then he rose to kiss Eva Braun on the lips, something he had never been seen to do in public before. With the help of the drugs administered by his valet, he achieved a kind of serenity. Later that day he received Speer, who had flown in from Hamburg to bid farewell to his patron. When Speer confessed that for weeks he had been striving to thwart Hitler's scorched-earth orders, the Führer showed no emotion.

Meanwhile the exodus continued. Keitel and Jodl, who had attended every one of Hitler's command conferences throughout the war, left the bunker on 22 April for the comparative safety of Fürstenburg, thirty miles north of Berlin, where they were close to Ravensbruck concentration camp which housed the so-called *Prominenten*, a group of well-connected foreign prisoners who were being held as hostages. Grand Admiral Dönitz had already removed himself to Plön, near Kiel on the Baltic, which had been his naval headquarters since March. Others came and went, the most spectacular arrival being that of General Robert Ritter von Greim, the commander of Luftflotte 6, based in Munich. Summoned to the bunker, he had arrived in Berlin on the 26th flying a Fieseler Storch light aircraft and accompanied by the woman test pilot Hanna Reitsch, a fanatical Nazi. Greim, who was at the controls, had been badly wounded in the foot just before touching down, leaving Reitsch to seize the stick and throttle to make a perfect landing on the road that forms Berlin's east-west axis, the broad street running from the River Havel on the west of the city to Unter den Linden in the centre. No sooner had Greim arrived in the bunker than he was appointed Field Marshal, a promotion that could equally well have been made by telephone. Now the new commander of the Luftwaffe was stranded, badly wounded, in the Führerbunker.

His predecessor, Göring, had secured his own dismissal on 23 April when he sent a telegram to Hitler from Berchtesgaden:

My Führer, In view of your decision to remain in the fortress of Berlin, are you agreed that I immediately assume overall leadership of the Reich as your Deputy, in accordance with your decree of 29 June 1941 with complete freedom of action at home and abroad? Unless an answer is given by 10pm I will assume that you have been deprived of your freedom of action. I shall then regard the conditions laid down by your Decree as being met, and shall act in the best interests of the people and the Fatherland. You know my feelings for you in these hardest hours of my life. I cannot express them adequately. May God protect you and allow you to come here soon despite everything. Your loyal Hermann Göring.

Göring was planning to fly to meet Eisenhower to ask for peace terms, although what worried him most was which of his many splendid uniforms he should wear for this momentous occasion. Hitler issued orders for Göring to be placed under house arrest. He then telegraphed his erstwhile colleague: 'Your actions are punishable by the death sentence, but because of your valuable services in the past I will refrain from instituting proceedings if you will voluntarily relinquish your offices and titles. Otherwise steps will have to be taken.' Hastily, the Reichsmarschall laid down his baton.

While these charades were being played out in the bunker, the people of Berlin were taking to their cellars. Vera Bockmann remembered:

The artillery was getting heavier and heavier, so we began to congregate in the basement during the day. . . . Someone put up a kerosene lamp. It was dim and smelly but we all grew to treasure that beacon of light burning night and day. No electricity, no more radio. Someone had brought a chiming clock – it was a normal sound from the normal world. Otto [her husband] had a small iron stove put in the coal cellar and that is where we set up our communal kitchen. Quite remarkable how it all functioned. After all, there were forty-one of us. We no longer dashed up to our flats indiscriminately, but at five in the morning there was usually a respite when we went up to have a wash. The water supply had been cut off but, just as our old-fashioned stove had been our only source of warmth, something far more important had been discovered. The streets of Berlin still had pumps, relics from the old-horse-and-buggy days. The water came up from wells, and as far I know were never used after the horse-and-buggy era. Now they proved invaluable. As they were so ornate, they had never been dismantled. The water was brackish, but it was uncontaminated, and wealth was counted by the number of buckets of water you had standing around.

In the bunker hopes now rested on General Walther Wenck's Twelfth

Army, to the west of Berlin. In the early hours of 23 April Keitel arrived at
Wenck's headquarters in the Weisenberg Forest, south-west of Berlin.
With much pointed waving of his field marshal's baton, Keitel ordered
Wenck to turn east and drive through Potsdam to Berlin, declaring por-
tentously, 'The Battle for Berlin has begun'. In truth it was already over,
as Wenck well knew. He heard Keitel out but had made his own plans.
Twelfth Army was to 'play it by the book', shifting towards Berlin but not
abandoning its position on the Elbe. In this way a corridor could be kept
open to the west. Wenck's army was surrounded by half a million
refugees, and appeals to save Hitler's life from Keitel, a desk general
if ever there was one, no longer had any meaning. In the bunker the
unanswered cry of '*Wo ist Wenck?*' was to echo round the walls of Hitler's
cubby hole as the Third Reich slid into oblivion.

At the same time that Keitel was haranguing Wenck, Stalin issued the
order which decided who was going to win the race to Berlin. Stavka
Directive No.11074 set a boundary between First Belorussian and First
Ukrainian Fronts which ran along a line from Lübben to the Anhalter station in the centre of Berlin, placing Konev's front a crucial 150 yards to
the west of the Reichstag, the pre-eminent symbolic objective in the
assault on Berlin. The 'conqueror of Berlin' was, after all, to be Zhukov,
exactly as Stalin had promised in November 1944.

On 24 April, Konev's front ran into a major obstacle, the Teltow Canal.
Most of its bridges had been blown, and the remainder prepared for
demolition. The northern bank was lined with bunkers and strongpoints
bristling with guns, dug-in tanks and Panzerfaust units. For the assault on
the canal, Konev assembled 966 guns to the mile, including the heaviest-
calibre pieces, rushed up on his orders, and under their fire the front's
assault troops swarmed across the Teltow without waiting for the barrage
to lift. A bridgehead established at Lankwitz by XI Mechanized Corps was
thrown back by determined German armoured and infantry attacks.
Others held, allowing Soviet engineers to bridge the canal while Konev
observed the action from the roof of a tall building. That day contact was
made between Eighth Guards and First Guards Tank Armies and Third
Guards Tank and Twenty-Eighth Armies in the south-eastern sector of
Berlin. There were now only three roads from Berlin open to the west,
and these were being constantly strafed by the Shturmoviki. Soviet casualties were mounting, however. Many companies had been reduced to
thirty men and regiments were fielding only two battalions rather than
three. The dead were consigned to graves hastily dug in gardens and
open spaces.

Zhukov, dismayed by the speed of Konev's progress, telephoned
Chuikov on the evening of the 24th, demanding to know exactly what

was going on. Somewhat taken aback, Chuikov told him that at 6pm units on the left flank of XXVIII Rifle Corps had made contact with Rybalko's tanks near the Schoenfeld aerodrome. Confirmation of the link-up soon arrived at Chuikov's command post in the form of Rybalko himself, who immediately put in a telephone call to the increasingly querulous Zhukov, who was still fearful of being beaten to the tape by his rival.

The battle for Berlin threw up weird constrasts: a delirium of fighting in some sectors and an almost eerie calm in others. In the early evening of the 24th the remnants of the Charlemagne Division – a Waffen-SS formation made up of French volunteers – fell back through the eastern outskirts of Berlin under the leadership of General Krukenberg. In its fifteen-mile march, the only troops encountered by Krukenberg's unit, now approximately battalion strength, was a trio of Panzerfaust-armed Hitler Youth on bicycles. All the bridges on their route were unguarded. They reached the empty Olympic stadium at about 10pm, looting an untenanted Luftwaffe canteen. Krukenberg then requisitioned a civilian car and drove with his adjutant down the Bismarckstrasse to the Brandenburg Gate and thence on to the Chancellery. The streets were uniformly quiet and the two SS officers saw little or no sign of any defensive works. They had crossed the city without once being stopped by sentries.

Gerhard Boldt had a similar experience when he reported to the bunker on the night of the 23rd:

> Darkness had fallen; the streets were almost deserted; the thunder of the battle for Berlin had almost died entirely away. The deeper we got into the city, the more lifeless the gigantic metropolis appeared. We reached the Wilhelmplatz without incident and turned into the Voss-strasse. The long frontage of the Reich Chancellery rose up dark and massive against the clear night sky. As we approached the Reich Chancellery, the dull burst of a shell shattered the illusion of peace. Everything appeared deserted. In front of the Party entrance lay a pile of rubble from a row of houses which had collapsed on the street. I ordered the car to stop near the Armed Forces entrance. There was no sign of the sentry who was usually on guard there. A hiss and a roar shattered the ... silence once again, and there was the bursting crash of a heavy shell which must have landed near the Potsdamerplatz. Beyond the ruins, in the direction of the firing, a faint burning glow grew even brighter.

Eight armies were now tightening the noose around Berlin. On the morning of the 25th, Chuikov arrived at his command post, which had been set up in a big five-storey building near the Johannistahl airfield:

> From a corner room with a jagged hole in the wall, I had a view of
> the southern and south-eastern parts of Berlin. It was impossible to
> see the whole of the city, which sprawled for scores of kilometres
> on either side of the Spree. All I could see were roofs and roofs,
> with gaps in them here and there, the work of high-explosive
> bombs. I also saw factory chimneys and church spires in the dis-
> tance. The parks and public gardens with the young leaves already
> out looked like spots of green foam. The morning mist mixed with
> the dust whipped up by the previous night's bombardment. In
> places the the mist blended with streams of greasy black smoke.
> Somewhere in the heart of Berlin ragged columns of yellow smoke
> and dust rose into the air as bombs exploded: our heavy bombers
> had already begun softening up the targets in preparation for the
> attack.

As Eighth Guards Army drove north to the centre of Berlin, the
Russians and Americans joined hands at the Elbe. At 1.30pm on
the 25th, in the Strehla sector, units of 58th Guards Rifle Division from
General A.S. Zhadov's Fifth Guards Army made contact with a reconnaissance group from US 69th Infantry Division, attached to V Corps of
First Army. On the same day, 173rd Guards Rifle Regiment bumped into
an American patrol in the area of Torgau. At about 1pm that afternoon
Lieutenant Albert Kotzbue of US 69th Division met a lone Red Army soldier near the village of Leckwitz. Crossing the river, whose banks were littered with the corpses of civilians cut down in some terrible but
unexplained massacre, Kotzbue had encountered more Soviet troops.
Later that afternoon another 69th Division patrol, led by Lieutenant
William D. Robinson, met Red Army units at Torgau, celebrating the
'official' link-up at 4.40pm.

While the Americans and the Russians joined up in a brief demonstration of comradeship in arms, the Wehrmacht was thrashing about in
its Berlin death throes, doomed, but still with the firepower to inflict deep
claw marks on the Red Army. Formations which had been all but wiped
off the order of battle in the struggle for the Seelow Heights appeared on
the outskirts of Berlin, shredded but still fighting. Weidling's LVI Corps
was one such. Indeed, so great was the confusion which now reigned in
the bunker that Hitler issued orders for Weidling's arrest on charges of
desertion. Weidling protested his innocence from a public telephone,
rushed to the bunker and, instead of facing a firing squad, found himself
appointed battle commandant of Berlin. Grimly, he observed that the
firing squad might have been a better option.

In Berlin the situation was desperate. Water and public transport systems had finally broken down. Food warehouses in the suburbs had been overrun by the Russians, and in the city stocks were down to two or three days. On 22 April the telegraph office had closed down after receiving its last message from Tokyo, 'Good Luck to You All'. Looting broke out. The huge Karstadt department store in the Hermannplatz was ransacked by a mob before it was dynamited by the SS, who were determined to deny the Russians the vast quantities of supplies salted away in its basement. Flying SS court-martial squads roamed the streets, shooting or stringing up from lampposts those they deemed to be deserters. An officer in the Müncheberg Panzer Division, now being shovelled back towards the centre of Berlin from the Tempelhof airfield (which fell to 39th and 79th Guards Divisions on the 26th), wrote in his diary:

> The wounded that are not torn apart are hardly taken in anywhere. The civilians in their shelters are afraid of them. Too many of them have been hanged as deserters. And the flying courts martial drive the civilians out of the cellars where they pick up deserters, because they are accessories to the crime. These courts martial appear in our sector particularly often today. Most of them are very young SS officers. Hardly a medal or a decoration on them. . . . General Mummert [Weidling's successor commanding LVI Corps, of which Müncheberg Division was a part] requests that no more courts martial visit the sector. A division made up of the largest number of men with the highest decorations does not deserve to be persecuted by such babies. He is resolved to shoot down any court martial that takes action in our sector.*

Now the Soviet armies which had encircled Berlin – 464,000 men supported by 12,700 guns, 21,000 rocket launchers and 1,500 tanks – drove into the centre of the city in a series of relentless concentric attacks. At the heart of the defence system was the Zitadelle, an island formed by the Spree in the north and the Landwehr Canal in the south, with an eastern bastion around the Alexanderplatz commanded by Lieutenant-Colonel Seifert, and a western bastion around the Knie under General

---

* The courts martial were conducted by fanatical officers in SS General Mohnke's Leibstandarte Guard Regiment. Mohnke himself had been ordered to set up 'flying field and station tribunals' by Himmler on 23 April. It was by these methods that Himmler had sought to stiffen morale during his brief period in command of Army Group Vistula. After the war the West German government treated the executions as war crimes bringing a number of senior SS officers to trial, including General Max Simon, commander of 16th SS Panzergrenadier Division.

Krukenberg. In overall command was SS General Mohnke, at thirty-four the youngest general still serving in the SS, and one of the founding members of Hitler's personal bodyguard, the Leibstandarte. For the defence of the Zitadelle, Mohnke's battle group consisted of the Leibstandarte Guard Regiment, a 1,200-strong detachment of combat veterans from its parent formation, the Leibstandarte Division;* Hitler's personal bodyguard, the Führer Begleit Kompanie or FBK; Himmler's bodyguard battalion; and a 2,000-strong Freikorps Adolf Hitler, all of them volunteers who had chosen to fight to the last for their Führer. During the last days of the battle the secretaries and female staff of the government departments Mohnke was defending were encouraged to join the ranks of the battle group, which was strung out along the southern perimeter of the Zitadelle around the Potsdamerplatz. These combatants were dubbed the 'Mohnke Girls'.

Berlin's S-bahn ring was breached on the 26th, and by nightfall on the 27th 'Fortress Berlin' had been squeezed down to an east-west belt ten miles long and three miles wide. The streets were strewn with dead – Volkssturm, Red Army soldiers, and women who, like Vera Bockmann, had crept up from their cellars to fill pails with water from a pump or standpipe and had been blown apart by Russian shells. In many districts at the heart of the fighting, elderly women, dressed soberly and wearing hats, queued patiently for food and other necessities while the battle boiled around them, T-34s looming out of the smoke to disappear into the murk, their guns firing at some unseen target. A position in the queue was not to be lost by seeking cover from high-explosive. These Berliners had been hardened by Allied bombing and had become inured to fire and sudden death. Only when machine-gun fire swept over their heads did the lines break up as individuals pressed themselves into doorways or hurried down steps to nearby cellars.

The cellars themselves sooon offered scant safety as the Russians attempted to outflank the street defences of the Zitadelle by smashing their way through courtyards, buildings and basements, blasting through party walls and leaving a trail of rape and destruction behind them. A stunned populace submitted with bewilderment to that characteristically Russian mixture of savagery and sudden, unexpected generosity. A Red Army man might rape a woman and then reappear, bearing presents of food, to protect her against the other soldiers. Dazed Hitler Youth were disarmed, given a cuff round the ear and packed off home. Near Potsdam, Russian infantrymen looted the UFA film studios, dancing

---

* 1st SS Division Leibstandarte Adolf Hitler fought its last major action in the Lake Balaton offensive in Hungary in March 1945.

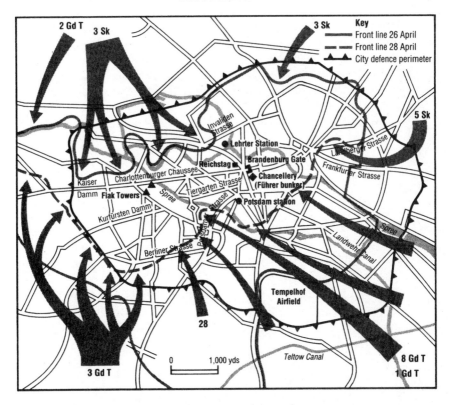

The Red Army's thrusts towards the Zitadelle in central Berlin

crazily in the streets in a bizarre assortment of costumes while bullets whistled around their heads.

On the night of the 26th the first Russian shells struck the Chancellery, sending vibrations through the Führerbunker as tons of masonry toppled into the street below, while the bunker's ventilators sucked in sulphurous fumes from the shell blasts, further poisoning an atmosphere rank with unwashed bodies, sweat and fear. The defences inside the Zitadelle buckled and threatened to give way. By now Müncheberg Division had been driven back from its front on the Tempelhof airfield, just inside the S-Bahn ring, to improvised positions around the Anhalter station, less than half a mile from the Chancellery. The division's diarist recorded:

> April 26. The night is fiery red. Heavy shelling. Otherwise a terrible silence. We are sniped at from many houses – probably foreign labourers. About 5.30am another grinding artillery barrage. The Russians attack. We have to retreat again, fighting for street after street. . . . New command post in the subway tunnels under the

Anhalter railway station. The station looks like an armed camp.
Women and children huddling in niches and corners listening for
the sounds of battle. Shells hit the roof, cement is crumbling from
the ceiling. Powder smell and smoke in the tunnels. . . . Late afternoon we change position again. A terrible sight at the entrance of
the subway station, one flight below street level: a heavy shell has
pierced the roof, and men, women, soldiers, children are literally
squashed against the walls.

In this sector Müncheberg Panzer Division joined the Nordland
Division, part of Krukenberg's command and of little more than battalion
strength. As a sector commander in the centre of Berlin, Krukenberg's
command post was a derelict subway carriage at the Stadmitte U-bahn
station beneath the junction of Mohrenstrasse and Friedrichstrasse. It had
no electric light or telephone but an abundance of food supplies looted
from the grocery shops in the nearby Gendermenmarkt.

Around Krukenberg's carriage swarmed hundreds of refugees seeking
the safety of the underground platforms. Overhead was the dull, regular
thump of impacting Soviet shells. Every so often a close hit would send
chunks of masonry spinning into the crowds on the platforms. A surreal
touch was added by the occasional arrival of a train, rolling slowly on to
an unknown destination.

Then water began to flow through the tunnels. In a bid to prevent the
Russians from advancing through them, engineers had been ordered to
blow the bulkheads which separated the tunnels from the Landwehr
Canal. There was a mad scramble to get above ground – a scene graphically reconstructed after the war in G.W. Pabst's film *Der Letzte Akt* (*The
Last Act*). Thousands were reported to have died in the tunnels that day,
but it is likely that the casualties were far fewer. After the initial alarm the
waters subsided and then the tunnels filled up gradually. The official who
was in charge of pumping out the subways in the autumn of 1945 stated
that the majority of the bodies recovered were those of people who had
died of their wounds before being placed in the tunnels.

On the night of the 28th, with the Red Army less than a mile away,
Hitler was dealt the final blow. At about 10pm an officer of the
Propaganda Ministry handed him a copy of a Reuters report that
Heinrich Himmler had contacted the Swedish diplomat Count
Bernadotte in order to negotiate a surrender in the West. Hitler was
beside himself with rage. Göring's treachery could be dismissed as the
aberration of a preposterous drug addict. But the defection of '*der treue
Heinrich*' – the one subordinate on whose loyalty Hitler could depend
absolutely – was the bitterest stroke of all. It had been a week since the

Führer had admitted to his commanders that the war was lost and that he intended to commit suicide. Now, after a characteristic period of hesitation and wavering, he made up his mind.

The first victim of Himmler's treachery was Eva Braun's brother-in-law, SS General Hermann Fegelein, an illiterate former jockey who had become the Reichsführer's personal liaison officer with Hitler. On the night of the 27th Fegelein had been apprehended in his foreign mistress's apartment, his pockets stuffed with Swiss francs and diamonds. He had been missing from the bunker complex for two days and, it seemed, had every intention of taking flight from what the hapless General Koller realized was a 'lunatic asylum'. Fegelein was frog-marched to Mohnke's command post under the Voss-strasse and then hauled, roaring drunk, before a court martial. Mohnke decided that he was in no fit state to stand trial and handed Fegelein, who was now sticky with his own excrement and urine, over to General Johann Rattenhuber, the Chancellery's Security Chief. In the early hours of 29 April Fegelein was shot.*

The new Commander-in-Chief of the Luftwaffe, Ritter von Greim, was now ordered to fly out of Berlin with Hanna Reitsch to arrest Himmler.[†] They took off from Berlin's east-west axis in a small Arado, scraping over the Brandenburg Tor, shells bursting around them, a sea of fire burning below as a furious fight raged around the Ministry of Interior building, or the 'Himmler House' as the Russians called it.

After the departure of Greim and Reitsch, and the disposal of Fegelein, Hitler married the late liaison officer's sister-in-law. The ceremony, conducted in the small hours of the 29th by a minor official in the Propaganda Ministry, Walter Wagner, was a model of *petit-bourgeois* respectability. Hitler and Eva Braun affirmed that they were of pure Aryan descent and were free of hereditary diseases, and were declared man and wife. In her excitement Eva Braun began to sign her maiden name on the wedding certificate, then crossed out the letter B and wrote 'Eva Hitler, née Braun'. With prim bureaucratic efficiency, Wagner changed the incorrectly entered date on the certificate from 28 to 29 April. Within an hour, once more back on duty with the Volkssturm, he was fatally shot through the head.

---

* In his book *The Berlin Bunker*, James P. O'Donnell has suggested that Fegelein's mistress was a spy, and that suspicion about this and information leaked from the bunker sealed his fate.

[†] Reitsch and Greim failed to arrest Himmler, but at Plön, after Hitler's suicide Reitsch angrily confronted him for betraying the Führer. When Himmler protested that Hitler was insane, Reitsch retorted: 'Hitler died bravely and honourably, while you and Göring and the rest must now live branded as cowards and traitors.'

After the wedding there was a melancholy little reception in Hitler's suite attended, among others, by Goebbels and his wife, Bormann, General Burgdorf, Ambassador Walther Hewel, Artur Axmann, the head of the Hitler Youth, Colonel Nikolaus von Below, the Luftwaffe liaison officer, Gerda Christian, one of the Führer's secretaries, and Heinz Linge, his personal servant. Amid the clink of champagne glasses the conversation ranged for the last time over the glories of past years. A surgeon, Professor Schenck, who had been assisting in the hospital under the Voss-strasse, found himself a slightly bemused guest at the wedding reception. Later he recalled Hitler's physical appearance:

> I could see Hitler's hunched spine, the curved shoulders that seemed to twitch and tremble. Somehow his head seemed withdrawn into his shoulders, turtlelike. . . . His eyes, although he was looking directly at me, did not seem to be focusing. They were like wet pale-blue porcelain, glazed, actually more grey than blue. They were filmy, like the skin of a soft grape. The whites were bloodshot. I could detect no expression on his vapid, immobile face.

Observing the Führer's uncontrollably shuddering left arm and leg with his doctor's eye, Schenck concluded that Hitler had the classic symptoms of Parkinson's disease and, had he lived, would soon have become a hopeless cripple.

At about 2am, Hitler retired with a secretary to dictate his personal testament. Like the Bourbons, he had learned nothing and forgotten nothing. The testament concluded: 'Above all I charge the leaders of the nation and those under them to scrupulous observance of the laws of race and to merciless opposition to the universal poisoners of all peoples, international Jewry.' Other provisions stated that Speer, Göring and Himmler were expelled from the Party and deprived of their now meaningless offices of state. Grand Admiral Dönitz was named as Hitler's successor in the posts of President, Minister of War and Supreme Commander of the Armed Forces. Goebbels and Bormann – whose insinuating influence runs through the document – received their own empty rewards, the Chancellorship and the post of Party Minister, respectively.

Three men were selected to deliver copies of the testament to Dönitz's headquarters at Plön in Schleswig-Holstein and to the last wartime Commander-in-Chief of the German Army, Field Marshal Schörner, who was now in Munich. An additional message was despatched to

Keitel, a stinging dismissal of the General Staff from their Supreme Commander:

> The people and the Wehrmacht have given their all in this long and hard struggle. The sacrifice has been enormous. But my trust has been misused by many people. Disloyalty and betrayal have undermined resistance throughout the war. It was therefore not granted to me to lead the people to victory. The Army General Staff cannot be compared with the General Staff of the First World War. Its achievements were far behind those of the fighting front.

During the course of the day news arrived of the death of Mussolini and his mistress Clara Petacci – summarily executed by partisans near Lake Como and then suspended by their heels from the roof of a Milan garage, to be mutilated and spat on by a jeering crowd. On the same day German forces in Italy capitulated at Caserta, the culmination of the negotiations between Allan Dulles and SS General Karl Wolff. Hitler now set about preparing his own end. The effects of the poison capsule he intended to use were tested on his German shepherd bitch, Blondi.

Late in the evening General Weidling reported that ammunition and supplies were now all but exhausted. The air drops on which so many false hopes had been placed had delivered only 6 tons of supplies, including just twenty Panzerfausts. Communications with the outside world had been cut as the balloon which supported the bunker's radio transmitting aerial had been shot down that morning and the telephone switchboard had ceased to work. To the north of Berlin, Manteuffel's Third Panzer Army was retreating westward.* Of Wenck there was no sign. Weidling told Hitler that resistance in Berlin would end within the next twenty-four hours. After an interminable silence Hitler, in a weary voice, asked Mohnke for his assessment of the situation. Mohnke replied that he could only agree with Weidling, who then raised the subject of a breakout in some of the few remaining armoured vehicles. Hitler, looking like 'a man completely resigned to his fate', merely indicated a map on which the dispositions had been marked by means of listening in to enemy radio stations, since German staffs no longer replied and German formations no longer obeyed the Führer's orders. Weidling pressed Hitler about what would

---

* Manteuffel told Weidling that he had seen nothing like it since 1918. At least 100,000 men were streaming to the west. It would have taken hundreds of officers to stop them.

happen when his troops ran out of ammunition. After consulting Krebs, Hitler replied that they could break out in 'small groups* but that there would be no surrender of Berlin. The conference had not long broken up when Keitel informed Hitler that Wenck's army was stuck fast south of the Schielow Lake and could no longer continue its attack towards Berlin. Ninth Army, which had been trying to batter its way out of the trap south-east of Berlin, was now encircled. Time had run out.

On the 30th, while fighting raged in the Tiergarten and Potsdamer-platz, only a few blocks away from the Chancellery, Hitler took lunch with his two secretaries and his vegetarian cook, Fräulein Manzialy. While they toyed with spaghetti and tossed salad, Hitler rambled on about the proper breeding of dogs and ventured the observation – both sinister and ridiculous – that French lipstick was made from grease collected from the Paris sewers.

The 'Himmler House' had been captured at about 4.30 that morning. Seven hours later the regiments of the Soviet 150th and 171st Rifle Divisions took up their positions for the final assault on the Reichstag. The day was sunny, though little of the sun could be seen through the dense clouds of black smoke hanging 1,000 feet above the city. In 150th Division's forward positions Red victory banners were distributed among the assault squads to be hoisted over the last objective as symbols of victory. Red Banner No.5 was passed to 1st Battalion, 756th Regiment, led by Captain Neustroyev. At 1pm, after an artillery preparation by 152mm and 203mm howitzers, tanks, self-propelled guns, Katyusha rockets and captured Panzerfausts firing at point-blank range, the three assault battalions launched themselves through the smoke and across a flooded anti-tank ditch to the steps of the Reichstag, defended by over 5,000 SS men, Hitler Youth and Volkssturm. As the Red Army men blasted their way in with submachine-guns and hand grenades, Captain Neustroyev attached his Red banner to a column at the entrance.

Two hundred yards away, in the Führerbunker, Hitler was saying farewell to Goebbels, Bormann and the others who were there. Traudl Junge recalled:

> The Führer looked more stooped than ever as he came out of his room and moved slowly towards us. He offered his hand to each of us, and as he shook hands he looked straight at me, but I knew he didn't see me. His right hand was warm. He seemed to be a

---

* Hitler later supplied Weidling with written confirmation of this decision.

thousand miles away. He whispered some words that I couldn't make out: I've never known what his last words to us were.

At about 3.20pm Hitler withdrew into his suite with Eva Braun, who was wearing the Führer's favourite dress, black with pink roses at either side of a low square neckline. Her hair was perfectly coiffed. The heavy iron door shut behind them. Outside, the inhabitants of the bunker waited. One of them was Major Otto Günsche, Hitler's senior SS adjutant and faithful shadow:

> Hitler had stood back to let Eva go through first. I was busy giving instructions to the men and officers who were to carry the two bodies outside. Hitler had told me to wait ten minutes before entering the apartment. They were the longest minutes of my life. I stood by the door like a sentry. Suddenly Magda Goebbels [Goebbels's wife] came rushing towards me, as if to force her way through. I couldn't push her back, so I opened the door to ask Hitler what I should do. She practically knocked me over in her desire to get into the room, but she came out again immediately. Hitler hadn't wanted to listen to her and she left sobbing. A moment later Axmann . . . arrived. This time I was firm and told him: 'Too late!'
>   Ten minutes later, after hearing the shot, I went into the room. Hitler's body was crumpled up, his head hanging towards the floor. Blood was running from his right temple on to the carpet. The pistol had fallen to the ground. Eva, who was sitting in the other corner of the sofa, her legs curled under her, had stayed in the same position. She showed no trace of any wound. Her pistol was beside her. A vase of flowers had fallen to the floor. . . .

Hitler had shot himself with his Walther 7.65mm pistol, which he had been carrying in his jacket for several weeks, in all probability simultaneously biting into a cyanide capsule. Eva Braun took the poison. Günsche had the table and chairs cleared out of the way and blankets spread on the floor. Three guards took Hitler's body, wrapped it in a blanket and carried it away. Martin Bormann lifted Eva Braun's body before Günsche took it from him and handed it over to the guards. While they were walking up the stairs to the Chancellery garden, Erich Kempka, Hitler's chauffeur, arrived with a detail of men carrying about forty gallons of petrol in jerrycans.

The two bodies were placed in a trench, doused with petrol and set on fire with pieces of flaming paper. Günsche recalled that, as the flames shot up, 'all the men present raised their arms in the Nazi salute'. Once the flames had died down, the bodies were buried in a deeper trench dug out of shell crater. On 3 May they were unearthed by an alert Red Army private, although the credit for the discovery was taken by an NKVD interrogator, Lieutenant-Colonel Ivan Klimenko, who on 5 May exhumed the charred remains of the Führer* and his mistress from the slime and rubble outside the bunker.

---

* Hitler's skull and teeth are now said to reside, in separate cardboard boxes, in a Moscow archive.

CHAPTER 10

Aftermath

On the station platform at Halle. A dreadful scene of destruction, with beings from another world wandering among the ruins. Soldiers, homeward bound, in tattered, padded tunics, covered with sores, staggering along on home-made crutches. Just living corpses. We gave them the last of our bread. The Lord God did indeed cast them down, horse, foot and artillery.

Ursula von Kardorff, September 1945

TRAUDL JUNGE WAS consoling herself with a stiff glass of schnapps on the upper level of the bunker when Otto Günsche returned, his normally suave features ashen and his hands trembling, to tell her that he had carried out the Führer's last orders.

Junge was drawn downstairs for the last time to Hitler's suite. The door was still open:

On a side table stood Eva's little revolver, beside a square of pink silk chiffon. I saw the cyanide capsule of yellow metal on the floor beside her armchair. It looked like an empty lipstick tube. Spread over the armchair, which was upholstered in a blue and white patterned fabric, was a large bloodstain. It was Hitler's blood. A feeling of nausea came over me. I couldn't stand the heavy smell of bitter almonds from the poison. My hand automatically reached to my own cyanide capsule: I wanted to throw it as far as I could and get out of this horrible place immediately.

Bedlam quickly took over in the bunker. Goebbels was hysterical and Mohnke and Rattenhuber in tears. Goebbels eventually got a grip on himself and, as the new Reich Chancellor, called a meeting with Bormann, Mohnke, Burgdorf and Krebs to decide on a plan of action.

The Führer was dead but the fighting continued. By about 2.30pm on the 30th a Red banner had appeared on the second floor of the Reichstag, but it was not until nearly 11pm that Sergeants Yegorov and Kantariya penetrated the upper floors to plant another Red banner high over the 'the Lair of the Fascist Beast', in whose basement there still lurked a well-armed and desperate pocket of resistance. Throughout the night Red Army men and the defenders of the Reichstag stalked each other through its shattered halls.

The defenders of Berlin had been squeezed into four isolated groups while the fighting reached a new intensity in the Tiergarten and the Zoological Gardens, where Soviet artillery was pouring fire at the great flak tower rearing up into the hellish purple glow set up by fire and gun flash. General Weidling was at the end of his tether. It would only be a matter of hours before the the Soviet armies driving towards each other from north and south would join hands at the Zoo station. Their assault groups were fighting their way across the Potsdamerplatz and the Anhalter station and a gaping hole now yawned in the German line between the Alexanderplatz and the Spittelmarkt. Weidling agonized about whether to organize a break-out in small groups, for which Hitler had given an authorization, though it had been rescinded at the last minute.

Weidling was put out of his agony by a summons to the bunker, a journey of less than a mile from his headquarters in the Bendlerstrasse, but one which took him an hour to negotiate. In the bunker he met Goebbels, Bormann and Krebs, who told him that the Führer was dead and his body had been burned. Having been sworn to secrecy, Weidling was then informed that Colonel Seifert, Mohnke's subordinate commander in the Zitadelle, was to cross the lines to arrange a meeting with Colonel-General Chuikov at which he would give an account of the recent melancholy events in the bunker, provide details of the successor government nominated by Hitler in his testament, and seek a cease-fire while this government assembled in Berlin to negotiate capitulation terms with the Russians.

Seifert's mission was accomplished late in the evening of 30 April. A little before 4am Krebs, with Weidling's new chief of staff, Colonel von Dufving, and an interpreter, Sonderführer Neilands, was escorted through Eighth Guards Army's lines to Chuikov's forward command post. The Russian commander had been enjoying supper with members of his political staff, two war correspondents and the composer Blanter, who had been sent to Berlin to compose a victory anthem. When Krebs arrived, Chuikov airily passed off his guests as members of his war council, with the exception of Blanter, who was dressed in civilian clothes. He had been hastily bundled into a cupboard, where he spent much of the ensuing discussions before passing out through lack of air and crashing into the room at the feet of the astonished Krebs.

Chuikov recalled: 'At 03:55 hours the door opened and a German general with an Iron Cross and a Nazi swastika on his sleeve entered the room. He was a solidly built man of medium height, with a shaven head and a scarred face. He flung out his right hand in the Nazi salute and with the other held out his identification card.'

In the days of the Nazi-Soviet Pact* the Russian-speaking Krebs had been publicly embraced by Stalin. Now the grip of the Russian bear was less friendly. Nevertheless, Krebs opened the proceedings with what he clearly felt would be a bombshell, telling Chuikov that Hitler was dead. The defender of Stalingrad played this fast delivery straight back again, calmly replying 'We know that'. Wrongfooted, Krebs insisted on explaining in detail what had happened in the bunker, while Chuikov opened a four-sided conversation with the German emissary in front of him and, by telephone, with Stalin and Zhukov. Stalin, roused from his bed, expressed gruff satisfaction at Hitler's death – 'So that's the end of the bastard' – while regretting that he had not been taken alive, as well as showing a lively interest in the whereabouts of the body. Having instructed Chuikov that there were to be no negotiations with Krebs, only an insistence on unconditional surrender, Stalin returned to bed to snatch some sleep before the May Day parade in Moscow.

The talks dragged on for twelve hours, during which Krebs unavailingly attempted to wriggle off the hook of unconditional surrender and secure some form of legitimacy for the Hitler-nominated government, an impossible task given that Dönitz, the Führer's successor, was as yet unaware of his death. Zhukov, tiring of this interminably circular argument, broke off communications and despatched his deputy, Sokolovsky, in his stead. Chuikov and Sokolovsky persevered, but to Krebs's pleadings there was only one answer – unconditional general surrender. Krebs was sent away empty-handed, and at 6.30am a new and ferocious Soviet artillery barrage descended on the Reichstag and the Chancellery.

The exhausted Krebs reappeared in the bunker shortly before Dönitz was informed of Hitler's death. Meanwhile, Mohnke and Günsche were working on an escape plan, propelling the inhabitants of the bunker into

---

* Signed in Moscow on 23 August 1939, and ended by Hitler's invasion of the USSR on 22 June 1941.

a last bout of feverish activity. Traudl Junge volunteered to join the first party to leave the bunker, which Mohnke was to lead himself:

> The depots were emptied of supplies accumulated by the commissariat, but there were hardly enough takers for the quantities of jam, wine, champagne, schnapps and chocolate. Under the circumstances, none of that held any great attraction: we were concerned with saving our lives. General Mohnke gave out weapons to everyone. Even the women were issued with pistols. . . . We were also supposed to be given more suitable clothes for our escape, for which purpose we had to go to the depot in a bunker beneath the Voss-strasse. . . . To get them we had to pass through the operating room of the medical centre. I had never seen a dead body, and I'd always hated the sight of blood, but that day I saw the horribly disfigured corpses of two soldiers lying on stretchers. Professor Haase didn't even glance up as we passed him: he was busy amputating a leg.

At the depot Traudl Junge was given a tin hat, a pair of trousers and a pair of heavy shoes. When she went back to the bunker she noticed that 'even the men had made changes to their clothing: many of them had taken off their medals and insignia of rank. Captain [*sic*] Hans Baur,* Hitler's personal pilot, was rolling up the portrait of Frederick the Great which Hitler used to take everywhere with him . . . and which he had given to Baur as a memento on the eve of his death.'

While the escape parties were waiting for nightfall, Goebbels came and went, chain-smoking and looking like a bankrupt restaurauter waiting for the last guests to leave. At about 8.30pm Magda Goebbels administered poison to her six children and then joined her husband in the Chancellery garden, where they took poison together. Like Hitler, Goebbels shot himself in the head as he bit on the capsule. A perfunctory effort was made to burn their bodies, the corpses being horribly charred but remaining recognizable.

At 11pm on 1 May Mohnke led the first escape party from the underground fire brigade garage of the Chancellery cellar complex facing the Wilhelmstrasse. The mixed bag of twenty men and women threaded their way through streets which seemed to have sprung straight from a canvas by Hieronymus Bosch. In the livid glare of the fires raging all around, Berliners were carving up the carcasses of dead horses in the Wilhelmstrasse. Near the Charité Hospital drunken Russian soldiers, inflamed by ethyl alcohol, pursued a naked woman across

---

* Baur was in fact a lieutenant-general.

the rooftops until she plunged to her death five storeys below. From an elevated position on the twisted girders of the wrecked S-bahn overhead railway, Mohnke had a panoramic view of the Berlin night battlefield:

> ... even to a hardened soldier it was most unreal, phantasmagoric. Most of the great city was pitch-dark; the moon was hiding; but flares, shell bursts, the burning buildings, all these reflected on a low-lying, blackish-yellow cloud of sulphur-like smoke.... This is one of the moments I still remember most clearly, for the reflections of the burning ruins were mirrored back from the water of the river, itself rippled by a steady night-time breeze. The Spree was now black, now red, very eerie. Again it was deathly quiet. Only the ghosts of the shadows, sometimes real, sometimes imagined, lurked in the streets leading to the stone quays on both sides of the river.

Mohnke's original escape route through the underground railway tunnels had foundered when his party ran into a bulkhead door firmly closed and guarded by two employees of the Municipal Transport Company. It was, it seemed, their job to close the door after the last train had gone through at night, and it mattered little to them that this had been over a week ago and normal service was unlikely to be resumed for some time. They refused to open up, even for an SS general waving a pistol in their faces. Mohnke had shot men for less, but he later confessed that it had been 'my own ingrained sense of duty that led me to respect theirs'.

After four hours of fruitless effort Mohnke's party, now swollen to more than a hundred, halted to rest at the Stettiner Bahnhof railway terminal. The motley column moved off again at about 9am on 2 May, almost immediately stumbling across a fantastic sight at the Humboldthain flak tower, around which were assembled companies of German troops armed to the teeth and in pristine battledress, supported by ten Tiger tanks, armoured personnel carriers and artillery. All dressed up and with nowhere to go, they were awaiting the order to attack.

The order never came, for at 10am an officer's radio picked up the news that Weidling had ordered a surrender. Berlin's battle commandant had taken matters into his own hands, and at 6am on the morning of 2 May he and his senior staff officers had surrendered to the Russians, colliding at Chuikov's headquarters with another German delegation (one of them incongruously attired in morning dress), led by Hans Fritzsche, Goebbels's radio chief.

After declaring that to waste more lives would be madness, and having given a brief account of his own military career – he had joined the army as a private in 1911 – Weidling broke down in tears. When he had recovered, Sokolovsky suggested to him that he write an order for a general surrender. After some hesitation Weidling composed the following:

> On 30 April 1945 the Führer took his own life and thus it is that we who remain – having sworn him an oath of loyalty – are left alone. According to the Führer's order, you, German soldiers, were to fight on for Berlin, in spite of the fact that ammunition has run out and in spite of the general situation, which makes further resistance on our part senseless. My orders are: to cease resistance forthwith. (Signed) General Weidling, General of Artillery, former Commandant of the Berlin Defence Zone.

Chuikov and Sokolovsky changed just one word, deleting 'former' from Weidling's description of himself.

As a chilling drizzle fell on the city, the remnants of its garrison surrendered one by one. In the west of Berlin a huge press of pedestrians and motor traffic converged on the bridges which crossed the Havel, making for the Elbe. Only one bridge remained in German hands, and those making for it were unaware that, on the Elbe, the Americans and Russians had joined hands. Running the gauntlet of sporadic Russian artillery fire and strafing, and swerving along a slalom course of craters, carts, trucks and motor cars crawled forward over the bodies of the dead and dying, their progress congealing into a nightmare traffic jam. A German soldier recalled:

> To the east hidden under clouds of smoke that rose black and yellow into the sky is Berlin. Underfoot are the bodies of those who had not made it as far as the bridge. Sod their luck; let's hope ours is better for in a minute or two it will be our turn to race across. Every man on our lorry is firing his weapon; machine-gun, machine-pistol or rifle. We roll on to the bridge roadway. The lorry picks up speed and races across the open space. It is not a straight drive but a sort of obstacle race, swerving to avoid the trucks, tanks and cars which are lying wrecked and burning on the bridge roadway. There is a sickening feeling as we bump over bodies lying stretched out, hundreds of them all along the length. At a collecting point SS military police armed with machine-pistols halt us. 'Arm of service?' they ask, 'Grenadier'. 'Over there; join that group, collect ammunition.' A battle group is being formed, an 'alarm

unit' was its proper name. The struggle for Berlin may have ended for some, but the war continues for the rest of us.

One person for whom the war was over was Martin Bormann, who had joined the third escape party to leave the bunker. With the death of Hitler, Bormann's authority had evaporated. When he had attempted to countermand one of Mohnke's orders, the SS general had told him to 'get lost', to the delight of all in the bunker. Bormann eventually found himself in a breakaway group with Artur Axmann and his aide Major Wetzen, Dr Stumpfegger and Hans Baur. Near the Reichstag they had come under fire and had lost contact with Baur. Bormann and his companions pressed on, crossing the railway bridge in the docks area of Humboldthafen and then dropping down on to the roadway beneath the Lehrter S-bahn station, to find themselves in the middle of a party of bivouacking Russian infantry. The Russians were not hostile, taking the group for members of the Volkssturm who had thrown their weapons away and were now returning home. Nervously, Bormann and Stumpfegger edged away before breaking into a run. Axmann and Wetzen followed but quickly lost them. However, they were soon reunited. Walking along the tracks leading out of the Lehrter railway station, they found the bodies of Bormann and Stumpfegger, both of whom had apparently committed suicide.

Their end was confirmed on a snowy winter's day in 1972 when workers constructing an exhibition park on the site of the Lehrter station uncovered two skeletons in a shallow grave, one of a tall man, the other short and burly. Lodged in their jawbones were splinters from glass cyanide ampoules. Forensic examination confirmed that here was the last resting place of Martin Bormann.

Others, including Krebs and Burgdorf, also committed suicide rather than face capture and imprisonment – or worse. Mohnke was taken prisoner in the huge Schultheiss-Patzenhofer brewery, where several hundred soldiers and civilians had either rendered themselves dead drunk or had joined a group sex orgy on one of the upper floors. At 8pm Mohnke emerged from the brewery cellars, and he and twelve other SS officers, were driven off at high speed to Chuikov's headquarters. There they were treated to a stupendous banquet before being handed over to the NKVD, who flew Mohnke to Moscow and less agreeable lodgings in the Lubyanka prison.

Earlier on 2 May Vera Bockmann had her long-anticipated rendezvous with the Red Army. The first troops to arrive in her district relieved her and her companions in the cellar of their watches:

It wasn't long before another batch came, cursing roundly on see-
ing bare arms and ringless fingers (everything not taken had been
hidden), but they did not molest us in any way. A . . . friend had
advised me to say '*Ja Anglichanka*' [an English woman] to the
Russians, but I doubted whether it would have any effect. Anyhow,
when the fourth lot came that day I decided to put it to the test.
Instead of waiting for them to approach me, I went up to them,
saying, '*Ja Anglichanka*'. The effect was startling. '*Anglichanka?*'
they repeated incredulously, pointing at me with the forefinger. I
nodded vehemently and we shook hands over it. Soon I became
bold enough to sit on a box in the courtyard. We were all starved
of fresh air. . . . All day long the Russians came and went and by
now their gait convinced us that they were very drunk. This time
they hauled the remaining older men out of the cellar. They
then picked out the most prosperous-looking one. . . . They made
him stand against the wall and the youngest of them put the
muzzle of his gun against the man's chest. 'Capitalist?' '*Nein*.'
'National Socialist?' '*Nein*.' It was a bit frightening and something
had to be done about it. So I went up to the young Russian,
shaking in my shoes, and said again, '*Ja Anglichanka*'. He wheeled
around and, drunk as he was, looked at me as though I had
dropped off the moon. When he found that I couldn't understand
a word of his voluble Russian, he laughed and said, 'Stalin *gut*,
Churchill *gut*, Hitler *schlachten*'. To this I heartily agreed and we
shook hands on it. Under my breath I told his 'captive' to get out
while the going was good. But he needed no telling.

At 3pm on the afternoon of 2 May Soviet artillery had ceased to fire
on Berlin. An all-enveloping silence descended on the city. Russian
troops raised a great cheer and broke out the food and drink. Past lines
of T-34s drawn up in parade-ground order, long columns of German
troops began the trek eastward. The Russians claim to have taken 134,000
prisoners on 2 May alone, but this represented a huge round-up of all
able-bodied men and women destined for the labour camps in the Soviet
Union. Vera Bockmann noted in her diary that on 2 May NKVD troops
had lined up and marched away all the German men under fifty in the
district in which she lived.

It was time to count the cost of Operation Berlin. Between 16 April and
8 May (the final German surrender), Zhukov, Konev and Rokossovsky's
fronts had sustained losses of 304,887 men killed, wounded and missing,
10 per cent of their strength and the heaviest casualties suffered by the
Red Army in any battle of the war with the exception of the great encirclements of the summer of 1941. For its part, the Soviet high command
estimated that in the capture of Berlin and the drive to the Elbe and the

Baltic it had destroyed seventy German infantry divisions, twelve armoured divisions and eleven motorized divisions. Some 480,000 officers and men had become prisoners of war, 1,500 tanks and self-propelled guns had been captured, plus 10,000 guns and fleets of aircraft. In Berlin itself up to 100,000 German soldiers and civilians had died in the fighting. Thus even by the most conservative calculation it would appear that, in John Erickson's words, the battle for Berlin 'cost half a million people their lives, their well-being and their sanity'.

'It was quiet in Berlin at last,' Chuikov wrote in his memoirs. 'We went out into the street. We could see the Red flags, the banners of victory flying over government buildings, the Reichstag and the Imperial Chancellery. All was quiet. . . .' Loudspeaker vans picked their way to every corner of the shattered city relaying Weidling's order to surrender, which he had tape-recorded in an old film studio in the south of Berlin. At the very heart of the capital of the Third Reich a sickening stench rose from the Führer's bunker.

No mourning had accompanied the announcement of Hitler's death. At 9.30pm on 1 May, Hamburg Radio had warned the German people that 'a grave and important announcement' was about to be made. Then, to the strains of Bruckner's Seventh Symphony, came the news of Hitler's death. 'It is reported from the Führer's headquarters that our Führer, Adolf Hitler, fighting to the last breath against Bolshevism, fell for Germany this afternoon in his operational command post in the Reich Chancellery. . . .' At 10.20 Admiral Dönitz came on the air to announce Hitler's death and his own succession.

Near the Baltic port of Lübeck a British prisoner of war, Lieutenant-Commander John Casson, heard Dönitz's announcement in interesting circumstances. Casson and hundreds of other POWs had been taken on a long forced march, under armed guard, away from the Russians and towards British Second Army. While they rested, one of the guards asked the German-speaking Casson if he would like to listen to the latest news bulletin from Hamburg. (Casson did not inform him that the POWs had been keeping in touch with events by listening to the BBC on their own home-made receiver.) After entertaining his guards with some conjuring tricks while they tuned in, Casson and his captors listened to Dönitz's broadcast. There was silence until the words '*Der Führer ist tot*', whereupon one young German soldier swore '*Scheisse*', an older one murmured '*Gott sei dank*', and a third merely threw his cap on the floor. Within an hour British troops had liberated Casson and his fellow POWs. Now the captured were the captors, and that night Casson sat around a campfire with some of his former guards, talking in German about philosophy.

Also among the first to hear the broadcast were men of the 6th Battalion, Royal Welch Fusiliers, who were advancing on Hamburg. Huddled around their command radio set in a captured farmhouse, they listened in to the announcements from Hamburg. The following morning they decided to leave behind a memento of the occasion on the village monument, which commemorated a visit by Hitler in 1935. One of the fusiliers – a stonemason in civilian life – chipped out the end of the story: 'KAPUT 1945'.

During his broadcast Dönitz had declared, 'My first task is to save Germany from destruction by the advancing Bolshevik enemy'. In his possession was a captured copy of the Allied plans for the post-war dismemberment of Germany. On 1 May German forces still controlled territory on both sides of the map's east-west demarcation line, holding out the hope that the Eastern armies and a huge number of refugees might yet make their way to the zones controlled by the British and Americans. On 1 May Wencks's Twelfth Army, and the remaining fragments of Busse's Ninth Army, had fallen back on the Elbe near Tangermünde with several hundred thousand refugees in tow. Wenck negotiated a surrender with the commander of US Ninth Army, General Simpson, who agreed to allow the German soldiers – or as many as were able to – to make their way across the river, and offered assistance with the wounded. However, Simpson flatly refused to take any civilian refugees, possibly because he felt unable to feed them all. The refugees would have been abandoned to the Russians had not the Red Army intervened with an artillery barrage on the crossings which forced the Americans to withdraw, leaving the Germans in control of them. With his XX Corps covering the crossings, Wenck estimated that in the first week of May he was able to pass about 100,000 soldiers and 300,000 civilians over the Elbe.

Meanwhile, Dönitz attempted to surrender in the West while holding off the Russians in the East. Eisenhower would have none of this, however, although on 4 May there was a partial surrender in northern Germany, where Army Group Vistula's line of retreat into Schleswig-Holstein had been severed by Montgomery's advance to Lübeck.

The last major hurdle for Montgomery, and the first major German port that was to fall into Allied hands, was Bremen on the River Weser. The preparation for the attack by Horrocks's XXX Corps had been made on the night of 22 April by Bomber Command. In one of Harris's last big raids 767 aircraft were despatched to attack the south-eastern suburbs of the city. The raid was hampered by cloud and the Master Bomber ordered the raid to halt after 195 Lancasters had bombed the target. Incredibly, in Bremen officials were still conscientiously recording the effects of the bombing in copious detail, even though the city would be in British hands within five days and the intervening period would be filled with continuous artillery bombardment, fighter-bomber attacks, and Horrocks's assault. Some 3,664 houses had been carefully listed under five categories of air-raid damage from 'destroyed' to 'broken windows'.

Bremen fell on 27 April after three days of ground attack by 43rd (Wessex) and 52nd (Lowland) Divisions north of the Weser, and 3rd Division attacking from the south. Six thousand German troops went into the bag, including two generals and an admiral. Brigadier Essame left a vivid picture of Bremen at the end of the war:

> In the falling rain the city presented a scene of sordid horror. Great piles of rubble blocked the streets, the twisted lamp standards were silhouetted grotesquely against the sky, the stench of build-ings still burning offended the nostrils and the open sewers stank to heaven. The people were broken-spirited and listless – many of them were literally green in colour for the ventilation in the big air-raid bunkers had broken down and the sanitary arrangements had collapsed. They were docile, bewildered and hopeless. By early afternoon a Military Government Detachment had established itself in each of the four police areas with a headquarters in the Polizei Praesidium. The fighting had released thousands of slave labourers from Eastern Europe and the USSR who broke loose and fell without restraint on the large stores of wines and spirits in the city. Some even drank the commercial spirit in the docks. Fighting, rape and murder broke out and the troops had to intervene to pro-tect the civil population. None of them were sorry, when they had restored order, to move out from this charnel house which had once been a gracious city into the clean air of the Cuxhaven peninsula.

Contact with the Red Army was made by 6th Airborne Division at Wismar, on the Baltic coast, on 2 May, and on the following day Hamburg was surrendered without a fight by its commandant, General Wolz. An assault on Hamburg like that on Bremen had been avoided when, on 29 April, a delegation from Wolz had arrived in the lines of 7th Armoured Division with a request that the city's hospitals be spared artillery fire. The talks quickly developed into proposals for the general surrender of the city. A message was sent to Wolz by the commander of 7th Armoured

Division, Major-General Lyne, in which it was chillingly pointed out that

> The population of Hamburg will not easily forget its first large-scale raid by over one thousand heavy bombers.* We now dispose of a bomber force five to ten times greater numerically and operating from nearby airfields. After the war, the German people must be fed: the more Hamburg's dock installations are damaged, the greater are the chances of famine in Germany.

Wolz's reply was a masterpiece of understatement:

> The thoughts for which you have found so lucid an expression ... have been considered by myself and by countless other responsible commanders; not unnaturally, considering the present military and political situation ... I am prepared ... to discuss with a representative empowered by GOC Second British Army to make decisions on military and political matters, the eventual surrender of Hamburg and the far-reaching consequences arising therefrom. ...

According to the history of 7th Armoured, the German staff officer who delivered Wolz's message asked the senior officer returning him to the German lines, Brigadier Spurling, whether, 'as soldier to soldier', he ought to commit suicide on his return. The brigadier replied, 'That's entirely up to you'. A British colonel pointed to the scarf covering the German interpreter's eyes, asking him, 'Isn't that a Brasenose scarf?' 'No, Christ Church,'† came the reply, 'I was there studying the House of Lords.'

When Hamburg was handed over, it became clear that Wolz was able to deliver to Montgomery's headquarters a delegation from Dönitz led by Admiral Hans von Friedeburg, Dönitz's successor as Commander-in-Chief of the German Navy, with powers to negotiate the surrender all of north Germany and to press for special consideration for refugees and troops in flight from the Russians.

On the afternoon of 3 May, Hamburg was handed over to 7th Armoured and 53rd (Welsh) Divisions, the route into the ruined port lined at regular intervals by white-coated German policemen standing by the neatly stacked piles of rubble to which Bomber Command and

---

* A reference to the raids of July 1943.
† Both colleges at Oxford University.

US Eighth Air Force had reduced much of the city. At 5pm on the 4th, Admiral Friedeburg and his delegation arrived at Montgomery's headquarters on Lüneburg Heath to surrender all German forces in Holland, north-west Germany and Denmark. Photographs of the event show the grim-faced German officers creaking their way across the windy heath in their long leather overcoats, escorted by mild-looking British counterparts who seem like bank managers in uniform. For the signing, Montgomery was at his most brisk and schoolmasterly. As he recalled, the business was conducted on 'a trestle table covered with an army blanket, an inkpot, an ordinary army pen that you could buy in a shop for twopence. The Germans were clearly nervous and one of them took out a cigarette ... I looked at him and he put the cigarette away.'

The surrender was to take effect from 8am British Summer Time on Saturday 5 May. Paragraph Three of the surrender document stated that the German high command was to 'carry out at once, without argument or comment, all further orders that will be issued by the Allied Commanders on any subject'. From Lüneburg, Admiral Friedeburg travelled to Eisenhower's headquarters at Reims where, on 6 May, he was joined by Colonel-General Jodl. Taken to the room where Friedeburg was waiting, Jodl greeeted the Admiral with a cryptic 'Aha'. A few minutes later Friedeburg emerged to request coffee and a map of Europe. The Germans were playing for time, and Eisenhower issued a sharp ultimatum. Whether or not the Germans delayed, he would close his lines within forty-eight hours of midnight on 6 May, 'so that no more Germans can get through'. At 2.41am on the morning of 7 May, Colonel-General Alfried Jodl signed the instrument of unconditional surrender in Eisenhower's war room which, appropriately, was dominated by a giant mock thermometer mounted on a background of swastikas and bearing a running total of German prisoners in Allied hands. An hour later Eisenhower brought matters to a close with a brief but eloquent cable to the British and American Chiefs of Staff: 'The mission of the Allied force was fulfilled at 0241, local time, May 7, 1945.'

Early on 8 May, Victory in Europe Day, Air Chief Marshal Tedder and USAAF General Spaatz flew to Berlin to participate in the formal German surrender to the Russians. Driving through Berlin to Zhukov's headquarters in an engineering college in the north-eastern suburbs of the city, Tedder sensed that the city 'was in a coma. The only sign of life was in the queues at water standpipes in the streets'. At the college there was an interminable delay while Zhukov, with Andrei Vyshinsky, the Soviet Deputy Commissar for Foreign Affairs, hovering at his shoulder, sorted out the details of the draft instrument of surrender, similar to the one signed in Reims, which Tedder had brought with him. Captain Harry Butcher, US Navy, a member of Eisenhower's personal staff, was struck by the presence of Vyshinsky: 'I was surprised by the way a civilian . . . dominated the entire proceedings, deferred to even by Zhukov. Even in this moment of Soviet military victory, the Kremlin was stepping in to take charge'.*

It was not until 11pm that the Allied commanders were ready to present the surrender terms to the Germans. The hall in which the ceremony took place was a remarkable sight, as Butcher remembered:

> The huge room was banked with klieg lights, blinding as we stepped in from the dim hallway. Everything seemed to be set up for the convenience of the Russian press, who numbered close to a hundred and swarmed around in a shouting bedlam. Movie cameras were ready in almost every conceivable spot. Microphones sprouted from the floor, hung from the ceiling; they and the klieg lights created a veritable spider web of wires and cables.

Silence fell as Keitel, accompanied by Friedeburg and Colonel-General Stumpff (representing the Luftwaffe), made his appearance. Tedder later wrote that Keitel was 'tall and arrogant, holding his baton high and looking in every way the personification of the horrid blend of Nazi and Prussian'. Noticing the French General Jean-Marie de Lattre de Tassigny, commander of French First Army, Keitel was heard to mutter, 'The French are here! That's all we need'. Then, recovering his icy demeanour, he jerked up his field marshal's baton in a salute and took his place at the table, eyeing the jostling journalists with contempt. As he signed the document the press kicked and fought to get a better view. Keitel's steely gaze bored through them as Friedeburg and Stumpff added their signatures. The three of them rose as one and, with Prussian military precision, stalked from the room.

The celebrations now began in earnest, and in true Russian style. An hour after the departure of what remained of the German high command the surrender hall had become a banqueting hall, with an orchestra installed on the balcony. The eating, and toasting, went on for four hours. Several Russians slid under the table into comradely oblivion. Eisenhower's secretary, along for the ride, contrived to remain sober by drinking water rather than vodka: 'As the party broke up just before dawn

---

* As Vyshinsky was the feared prosecutor in Stalin's purges in the 1930s, Zhukov was quite right to respect him.

(we women) agreed that there had been between 24 and 29 individual toasts, each requiring five to ten minutes for translation, plus the musical chord and the final, deadly bottoms-up.'

The official interpreter had gallantly kept abreast of the toasts for most of the banquet, but towards the end even he could make no sense of them. In a final display of characteristically erratic Russian hospitality, the visiting party was taken on a dawn tour of the ruins of Berlin, a sight calculated to sober up even the most inebriated member of the delegation from Reims. They took off from Tempelhof airport at seven in the morning.

On 9 May there remained only one pocket of German resistance, in Slovakia. The Czechoslovak National Army had planned a rising for 7 May, but it was pre-empted on 4 May by the citizens of Prague who, excited by the news of the 'American advance into Bohemia, took to the streets. The next day the National Army rose in open revolt against Schörner's Army Group Centre. Even at the fag-end of the war the Waffen-SS moved with its old ferocity. As its tanks closed on Prague – a city which had survived the conflict physically unscathed – a Czech radio station, broadcasting in English and Russian, made an appeal for air support to hold off the German armour. On 6 May the calls became increasingly desperate – 'Send your tanks, send your aircraft, help us save Prague'.

The Americans held back. On 7 May advanced elements of Patton's Third Army had reached the outskirts of the city, but Eisenhower had already been told by Roosevelt's successor as President, Harry S. Truman,* that no American lives were to be risked in so volatile a situation. The US troops in Prague were ordered to drive back fifty miles to rejoin Third Army on the Pilsen Line. Patton's heartfelt and openly stated desire for his men to fraternize with Czech women – German women being officially out of bounds – had been denied.

For the next thirty-six hours murderous confusion reigned. Heavy street fighting raged in Prague. To the east, German units falling back before the Russians left behind them a trail of destruction. The small town of Konetopy, twenty-two miles north-east of Prague, was burned to the ground and its inhabitants mown down by firing squads. Vlasov's army arrived on the scene and threatened to turn on its German masters. To the west, German formations were racing Russian spearheads to the safety of the American lines. It was left to Marshal Konev to finish the matter. At 8pm on 8 May he transmitted details of the capitulation to all

---

* Roosevelt had died from a cerebral haemorrhage at Warm Springs, Georgia, on 12 April.

German units in western Czechoslovakia, giving their commanders there three hours to reply. When no reply came, Konev ordered a pulverizing artillery bombardment and, as it lifted, the armies on his front resumed their westward progress. In the small hours of 9 May, armoured units of General Lelyushenko's Fourth Guards Tank Army reached the outer suburbs of Prague. At the same time the German garrison was streaming west in an attempt to escape the jaws of the Red Army encirclement closing around them. Later in the day Soviet tanks entered the ancient city, their tracks rolling over a carpet of lilacs thrown in their path by its jubilant population. In the city whose annexation had started the inexorable slide to war, the European struggle against Nazism had come to an end.

Among the victors, there was a strange sense of anticlimax at the end of the war. For 43rd (Wessex) Division peace broke out on the morning of 5 May as Major-General Thomas prepared to take Bremerhaven. He was at Westerimke, where 214 Brigade had set up its headquarters on the edge of a German prisoner-of-war camp that housed captured merchant seamen. His briefing, in the brigadier's caravan, was interrupted by an urgent message from Horrocks: 'Germans surrendered unconditionally at 1820 hrs. Hostilities on all Second Army front will cease at 0800 hours tomorrow 5th May 45. No repeat No advance beyond present front line without further orders from me.'

Without comment, General Thomas rose and left the caravan. In silence he walked over to where his Buffalo waited, twenty yards away. Then he turned to the brigadier and said, 'The troops have done us damn well'. The steel door of the Buffalo slammed shut and the major-general sped away in the early summer twilight. From the direction of Osterimke a few Very lights arced into the air. To the south, tracer fire briefly flashed in the overcast sky. In the bridgehead beyond the Hamme Canal 130 Brigade put up a few mortar flares. There was no spontaneous outbreak of wild rejoicing.

For the last two days of the war part of Das Reich Division's panzer regiment had been stranded at Kirchberg am Wagram in Austria. The final days of the war came and went without the unit's commander being given any news or orders. He recalled:

> The company was quite isolated. It was odd that at the end of the war we had a full establishment of vehicles. We had 22 Panthers, a Tiger II (all completely equipped) and five Panther recovery vehicles. We were all determined that none of these would fall into the hands of the Russians. We blew up the recovery vehicles near

a village and drove the remaining machines to a small stretch of road and positioned them on the verge, in single file, with their guns pointing eastwards. My own panzer was close to the road and located to shoot at and destroy the other vehicles when the time came. The unit's wheeled transport, held in the main square of the town, would be used to carry the panzer crews once our mission had been completed. We removed all surplus fittings and equipment from the lorries to give us more space. There was a final pay parade and the last canteen supplies were handed out. When that had been done No.2 Company of Das Reich Panzer Regiment paraded for the last time.... Then it was time for us to begin our work. With a lump in our throats we fired at and destroyed our panzers one after the other. The feeling which this aroused in us cannot be described in words. The Tiger II would not die and we had to fire several rounds into it before it caught alight. As a final act the No.1 on the gun blew our own machine. For some time we could not move from the place in which our vehicles were burning. Again and again the wall of flames was split by one mighty detonation after another as the ammunition inside the panzers exploded. The death throes of vehicles which had become part of ourselves seemed to be a symbol of our defeat. We loaded a few Panzerfausts in the truck, just in case we had to fight our way past Russian tanks, and then away we went towards Zettl.

Until 22 May the Dönitz government exercised a phantom authority from his headquarters at Flensburg, near the Danish border. Its initiatives included the establishment of an 'information service' consisting of an old radio set housed in a school classroom. The Minister of Food's sole function was to supply the desultory meetings with a constant supply of whisky. The author and wit Arthur Calder-Marshall – then a colonel in Army Intelligence – recalled the bizarre atmosphere which hung over Flensburg. Every day he found himself exchanging punctilious salutes with Field Marshal Keitel, soon to stand trial at Nuremberg. Lunching one day on the *Patria*, a liner moored to the quay at Flensburg, Marshall watched an officer of the German Navy instructing a group of young officers in U-boat tactics. Presiding over the scene was a huge bust of Hitler. Shortly afterwards a gang of workmen arrived and sawed off the Führer's head.

In May 1945 Europe lay in ruins, and in the middle of this sea of misery lay Germany. The writer and illustrator Mervyn Peake, despatched to Germany as a war artist, wrote home to his wife about the cities through which he had passed:

They are no more. They are relics. Terrible as the bombing of London was, it is as absolutely nothing – nothing – compared with this unutterable desolation. Imagine Chelsea in fragments with not a single house with any more than a few weird-shaped walls where it once stood, and you will get an idea in miniature of what Mannheim and Wiesbaden are like – yet these are only two of the towns we have seen.

In the British occupation zone alone there were at least 1 million 'displaced persons', known to everyone as DPs, among them former slave labourers, released prisoners of war, and German refugees ejected from the East. For two weeks in May a hated figure slid unrecognized in the midst of this human tide. On 5 May, at Flensburg, Heinrich Himmler held his last staff conference. Although Hitler's testament had stripped him of all his many offices, and at Flensburg he had had been openly snubbed by Dönitz, Himmler still nursed fantasies of establishing a 'reformed' Nazi administration in Schleswig-Holstein which would then negotiate with the Allies as a sovereign government. The historian Hugh Trevor-Roper (now Lord Dacre) has painted a sardonic picture of the twilight of Himmler's dwindling empire as, surrounded by his retinue, the former Reichsführer SS lingered on the outskirts of Flensburg:

> Like obsolete dinosaurs, moving inappropriately in the wrong geological age, they gathered at his headquarters – high SS and police leaders, Obergruppenführer and Gruppenführer, heads now of defunct organizations, sustained only by portentous titles, the memory of vanished authority, and absurd illusions.

The illusions were swiftly shattered. After the German capitulation Himmler's jellified powers of decision deserted him completely. He dithered, vacillated, drove aimlessly around the surrounding country-side, sometimes sleeping in station waiting-rooms. To disguise himself, he had shaved off his moustache, donned an eyepatch and wore the uniform of a sergeant in the Geheime Feldpolizei,* a fatal error as the organization was on an Allied blacklist: sergeants and above were subject to automatic arrest. The British had also been tipped off by the Danes that Himmler was moving south, with a view, perhaps, to finding the mythical National Redoubt, and they were on the lookout for him.

On 21 May Himmler and two companions blundered into a British

---

* Secret Field Police, as distinct from the Geheime Staats Polizei (Secret State Police) – the Gestapo.

control point near Bremervörde, halfway between Hamburg and Bremen, and were arrested. At first he went unrecognized, but on the 23rd, while at an interrogation centre at Barfeld, he revealed his identity to the centre's commanding officer, Captain Selvester. Himmler was strip-searched while Selvester summoned a senior Intelligence officer, Colonel Michael Murphy. While they waited for Murphy to arrive, Selvester showed Himmler photographs of the victims of the death camps. Coolly, the ex-Reichsführer declared 'Am I responsible for the excesses of my subordinates?'

Himmler was offered a British Army uniform but declined it, remaining huddled in a blanket, expressing the hope that he would soon be negotiating with Montgomery or even Churchill, his eyes 'steely and bereft of all expression'.* When Murphy arrived, he was unceremoniously bundled into a car, still clutching his blanket, and whisked away to an interrogation centre near Lüneburg. Once again he was stripped and searched. As the fingers of the Army doctor, Wells, groped in his mouth, Himmler bit on the cyanide capsule concealed there. Major N. Whittaker witnessed the ensuing commotion:

> Himmler wouldn't open his mouth wide, so I shone the standard lamp into it. And then I heard the Doc say, 'My God! It's in his mouth and he's done it on me'. Himmler gave a shake of his head (the Doc later told me that he had bitten his finger). Himmler pitched forward immediately and at once I smelt cyanide and knew that it must be a very strong dose. And we immediately upended the old bastard and got his mouth into the bowl of water that was there to try to wash the poison out. There were terrible groans and grunts coming from the swine. Colonel Murphy and I were taking it in turns to get hold of his tongue. But have you ever tried to keep hold of a slippery tongue? All this time we were working on artificial respiration and calling for cardiac stimulant, while Keith was vainly trying to get by telephone to Rear HQ. But the telephone wouldn't function. . . . We now had procured a needle and cotton to fix his tongue, but the first thing we did was to get the needle through his lip. So we had to get it out. But finally we got his tongue fixed. But it was a losing battle we were fighting and the evil thing breathed his last at 2314. We turned it on its back, put a blanket on it and came away. . . . Jimmy the dentist badly wanted to take a couple of teeth as souvenirs, but I said No!

---

* The recollection of Chaim Herzog, then a British Intelligence officer, later President of Israel.

On 26 May, Himmler's body, wrapped in camouflage net, was buried in secret on Lüneburg Heath. The press were still asking when the funeral was to be held.

In Berlin, Vera Bockmann was already at work clearing up the rubble:

> We had survived: no use to moan about the task. It made sense and we got on with it, loading everything on to trucks. Within a few days our street almost looked presentable again, and although our backs ached and our stomachs rumbled for the lack of food we were proud of our achievement. A cannon was still in the middle of the street and a centre of interest for children. Burned out tram-cars round the corner – almost an El Dorado for children who liked slamming doors of broken-down vehicles or sitting at the steering wheel.

Lieutenant-Colonel R.L.H Nunn, a member of the military administration of the British zone in Berlin, found that in the early summer of 1945

> It was just possible to motor down the principal streets past the corpses of burnt-out tanks and cars, but the side streets were generally quite impassable owing to the accumulation of debris which blocked the way. Everything was there – tanks, lorries, cars, guns, uniforms, rifles, equipment, furniture and, above all, bricks and rubble from demolished buildings. In the Tiergarten park itself where the fighting had been heaviest, the trees were cut down and maimed, with branches hanging limply, severed by shell or bomb from the trunks. The monuments of famous Prussian statesmen and generals were occupying quite fantastic positions. One would find the figure of a portly Prussian with his head decapitated, lying under the nearest garden seat. . . . Above all there was a frightful stench, a combination of drains (the broken sewers had not been repaired) and unburied corpses. Flies swarmed everywhere.

Under the shattered roof of the Lehrter station, near which Martin Bormann had met his end, Nunn saw

> crowds of desolate, desperate people trying to leave the stricken city, most of whom had not been able to make any arrangements anywhere else and were simply obsessed with the one idea of getting away. Inevitably they found the situation no better in other

cities . . . so many came back again. Consequently in those first few months there was a constant whirligig of humanity streaming back and forth across Berlin. Journeys even over short distances took days to accomplish . . . Crowded into cattle trucks without lights, suffocated if the doors were closed, frozen if they were open, with no sanitary arrangements, they trundled for days across the northern plain of Germany. It is hardly a matter of surprise that trains arriving at the Lehrter station, and others, often contained the corpses of those whose strength had at last succumbed under these intolerable conditions.

Berlin seethed with Russian deserters, who sold looted goods on the black market and preyed on the refugees arriving at the railway terminals. Nunn recalled that 'Clothing of all kinds and in fact in almost any condition, was at a premium . . . a first-class black market commodity. Women had their fur coats snatched from them in the streets and there was one case when a German turned up at my office literally clothed only in his underpants. He had been completely stripped in the Tiergarten'.

Nunn's relations with his Russian opposite number were lubricated with massive quantities of vodka:

Topokov always brought the discussion to a close by saying, 'We won't bother with that now, let's have something to eat and drink'. As a consequence we were continually adjourning to the inner sanctum to refresh ourselves. I found that these first days were a real physical as well as a mental strain. The Russian, when he drinks, is no mean performer.

Relations on the ground were less amicable. The Russians continually invaded Nunn's district on looting expeditions and were expert at stealing motor cars, often under the noses of the British military guard. German civilians working for the military government were snatched into the Russian sector where they were interrogated about the British administration. They often reappeared weeks later, reluctant to talk about their experience. Nunn observed, 'I would have been happy to explain our system of administration to any Russian officer if he had asked me and saved him this melodramatic kidnapping business.'

Sometimes shots were exchanged between British and Russian troops. In Spandau, Russian soldiers unsuccessfully attempting to hitch a lift back to their sector decided to open fire on the next vehicle to come round the corner. It was a truck filled with British infantry, and one man was killed and another wounded. In the ensuing firefight the Russians received a severe mauling. 'At times,' Nunn mused, 'it seemed rather like being stationed on the frontier of India, always ready to beat off an attack by Afridi tribesmen.' Indeed, Nunn had his own walk-on part in the mid-twentieth century variant of 'The Great Game' – the beginning of the Cold War.

Appendix 1

KEY ITEMS OF WEAPONRY IN THE BATTLE FOR GERMANY

Boeing B-17 Flying Fortress: In its main production variant, the B-17G Flying Fortress, with 'chin' turret for improved forward protection against head-on attacks, was the mainstay of the USAAF's strategic air effort in Europe from 1942 to the end of the war. Losses were particularly heavy in 1943, US Eighth Air Force's overall loss figures being 967 aircraft from 22,779 sorties, a casualty rate of 4.24 per cent compared with the 3.6 per cent sustained by Bomber Command (partly accounted for by the fact that the RAF mainly bombed by night, and the USAAF by day). In the autumn of 1943 average losses per mission were running at nearly 10 per cent and morale dipped to a dangerously low ebb. The situation improved in December 1943 with the introduction of the powerful North American P-51 Mustang long-range fighter, capable of accompanying the bomber formations deep into the heart of Germany, and also of mounting fighting patrols to seek out and destroy enemy fighters. The basis of USAAF bomber tactics was formation flying, which was both gruelling and dangerous. Extreme physical effort was required from the pilot to keep station in the turbulence generated by hundreds of propellers. Poor flying by wing leaders and the constant seesawing of positions often added to pilots' fatigue and increased the risk of collisions or the shaking out of part of the formation. Towards the end of the war, however, when the greater threat was posed by massed anti-aircraft batteries, Eighth Air Force's formations loosened up to provide a more difficult target for the German gunners.

Wing span: 104 feet *Engines*: 4 × 1,200hp radial: *Maximum speed*: 299 mph *Service ceiling*: 37,500 feet *Normal range*: 1,300 or 2,200 miles *Maximum range*: 2,680 or 3,800 miles *Normal bombload*: 6,000 pounds *Maximum bombload*: 13,600 pounds *Crew*: 10 *Defensive armament*: 13 × .5 inch machine-guns

Avro Lancaster: RAF Bomber Command's best heavy bomber of the war. A total of 7,374 had been built by February 1946 and 3,345 were reported missing during the course of the war. Originally designed to carry 4,000-pound bombs, the Lancaster was adapted to carry an 8,000-pound bomb, then the ballistic 12,000-pound Tallboy bomb, the bouncing bomb which breached the Ruhr dams in 1943, and finally, the huge 22,000-pound Grand Slam or 'earthquake' bomb, which demolished the Bielefeld Viaduct on 14 March 1945. Bomber Command losses reached a peak in February-March 1944, when Air Chief Marshal Sir Arthur Harris briefly considered a plan for night-fighters to escort his bombers to their targets. However, by early 1945 huge formations of Lancasters were flying daylight raids in the face of reduced Luftwaffe opposition.

Wing span (MkIII): 102 feet *Engines*: 4 × 1,460hp in-line Rolls-Royce Merlin *Maximum speed*: 287mph *Service ceiling*: 24,500ft *Range*: (with 14,000-pound bombload) 1,660 miles *Crew*: 7 *Defensive armament*: 8 × .303-inch machine-guns

Messerschmitt Me262: Work on the design of the Me262 jet fighter began a year before the outbreak of war. However, because of delays in the development and delivery of satisfactory engines, the damage caused by the Allied bombing offensive, and Hitler's refusal to be advised as to the aircraft's appropriate role, it was six years before the aircraft entered Luftwaffe squadron service, and then only in limited numbers. The principal operational versions were the Me262A-1A *Schwalbe* (Swallow) interceptor and the Me262A-2A *Sturmvögel* (Storm Bird). The Schwalbe was built in a number of sub-types with alternative armament installations; the Sturmvögel, which on Hitler's orders was produced as a bomber, was fitted with external bomb racks. By the end of the war about 1,400 Me262s had been produced, although only a quarter of them saw front-line combat service. Losses among them were heavy, many being destroyed in air-to-air combat by Allied piston-engined Mustang, Thunderbolt, Spitfire and Tempest fighters whose maximum speed was about 100mph slower than the Me262. Neverthe-less, Me262s caused great apprehension among the crews of American bombers. One rear gunner recalled his feelings of 'sheer terror' when encountering Me262s. His B-17 could not turn inside the jets, and he had to sit and watch them 'rip through the for-mation firing their rockets and cannon' while his shaking hands held machine-guns with which he was incapable of tracking the German aircraft. His most vivid memory was that of the breakdown of radio discipline at the appearance of 'the nightmare fighter which we had all hoped was a propaganda myth'. The tactic used by Me262 pilots when attacking US bombers was generally to place themselves about three miles behind the bomber formation and about 6,000 feet above. From this position they began a dive to reach a speed of over 540mph, at which they burst through the fighter screen. Diving down to about 1,500ft below the formation, the Me262 pilots would then pull up, throttle back in order to lose some of this forward speed, then level out 1,000 yards behind the target, ripple-firing rockets at 600 yards to form a dense pattern and following up at closer range with 30mm cannon. There is little doubt that had the Me262 been introduced at an earlier stage in the war, it would have played havoc with American bombers. The most advanced fighter of the war, it was a delight to fly, but its principal drawbacks were the unreliability of its immature engines and its endurance of only an hour.

Wing span: 41 feet *Engines*: 2 × Junkers Jumo turbojets *Maximum speed*: 540mph *Service ceiling*: 40,000 feet *Range*: 650 miles *Armament* (Me262A-1A): 4 × 30mm can-non, 24 × R4M air-to-air rockets

Ilyushin Il-2: The *Shturmovik* ground-attack aircraft was built in larger numbers than any other combat aircraft of the war. By May 1945 over 35,000 had rolled off the pro-duction lines in three huge factories. Constructed around an armoured steel 'bath' which housed the engine and the cockpit, the Il-2 was almost impervious to light ground fire. Originally built as a single-seater, the early Shturmoviks lacked power and manoeuvrability and were vulnerable to attack from the rear. By the summer of 1943 they had been replaced by the Il-2m3 with a more powerful engine and a second seat for a rear gunner firing a 12.7mm machine-gun. The Il-2m3 also carried two 37mm can-non in its wings which were capable of penetrating the armour of most German tanks. Rocket-propelled missiles could be carried under the wings and anti-personnel or hol-low-charge anti-tank bombs were housed internally in a number of small bomb bays. German fighter pilots dubbed this rugged aircraft, superbly suited to the Soviet way of waging war, the *Zementer*, or 'cement bomber'.

Wing span: 48 feet *Engine*: 1 × 1,600hp in-line *Maximum speed*: 257mph *Crew*: 2 *Armament*: 2 × 37mm cannon, 3 machine-guns, 8 rockets or 1,300 pounds of bombs

PzKpfw V Panther Battle Tank: The German response to the Red Army's T-34, the Panther entered production in November 1942 and first went into action at Kursk in the summer of 1943, but was initially plagued by mechanical problems stemming from its rushed introduction to service. Subsequent modifications ironed out most of the Panther's teething troubles, and it quickly acquired a formidable reputation, equipping one of each panzer regiment's two battalions. Three major versions were produced – the D, A, and finally the G – which incorporated successive improvements without altering the Panther's basic characteristics, the most notable of which were its 75mm L/70 gun, sloped glacis, wide tracks and interleaved suspension. A total of 5,508 Panthers were built during the war, of which 3,740 were Model Gs. The Panther's most successful derivative was the *Jagdpanther* heavy tank destroyer, armed with an 88mm gun, housed in a well-angled enclosed superstructure, which was capable of penetrating the armour of every Allied tank in service.

Panther G – *Crew*: 5 *Weight*: 45 tons *Maximum road speed*: 29mph *Cross-country speed*: 15mph *Range*: 110 miles *Armour*: 20–120mm *Armament*: 1 × 75mm L/70 gun, 2 × 7.92mm machine-guns

PzKpfw VI Tiger I Heavy Battle Tank: At the time of its introduction to service in the late summer of 1942, and for some time afterwards, the Tiger was the most powerful tank in the world. Its 88mm gun, for which the tank carried 92 rounds of ammunition, outranged and outpunched all Allied types, and although its armour was not well sloped, as was that of the Panther, it was 100mm thick at the front and 80mm thick around the sides. In spite of its weight, overloaded engine and transmission, and slow speed, the Tiger was highly effective when used in battalion-sized formations of about thirty vehicles under the control of an army or corps headquarters. The Tiger's firepower could overcome all but the most skilfully handled opposition and forced the Allies to develop new tactics to deal with it. The rule of thumb was that it took at least five American M4 Sherman medium tanks to knock out a cornered Tiger. The Tiger I was phased out in the summer of 1944 after 1,300 had been built, a relatively small number when one considers the effect the tank had on Allied morale. The Tiger was followed into service by the Tiger II or *Königstiger*, known to the Allies as the Royal Tiger. Introduced in the autumn of 1944, it was the heaviest, best protected and most powerfully armoured tank to see service in the war; indeed, its armour and gun would do justice to a main battle tank today. Some 485 Tiger IIs were produced before the end of the war. Although ponderous and liable to be stranded in a fast-moving battle, they were capable of fighting against heavy odds and of knocking out numerous enemy armoured vehicles while suffering little damage themselves.

Tiger I – *Crew*: 5 *Weight*: 56 tons *Maximum road speed*: 24mph *Cross-country speed*: 12mph *Range*: 62 miles *Armour*: 26–110mm *Armament*: 1 × 88mm L/56 gun, 2 × 7.92mm machine-guns

Tiger II – *Crew*: 5 *Weight*: 68 tons *Maximum road speed*: 24mph *Cross-country speed*: 11mph *Range*: 68 miles *Armour*: 40–185mm *Armament*: 1 × 88mm L/71 gun, 2 × 7.92mm machine-guns

T-34: The mainstay of the Soviet Union's tank armies, the T-34 was a superb fighting machine whose basic excellence was underlined by the fact that it went through the war without major modification. Its broad tracks reduced ground pressure to a minimum and it was fast and agile even in the roughest terrain. A rugged all-weather diesel engine gave the T-34 an excellent power-to-weight ratio and a range of 186 miles, nearly twice that of the Panther and three times that of the Tiger. Sloping armour considerably increased resistance to shell penetration – a feature which was copied in the Panther – and an innovatory long-barrelled high-velocity 76.2mm gun completed a well-balanced design which combined the fundamental requirements of firepower, mobility and protection with the facility of rapid mass production and easy repair and maintenance in the field. The T34/76, which entered service in 1941, was followed in the spring of 1944 by the upgunned T-34/85, equipping independent tank brigades. During the war the T-34 accounted for 68 per cent of Soviet tank production, and the T-34/85 went on to see service in the

Korean War (1950–3), the Arab–Israeli Wars (1967 and 1973) and numerous other conflicts.

Crew: 5 *Weight* (T-34/85): 36 tons *Maximum road speed*: 31mph *Range*: 186 miles *Armour*: 18–60mm *Armament* (T-34/85): 1 × 85mm gun, 2 × 7.62mm machine-guns

M4 Sherman: More Shermans were manufactured than any other single tank during the war, a tribute to the American genius for mass production. When production ceased in June 1945, 49,234 had been built, a figure which exceeded the combined British and German tank output. Combat experience quickly revealed that the Sherman was undergunned in comparison with the German Tiger and Panther, and later models of the M4A1, M4A2 and M4A3 were armed with a 76mm gun which improved armour-piercing capability, but nevertheless fell short of that possessed by the British Firefly conversion, which had a 17-pounder gun. Active service also revealed that the Sherman had an alarming propensity for 'brewing up' if penetrated by a shell. To overcome this fault, attempts were made to provide wet stowage for the ammunition, the bins being surrounded by water jackets. As well as providing the backbone of the US Armoured Force during the war, the Sherman was also the mainstay of British armoured divisions, which counted on its general reliability in action, ease of maintenance and sheer weight of numbers to offset its inferiority against Tigers and Panthers. The many Sherman derivatives included the DD Duplex-Drive swimming tank, the mine detonating Crab flail tank and the M18, M19, M36 and M40 tank destroyers. Like the T-34, the Sherman had a long post-war life.

Crew: 5 *Weight*: 31 tons *Maximum road speed*: 26mph *Range* (road): 100 miles *Armour*: 15–100mm *Armament*: 1 × 75mm gun, 2 × 0.3-inch machine-guns, 1 × 0.5-inch machine-gun

Katyusha: The nickname (Little Kate) given to the Red Army's fin-stabilized rockets, which were launched from rails mounted on a heavy truck. A Katyusha division was capable of firing a barrage of 3,840 projectiles (230 tons of high-explosive) up to a range of 3.5 miles.

Panzerfaust: A German hand-held recoilless anti-tank weapon fired by one man. It consisted of a short steel tube containing a propelling charge and with the tail stem of a shaped-charge bomb inserted in the mouth of the tube. The firer tucked it under his arm, took aim across the top of the bomb and pressed a trigger to fire the charge, which in turn blew the bomb forward while expelling the gases from the rear of the tube to counteract the recoil. The first model appeared in 1942, but had a very short range of about 100 feet. By the end of the war the hundreds of thousands of Panzerfausts issued to the Volkssturm were effective against tanks at up to 500 feet provided the bomb hit the side or the rear – the weapon was useless against frontal armour. In terms of cost-effectiveness, a Panzerfaust in the hands of a determined soldier was one of the most successful weapons of the war. During the closing months of the conflict British 11th Armoured Division suffered significant losses from simple Panzerfaust tactics. The firers concealed themselves beside a road or in a defile and waited for the leading tank to arrive; infantry support and the spraying of likely-looking hiding places with machine-gun fire failed to prevent the Panzerfaust taking a regular toll. As a member of 11th Armoured reflected: 'That machines costing many thousands of pounds and requiring a high order of craftsmanship and a considerable number of man-hours to produce, should be so persistently destroyed by a small tube which looks like a toy bought at a department store would seem to be a matter demanding very serious attention in high quarters.'

Appendix 2

NOTES ON PERSONALITIES

Antonov, General A.I. Chief of Operations, Soviet General Staff, from December 1942. From April 1943 he served simultaneously as First Deputy Chief of Staff. Chief of the General Staff, February 1945–March 1946.

Axmann, Artur Leader of the Hitler Youth and present in the Führerbunker during the final days. On 30 April 1945 he examined the dead bodies of Hitler and Eva Braun. Broke out of the bunker on 1 May and later saw the bodies of Bormann and Stumpfegger.

Boldt, Captain Gerhard ADC to Colonel-General Krebs. Tried and failed to commit suicide after breaking out of the bunker. Later wrote an interesting personal account of the closing days of the war, *Hitler's Last Days*.

Bormann, Martin Bormann was one of the first to join the Nazi Party and from 1943 was Hitler's Secretary, exercising complete control of access to the Führer. He shared Hitler's strategic views and it has been suggested that some of the Führer's more spectacular blunders stemmed directly from Bormann's insinuating advice. During the closing weeks of the war Bormann opened secret negotiations with the Russians, an initiative he successfully concealed from his master, at whose side he remained until the end. He committed suicide on 1 May after breaking out of the bunker.

Bradley, General Omar N. After serving as commander of US 82nd and 28th Infantry Division in 1942, Bradley became deputy commander, then commander of US II Corps in Tunisia and Sicily, 1943. He commanded US First Army in the Normandy landings, broke out from the bridgehead at St Lô on 25 July 1944, and on 1 August was appointed commander of the newly formed US 12th Army Group which breached the Siegfried Line. He ordered Patton to make his dramatic shift in direction against the German southern flank in December 1945 during the Ardennes offensive. Men of his army group took the Remagen bridge over the Rhine, 7 March 1945, and invaded southern Germany to reach Prague by the end of the war. Bradley was the US Army's Chief of Staff 1948–9 and served as Chairman of the US Joint Chiefs of Staff from August 1949 to August 1953.

Brooke, Field Marshal Sir Alan (First Viscount Alanbrooke of Brookeborough) Brooke served as the commander of II Corps, British Expeditionary Force in France, September 1939–June 1940 and then as C-in-C Southern Command, June-July 1940. After a spell as C-in-C Home Forces, he was appointed Chief of the Imperial General Staff (CIGS) in December 1941. He held this post until June 1946, combining the function of CIGS with that of Chairman of the British Chiefs of Staff Committee from March 1942. His close relations with Churchill – he was effectively the Prime Minister's executive officer – were fundamental to Allied strategy, and he played an important role both in negotiating tactfully with the Americans and ensuring that some of Churchill's wilder schemes never saw the light of day. Brooke had a sure grasp of strategy, and the vital ability to translate the wide-ranging strategic ambitions of the British Prime Minister into hard reality in terms of Britain's stretched military resources.

Chuikov, Marshal V.I. One of the outstanding fighting generals of the Second World War, Chuikov, a man of peasant origins, joined the Red Army in 1918, rising to command Fourth Army from 1938–40. He took part in the occupation of Poland (1939) and the Russo-Finnish War (November 1939–March 1940) before his appointment as military attaché in China and adviser to the Chinese leader Chiang Kai-shek, 1941–2. As commander of Sixty-Second (later Eighth Guards) Army he played a major role in the defence of Stalingrad in the winter of 1942–3, and later in the assault on Berlin. From 1946–53 Chuikov was the Deputy Commander and then Commander-in-Chief of Soviet occupation forces in Germany. His book, *The End of the Third Reich*, is an immensely readable, no-nonsense personal account of the Vistula-Oder and Berlin operations.

Crerar, Lieutenant-General Henry The commander of Canadian I Corps in Italy in 1943, Crerar later led Canadian First Army in the invasion of Normandy and the campaign in North-West Europe. His army's operations on the left flank of the Allied advance included the capture of the V-weapons sites, the Pas de Calais and Antwerp. Crerar's army also executed the encirclement of all German forces in the Netherlands.

Dietrich, SS Colonel-General Sepp In 1928 Dietrich, a diehard Nazi, was given command of Hitler's bodyguard, which in June 1934 became the Leibstandarte SS Adolf Hitler. He continued to command this formation in the war, as it expanded to a division, fighting in Poland, France, the Eastern Front and Normandy, where in 1944 he was promoted to Colonel-General and awarded the Diamonds to the Knight's Cross. Dietrich then led Sixth SS Panzer Army in the Ardennes offensive in December 1944 before being transferred to Hungary in March 1945 in a vain attempt to retake Budapest. Dietrich retreated into Austria, doing his best to ensure that his men did not fall into Russian hands, and surrendered to the US Army. He was tried as a war criminal by the Americans and in 1946 sentenced to twenty-five years' imprisonment for the murder of US prisoners-of-war at Malmédy, Belgium, in 1944. Released in 1955, he was then sentenced to eighteen months' imprisonment by a German civil court for his role in the 'Night of the Long Knives' (the elimination by SS units of the older and more radical Nazi SA) in 1934. Dietrich was no military theorist, and he had little training to equip him for high command, but he was a tough fighting general with a keen grasp of man management and leadership, which inspired loyalty among the men he commanded.

Dönitz, Grand Admiral Karl A submariner who commanded the German U-boat service from the outbreak of war until January 1943, when he succeeded Grand Admiral Erich Raeder as C-in-C of the German Navy. On 29 April 1945, Hitler nominated Dönitz as his successor. On 4 May, Dönitz's emissary, Admiral Friedeburg, surrendered German forces in the north-west of Germany and other areas at Montgomery's headquarters. Dönitz, who wished to make peace with the Western Allies while continuing to fight the Russians, was arrested on 23 May and sentenced to ten years' imprisonment (in Spandau) at the Nuremberg trials.

Eden, Anthony (First Earl of Avon) Eden served as the British Foreign Secretary from September 1939 to May 1940, when he briefly became Churchill's Secretary of State for War before resuming his post as Foreign Secretary. He enjoyed a close working relationship with Churchill, being seen as the Prime Minister's unofficial heir, and was a key figure at all the wartime conferences. In May 1945 Eden led the British delegation to San Francisco to participate in the establishment of the United Nations Organization. Eden served as British Prime Minister from 1955 to January 1957, when he resigned following the Suez Crisis of late 1956.

Eisenhower, General Dwight D. Eisenhower was Chief of the War Plans Division in the US War Department from February to June 1942, when he laid down the first plans for the invasion of North-West Europe. He was Commanding General US Forces, European Theatre, until November 1942 when he was appointed C-in-C Allied Forces

North Africa for the Torch landings in French North-West Africa and subsequent Tunisian campaign. On 20 January 1943 he became Supreme Allied Commander Mediterranean. In December 1943 he was appointed Supreme Commander Allied Forces Europe after President Roosevelt decided that General Marshall, the US Army Chief of Staff and his first choice, was indispensable in Washington. Eisenhower accepted the unconditional surrender of Germany on 7 May 1945. He succeeded Marshall as US Army Chief of Staff in late 1945, holding the position until 1948. He was subsequently Supreme Allied Commander Europe (SACEUR), 1950–2, and US President 1953–61.

Guderian, Colonel-General Heinz The German Army's leading expert in armoured warfare, and a key figure in the German conquest of France in 1940, Guderian was appointed Inspector-General of Armoured Troops in March 1943. In July 1944 he replaced Colonel-General Zeitzler as Chief of the Army General Staff after the purge of officers involved in the 20 July bomb plot against Hitler. Long at loggerheads with the Führer over strategy – he had been removed from the command of 2nd Panzer Group in December 1941 after making a tactical withdrawal on the Eastern Front – Guderian's time as Chief of Staff was marked by a series of blazing rows with Hitler, during some of which they nearly came to blows. The last confrontation came on 28 March 1945, after which Guderian was dismissed. His autobiography, *Panzer Leader*, is somewhat self-serving but full of detail about the German high command and its leading personalities. Guderian, who had been involved with the training of panzer forces since 1934, is generally credited with having perfected the technique of the *Blitzkrieg* (lightning war).

Harris, Air Chief Marshal Sir Arthur Harris served as Air Officer Commanding 5 Group in 1939–40 and was then appointed Deputy Chief of Air Staff at the Air Ministry. He led the RAF delegation to Washington before replacing Sir Richard Peirse as Air Officer Commanding-in-Chief, Bomber Command, in February 1942. Harris's flair for publicity, equalled only by Montgomery's, was quickly demonstrated in the 1,000-bomber raid on Cologne on 30/31 May 1942. Blunt to the point of rudeness, and an unwavering advocate of area bombing, a policy which he had inherited rather than originated, Harris always cut a controversial figure, but he remains one of the great operational commanders of the war. He was nicknamed, though not unaffectionately, 'Butch' (short for 'Butcher') by his crews, though this was superseded by the now common 'Bomber'.

Heinrici, Colonel-General Gotthard A leading expert on defensive warfare, Heinrici had commanded First Army's XII Corps in France in 1940 and XLIII Corps in the invasion of the Soviet Union in 1941. He was promoted to command Fourth Army in May 1942, and in May 1944 he assumed command of First Panzer Army on the Carpathian front, conducting a skilful retreat to Silesia early in 1945. In March 1945 he replaced Himmler as commander of Army Group Vistula. At the end of the war he was captured by the Russians and imprisoned until 1955.

Hodges, General Courtney An infantry officer, Hodges was appointed the US Army's Chief of Intelligence on the outbreak of war, a post he held until 1942. After commanding the Army's Replacement and Training organization he took over X Corps in late 1942. Promoted Lieutenant-General in 1943, he commanded Third Army, then training in Texas, before being appointed Deputy Commander of First Army under Bradley. Hodges was responsible for First Army's landings on Utah and Omaha beaches on D-Day, 6 June 1944. In August 1944, when Bradley was given command of 12th Army Group, Hodges succeeded to the command of First Army.

Horrocks, Lieutenant-General Sir Brian Known throughout the British Army, and the Allied high command, as 'Jorrocks', Horrocks commanded a battalion of 3rd Division in France in 1940, where he caught the eye of the divisional commander, Montgomery. In 1942 Montgomery sent for Horrocks and gave him command of XIII Corps, which he led during the second Battle of El Alamein. Horrocks then commanded X Corps before transferring to British First Army where he handled the capture of Tunis in May 1943. Just before the end of the Tunisian campaign Horrocks was wounded in an air raid and returned to England. When he recovered, Montgomery gave him XXX Corps, which he led from Normandy to the end of the war. Horrocks was an effective and popular corps commander, through hindsight shows that he was fatally over-cautious during XXX Corps' drive to link up with British 1st Airborne Division at Arnhem in Operation Market Garden.

Jodl, Colonel-General Alfried Chief of Staff of the High Command of the German Armed Forces (OKW) 1939–1945, Jodl was Hitler's executive officer, though he had no active experience of command. His importance rested in the fact that throughout the war he was the officer closest to the Führer, personally briefing him every day and discussing the plans and operational orders which he drafted in Hitler's name. Jodl's loyalty to Hitler, whom he considered a military genius, overrode the private misgivings he had about the conduct of the war from 1942. Content with such submissiveness, Hitler told Göring that he considered Jodl 'a very good and solid worker with an excellent general staff training'. Late in the war, however, Hitler called Jodl a 'worn-out fuddy-duddy', but Field Marshal Kesselring regarded him as one of the ablest men in the OKW, observing that no man could have done better in that impossible situation. Jodl signed the German surrender at Reims on 7 May, 1945. He was tried for war crimes at Nuremberg and hanged on 16 October 1946.

Keitel, Field Marshal Wilhelm Chief of the High Command of the German Armed Forces (OKW) from February 1938 to May 1945. Keitel exercised no influence over operations, acting as a functionary and carrying out Hitler's orders in a slavish fashion which earned him the nickname '*Lakaitel*', a pun on his name and *Lakai*, the German for servant, or 'nodding donkey', a reference to his constant readiness to agree with the Führer. Mussolini observed that Keitel was a man very pleased to be Keitel. Hitler thought he had 'the brains of a cinema commissionaire'. Keitel signed the German surrender in Berlin on 8 May 1945. He was tried for war crimes at Nuremberg and hanged on 16 October 1946.

Konev, Marshal I.S. In the battle for Moscow in the winter of 1941, Konev was commander of Nineteenth Army and Western Army Front. From 1941 to 1943 he commanded Kalinin Front before taking over Steppe Front, Stavka's strategic reserve at the Battle of Kursk in July 1943. He went on to command Second and then First Ukrainian Fronts in the Red Army offensives in the Ukraine, Poland and the battle for Berlin. He was obliged to cede the prize of Berlin to Zhukov, but in the political switchback of the post-war years Konev fared better than his great rival. His post-war appointments included Commander-in-Chief of the Soviet Ground Forces and Deputy Minister of War, 1946–50, and First Deputy Minister of Defence and Commander-in-Chief of Warsaw Pact Forces, 1955–60.

Malinovsky, Marshal R. Malinovsky commanded the Russian South-West Front in December 1941 and a year later frustrated German attempts to relieve their Sixth Army, trapped in Stalingrad. He then took over Third Ukrainian Front, completing the liberation of the Donbass and the western Ukraine. He led Second Ukrainian Front in Romania and Hungary, taking Budapest in February 1945 and liberating Slovakia.

Malinovsky then commanded the Transbaikal Front in the brief war with Japan in 1945. In 1945–6 he served as C-in-C Soviet Forces Far East, and in 1956–7 was briefly C-in-C Soviet Ground Forces.

Manteuffel, General Baron Hasso Eccard von An expert in armoured warfare, Manteuffel rose to prominence in 1943 as the commander of 7th Panzer Division, later leading Grossdeutschland Division. On 12 September 1944 he was appointed commander of Fifth Panzer Army, which he led in the Ardennes offensive. Early in March 1945 he assumed command of Third Panzer Army, holding this appointment to the end of the war. Diminutive and hard-driving, Manteuffel was also a superb horseman and sometime gentleman jockey.

Mellenthin, Major-General F.W. von After holding a number of staff jobs in the Polish, French and Balkan campaigns of 1939–41, Mellenthin went to the Western Desert as Third General Staff Officer to Panzer Group Afrika in June 1941. After holding the post of Deputy First General Staff Officer in 1942, during which he suffered a period in hospital, Mellenthin went to the Eastern Front in November 1942 as Chief of Staff, XLVIII Panzer Corps. He later served as Chief of Staff, Fourth Panzer Army, August-September 1944, and then took over as Chief of Staff Army Group G until 5 December 1944. He was attached to 9th Panzer Division in January-February 1945 before finishing the war as Chief of Staff, Fifth Panzer Army. His book *Panzer Battles* is full of insights into armoured warfare on six fronts in the Second World War.

Model, Field Marshal Walther Model served as Sixteenth Army's Chief of Staff during the 1940 campaign in France. During the invasion of the Soviet Union in 1941 he led 3rd Panzer Division and then XLI Panzer Corps. He commanded Ninth Army at Kursk in July 1943 and from October 1943 was, successively, the commander of Army Groups North, South and Centre. He was appointed C-in-C West in August 1944. He was replaced by Rundstedt at the beginning of September but remained in command of Army Group B. He committed suicide in the Ruhr pocket on 21 April 1945.

Mohnke, SS General Wilhelm A founder-member of the Leibstandarte SS Adolf Hitler, Mohnke commanded the inner defensive ring of Berlin, the *Zitadelle*, and the Führerbunker, during the battle for the German capital. On 2 May 1945, he went into a ten-year captivity in the Soviet Union. In the post-war years *prima facie* cases were made which implicated Mohnke in the commission of war crimes as a battalion and a regimental commander in France, respectively, in 1940 and 1944, and as the divisional commander of the Leibstandarte Division during the Ardennes offensive. All these charges involved the murder of prisoners of war; the last, concerning an incident in December 1944, also involved the issuing of orders to execute defenceless Belgian civilians. Mohnke was also suspected of complicity in the flying courts martial (*Stadgerichte*) set up during the final stages of the battle for Berlin. After he returned from captivity in Russia, he was not called to account for any of these alleged crimes, although he remained on the wanted lists of the British, Canadian and American governments and the United Nations War Crimes Commission. Mohnke had a moulded wooden foot, the result of a war wound suffered in the Balkans.

Montgomery, Field Marshal Sir Bernard Law (First Viscount Montgomery of Alamein) In 1939–40 Montgomery commanded 3rd Division in France and Belgium and in the final stages of the campaign assumed command of II Corps during the retreat to Dunkirk. He then successively commanded V Corps, XII Corps and South-Eastern Command before replacing General Sir Claude Auchinleck as commander of British Eighth Army in Egypt in July 1942. Montgomery threw back Field Marshal Erwin Rommel's attack at Alam al Halfa, 31 August–2 September 1942, and then defeated him at the second Battle of El Alamein, 23 October–4 November 1942. After the clearing of North Africa, Montgomery led Eighth Army in the assault on Sicily, July 1943, and in the invasion of Italy in the following September. In December 1943 he was chosen to command Allied ground forces in the invasion of Normandy, 6 June 1944. In September 1944 he surrendered overall command to Eisenhower, retaining command of British 21st Army Group until the end of the war. On 4 May 1945 he received the surrender of all German forces in northern Europe on Lüneburg Heath. Montgomery's post-war appointments included Chief of the Imperial General Staff, 1948–51, and NATO's Deputy Supreme Commander in Europe, 1951–8.

Novikov, Marshal A. C-in-C of the Soviet Air Force from 1942, and responsible for air operations during the battles of Stalingrad, Kursk, Belorussia and Königsberg. In charge of Soviet air operations in Manchuria in August 1945. Imprisoned by Stalin in 1946.

Patch, Lieutenant-General Alexander Patch began wartime field service commanding US forces in New Caledonia, in the Pacific, in 1942. In December 1942 he was appointed commander of US XIV Corps on Guadalcanal, where he remained until February 1943. In March 1944 he was appointed commander of US Seventh Army, which in August of that year landed in southern France. Seventh Army advanced up the Rhône valley to Alsace, crossed the Rhine on 26 March 1945, and took the surrender of Army Group G on 5 May.

Patton, General George S. Patton commanded Western Task Force in the Torch landings in North Africa, November 1942. In March 1943 he was appointed commander of US II Corps in Tunisia, linking with Montgomery's Eighth Army for the final advance on Tunis, but was replaced by Bradley in late April in order to take command of US forces preparing to invade Sicily, where he led US Seventh Army, July–August 1943. Patton commanded US Third Army in the Normandy campaign, played a major role in the defeat of the German offensive in the Ardennes, and crossed the Rhine at Oppenheim on 22 March 1945. Advancing south of Berlin, he had reached the Danube by the end of April. Patton always courted controversy, notably in the infamous incident in Sicily when he struck a soldier suffering from combat fatigue. At the very end of the war he was involved in a highly questionable venture. On the night of 26/27 March 1945, he sent an armoured column deep behind enemy lines to a POW camp at Hammelburg, forty miles east of Frankfurt. The column reached the camp but was cut to pieces as it made its way back to the American lines. Patton claimed that his aim had been to confuse the enemy, but it emerged that his son-in-law, Lieutenant-Colonel John K. Waters, who had been captured by the Germans in North Africa early in 1943, was an inmate of the Hammelburg camp. The suspicion remains that Patton's principal purpose was to rescue him. In this he failed; Waters was wounded and recaptured by the Germans during the operation. Patton himself was killed in a road accident in occupied Germany, 21 December 1945, while commanding US Fifth Army.

Rokossovsky, Marshal K.K. Rokossovsky had been arrested and imprisoned for three years during Stalin's purges of the 1930s. Released in 1940, he was appointed commander of V Cavalry Corps. He led Sixteenth Army in the battle for Moscow in December 1941 and by the following winter had risen to command Don Front during the Battle of Stalingrad. At Kursk, in July 1943, Rokossovsky commanded Central Front. He subsequently commanded First and then Second Belorussian Fronts. As the commander of First Belorussian Front, he denied the Polish Home Army assistance when it rose against the Germans in Warsaw (August–October 1944). His troops remained in their positions, barely twenty miles south of the city, while the Germans ruthlessly put down the insurrection. Soviet historians later claimed that Rokossovsky's resources were exhausted and that the rising – itself encouraged by Soviet radio broadcasts – had been premature. It was not until January 1945 that Rokossovsky, now in command of Second Belorussian Front, entered Warsaw before advancing across Poland to take Danzig and encircle the German forces in East Prussia. Leading elements of Second Belorussian Front made contact with British units at Wismar on 5 May. Rokossovsky's post-war appointments included C-in-C Soviet Forces in Poland (a snub from a still suspicious Stalin) and Deputy Minister of Defence, 1956–62.

Rybalko, Colonel-General P. Rybalko's Third Tank Army saw heavy fighting in the Soviet offensive of January 1943 and in the counter-offensive which followed the Battle of Kursk in August–September of the same year. Rewarded with the honorific title 'Guards', it then took part in the liberation of Kiev in the autumn of 1943, and in December was involved in the tank battles in the Zhitomir sector. In July 1944, Rybalko took the old Polish city of Lvov and during the Vistula-Oder operation Third Guards Tank Army captured Cracow. During the battle for Berlin, Third Guards Tank Army took Zossen, the headquarters of OKW and OKH. Redeploying, it then drove south against Dresden and Prague, entering the latter on 9 May. Rybalko was an outstanding example of the battle-hardened military professionals who carried the Soviet Union to victory following the reform of the Red Army in 1942–3.

Schörner, Field Marshal Ferdinand A longstanding Nazi, Schörner commanded 6th Mountain Division in northern Norway where, in late 1941, it took part in the advance on Murmansk. Subsequently he commanded XIX Mountain Corps in Finland and in 1943 returned to the Eastern Front in command of XL Panzer Corps. In March 1944 he was promoted to command Army Group South Ukraine, and in July became commander of Army Group North on the Baltic coast. His final command was Army Group Centre in Czechoslovakia, and he was promoted to the rank of Field Marshal on 5 April 1945. In his testament, Hitler appointed Schörner the last C-in-C of the wartime German Army. When he received Keitel's order to surrender on 7 March, Schörner refused to obey for three days. He was imprisoned by the Russians for nine years after the war, and was sentenced to a term of forty-one years on his return to Germany for his part in instigating the flying courts martial during the final days of the Third Reich.

Simpson, Lieutenant-General William H. Popularly known as 'Big Bill', Simpson first saw action in 1916 against the Mexican revolutionary leader Pancho Villa. Eisenhower brought him to Europe in the summer of 1944 in command of US Ninth Army, which liberated Brest on 18 September and then moved into the line on the Western Front between US First and British Second Armies. In February 1945, Ninth Army mounted Operation Grenade, which took it over the River Roer and on to the west bank of the Rhine. Simpson's army crossed the Rhine between Düsseldorf and Duisburg in March, and by 11 April 1945 had reached the Elbe near Magdeburg.

Sokolovsky, Marshal V. Sokolovsky commanded Western Front in the Soviet counter-offensive following the battle of Kursk in the autumn of 1943. In 1944 he transferred to First Ukrainian Front as Chief of Staff. During the assault on Berlin he was Deputy Front Commander with First Belorussian Front. Sokolovsky reportedly identified Hitler's charred corpse from the Führer's dental records.

Spaatz, General Carl Spaatz was Commanding General US Army Air Forces, Europe, 1942–3. In February 1943 he was appointed commander of the North-West African Air Force in Tunisia, remaining Mediterranean Commander for the subsequent operations in Sicily and Italy. In January 1944 he became C-in-C of the US Strategic (Bombing) Air

Forces, North-West Europe. In March 1945 he moved to the Pacific to lead the US Strategic Forces in that theatre. In 1947–8 Spaatz was the US Air Forces's Chief of Staff.

Tedder, Air Chief Marshal Sir Arthur (First Baron Tedder) In 1940–1 Tedder served as Deputy Air Officer Commanding-in-Chief Middle East before taking over as Air Officer Commanding-in-Chief in that theatre. Following the Casablanca Conference in January 1943, Tedder was appointed C-in-C Mediterranean Air Command, later co-ordinating land and air operations during the invasions of Sicily and Italy. In 1944 he served as Eisenhower's Deputy Supreme Commander during the invasion of Normandy and was responsible for integrating the Allied tactical and strategic air offensives against the enemy's communications. After the successful conclusion of the Normandy campaign, Tedder co-ordinated the operations of the Allied tactical air forces and arranged intervention by the strategic air forces to aid ground forces. On 8 May, Tedder ratified the instrument of German surrender in Berlin on Eisenhower's behalf. In September 1945 he was appointed Marshal of the RAF and on 1 January 1946 became Chief of Air Staff and was created Lord Tedder.

Tolbukhin, Marshal V.I. Tolbukhin was Chief of Staff to Transcaucasian Front and then Crimean Front in 1941–2, and commanded Fifty-Seventh Army during the Battle of Stalingrad in 1942–3. As commander of Southern Front (later renamed Fourth Ukrainian Front) Tolbukhin liberated the Crimea and was promoted marshal. In May 1944 he assumed command of Third Ukrainian Front, which he led to the end of the war. He commanded Soviet forces in South-Eastern Europe in 1945–7, and served as commander of the Transcaucasian Military District, 1947–9.

Vasilevsky, Marshal A.M. Vasilevsky was appointed Chief of the Soviet General Staff in June 1942, in which capacity he served almost to the end of the war. Of his thirty-four months in the post he spent twenty-two at various fronts. In February 1945 he assumed command of Third Belorussian Front after the death of General Chernyakhovksy. He commanded the Soviet armies in the Far East in the August 1945 campaign against the Japanese in Manchuria and Korea, before reassuming direction of the General Staff in 1946. From 1949 to Stalin's death in 1953, Vasilevsky served as Minister of Defence.

Zhukov, Marshal G.K. Zhukov was appointed First Deputy Supreme Commander-in-Chief Soviet Armed Forces in August 1942, serving in this post to the end of the war. He exercised key responsibility for the planning of the Battles of Stalingrad and Kursk. He co-ordinated First and Second Ukrainian Fronts in the winter offensive of 1943–4 before moving on to command First Ukrainian Front in the spring of 1944, and to co-ordinate the operations of First and Second Belorussian Fronts in the summer offensive of 1944. Zhukov commanded First Belorussian Front in the final assault on Germany and in 1945–6 was C-in-C of the Soviet occupation forces in Germany. From 1947 to 1952 he was removed from the centre of power by a jealous Stalin and relegated to the obscurity of commanding the Odessa and Ural Military Districts. He returned to favour after Stalin's death, but in 1957, while serving as Minister of Defence, he was summarily dismissed and disgraced, allegedly for challenging the Communist Party leadership of the armed forces.

SELECT BIBLIOGRAPHY

Ahlfen, H. *Der Kampf um Schleisen 1944–45* (1977)

Allen, P. *One More River: The Rhine Crossings of 1945* (1980)

Bagramyan, I.K. 'The Storming of Königsberg' (in Erickson, J. *Main Front*, 1987)

Barclay, C.N. *The History of 53rd (Welsh) Division in the Second World War* (1956)

Bartov, O. *The Eastern Front 1941–45: German Troops and the Barbarization of Warfare* (1985)

Bekker, C. *The Luftwaffe War Diaries* (1967)

Bialer, S. *Stalin and His Generals* (1970)

Blumenson, M. (ed.) *The Patton Papers* (1974)

Bockmann, V. *Full Circle: An Australian in Berlin 1930–46* (1986)

Boldt, G. *Hitler's Last Days* (1973)

Bourke-White, M. *Dear Fatherland Rest Quietly* (1947)

Bradley, O. and Blair, C. *A General's Life* (1983)

Byford-Jones, W. *Berlin Twilight* (1947)

Bullock, A. *Hitler, A Study in Tyranny* (1967)

Chuikov, V.I. *The End of the Third Reich* (1978)

Cole, H.M. *The Lorraine Campaign* (1950)

De la Mazière, C. *The Captive Dreamer* (1974)

Duffy, C. *Red Storm on the Reich: The Soviet March on Germany, 1945* (1991)

Eisenhower, D.D. *Crusade in Europe* (1948)

Ellis, J. *Brute Force: Allied Strategy and Tactics in the Second World War* (1990)

Elstob, P. *Hitler's Last Offensive* (1972)

Erickson, J. *Stalin's War With Germany* (2 vols. 1975–83)

    Main Front: Soviet Leaders Look Back on World War II (1987)

Essame, H. *The 43rd Wessex Division at War* (1952)

    The Battle for Germany (1969)

    Patton the Commander (1974)

Fest, J. *Hitler* (1977)

Gavin, J.M. *On to Berlin* (1979)

Gellermann, G.W. *Die Armee Wenck – Hitlers letzte Hoffnung* (1983)

Gilbert, M. *The Holocaust: The Jewish Tragedy* (1986)

Glantz, D. (ed.) *Art of War Symposium: From the Vistula to the Oder: Soviet Offensive Operations, October 1944–March 1945* (1986)

    Soviet Military Deception in the Second World War (1989)

Goebbels, J. *The Goebbels Diaries* (1977)

Görlitz, W. *The Memoirs of Field Marshal Keitel* (1965)

Guderian, H. *Panzer Leader* (1952)

Halder, F. *Hitler as War Lord* (1950)

Horrocks, B. *A Full Life* (1974)

    Corps Commander (1977)

Irving, D. *The Destruction of Dresden* (1963)

    Hitler's War (1977)

Kardorff, U. von *Diary of a Nightmare* (1965)

Katukov, M.E. *Na Ostrie Glavnovo Udara* (1976)

Keegan, J. *The Second World War* (1989)

Koch, H.W. *The Hitler Youth* (1976)

Koller, K. *Der letzte Monat* (1985)

Konev, I.S. *Year of Victory* (1969)

Koriakov, M. *I'll Never Go Back* (1948)

Kuby, E. *The Russians and Berlin 1945* (1964)

Lamb, R. *Montgomery in Europe 1943–45: Success or Failure?* (1983)

Lasch, O. *So fiel Königsberg* (1977)

Lelyushenko, D.D. *Moskva-Stalingrad-Berlin-Praga* (1970)

Longmate, N. *The Bombers* (1983)

Mabire, J. *La Division Nordland* (1982)

MacDonald, C. *Company Commander* (1958)
 The Siegfried Line Campaign (1963)

McKee, A. *The Race for the Rhine Bridges* (1971)
 Dresden 1945 (1982)

Montgomery, B.L. *Normandy to the Baltic* (1946)
 Memoirs (1958)

Nobuesch, J. *Zum Bitteren Ende* (1979)

O'Donnell, J.P. *The Berlin Bunker* (1979)

Overy, R.J. *The Air War 1939–45* (1980)

Paul, W. *Der Endkampf um Deutschland 1945* (1978)

Padfield, P. *Himmler* (1990)

Powell, G. *The Devil's Birthday: The Bridges to Arnhem 1944* (1984)

Ryan, C. *The Last Battle* (1966)

Salisbury, H.E. *Marshal Zhukov's Greatest Battles* (1969)

Salmond, J. *The History of 51st Highland Division*

Selzer, M. *Deliverance Day* (1980)

Sayer, G. *The Forgotten Soldier* (1971)

Sayer, I. and Botting, D. *Hitler's Last General* (1989)

Schramm, P.E. *Kriegstagesbuch des OKW 1940–45*, Vol. IV (1961)

Seaton, A. *The Russo-German War 1941–45* (1971)
 Stalin as Warlord (1976)

Shtemenko, S.M. *The Last Six Months* (1977)

Speer, A. *Inside the Third Reich* (1970)

Stacey, C.P. *The Victory Campaign* (1962)

Strawson, J. *The Battle for Berlin* (1974)

Studnitz, H. *While Berlin Burns* (1963)

Thorwald, J. *Das Ende an der Elbe* (1950)

Van Creveld, M. *Supplying War: Logistics from Wallenstein to Patton* (1977)
 Fighting Power: German and US Performance 1939–45 (1983)

Weighley, R.F. *Eisenhower's Lieutenants: The Campaigns of France and Germany 1944–45* (1981)

Westphal, S. *The Fatal Decisions* (1956)

Whiting, C. *The Battle of the Hürtgen Forest* (1989)
 Siegfried: The Nazis' Last Stand (1983)
 Werewolf (1972)
 Death of a Division (1981)

Williams, J. *The Long Left Flank: The Hard-Fought Way to the Reich 1944–45* (1988)

Wilmot, C. *The Struggle for Europe* (1952)

Zhukov, G.K. *The Memoirs of Marshal Zhukov* (1971)

Ziemke, E. *Battle for Berlin* (1968)
 Stalingrad to Berlin: The German Defeat in the East (1984)

Index